Not at All What One Is Used To

University of Missouri Press   Columbia and London

Marian Janssen

Not at All What One Is Used To

The Life and Times of Isabella Gardner

Copyright © 2010 by
The Curators of the University of Missouri
University of Missouri Press, Columbia, Missouri 65201
Printed and bound in the United States of America
All rights reserved
5 4 3 2 1   14 13 12 11 10

Cataloging-in-Publication data available from the Library of Congress
ISBN 978-0-8262-1898-8

●○™ This paper meets the requirements of the
American National Standard for Permanence of Paper
for Printed Library Materials, Z39.48, 1984.

Design and composition: Jennifer Cropp
Printing and binding: Thomson-Shore, Inc.
Typefaces: Minion, Berkeley, and Florentine

Contents

Of Belle

She was tall and gawky—long legs like a stork and her gait reflected that. She was not clumsy or awkward, however. She did stoop somewhat sometimes to accommodate shorter persons—in a gracious socially polite way. Her manner was schooled. The politeness of a properly trained upper class girl.

Her voice was a marvel. Enormous range of tones—and very melodic in quality. When she read her poetry there was a sensation of having heard music and she was aware of this. Once she was reading me something recent at my request and I found myself very moved. She watched me wipe my eyes and said "It's not really that good Annie—it's the *voice*." This was true. She read without flourishes or drama but the modulations, the tones created a line that *held* one absolutely transfixed. Once I saw a woman go up to her after a reading and just kiss her. Not a friend: a stranger.

Physically she was slender—a long body not thin but not fleshy—and with those long arms and legs and amazing small hands that looked absolutely useless—like a child's. Not w[ith] long nails and never any polish. She was tremendously proud of her *small* feet. Normally a person of her height would have large long feet. She seemed to me to indicate somehow that the small-ness of her feet proved she was—what?—. . . a princess? I never knew quite but it was a big plus to her. You probably know her sister (Kitty) was a "Great Beauty" and this ranked her as *the one* and Belle was nowhere. A portrait of Belle when she was at RSDA [Royal Society of Dramatic Acting] in London (age 20 something I suppose) gives her Blonde coloring and a pretty face in which I see a resemblance to [her daughter] Rosie when young.

By the time I met her in Chi[cago] she was 27 and pregnant w[ith] Daniel. Her face had assumed its adult form and remained the same except for the effect of drinking. She called that "John Barleycorn" when I observed that the shapes of cheek and contours were "different." The nose a bit bulbous etc. . . . She was wearing her hair drawn back into a v. short pony-tail i.e. a ribbon to hold it back from her face. To watch her do her face or hair was a surprise—that she *could!* Those tiny hands powdering etc. They seemed positively unnatural except holding a cigarette habitually raised to her mouth.

She was always in a highly emotional state—plus or minus. I wrote Myra recently and found I had described Belle as hysterical and her ambience— "feverish and anguished."

She dressed expensively and elegantly. She wanted to be accepted for herself and as one of us, yet the fact of her enormous wealth in the background of which she was unconscious, obtruded in odd ways. Assumptions she made as to how things were done or could be—such as Rosie being called for and taken to a private school by age 4. Endless entertaining, no trouble—called a favorite restaurant and had one of their special delicacies delivered in *quantity* for all to "nosh" on and unlimited supply of drink. Simply taking cabs all over the place—Chicago, New York, Florence etc.

No need *ever* to count the cost of anything and NEVER HAD BEEN! Therefore no need or ability to plan ahead or think about consequences. So she could easily remain childlike. She tried *very* hard to be on a par with the rest of us who were in school of one kind or another—those who were married were making their way (counting pennies) and all were more knowledgeable than Belle, having lived with reality all their lives. I was more like her having been extraordinarily *sheltered* by my parents—not a matter of wealth or caste. She was a creature of the most privileged class and was fighting for her life . . . to escape. This explains much: her marriage to Seymour for one. She did not know who she was or where she belonged and so was an impossible mother. Raised by nannies and governesses with a mother from whom she was alienated there was a real gap in her experience. Her many analysts and much therapy were keeping her on an even keel but all the time in her social and private persona there was an intensity that was scary. I was not responsible for or to her nor was I emotionally depend[e]nt on her. However, anyone who was in either of those conditions was in for a real roller coaster ride. *Her poetry probably saved her sanity.*

The money made it possible for her to marry and divorce at will—Each time she went from one state to the next she created an entire household anew. All the furniture and rugs, drapes, pictures etc. were bestowed on friends whose houses were vastly enhanced—and whatever the new husband or *his* style called for would be selected and appear like magic and was often elegant and expensive beyond my ken. Chairs by Mies (Van Der Rohe) or no—the [building] was Mies—the chairs were those leather steel Barcelona ? ones of some other very important architect / designer. The name is gone—

There was always something *unreal* about her *lives.* The presence of famous actors, male and female, at her parties added to the unreality. My husband Josh called her Mehitabel the cat after the Damon Runyon verse—and it was true.

She lived at total risk—and took no care for herself nor for others. At the time it seemed to me perfectly natural as I was living that way myself—but now at age 70 I read what I have written and I see that I am looking at her askance—at the time I was smart enough to be wary—and to go my own way. I did not agree to go with her and Seymour to Mexico where Belle's brother would be coming to stay with them . . . a *very* attractive fellow I had already met. They were very puzzled! The fact that I was at school at the time meant nothing.

During the Allen Tate period, or after I suppose, she adopted "Carpe Diem" as a motto—as if she hadn't always lived that way.

I stayed w[ith] Belle and Allen in Truro for a short time—Rosie was there—after her time in Spain—and at some point, Daniel who was not yet a teenager. Allen had no connection with them—I had never liked Allen and did not tell Belle. McCormick seemed to me a wreck—with the same shape and prep school accent as her brother [George] and her father.

Belle was a devourer of books as was I (and Myra) so we had a great deal of shared background and much to talk about. We endlessly critiqued every book, film, play, person and political event. Belle kept the Rhine wine flowing. I did not drink. One glass per evening or meal was enough. Later years she met me in Washington at a bar and double vodka's were her style. None of it affected her—Myra explained to me—it meant she was inured and drinking much too much.

I am recollecting in tranquillity because I am losing vision in my right eye and can't read too much. Also my heart now requires a rather sedentary daily schedule when I am not out—going to *Doctors!*

My script is deteriorating.

Sorry—Please forgive.

Anabel Holland to the author, January 17, 1995

Prologue

It all started in the rare book room of Washington University in St. Louis. I was reading John Crowe Ransom's editorial correspondence for my study of his literary magazine the *Kenyon Review,* and Holly Hall, the manuscripts librarian, told me that the university had recently acquired the correspondence of Isabella Gardner.[1] She asked me if I would like to see this collection, which no researcher had yet looked at closely. For me, Gardner had been merely one of the few women poets to be published in Ransom's male-dominated review. But in reading hundreds of letters to her I realized I had been shamefully inattentive to a poet whose first book of poems, *Birthdays from the Ocean* (1955), had been praised by Wallace Stevens as "the freshest, truest book of poetry that [he] had read for a long time"; whom William Carlos Williams had praised for "her straightforwardness and the unflinching character of her mind"; and whom Delmore Schwartz had called "a direct descend[a]nt of Emily Dickinson spiritually as well as poetically."[2] Here was a poet whose books had been nominated for National Book Awards and the Pulitzer Prize, and whom Sylvia Plath saw as a rival to the title of "The Poetess of America."[3] Yet, when I first made Gardner's superficial acquaintance in the pages of the *Kenyon Review,* she had been virtually forgotten. What on earth had happened to her? Where did she spring from, and why had she sunk into oblivion?

When Gardner started writing in the 1940s, poetry was very much a man's preserve; poets often were professors, and the few women who were admitted to the contemporary canon exemplified the tradition of intellectual, academy-trained writers who unequivocally distanced themselves from feeling, laid bare on the page. Gardner did not fit that mold. As a beginning poet she was married to an uneducated immigrant and had two children. She did not have a college education, did not belong to a group of fellow aspiring poets, with whom she could critique and compete, and did not have influential academic mentors willing to go to bat for her work. Self-educated, she had steeped herself in the classical and romantic poets, but, as she wanted to find her own voice, had refrained from reading her American contemporaries. She did admire such male modernist writers as Ransom and Allen Tate, who had started writing a generation earlier, for their craftsmanship, wit, and veiled passion, and, like them, she by and large looked down on her immediate female precursors, from Amy Lowell to Edna St. Vincent Millay. But unlike many male modernist writers, Gardner was not touched by Marianne Moore, although in her own poetry, too, wonderfully detailed animals figured. In fact, Moore and Gardner were poles apart; whereas Moore armed her poems, her animals, herself, at all points, Gardner stressed in poetry as in life the "necessary nakedness," "the democracy of universal vulnerability."[4] And where Moore experimented with the visual appearance of her poems, Gardner always concentrated on the sound, her poems "a ballet for the ear."[5]

Birthdays earned glowing reviews from the foremost critics of her day because Gardner had clothed naked feelings of sex, terror, and death in suitable forms, as she had taught herself to write perfectly crafted, intense lyric verse. A past master at poetic styles, from simple sonnet to sophisticated sestina, Gardner had not submitted to absolutist formal dictates, but controlled human chaos intuitively through end rhyme, assonance, and, often, strictly metered iambic lines. So, in the 1950s when most women poets were sidelined by poet-critics, Gardner was hailed as one of the foremost American writers of her day. (The one exception was ruthless Randall Jarrell, who felt threatened by Gardner and used his caustic, gender-based smartness to ridicule her.) She became an admired member of the poetic generation born in the 1910s, which included John Berryman, Elizabeth Bishop, Robert Lowell, Theodore Roethke, and Karl Shapiro. Everyone in the literary world knew her name.

When W. D. Snodgrass's moving *Heart's Needle* (1959) and Robert Lowell's groundbreaking *Life Studies* (1959) came out, their kind of exposed confessional poetry soon overshadowed Gardner's, whose craftfully formalized vulnerability no longer seemed personal or painful enough; and when political poetry became fashionable in the turbulent 1960s, Gardner rarely engaged in it. As a writer of passionate poems about the danger and suffering of human relationships rather than of inhuman wars, and of disciplined, unsentimental, personal accounts rather than (self-) flagellating confessions, Gardner lost touch with poetic vogues. Her constrained elegies were not tear-jerking enough, her sensual love poems not explicit enough, her domestic poems about children of little interest. Nevertheless, although her second book, *The Looking Glass* (1961) received far fewer reviews than *Birthdays* had, those it did get were again almost without exception laudatory. James Wright, for one, bracketed her with Denise Levertov as "two of the best living poets in America." He praised Gardner's "power of incantation," her poetry as "sensitive and civilized," but, he warned, "you are not advised to hold a lighted match near it."[6]

As Gardner's poems became unfashionable both in theme and style, periodicals which had eagerly solicited her work now turned her down, even *Poetry Magazine,* to which she had devoted years of her life as an associate editor under Karl Shapiro. But, then, her output was minimal and her third book, *West of Childhood* (1965), contained only three new poems. For while male poetic rivals such as Berryman, Jarrell, and Lowell were unabashedly competitive and put their lives and loves in the service of their art and in pursuit of being number one, Gardner had internalized many of the values of her time, and the men in her life came first. It was not until 1979, shortly before her death, that her last volume, *That Was Then* appeared, with sixteen poignant new poems once more communicating raw emotions through structured form. The tide had turned, and this slim book was nominated for the National Book Award and made Gardner, posthumously, New York State's first Poet Laureate.

It took me longer than my initial brief meeting with Gardner in St. Louis to come to know and love her multifaceted, brilliant poetry and to understand her seesawing reputation, but from the first I was captivated by Gardner herself. Letters to her showed not only that she knew everybody in the literary world, from T. S. Eliot to Erica Jong, but the fascination was how unreservedly intimate her correspondents often were. I was used to reading the editorial and personal correspondence among lifelong friends such as Ransom, Tate, and Robert Penn Warren, or their protégés Lowell and Jarrell, but those letters were dryly impersonal compared to the ones Gardner received. She called forth inordinate openness in her contacts and friends, who told her about their loves and lusts, their marriages and money problems, their ambitions and abortions. This collection seemed made to measure for a book about the neglected poet Isabella Gardner and her literary friends.

Yet, when I got to know Gardner better, I found that the drama of her life encompassed much more than her being a neglected writer in her own right and the focal point of an intimate literary circle. Born into one of the first families of Boston, cousin to Robert Lowell and the painter Billy Congdon, she was a child of wealth who rebelled against her privileged upbringing. Before she became a poet, she was an actress on Broadway. She married into the theater world, then wedded a Russian-Jewish photographer with connections to the mob, turned next to one of the millionaire Chicago McCormicks, then cast him aside for the southern writer Allen Tate, who then deserted her. During her last years, spent at the Hotel Chelsea in New York, she suffered from the tragic fates of her children, and struggled with enemies, friends, lovers, and the bottle. Gardner's complicated, compelling life among descendants of the first settlers, first-generation immigrants, and unreconstructed southerners, reaching from the Atlantic to the Pacific and often to Europe, offers a wonderful panorama of the intellectual concerns and social experiences of the last century. It was a story begging to be told.

Chapter One

"The Walled Garden," 1915–1933

Brother do you remember the walled garden, our dallies
    in that ding dong dell
where my fistful of violets mazed the air we moved
    through and upon
and a swallow of brook skimmed your tabloid sloop to sea
    and gone?
("West of Childhood")

"My birth was a disaster to my mother," Isabella Gardner told a prospective biographer when she was in her fifties. "It was desperately important to her (because of another woman my father loved) to bear a son. I was the 2nd daughter. She has (but I love her) rejected me all the years of her life."[1] And around that time Gardner's aunt Catherine Gardner Mayes wrote her niece: "I remember that though you were a perfectly healthy baby you cried continually most of the time you were awake. None of the others did. Maybe you had some sort of premonition of what a world you had come into and what a hard road you had to travel."[2]

Isabella Stewart Gardner was the second child born to Rose Grosvenor Gardner and George Peabody Gardner. She was called "Belle" after her godmother, the Isabella Stewart Gardner known in Boston as flamboyant "Mrs. Jack," who had founded the wonderfully idiosyncratic Isabella Stewart Gardner Museum. On September 7, 1915, proud father George wrote to "Dear Aunt Belle": "Little Isabella Gardner arrived this morning and seems a very healthy specimen. Rose is feeling very happy and well. She sends her love and says you may see your namesake anytime and hopes to see you the first of next week sometime. The doctor is going to be very strict about her seeing people. Much love from all

1

three of us, we are so pleased that we can call her Isabella for we are very fond and proud of her namesake." His great-aunt Belle noted on the letter: "Time of arrival 10.30 A.M., weight 7 3/4 lbs."[3]

Isabella Gardner's parents were both in their mid-twenties and had been married since January 1913; their first child, Katherine, "Kitty," had been born in December of that year. Rose Grosvenor proudly traced her ancestry back to John and Esther Grosvenor, who came from Cheshire, England, in 1640 and settled in Roxbury, Massachusetts. In 1836, her grandfather, the physician William Grosvenor, married Rosa Anne Mason, a descendant of John Brown, the wealthy and socially prominent merchant of Revolutionary fame, who had led the expedition which ended in the burning of the British warship *Gaspee.* Dr. Grosvenor moved to Providence, Rhode Island, and soon turned from a practicing physician into a wholesale dealer in drugs and dyes and, later, a manufacturer of cotton and calico, owning most of the stock of the steadily prospering Grosvenor-Dale Company. The eldest son, William, attended Brown University, the college founded by his maternal forebears, and became one of the chief executives of the Grosvenor-Dale Company. He married attractive red-haired Rose Diamond Phinney in 1882, but according to her grandson William Congdon, she was crazy: "The Phinney family were all mad."[4] Successful William Grosvenor and his beautiful Rose had seven children, the fourth of which, Gardner's mother Rose, was born on October 13, 1888. "Without money my mother's brothers would have been skid row bums," Gardner wrote much later, for in her view, too, her mother's line had "[t]emperament without what it takes."[5]

George Peabody Gardner Jr. had been born on January 27 of that same year, with, as he later wrote in his Harvard twenty-fifth yearbook, "a silver spoon in his mouth."[6] In America's famously classless society, George Peabody Gardner Jr. was even more blue-blooded than his wife. Ten generations earlier, his forefather Thomas Gardner, sailing from England on the *Zouch Phenix,* had settled in Cape Ann in 1624, moving to Salem two years later. His descendants intermarried with other early and increasingly prominent New England families like the Coffins, Endicotts, Lowells, Putnams, Pickerings, and Peabodys, building a firm Boston Brahmin background for their heirs.[7] Where Thomas Gardner had been a planter, his lineage branched out into shipping, manufacturing, and financing, prospering in the China trade and securing a strong financial base, even if by the early twentieth century their fortunes had been eclipsed by those of the more recent *nouveau riche* Rockefeller, Frick, or Carnegie families.

Isabella Gardner's paternal grandfather, George Peabody Gardner, was born in 1855 in Boston, and he went on to be "actively and intimately connected with the development of two of the largest industrial concerns in the country, namely the General Electric Company and the American Telephone and Telegraph Company."[8] When George was still a boy, his uncle John Lowell Gardner, hardly penniless, had married new money in the person of Isabella Stewart from New York City, the daughter of an enterprising businessman. Extravagant, magnetic Mrs. Jack Gardner would soon scandalize good old Boston, filling the tabloids with tales of her real and imagined eccentric behavior: terrifying crowds by taking out a lion on a leash; recommending a show, "The Red Moon," with black participants, which true ladies should not attend even in disguise; and strutting with two enormous diamonds mounted on waving antennae in her hair. Most shocking to Boston's eagle-eyed, judgmental matrons was her obvious partiality, when she grew older, for creative younger men such as the popular novelist Francis Marion Crawford. Mrs. Jack allowed herself to be painted by John Singer Sargent in a tight black dress that displayed a hint of cleavage with her famous pearls wound around her wasplike waist, but her affable husband locked the portrait up for his lifetime after an ill-bred scoundrel had hinted at her liaison with Crawford by alluding to a steep and narrow gorge in the White Mountains: "Sargent has painted Mrs. Gardner all the way down to Crawford's Notch."[9] Belle Gardner remained unperturbed and with her "quaint habit of doing as she pleased" was described admiringly in a Florida journal as "[t]he Boston woman who is getting columns upon columns of free advertising out of her love of privacy . . . a genius in her way."[10] By 1915, when her godchild Isabella Stewart Gardner was born, Mrs. Jack, at seventy-five, had been grudgingly adopted by Boston society. That she and her husband had raised his brother Joseph Peabody Gardner's three children after their father's suicide had not quite won over Boston's staunch defenders of propriety, but her fabulous museum with its fine collection of paintings, her renowned admirers of impeccable station and repute, like Henry Adams and Henry James, and her friendship with noted artists Sargent and James McNeill Whistler, had finally guaranteed her her place among Boston's ruling class. And then, she had become simply too old to cause scandal.

When Gardner's father, known as Peabo, was still a schoolboy, he often hid out of embarrassment when his great-aunt Mrs. Jack came to see her favorite grandnephew at hockey practice. A "small, excited figure," she would be "cheering wildly on the side lines at every game his team played," sitting, "wrapped in furs, on an upended packing case to watch him skate with his . . . team."[11] He attended the proper schools in the Boston suburb of Southborough—Fay School, which prides itself on being the oldest junior boarding school in America, and the socially equally selective St. Mark's, founded by his maternal grandfather Joseph Burnett—then followed in his forebears' footsteps by entering Harvard. He belonged to the well-known class of 1910, where he excelled among a celebrated grouping of classmates as different as T. S. Eliot, Walter Lippmann, and John Reed. If he graduated *cum laude* from Harvard, his interests were hardly academic. "He was a member of the varsity track, hockey and tennis teams for three years and the varsity baseball team one year—doubtless the year when his [great-]aunt became a baseball fan. He won 'eight major and two minor H's in all,' and his countless trophies pleased her as much or more than as though she had won them herself."[12] An intercollegiate tennis champion, he also was president of Harvard's student council during the last half of his senior year and vice president of its union.

But there had to be time for relaxation, too, and at Harvard, where not making a club spelled ostracization from the magic circle of future leaders, Peabo was a member of the elegant, ritualistic, snobbish Porcellian Club, according to insider Cleveland Amory "the *ne plus ultra* of college clubs," clubs that were meant to keep people out as much as let the chosen few in.[13] Nelson Aldrich, another American aristocrat, noted that "Scott Fitzgerald and Tommy Hitchcock might be friends, but there was no way, even if he had gone to Harvard, that Scott Fitzgerald could belong to the Porcellian Club. To belong to the Porcellian Club it was not enough—it still isn't—that one be friends with a member. One has to have been friends with him always, and in that elusive past perfect tense of the verb *to be* the socially ambitious read their sad fate."[14] In "the United States membership in the 'Pork' was equivalent to a peerage in England," a Porcellian graduate said to one of his friends, whose son wondered which club he should choose; Franklin D. Roosevelt and Joseph P. Kennedy were among the many who were blackballed.[15] More central to Peabo's college experience, though, was his membership in and presidency of Harvard's superselect Hasty Pudding Club, which dated back to the eighteenth century and put on spectacular shows with its men playing both male and female roles. Here he could revel in his love for the theater.

A dashing man of enormous potential, after graduating Gardner was far too vibrantly energetic to buckle down straightaway to the restricted life of a Boston gentleman. He embarked on a grand tour, another crucial ingredient in the old money educational curriculum.[16] With friends, he visited the East and depicted their experiences in a privately printed book, *Chiefly the Orient*:

> In spite of my great enthusiasm for the trip which had lasted for a long time, when the time came for leaving it began to ooze rapidly until there was barely a drop left. How sad it was leaving my mother and the Boyers at Monument Beach on Tuesday and later my father in Boston! However, once on my way, it began to return and the words of my grandfather when he told me that he would not be alive when I returned bore less heavily on my mind and the sorrow at leaving my dear family became less poignant.
>
> Here and now I want to thank my father and mother for their generosity and absolute unselfishness in letting me go or rather in sending me. For it is not conceit on my part to know how much I am to them—much, much more than I deserve, for there never were two better, sweeter, or more loving parents.[17]

They traveled from Boston to Moscow, Peking, Seoul, Osaka, Kyoto, Manila, Batavia, Benares, Delhi, Karnak, and via Constantinople and Athens to London, visiting many cultural highlights, mingling with members of their class wherever they went. From Kyoto, on October 24, 1910: "After tiffin, we left our cards at the Minister of Foreign Affairs, met Mr. Schuyler, the first secretary, and Captain Summerlin, the second secretary of the American Embassy. We then had a few sets of tennis at the tennis club with an old Yale man, Condit. In the evening we dined with Curtice and Eldridge, two student interpreters."[18] Or from Singapore, on January 18, 1911: "At seven o'clock Mrs. Du Bois, the consul's wife, took us to the Economic Gardens, where they have an experimental rubber plantation."[19]

In this way his undigested, rather juvenile journal goes on for almost four hundred pages, ending in Europe, where Peabo visited the Paris Independent Exhibition of 1911, which brought the terms fauvism and cubism into common speech: "If all the lunatics were to be let loose in a paint shop they might be able to produce a result equally terrifying, but I doubt it." Nevertheless, "after a most delightful week" he left for London in the early summer, "to join my mother who had been waiting there some time for me." There he was swept up in a whirlwind of social events: he played tennis, danced—finding "charming girls," but also "numerous long, rather scrawny necked women, their heads bent forward under the weight of large but unlovely jewelry"—went to the Derby, nearly "died laughing at cousin John," and "spent one day at Mr. Astor's place, Clivenden with Bobbie and Priscilla Grant and Frank Paul."[20] On the very last page of his journal he briefly noted: "Rose Grosvenor was also in London some of the time with her mother and younger sister. We went to several plays and visited various galleries together which was most enjoyable."[21] Reading Peabo's travelogue in 1951, when Peabo Gardner was in his sixties, Gilbert Hovey Grosvenor, a distant relative of Rose's and the first full-time editor of *National Geographic*, was impressed with this "delightful record. . . . It is amazing to me that you at that early age should have been so observant and eager to see everything. I wish I had lured you into the National Geographic work before you got so intensely absorbed in Boston and Harvard affairs. The National Geographic Society would have at least 10,000,000 members instead of a measly 2,000,000. Think of all your energy and talent wasted on Harvard, American Telephone and Telegraph, General Electric, etc., and looking after the millionaires of Boston and Boston's museums."[22]

Belonging to the smart set at the beginning of the twentieth century, Peabo Gardner and Rose Grosvenor were frequently, often fawningly, mentioned in the gossipy society pages of local, even national, newspapers. Rose's parents had built a "substantial" summer villa in fashionable Newport, Rhode Island—according to *Town and Country*, with an "unrivaled ocean view," a "dainty library," and an "artistic . . . children's playhouse"—to ensure that their children would meet suitable marriage candidates. Rose Grosvenor was noted for her skills in driving small cars and playing tennis and bridge. She preferred the tango and waltzing to the old-fashioned cotillion, and even, daringly, with her friends stopped exiting directly into the water from the non-revealing bathing cabins and promenaded instead along the beach in their swimsuits, if fully covered by robes.[23] For "the benefit of the Italian Children's Summer Mission in New York city," she faithfully represented the actress Sarah Bernhardt in a Whartonian performance of tableaux vivants, wearing "a gown of brown chiffon and a gold sash;" and she "won the applause of the audience" as heiress Miss Cecily Cardew in an amateur performance, also for charity, of Oscar Wilde's *The Importance of Being Earnest*.[24] In 1910, too, she was one of the bridesmaids at the wedding of her beloved older sister Caroline to Yale man Gilbert Maurice Congdon; the description of their elaborate Edwardian gowns in "pink liberty satin veiled with pale blue chiffon" and "immense hats with accordion crowns and wide lace-edged brims with primroses and blue velvet ribbons" alone took up almost half a *New York Times* column.[25]

Though "one of the most popular girls in Newport, a clever whip, musician, and scholar" and "the most amiable girl in Newport society," Rose Grosvenor at that time still had no suitable beau.[26] Two years later, in September 1912, the *New York Times* captioned enthusiastically: "Grosvenor-Gardner Nuptials Expected," but had to admit that Mrs. Grosvenor, "when asked if the engagement of her daughter, Miss Rose Grosvenor, to George P. Gardner of Boston was to be announced," said "that there was no announcement to be made."[27] The next day, one step behind the *Times,* the *Washington Post* tattled that "Mrs. Grosvenor says no" to the gossip that her daughter was engaged to "George Gardner, the Harvard man and noted tennis player," but the paper was happy to chronicle some two weeks later that the rumors had been true.[28] Naturally, the wedding, set for January 1913, "was to have been a brilliant affair," but the bride's grandfather died in December, plunging the Grosvenors into mourning, and the couple had a subdued church wedding, followed, fortunately, by a "large reception at the home of the bride's mother."[29] Newspaper coverage was duly restrained.

Once married, the Peabody Gardners were far less fascinating to the editors of juicy society pages. Living in Newport, Massachusetts—an old-time suburb of Boston—Rose Grosvenor Gardner soon got caught up in the more humdrum social pleasures and responsibilities of a cultivated lady of a Boston family of prominence: breakfasting in bed, discussing menus with cook, arranging the flowers, lunching at, usually, the elegant Chilton Club (newly founded in response to the men's clubs, which did not allow women to be members or even to enter), playing tennis and bridge with other members of her social circle, and being involved in charity work. Her husband became private secretary to Harvard's President Lowell and secretary to the Harvard Corporation but had ample time for sailing, tennis, amateur theatricals, and his many exclusive clubs. His favorite was perhaps the Tavern Club of Boston, with its record of Elizabethan plays "capably done," according to society watcher Dixon Wecter in 1937, "without doubt the most aristocratic," and "[e]xcessively reactionary in the matter of electric lights and pedigrees."[30]

In Europe, in 1914, World War I had broken out, but it seemed remote to the young Peabody Gardners, whose main worry was the health of their daughters, Kitty and Belle. Kitty had to spend most of her youth as an invalid, crippled and flat on her back for months at a stretch because of spinal tuberculosis, aggravated by asthma, anemia, and other illnesses. Belle was miserable, a crybaby, suffering, in her aunt Catherine's words, from "one of the especially idiotic ideas, to which the medical profession seems prone . . . the dictum that babies were better left alone 'to cry it out' and held to strict hours of feeding and human companionship."[31] When Congress finally declared war on Germany, on April 6, 1917, Peabo immediately "went on active service as an ensign in the United States Naval Reserve Force—on transports whose hazardous duty it was to dodge German submarines and keep the supply lines open."[32] During this difficult period of her early married life, amidst uncertainty and horror, Rose was pregnant with their first son, George Peabody Gardner III, who was born in September 1917.

When, in 1918, Peabo returned to his wife and now three children, he was, as always, in wonderful physical shape, and he was eager to rejoin the life of Boston's social elite. He started working for the predecessor of the brokerage firm of Paine, Webber, Jackson and Curtis, a main player in the American financial market, later becoming a partner in that firm. But the separation caused by the war may have had its effect on the family; it was not until April 1923, more than five years after George's birth, that John Lowell Gardner was born; he was quickly followed by Rose Phinney in October 1924 and their last-born, Robert, in November 1925. The gap in ages, the siblings always felt, divided their family decidedly into two, the more so by Kitty's precarious health and her parents' frequent fears for her life. In the late 1920s, the teenaged Kitty still wore a steel brace that covered her upper body, which she was allowed to take off only for parties. Helped by Sully, a live-in nurse, Rose focused on Kitty's health and had hardly any time to spare for her younger children. Belle and George, thrown together, bonded closely and developed their own shared language. This "early thread of intimacy" wove all through their diverging lives: like her godmother, Belle would rebel against convention, while George would perfectly fit the mold of the proper Bostonian as an investment banker, living a life filled with directorships and carrying on the solid New England tradition of numerous trusteeships. When, again following custom, he went to St. Mark's as an adolescent, he wrote long letters to his sister, signed Pigwiggin, Gig, or Joe Wudge, filled with private-school essentials like grades, athletics, and classic mischief— "Promise not to tell anyone, but about 2 weeks ago or less Molly and Jackie came up and we went out to lunch to the little house. After they went Sunday afternoon 3 friends and I used up a full package of cigarettes between us, gee it was the best fun"—and constantly interspersed with remarks like "Really I love you;" "I love you. Come up prize day;" "P.S. I hear you may come up Prize day. Yeah;" "I *loved* your letter and read over when I am depressed."[33] Their kinship was especially profound, because they had no true friends outside their family.

Meanwhile, Peabo and Rose had moved their family to Brookline—known as "the rich men's town." The house, Green Hill, was situated in magnificent isolation on top of a hill with extensive grounds, far from the madding crowd. It had been the out-of-town house for the Jack Gardners, which they had in-herited on the death of his father in 1884. Mrs. Jack made Fenway Court— after her death called the Isabella Stewart Gardner Museum—both her summer and winter residence and turned Green Hill over to Peabo, "now returned from his sea duty during World War I and in need of a home."[34] According to Mrs. Jack's biographer, Louise Tharp, it was "a rambling farmhouse rebuilt until it fitted the family like a living shell. It stood on a knoll, overlooking fields and woodland. In the distance was the city of Boston with the golden dome of the State House clearly to be seen above the clustering Beacon Hill houses."[35] Green Hill was actually much grander than a sprawling farmhouse. During Isabella Gardner's childhood, there were, next to the main house, a number of small houses, among them one for the family chauffeur; there were stables, a swim-ming pool in the back, and two greenhouses famed since Mrs. Jack's times for their floral abundance, filled with azaleas and camellias, oranges and lemons. The hill burst into color in spring with its thousands of crocuses, daisies, tu-lips, and other bulbous flowers, and a little creek passed through this children's paradise. In March 1920, Gardner's father wrote to her godmother:

> I have been meaning for a long time to write to you and to tell you about our first winter at Green Hill. I do not suppose that there has ever been a much more severe winter or one that made it more difficult to get about and yet we would not have been in town for anything. It has been warm and comfortable. The chil-dren never have been better in winter. On Saturdays and Sundays it has been like being at St. Moritz for we have had skiing and coasting literal[l]y from our front door. . . . Kitty not withstanding some slight upsets has progressed famously and really is beginning to walk alone. Isabella grows sweeter and lovelier every day and George is the good natured and excessively active lord of all he surveys. It is a picture to see them both on snowshoes.
>
> Rose and I love Green Hill better than we ever dreamed we could love any place and we are extremely grateful to you for giving us the opportunity of living

here. Undoubtedly one of the reasons we like it so much is that there are so many things which remind us of you.[36]

The house was comfortable with two kitchens, a dining room with a striking black-and-white-checked wooden floor, a small study filled with Peabo's book-cases and sports trophies, where Belle's parents took their tea in the afternoons, and for the children a large playroom and a sleeping porch. The "Bird Room," named for the birds depicted in its wallpaper, boasted a large crystal chandelier, which, family lore has it, one of the maids, fainting dead away while cleaning it, did not let go off for fear of breaking it. There were, of course, works of art by Isabella Stewart Gardner's painter friends John Singer Sargent and Anders Zorn. The "Music Room," always filled with flowers from the conservatory, had French windows and could be divided in two by means of a curtain. Here the children played, indifferently, the piano, and performed, enthusiastically, lit-tle plays that Belle Gardner mostly wrote, produced, and directed. Once, the three youngest, whom she regarded as her "toy children," were recruited for a production of Rumpelstiltskin, which, however, never came to pass as just before opening night Robert succumbed to what probably was the chicken pox.[37] Peabo would join in wholeheartedly and "dress up and do sort of little skits, things like that. He would sort of put on little theatricals for his children," which would be at least as enjoyable for him as for his offspring.[38]

Green Hill was idyllic. Wistfully, George wrote from St. Mark's:

Yesterday after classes I went home and had lunch, and then went to the Milton Game with Daddy, Kitty and Mummy—with half of the top down on the big car. I got home at about 11:20 and had a swell time. You ought to see the pony. I rode him a lot bar[e]back and got some swell spills. . . . The place looks wonderfu[l]!! Everything is being seeded and sodded. The tennis court is being fixed, the house has been painted, the swimming pool has been painted, new pines are being planted, the rose garden has been fixed and the spring garden is wonderful and the grass is just like a carpet. . . . Flower-hill is the best it has ever been, and all the trees are out. We lost the game but it was worth coming home for.[39]

Peabo Gardner's home movies show the Gardner children skating, sledding, horseback riding, and in pony carts, always with Belle as his tomboyish movie star and favorite. Thanking "Aunt Belle" on behalf of her godchild for a gold mesh bag with "Isabella" spelled in precious stones, he wrote: "I trust that she will grow up to be worthy in every way of po[s]sessing such a beautiful and in-timate possession of yours. I think she will if she keeps on developing as she has so far but then Rose is continual[l]y laughing at me for what she chooses to call my partiality for Isabella. I do not admit that I am partial but I confess I do love her very dearly and what is more unusual she seems to really love me."[40] "You have more stuff in you than all the rest of my children put to-gether," Peabo would tell her later, "but you are a composite of opposing extremes."[41] Gardner indeed had a "magical relationship" with her father, was "dazzled" by him, and had "a high opinion of his largely untested promise as a writer, as an actor, as . . . humanitarian," for he seemed able to do all the things he wanted, showing her that life offered seemingly endless and always exciting possibilities.[42] One of Gardner's friends thought him a "gorgeous man," tall, athletic, and "abso-lutely breathtaking" even in his sixties, with a smile like movie legend Errol Flynn's.[43] He was charming, suave in manners and style, and if he sometimes "seemed quite stern," he was always indulgent with the apple of his eye, Belle, with whom he shared a silly sense of humor, a love of romance, of theatrics, preferring fantasy to reality.[44] Later, Gardner remembered

> The child I was went there nearly every night for a winter
> or more, half a century ago. My younger brother George
> slept in the same room. The muttering embers
> in the grate spoke quivering pictures to the ceiling.
> What a viewing! From these slipping shapes I construed
> a hill-side coastal village and staring hard I was transported
> to that primal coast I stood on the pier I climbed the steep
>   street.
> All the cobblestoned way up that hilly street every single
> tiny house was full of light. The little houses all alight
> by the light of whale oil lamps. All doors ajar.
> All the people in their houses shouted here you ARE
> Here's cookies, ginger people baked for you. Here's a
>   BOTTOMLESS
> pitcher of milk for you. From each glowing little house
> they beckoned me and they welcomed me and they hugged me.
> I was theirs. They were mine. Such Love!
>   Wolves bared their teeth at my little brother in his dark.
> Only to my father each bedtime, and to our Irish laundress
> those mornings she was there, did I recount the serial tales
> of where I'd been and gone. George, two years littler than I
> cried "Take ME Take ME why can't I
> go too?"
> ("Card Island or Cod Island?" 113)

In Isabella Gardner's enchanted world the laundress played a crucial role, but even more so the children's nurses: Ray, Carly, Suzie, and, particularly, Irish Molly Laughlin. Molly, magical faithful servant, nourished the "tremendous love that Belle had for fairy tales as a child. . . . [H]er mind was formed by the Irish fairy tales, the Norwegian fairy tales, the Chinese fairy tales, the Grimm fairy tales . . . every single possibility of a fairy tale she simply devoured . . . in having them read to her, or reading them to herself, or reading them to [the younger children]. . . . This was something that she just absolutely lived off . . . intellectually and mentally."[45] Stories told by their handsome Portuguese chauffeur, Johnny Silvia, who called Gardner "Bob," befitting the tomboy she was, also fed her yearning for a life beyond the pale respectability of Brookline. Robert remembered that Molly and Johnny had a love-hate relationship with Rose Grosvenor and therefore "tried to outlive my mother. And they both succeeded."[46]

With their Grosvenor relatives the Gardners often summered in Bristol, Rhode Island:

> The humming of the sun
> The mumbling in the honey-suckle vine
> The whirring in the clovered grass
> The pizzicato plinkle of ice in an auburn
> uncle's amber glass.
> The whing of father's racquet and the whack
> of brother's bat on cousin's ball
> and calling voices call-
> ing voices spilling voices . . .
> ("Summer Remembered," 66)

The family also spent some weeks of the summer on Roque Island, in part because Gardner's "lunatic great uncle was there with his keeper," howling at the moon.[47] True representatives of the Old Order, the Gardner dynasty owned this island off the coast of Maine, which had been handed down from generation to generation. There were no automobiles; the Gardners walked about in their oldest clothes or swam without, and sailed their boats, rode their horses, gathered wild blueberries, picnicked, ran around, and read, enjoying the simple pleasures of summer. Their island home was "comfortable and tasteful," but appearances need not be kept up and the family went native with the caretaking natives—paradoxically thereby once more reaffirming their social status.[48] Rose Grosvenor Gardner's outrageous, racy Rhode Island friend, the countess and writer Eleanor Palffy, regarded such a family island as "a suitable place in which to indulge the urge for squalid living, which seems inherent in the comfortably off from the Commonwealth of Massachusetts."[49] In fact Roque Island, with its small private harbor and curved sand beach, with bald eagles cruising, herons fishing, and seals sleeping upon sunny rocks, was "a terribly special place" to the Gardner family.[50] "[E]veryone who has visited or lived on Roque carries away his own set of sensations or incidents which most appeal to him," wrote John Peabody Monks in his history of the island: "it may be watching the ever-present lobsterman from Lakeman's hauling his traps attached to glass bottle floats and brilliantly painted wooden buoys. Or it may be the crackle as someone throws a green spruce branch on the hot evening picnic fire of guttering birchwood, while all around recline those whose stomachs are heavy with lobster meat. . . . Rare indeed has been the visitor who did not completely succumb to the charms and beauties of Roque."[51]

Here the Gardners were often joined by Rose's sister Caroline Congdon, her husband, and their sons, Gilbert, William ("Billy"), John, Robert, and Edward. Billy, born the night the *Titanic* sank, became Gardner's friend for life; both intuitive, impulsive, and intense, they bonded intimately also because of their common interest in literature and the arts, "the affinity of our creativity," as Congdon later described it. They came to trust each other so wholeheartedly that they confided their erotic awakenings to each other when adolescents. Congdon remembered how in the mornings they went swimming "on the big beach. That was a great pleasure. We all went naked; the women on one part and the men on another. . . . Belle and I used to ignore the icy water; everybody else was screaming, but Belle and I were just pretending it was hot. . . . We would go trailing in the afternoon. . . . Usually her father, who was a Spartan man who had projects of creating paths through the forests took long walks . . . and Belle would be with us. She did not stay with the mothers, she stayed with the brothers."[52] Only Kitty, never "very much of an outdoorsy girl," was bored on Roque Island, as there was nothing there but family, but even Gardner's mother was happy to "set herself up in the kitchen and make pajama cakes, a sort of pancake made out of cornmeal," which was atypical as "she didn't cook."[53] Every September, Belle's and George's birthdays were celebrated on Roque with charades; George got sealskin moccasins, and Belle, sweetgrass baskets, because an itinerant native American salesman had smelled out this annual celebration and showed up just a day or two before the festivities to peddle his wares.

"Somehow I hanker for the Roque of childhood," Gardner wrote her brother Robert when she was almost sixty.[54] Twenty years earlier she had told him that "in some way Roque despite tensions and absurdities renews me, I suppose what roots I have are there." But that same letter demonstrates that she yearned for a childhood that never was: "I told Mother on the telephone about a week ago that Rose, Dan and I wd. arrive at Roque on the 23rd. . . . .I told Mother we would love to stay at the Red House with you, and lunch and dine with her as we did last year. Her response was a Halloween-ish laugh preceding '*Well!* I can't feed the whole kit and caboodle, you know.' I wrote subsequently saying the trip meant a great deal to all of us; that *any* arrangement she made would delight us—that *she* should have joy of Roque and worry less about all of us—

etc. I told her I'd love to cook in the Red House or whatever seemed easiest. I am rather discouraged. I call her often with a gay and loving heart and she is *so* grim, so tense, *so* hostile that I am appalled, even frightened."[55] Indeed, from early on, family antagonisms had simmered beneath the paradisiacal surface, and the Gardner children were differently affected.

Kitty, the eldest, ailing daughter, was as taken with and involved in society as their conventional, proper mother and therefore usually cherished by her. Rose, her youngest daughter and namesake, found both her parents very distant and would just briefly see them in the mornings and evenings: "[o]ur mother and father had very little, or nothing to do with us."[56] Rose's one traumatically sad childhood memory was when her nurse went back to Scotland to marry her fiancé; but, on the other hand, when her parents left with the three eldest children on a long trip to Ireland, that was "just the way it was."[57] Then again, Rose Grosvenor Gardner poured such mother-love on her youngest son, Robert, that he described her, during his young adulthood, as hyperpossessive. She was always much more critical of the girls than of the boys, who could do more or less what they wanted.

Belle suffered the full force of their mother's censure. Even at Roque, where hardly any social rules applied, she managed to be late, tip over the pot, step into somebody's plate (leaving pools of sand on their food), eat corn too voraciously, and, generally, behave as unladylike as could be. Her physical awkwardness and especially her ungainly posture were "of utmost concern to the family. How can you stand this way? How can you slouch this way? How can you look so disembodied, or loose-jointed . . . being a sort of continual refrain."[58] Was it because both mother and daughter were "stormy" that Rose was so critical?[59] Or did Rose feel that her daughter, by behaving as she did, scoffed at society, which she held dear? George, though two years younger, vainly tried to shield his sister, for Gardner could do no good in her mother's eyes and consequently came to conduct herself ever more inappropriately. If, at age seven or so, Belle had still written a loving poem to both her parents—"you that rule within my heart / you and I shall never part"—she soon despaired of winning her mother's love.[60] In "The Music Room" (107)

> Behind the white doors plants
> Alone were smiled at, but with joyless pride that drained
>
> Odor and pollen. It was indifference drained
> The marrow from the bones of the piano,
> Gutted the child, but watered the tuneless plants.

By contrast, Peabo tended to be lenient, and his favoring of Belle may have exacerbated Rose's disapproval of her daughter. For theirs was not a happy marriage. Rose always remembered her Newport days as her "golden period" and like a true blue Rhode Islander had thought Boston inherently inferior to Narragansett Bay. Newly married, though, she had been snubbed by "very stodgy Boston" when she wanted to show off her trousseau, because "her beautiful new clothes were considered too fashionable, too fancy and so she just packed them all and sent them away."[61] She adapted quickly to her gilded cage, transforming herself from a smart, popular girl into an esteemed Bostonian of impeccable dignity. But Peabo Gardner soon dealt her a much more painful blow. It was not uncommon for men of his class to keep mistresses, and Peabo was no exception. That was "the reason for a good deal of tension.... If not his actual infidelity, his possible infidelity. Which is just as good a way of getting somebody's nerves on edge than actually going out and doing it."[62] There were screaming matches, and Peabo made his adored daughter, in effect his eldest child because of Kitty's fragile health, his reluctant accomplice, as Gardner recalled in a boozy, troubled letter to George:

> It was indescribably difficult and painful for me to survive the two years you were at St Marks, and I, alone, bore the brunt of our parents' tears, fights, struggles. Mother, leaving the table in tears and hysteria would go to the 'office'—the trophy room; Daddy would go to the 'library.' Mother would summon me and say, *scream*, "Your father does not love me." I *tried* to console her. *Daddy* would then summon me to the 'library'—"Did I *say* anything wrong—did I *do* anything wrong?" he would say. Torn apart I tried to console both; knowing Daddy had *said* nothing wrong, but also knowing that he *had* done "wrong" and had exposed me (*just* me) to his passion for Vivian Cochrane Pickman. He had taken me to see her (front row) to the Vincent Club Show where she showered him with yellow [illegible] or whatever. He took me to her *apartment*. You may remember that he had her for dinner at *Green Hill* and she sat in our Mother's place.
>
> It was impossible and intolerable for me. I could not and would not betray my mother *or* my father. I was a *child*. Years later our mother talked to me about the pain she suffered. The fact that I was born a girl and not a "scion" compounded her pain. She could not *help* resenting me. I understand that.[63]

Gardner may not have actively chosen her father's side on this fundamental issue, but she was much more intrigued, attracted even, by his exciting life—by the fact that he had a mistress on the side, an actress no less—than by her mother's dreary daily rounds of bridge, her emphasis on prudence and posture. It was distressingly clear to Rose Gardner where her daughter's loyalties lay. In the 1950s, in therapy like so many of her contemporaries, struggling to make sense of her parents' characters and her relationship with them, Gardner tried to be fair, but the balance still was clearly weighted in Peabo's favor:

I've been thinking a good deal about Mother and Daddy since I left Roque. Poor mother seemed so drained of energy, so *emptied*; I had the feeling that no conversation was possible for her without cocktails. She used to like to 'discuss' family affairs—(mine and hers) usually in order to direct or dispute and is now too spiritually tired to be combative—or even interested. And now instead of the . . . gayety which at first often and then occasionally flashed to warm and delight all of us there is a kind of embarrassing volubility about the extraordinary merit of the menu couched in the form of repeated questions to which we must respond in crescendos of applause and gratitude. If she could only many years ago have gotten outside herself a little and realized that her contribution and fulfillment consisted in the six different and quite wonderful children she *created* and not in the food she feeds them or in the décor she provides them. But it is not *her* response to her children but theirs to her with which she is primarily concerned, and inevitably and constantly she is disappointed.

Daddy "looked" well and his personality had substance, his manner was controlled and unfrayed but I felt he was sad, lonely and forlorn.

No real analogy intended, but, as was said in *Death of a Salesman* "Attention must be paid." Daddy whatsoever his faults and limitations has been desperately conscientious and loving to-ward and about his children. He has always tried to recognize and applaud the value and uniqueness of the *person* in each child. Of course he has made mistakes but he has tried, *often* unselfishly, and we must recognize and meet and greet and salute and reassure, and we must nourish and protect that ego as we would that of our child once we are even vaguely sure within ourselves of who we are. I think he feels that since my analysis and my marriage to Bob that I have withdrawn from him, and it is true that I now am equally attentive to Mother and make no special gestures in his direction.[64]

Peabo Gardner was, by all accounts, far more easy to get along with than his "cold and unsmiling," disappointed, difficult, argumentative wife.[65] He was a terribly handsome, talented, and many-sided man, and Peabo's golden years lasted, while his wife's waned after she married him and adopted the strict mores for women of her time and position. "[I]f she were only NICE one could easily put up with her tiny frame of reference—stupidity," Kitty complained. "And if she were only CLEVER one could put up with the jabs and barbs."[66] Rose Grosvenor Gardner's daughter Belle never belonged to Boston's world of intolerant moralism and outward appearances; from the first withdrawn, dreamy, she preferred her private magic island kingdom: "almost schizophrenically unaware and unobservant of people—I was part of a tree—part of a blade of grass—part of the sea but apart from people—except one brother."[67] George was her "only link to love and reality," Gardner remembered when she was almost sixty. "The games we played . . . the screened porch, the prayers, the Audubon charts, the ice hut we made, the squirrels we fed, collecting nuts for them with Mademoiselle [Voirol?]. . . . [O]ur vast household staff used to say I was so ethereal I was 'not long for this world.'"[68]

Family dynamics were the more central, because, her youngest brother, Robert, explained, "there was a wall around us, literally. And nobody came in or out of that place without a good deal of explaining. It was not because Lindbergh's child had been kidnapped and murdered. It was because there was a certain isolation, a feeling of wanting to be separate and on top of the hill. . . . And I had no idea who was living in the houses that were surrounding the house that I was in."[69] The wall, the hill separated the Gardners, both in reality and metaphorically, from the world most Americans knew in the early twentieth century. The security of their wealth protected them from economic worry and competition, fostering, according to the writer Mary Manning, in Gardner, as in many other members of the New England aristocracy, "an extraordinary basic innocence": "They can be easily cheated, they are idealistic, they are always wide open to hurt. They float, they are like doves and are usually brought down."[70]

The Gardner children went to small, privileged private day schools, their hill home remaining their secluded stronghold. Belle Gardner started out in nearby Park School, to which she usually walked with George; Kitty could not attend continuously because of her health. Even at this early age, Gardner was vulnerable to those who had less, and she would give away her lunch to the "dear embarrassed man who was sweeping up Warren Street," or perhaps to Officer Carroll, who, though they thought he was knighted "Sir Carroll," seemed to be in need of extra nourishment.[71] The personalities of his three daughters, Peabo Gardner maintained, were formed very early and could be measured "in the way they reacted to how they were driven to school. They had the chauffeur and the town car, which was a very stylish car, and they had this sort of truck. When [Kitty] was driven to school, she wanted to be in the town car, and if she had to go in the truck, she wanted to be dropped off two blocks before school. Belle was so much in the clouds that she never knew what car she was in and could not care less anyway. If Rose had to go in the town car, she asked to be dropped off two blocks before school."[72] Gardner's brother George told a slightly different story: "Kitty did not mind driving up in the car, but Belle used to get out, and make sure that nobody knew that she would come that way. She was always very mindful of the person less privileged."[73] Ever in favor of the underdog, Belle Gardner was fond of the least likeable teacher at Park School, the English teacher Mrs. Harrods, "the one that people thought was a little bit of a grunt."[74] She read ravenously and once fell out of a tree with her book and broke her arm because she was oblivious to her physical surroundings. "When you were a child," nurse Suzie Micklay wrote Gardner after her first book of poetry, *Birthdays from the Ocean,* had come out, "I used to tell Mr and Mrs Gardner . . . that some day you would be a poem writer, as you were always reading poems, especially when we were getting dressed for school. I must finish my poem first, Suzie?"[75] Gardner not only read, she wrote her own. Many of her juvenile poems are typical of children's verse in their themes and their conscientious rhyming: "Shadows now are falling low, / O'er the pureness of the snow, / Lonely Shepherds watch their sheep / In a silence strong and deep."[76] Now and then, though, the wit that would be evident in Gardner's later poems peeps through:

> Here lies a mouse: 'Twas George's pet.
> He died unattended by a parson or vet.
> God hath forever stilled the beat
> Of his tiny dancing feet.
> Now he lies in tranquil calm—
> Far from evil and alarm.
> With many a sigh and many a tear
> We take our leave of Mousie dear.[77]

As a teenager, Gardner transferred to Beaver County Day School, which had been founded some years earlier by affluent parents who wanted their children, particularly their daughters, to have a more progressive education than was usual, with much emphasis on creativity and the performing and visual arts. With her interest in the theater, her passion for reading, and her attempts at writing, Gardner should have fitted in brilliantly, but she did badly. Her report card of February 1930, when she was fourteen, reads that though her "creative ability is very good," her "mechanics of English have been weak all through, due in large manner to badly formed habits in her earlier grades." In Latin, the "[e]xamination was most unsatisfactory, showing lack of effort. Isabella is not meeting requirements of the course and cannot overcome her difficulties unless she is willing to work seriously." If her work in French was "fairly good," attitude and effort were only "fair." In mathematics she was "failing to meet the minimal requirements of the course." In art, it said, "[e]ffort not her best;" and in chorus she had "considerable ability but dislikes to make a real effort." In all, this was "a very poor report—one of the poorest in the Senior High School. Isabella has so much ability along so many lines that it is too bad to see her not achieving that of which she is capable. She is failing in mathematics, in Latin and in the technical side of English."[78] The evermore violent conflicts with her mother, in whose eyes Gardner was always lacking, made Gardner, who wore her skin inside out, dramatically unhappy and contributed to her bad performance at school. Never a compliant child, she made "a fetish out of preferring the kitchen to the saloon," refused to learn manners—a difficult feat at Green Hill—vexing her mother, who had come to regard the cultivation of social grace as imperative.[79] Caught up in the constant crises of her parents' marriage, misunderstood and lonely, Gardner succumbed to rebellious despair.

Not affected by the Great Depression, which had blanketed most of America in a gray fog of misery, Gardner's parents decided to send their ungainly, slothful, underperforming teenager away to the country's most expensive boarding school for girls, Foxcroft, situated in hunting country in Middleburg, Virginia.[80] At horsey, posh Foxcroft, "this absolutely outrageously privileged place to be," some eighty girls, in grades nine to twelve, were prepared for their futures as the refined wives of the country's upper class.[81] In this chic setting, the daughters of the Abbott, Amory, Auchincloss, Carnegie, Endicott, Frick, McCormick, Mellon, Olmsted, Pulitzer, Roosevelt, Saltonstall, Spaulding, and Whitney families mingled, making suitable friends for life. (Jacqueline Bouvier, later Kennedy, did not get in.) Extending over four thousand acres, Foxcroft boasted "its own stable . . . and accommodation for twenty-five horses privately owned by the girls," "a large gymnasium especially built for indoor basketball with two galleries which can hold two hundred spectators," "a large entertainment hall with movable stage," and also "its own electric laundry" and "chick-farm with all the latest improvements for chicken-raising, sow-breeding, etc."[82]

The school was founded in 1914 and led by the indomitable Charlotte Noland, from a First Family of Virginia, whose self-appointed task of finishing the daughters of the finest families was not an easy one as most of them had been spoiled by nurses, governesses, and chauffeurs. "Miss Charlotte Noland of the Foxcroft School may never have heard of [Plato's] *Symposium* . . .—she was not a literary woman, fancying instead a curriculum of equestrian sports, military drill, and good works for her girls—but generations of Old Money women learned at Foxcroft . . . the same fiercely loyal, sometimes romantic friendships that Peabody and Gardner thought one of the great benefits of a boarding-school education."[83] And if Miss Noland, grande dame and one of the "all-time greatest manner mentors" regretted the girls "rode astride, instead of side-saddle," she did succeed in keeping her pupils in line and instilling in them a sense of belonging and love, an achievement celebrated sixty years later in a panegyric by Gardner's classmate, Joan Ryerson: "Miss Charlotte was a great Head of a girls' school, a woman who represented everything that was finest in 'gentlewomen' of the south. She was ladylike, dedicated to values and principles, at the same time highly imaginative, a creative spirit with a lively sense of humor and she really cared for her student body as individuals. She saw each one as she was in her uniqueness and imagined her as she would be. She was extremely beautiful. She rode a big white horse named 'Winter Weather' and for years was Master of the local Fox Hounds ('MFH'). Tradition meant much to her, but as something inspiriting and joyful, not an inflicting of the past on the present. She had courage, wit and compassion."[84]

The boarders slept two to a cubicle, on open porches, and marched to school dressed in militaristic tan corduroy skirts and green blazers with gold buttons, with as finishing touch a "sort of Rebel's cap from the confederate war"; in spring they wore green one-piece dresses.[85] They had classes in the mornings; afternoons were devoted to athletics for which they had ranks and platoons and were divided into two teams, Foxes and Hounds, who competed against each other, playing tennis, lacrosse, hockey, or basketball. This most elite of girls' schools, with its "quaint mixture of riding to hounds and reveling in lacy-valentine crushes," was exceptionally secluded, and apart from shepherded Sunday outings to church in provincial Middleburg and hunts with some distinguished Virginian neighbors, the Foxcoft girls only interacted with their teachers and one another.[86] For most, the first months at this inward-looking school were daunting, the more so because the new girls were hazed and "had to braid [their] hair into ten pigtails, wear . . . clothes inside out and entertain the older girls who dealt with [them] meanly and with sarcasm and cruel remarks."[87] Gardner, too, was forlorn for months: "Mother dearest: I am feeling *so* depressed. A few minutes ago I called up home and I wanted to speak to *you so* badly! *Why, why* wouldn't you speak to me to-night? . . . I thought you'd be glad and excited and want to speak to me but you didn't seem to care at all, and it means an *awful* lot to me. We are in the middle of mid year exams and I suppose that is making me more homesick than usual. Please, please Mummy write to me more and tell me why you wouldn't talk to me. I love you."[88]

Gardner soon fell under Noland's spell, later describing her lovingly as "wildly illiterate," but "wonderfully ardent and hospitable . . . and a robust generous hearted tomboy."[89] And although she "*hated* . . . the school spirit girl scout Mary Blagden all round type" and was never sporty, Gardner had always enjoyed horseback riding and had brought her own horse to Foxcroft.[90] In February 1931 she went foxhunting for the first time in her life: "Cherry went beautifully but it was a stiff test for both of us, as . . . we got to the meet at 11.00 a.m. and got home at 7.15 p.m. . . . I couldn't think of asking you for $50 for hunting regularly (every [M]onday) unless you would promise to consider it my only and premature birthday present, that would be *divine?!*"[91] Gardner got her wish and, during her first year at Foxcroft, became a passionate member of the hunting crowd. The school's curriculum, though certainly not intellectually strenuous, encouraged boarders to excel in what they were best at, provided they chose pastimes appropriate for young ladies. "She could keep reading, that was all she wanted to do anyway, and they encouraged that, because that is a good southern thing to do: to steep yourself in literature."[92] Gardner also enjoyed writing, prose and especially poetry, and did well at it: her poems and stories won prizes and were published in the Foxcroft yearbooks. Just a teen-ager, she used different poetic forms, from sonnet to the complicated triolet, freely, knowledgeably, and musically, but subject matter hardly went beyond the average adolescent poem. Her sonnet "I Am Alone upon a Bleak High Hill" ends: "The earth is still and beautiful and bare—/ But yet I long to break away from all / That I have known. I want to do and dare / And seek and find, scale every craggy wall; / I want to leap into an unknown sky / And answer every age-old how and why."[93] But the prose "Portrait," describing Gardner's visit to her great-great-aunt Belle shortly before her death in 1924, foreshadows the theme that would pervade her poetry:

> While I stood wondering how anyone could live in such a room, I saw my Aunt Belle, a white-wrapped figure in a great carved chair, high-backed like a throne. I went up to her. Over her head hung a portrait, Sargent I think, of a very old lady huddled in a throne chair; her arms, beautiful arms I knew, outlined under the folds of white. I looked down at Aunt Belle, and then I saw her eyes. Pathetically young and challenging they were desperate in their vitality, as though she had tried to acknowledge death, couldn't, and was afraid—afraid, I knew, not of the physical pain of death, but of the agony of losing life.[94]

In her boarding school's protected, slightly inbred ambiance, Gardner came to feel at home, and she partook readily of the possibilities Foxcroft provided, becoming president of its dramatic club and costume closet, church monitor, and a member of the Horse Show Committee. And if she never wholly chimed in with Foxcroft's girl-scout coterie, Gardner felt she belonged, was happier than at home, the more so as she had found in Barbara Ransom from Atlanta, great-granddaughter of Confederate General Thomas R. Cobb, a friend for life. But to Rose Grosvenor Gardner's disappointment, even this preeminent finishing school failed to improve Gardner's poise; upon her graduation in 1933 she was still gauche and awkward, hardly ready for the marriage market for which Foxcroft alumnae were groomed. Indeed, many of Foxcroft's for-mer students were married within a year or two, after first having made their debut, of course. "A christening, wedding, or funeral may happen to any-body," Dixon Wecter wrote in his acute *The Saga of American Society,* which was published just four years after Gardner was a debutante, "but the modern début is a rite belonging to Society alone, or at least to those who covet its prizes."

> Serving notice upon the social world that a daughter has become nubile, the début has immemorial roots which may be traced to coming of age in Samoa and Polynesia. . . . The traditional purpose of the début is to introduce a girl to So-

ciety of all ages—especially the friends of her family—whom, as cynics remark, she knows already and probably never wants to see again. . . . The average cost for hotel rental, food and drink, service, music and flowers runs at present from $5000 to $10,000. . . . With cruel irony, the girl who most needs the fanfare of début often can afford it least, while the worldling who is already well known—from school at Foxcroft, Miss Chapin's or Brearley, and summers at Newport, Bar Harbor, or Southampton—will be invited to the best parties and treated as a débutante though her family makes few overtures or none. . . . The old *Town Topics* of horrid memory loved to grade débutantes like certified milk, into categories which are still current among the ruthless. Grade A was the girl who had three generations of family, with money and personal charm. Grade B was a mixed lot into which were swept girls with background but scant attractiveness, reckless girls with money and position, and nice girls whose antecedents were a little tarnished by the wrong kinds of divorces and financial scandals; it was in fact a class demoted largely on the score of behavior, either one's own or one's parents.' Stamped with Grade C were children of the new-rich, still odorous of oil, paint and varnish, or the stockyards; theirs was a frankly hopeful campaign for a step on the escalator.[95]

Contrary to the custom of her class and family, Gardner was briefly seduced by the thought of going to university and sat for and received certificates from the College Entrance Examination Board. Scoring badly, she decided she did "not feel prepared for the rigors of the academic intellectual world."[96] In fact, she would hardly have had the time to go to college, because being a debutante was time-consuming and, in its way, strenuous, as hopes were high, competition fierce, and heartbreak around the corner. Beautiful Kitty, who had come out the previous year, had been popular and victorious, having readily returned her parents' investment in her private education and debut by catching one of that season's most eligible, wealthy bachelors, Parmely Herrick Jr., grandson of a famous American ambassador to France and family friend of the Charles Lindberghs.

Now, at barely eighteen, with titian blonde hair and audacious blue eyes, it was Gardner's turn to be introduced to the wedding mart, glamorously enacted as a round of romantic festivities with debutantes at their center. Starting out in September 1933 in Philadelphia, Gardner danced her way through a dizzying swirl of parties in Long Island and New York City, reaching a crescendo in her hometown in November and December. One of the finest celebrations, preceding Gardner's official coming-out party, was given by the Richard Curtises at the fashionable Hotel Somerset, "[f]estooned with pink roses and Southern smilax," for their nieces Sarah Cary Curtis, Mary Burnett Grosvenor, Rosa Anne Grosvenor, and Belle Gardner:

This important social event will unite a large family of prominence in New England . . . it will be one of the few debutante affairs of the winter where the older group and their friends will participate almost to the same extent as the young group . . . a very nice custom dating back to the Victorian era. . . . The ushers' dinner for 100 will be held before the dance at the Ritz-Carlton, given by Mr. and Mrs. Charles Pelham Curtis, Jr., and among the guests will be college friends and intimate friends of Mr. and Mrs. Curtis. Mrs. Richard Cary Curtis and Mrs. George Peabody Gardner, Jr. are entertaining a group of their friends at dinner. . . . Miss Isabella, tall, slender, and blonde, will wear a gown of cloth of gold.[97]

On December 19, on the basis of answers returned on a questionnaire sent out to debutantes, the *Boston Globe* announced Gardner's official presentation to society the next day with a lengthy, but apparently riveting, listing of the names of invited guests who made up a roster of America's aristocracy:

Mr. and Mrs. George Peabody Gardner, Jr., of "Green Hill," Brookline, are having a dinner for 50 guests at their home before their dance at the Ritz-Carlton tomorrow evening for their debutante daughter, Miss Isabella Stewart Gardner. . . .

Mr. William A. Coolidge will be head usher at the dance which will be one of those delightful parties with about half older and half younger people. Others at the ushers' dinner at the Gardner residence in addition to Miss Katherine Gardner, whose 20th birthday is tomorrow, and her fiancé, Mr. Parmely Herrick, Jr., will be Mr. and Mrs. J. Hampden Robb, Mrs. Evans R. Dick, Jr., Mr. William Prescott Wolcott and Miss Mary Harris of Philadelphia, who will be the Gardners' house guests.

Other guests at the dinner will be the Misses Nancy Shaw, Nancy Whitman, Rose Whitman, Nina Phillips, Susanna Minturn, Isabel Lawrence, Alice Clark, Hortense Clark, Mildred Carter, Louise Amory, Dorothy West, Gwendolen Livermore, Phyllis Forbes, Dorothy Forbes, Beatrice de Menocal, Emily Dick and Miss Lorraine Young.

Also dinner guests before the dance will be Messrs. Francis H. Burr, Nelson Alden, Charles Stockton, Benjamin Bacon, James T. Lee, Jr., Malcolm Stewart, Nelson B. Jay, Charles F. Adams, Jr., G. H. Kinincott, Jr., Thomas Jefferson Davis, Jr., Edward H. Robbins, Charles Woodard, Warren Delano Robbins, Robert Minturn, Robert Grant, 3d, William Gardner Davis, Louis Class Ledyard and Mr. Gilbert M. Congdon, Jr., of Providence.[98]

The Gardner party ("a great success. . . . Practically every head had a tiara perched on it") was part of the "last whirl before Christmas. . . . Last, because 'the Harvard boys' went home straight afterwards." Gardner "made an extra attractive debutante causing thereby a good many poor but happily received puns on her nickname 'Belle' and 'belle of the ball.'"[99] That night, Gardner was wearing a white taffeta dress with gardenias, as was Kitty, while their mother Rose was dressed in green, carrying green orchids. The Ritz was smothered in buddleia, Ruby Newman's society orchestra played the waltzes it would still perform sixty years later, and Gardner's ball-book was filled. Her debut seemed quite equal to her sister's in success: she was written up as "very tall, blonde and BEAUTIFUL . . . the most outstanding debutante we have seen so far this season," and as "one of the daintiest mannequins in the debutante ranks . . . always in demand at fashion shows. . . . Miss Gardner is one of the most popular of the new season's crop of debbies."[100] Among her ardent suitors were William Burnham, who hogged her dances, and Samuel Atkinson, who later chased her all over Boston.[101]

Exhilarated by the attention, and liberated from the protected confines of thoroughbred Foxcroft, Gardner partied with abandon: flirting, dancing, and drinking. (With her fellow graduates of the Class of 1933, enlisted by Noland, Gardner had wrapped candies with texts in favor of Repeal and distributed them, but they had not been allowed to drink a drop themselves. Noland, herself, was an outspoken opponent of Prohibition who always found ways to keep on drinking her cocktails.) In March 1933 the making and selling of beer and wines had again been allowed, but it was not until December 5, conveniently just before Gardner's coming-out party, that the dry years were over and alcohol could again be legally served in public. And where before Prohibition "a gentleman was expected to hold his liquor, which is why he got 'stiff' with the effort (ladies, of course, were not allowed to get drunk at all); after Prohibition, there was a pronounced relaxation of the 'stiffness' and of the double standard, and it became permissible, if not actually amusing, to get uninhibitedly drunk."[102]

Gardner, who had always been shy, withdrawn even, found that alcohol loosened her up and made her the life of the party. Alcoholism had always been a problem with the Gardners, Grosvenors, and Phinneys; reflecting on her own excessive drinking in the 1970s, Gardner tallied up a number of alcoholic uncles, some suicides, and "innumerable eccentrics with a capital E on . . . all sides of the family. For a family, that is, except for money and longevity, a *terrible* track record."[103] Her own parents "were able to control the amount that they drank," their youngest son recalled. "In fact they spent a great deal of their time doing exactly that. But to do that, and to spend a lot of your time doing that, indicates that there is a problem somewhere. Why else would you be putting so much effort in these little ritualistic rules and regulations and preventions, which were observed absolutely scrupulously, like you cannot drink until it is exactly seven o'clock in the evening? And then this immense cocktail shaker full of gin and vermouth appeared and [you would have to] start throwing them down as quickly as you can, because you only have a certain amount of time before the person comes in to tell you dinner is ready. You have to make hay in that. They could keep on drinking because they got wine at dinner, of course."[104]

All the ingredients for disaster were at hand: a debutante who had not been allowed to drink at boarding school; the end of Prohibition and the resulting overflow of alcohol; days starting with drinks at lunch and martinis during cocktail hour, running over into wine-drenched dinners and bibulous balls which went on until early the next morning. And although Peabo Gardner usually sent the family's driver to pick his daughter up from parties, she disliked making use of this service, preferring to drive home by herself, as having the car gave her freedom to experiment sexually; making out, however innocently, in the back of the car with the family chauffeur up front being out of the question. (The Gardner children slept with aluminized mittens on, so that they could not touch themselves, and around the Gardner daughters "sex was not mentioned at all," certainly not by Rose Grosvenor Gardner, who even left the subject of menstruation to their nurses.[105]) Belle Gardner was an inexperienced driver, and one night, driving a car full of revelers when she had definitely had too much to drink, she caused an accident in which a woman was grievously injured.[106] Robert Gardner, who was only seven or eight at the time, recalled "very, very vividly the mood in the house when this was happening. This was a situation which had to be met and had to be dealt with."[107] Proper Bostonians with an absolute dread of scandal and with clout, the Gardners hushed up the tragedy, and legal action was not taken. In fact, the disastrous accident was covered up so completely that it is impossible to find out, after all these years, what happened to the woman who was hit and whether she survived. If Gardner "felt so responsible" that she hardly ever got behind the steering wheel of a car again, from then on relying on chauffeurs, friends, or taxis to take her places, and if the accident touched her deeply, causing her "enormous unhappiness," as a Gardner she did not, like lesser mortals, have to face the (legal) consequences of her acts.[108]

Chapter Two

"Not at All What One Is Used To . . . ," 1934–1942

> Not long ago
> I portrayed a madwoman (but gentle and sentimental)
> I curtseyed, sang a short song as I did not
> stammer when I sang, and fondled a telescope that
> had belonged to a sea-going ancestor. It was agreed
> that at last, despite previous successes, I had indeed
> and finally found my niche.
> ("Not at All What One Is Used To . . .")

Isabella Gardner's debut ended dramatically in tragedy. She had been one of the most sought-after debutantes of her year, glamorous, vivacious, intelligent, and talented. Within her mental makeup, however, was a self-destructive streak; feeling always that her birth had been a disaster to her mother, Gardner seemed bent on proving it so. Peabo Gardner had the clout to protect his daughter from the law and from headlines in tabloids, but Boston knew that Belle Gardner was damaged goods. Her chances of an excellent match evaporated; what proper Harvard man would want to marry a girl who, driving while drunk, had caused a horrific accident? Far more fundamentally, Gardner could not cope with her feelings of guilt. Generally excessively vulnerable to even the smallest hurt done to others, she wiped this catastrophe consciously, rigorously from her mind; whereas she eventually mentions most of the incidents and accidents of her youth in her correspondence, this one calamity is omitted.[1]

What was left for a guilt-laden debutante who had been educated at a finishing school, then, finished, had bungled her debut—a debutante who had decided not to go to college even though "she clearly had the mind to deal with college and way beyond?"[2] The dea ex machina was an enchanting divorcée, Mrs. Edith Forbes Kennedy. In her early forties, with three sons to raise in a shabby genteel house on Shepard Street in Cambridge, Massachusetts, Mrs. Kennedy tried to make ends meet by proofreading and tutoring society girls who had not yet assumed their rightful positions as wives and mothers. In the words of a Brahmin, she "took young ladies under her wing . . . and usually built them up a little bit over what they were."[3] In the 1930s many girls and women came under her spell, the writer May Sarton most outspokenly and sentimentally, even though her passionate lesbian love for Kennedy was not reciprocated. Sarton fictionalized Kennedy as the protagonist's muse and mentor Willa MacPherson in her autobiographical *Mrs. Stevens Hears the Mermaids Singing* (1965) and she celebrated her in a memoir, *A World of Light* (1976), as "extremely tolerant, compassionate," a "tiny elegant presence" holding court and transfixing her manifold visitors by her charm, erudition, and conversation. "One cannot have brilliant conversation without a wide frame of reference. Edith had had no formal education, but she had read enormously and listened to music passionately and critically all her life, so she could hold her own with, and stimulate, friends as various as Ernest Simmons, Edwin Cohn, George Sarton, Nancy Hale, or Elliott Carter. Yet she was never pedantic, used slang in a pointed and witty way, and could be extremely funny." Sarton described how around ten in the morning Edith Kennedy "usually met with a group of young women who came to get her criticism on their short stories, or in private session with a single pupil. . . . . To each of them she was a touchstone."[4] Gardner, one in the "group of young women," concurred, calling Kennedy "a remarkable woman, whom I adored; I studied Dante, Chaucer, short story writing etc."[5]

Besides teaching her students classical authors, Edith Kennedy introduced them to a different range of books, from psychology to autobiography, depicting strata of society with which her sheltered protégées usually did not come into contact. Gardner saved her assignments dealing with these subjects, such as a sloppy report, citing both Carl Gustav Jung and Rabindranath Tagore while pouring scorn on Harry Allen Overstreet's trendy best-seller *About Ourselves* (1927), which intended to awaken its readers to the "revelation" that people need to know much more about themselves in order to function well spiritually and mentally; and an essay about Booker T. Washington's potent *Up from Slavery* (1901), in which she expressed amazement at its being "so refreshingly free from bitterness and hurt pride"; and she identified with Mary Antin's autobiographical account of her Russian-Jewish family's immigration to the Boston slums in *The Promised Land* (1912): "we too are Jews, sensing that we are a people apart, knowing we are despised and not understanding why."[6]

Kennedy was regarded by some as a dilettante, a Boston Forbes fallen on hard times to whom you sent your problem daughters to keep them out of mischief (and her, charitably, in funds), but Gardner felt indebted to this woman who "meant so amazingly much to me and taught me so much," opening up new literary vistas. Gardner had always read a few books a day indiscriminately, but neither at home, nor at Beaver Day or Park schools, or even at Foxcroft had she been guided.[7] Besides pointing her pupils to important books, Kennedy was an excellent reader of their own work and precisely pinpointed their shortcomings. Scoffing at sentimentality, Kennedy put her finger on Gardner's weak spot as a beginning poet, causing Gardner to "[stop] writing *poetry* then because I felt I was too facile."[8]

Another influential older woman in Gardner's life at this time was nimble-brained, acid-tongued Mary Manning, another friend of May Sarton's in small-town Boston. Born in Ireland in 1905, Mary Manning had left her homeland at sixteen to study theater in London, and worked in Dublin as an actress and playwright in the 1920s and early 1930s, also writing film criticism and collaborating regularly with her childhood friend Samuel Beckett. After she was jilted by her lover, the novelist Anthony Powell, for Lady Violet Pakenham—also Anglo-Irish and similarly blessed with an infectious curiosity and sharp wit, but with money and a title to boot—Manning immigrated to America in 1934, to direct drama at Radcliffe College. Soon after, in February 1935, she married the liberal Boston lawyer and writer Mark De Wolfe Howe.

Connections between the upper-class Irish in Ireland and those in Boston were strong, reaching into the higher echelons of the Brahmins; in the right circles, everybody knew everybody else. Manning's family in Ireland was close to Mollie Osgood Childers, who was Boston-born, had been one of Isabella Stewart Gardner's young protégées, and was Robert Erskine Childers's widow. In January 1904, after a three-week courtship, Osgood had married Childers, the Protestant Anglo-Irish writer of, reputedly, the first espionage novel ever, *Riddles of the Sand* (1903). A driven idealist, actively encouraged by his wife, Childers ardently took up the cause of Irish independence, even conspiring with the German kaiser during the Great War, for to him, as in the old Irish adage, "England's crisis was Ireland's opportunity." Wholly English in bearing, he was the implausible secretary-general of the Irish delegation negotiating the Anglo-Irish Treaty of 1921. Its outcome, particularly the oath of allegiance Irish leaders had to pledge to the British king, bitterly wounded him, and he became one of its fiercest opponents. When Ireland subsequently plunged into Civil War, the government of the recently founded Irish Free State—based on the treaty—branded him a traitor, arrested him, and had him shot while appeal of his death sentence was pending. Till the last the romantic revolutionary, Childers, in his cell, made his teenaged son, Erskine Hamilton Childers, promise to "approach those who had signed his death-warrant and person-ally convey his forgiveness, a daunting task which was faithfully undertaken."[9] Childers himself clasped hands with the members of the firing squad, and his last words were: "Take a step or two forwards, lads. It will be easier that way."[10]

On both sides of the Atlantic the De Wolfe Howes, Mannings, and Gardners also mingled with the Farley family, George Peabody Gardner Jr. being "great pals" with Farley Senior at their Somerset Club. As their wealth had apparently been made in shipping only in the nineteenth century, the Farleys did not quite belong to Boston's First Families, and though the men fraternized convivially at their club, for Mrs. Farley there was, "naturally, no speaking to the Gardners."[11] Still, in 1935 Belle Gardner was given permission to travel to Ireland in the company of the Farleys' witty, beautiful daughter Betty, with, as their unlike-ly chaperone, unconventional Mary Manning, at least now safely married. "It was in the nature of things that Bella and Beth would become friends," Farley fictionalized in "A Lack of Decorum." "They were the same age and attended the same parties, but, more than that, they considered themselves, and were considered, non-conformists. They had been brought up in much the same manner and they shared the same disdain for the precepts and codes of their parents. . . . They merely wanted to be 'fast.'"[12]

Sailing to Ireland, Gardner had the requisite seaboard romance with a darkly handsome Italian diplomat, for, perhaps to shield herself from disappointment after the car accident, she was no longer interested in pedigreed Boston suitors, whose respectable futures as bankers, directors, trustees, and philanthropists were foreordained, and whose wives would duplicate her mother's fashionable Boston drawing-room existence. "They seemed very pale to her . . . she may not have been attracted to the white-bread men, the WASPs."[13] When asked around this time to characterize her sister Kitty, who was steeped in respectability and the living embodiment of her mother's social aspirations, Gardner answered cattily that "the best description would be to say that she thinks a suitable hus-band might come from Harvard or Yale and very few from Princeton."[14]

Ireland, which Gardner had not visited since childhood vacations with her family, promised to be full of the warmth and color of her nurses' stories, of myths, folklore, and heroes, all of which to her had always been more real, cer-tainly more romantic, than everyday life at Green Hill. "As a child of 8 or 10 years and for years I *identified* with Artemis as a child. There were times when I *was* a naiad . . . a dryad. Afterward the Greek and Norse deities were more 'fa-miliar' to me than even my own family and friends and when I was older and in Ireland the Sidhe—and Oisin, Naoisi, Cuchulain and so on—still later Graves' White Goddess—the Golden Bough—From Ritual to Romance, Brinton's and Campbell's The Hero with a 1,000 Faces—Myths of the New World. To deny myth, and its life long importance to me would be like denying nature."[15]

Farley and Gardner stayed with Irish Farley and Manning relatives, spent time in Dublin at the stately Shelbourne Hotel, and generally were in a buoyant holiday mood, intending to have fun and perhaps meet interesting men. Manning duly introduced the young American heiresses to her friends, among them Mollie Osgood's son, Erskine Hamilton Childers, who was to become Gardner's first true love. Born in London in December 1905, Childers had spent most of his youth with his parents in Wicklow, Ireland.[16] After his father's execution, he had immediately left Ireland, returning permanently ten years later at the request of one of its leading political figures, Éamon de Valera. Like his close political confidant Robert Erskine Childers, de Valera had recoiled from the Anglo-Irish Treaty of 1921. Having spent some time in prison for his anti-treaty activities, de Valera became prime minister in 1932 when his Republican Party, Fianna Fáil, won the election. It is hard to untwist the tangled threads of the Irish political situation in those days, but de Valera's government was initially supportive of the (anti-treaty) Irish Republican Army. He legalized the IRA and freed its political prisoners during his first two years in office; its membership grew fivefold to 10,000. The Great Depression, which had hit Ireland hard, had fueled the growth of radical groups like the IRA and the opposing quasi-fascist Blueshirts, whom de Valera quickly tried to neutralize. By 1935, the IRA had come to regard him as too soft, because he put up with the separation of Ireland, while de Valera found the IRA, with its continued guerrilla tactics, too confrontational and belligerent, as he tried to make Ireland an independent republic by legal and official methods only. He was soon to ban the IRA again.

It was at this time, in this divided country, that Gardner met charismatic Erskine Childers, whose life and thought had been shaped, from the first, by his parents' strict moral, idealistic code and their passionate devotion to Ireland. A few weeks after his father's death, Childers, at seventeen, had met the worldly-wise American Ruth Ellen Dow, then twenty-three, and they became involved. In 1924 he enrolled in Trinity College, Cambridge, to study politics and history and acquired a striking upper-class British accent. Although not yet twenty, he overcame his family's initial resistance and married Ruth Dow. The couple soon left for Paris, where Childers worked for a travel agency, for a few years free from the burden his parents had put upon him; "English by birth and upbringing, Irish through filial devotion, he was perhaps a Parisian by inclination and temperament."[17] But the tourism trade collapsed because of the Great Depression, de Valera beckoned, and Childers, ruled by his promise as an adolescent to his father "to do everything possible to effect reconciliation between Irishmen and between Britain and Ireland," returned to Dublin in 1932, accompanied by his wife and, by that time, three children.[18] With his conspicuous name, he chose deliberately "to live in the same corner of the same city as had his father," executed only ten years before.[19]

For Childers, living symbol of Irish martyrdom, Ireland always came first. He joined de Valera's Republican Party and worked for the newly founded Irish Press; cloaked in the tragedy of his father's life, he was almost more Irish than the Irish. He was good-looking, courteous, vibrant, and genuinely interested in music and the arts; his biographer John Nichols Young noted that "poetry was already an essential ingredient in his life and he frequently wore the thoughtful, abstracted look of a poet searching for a vital stanza."[20] Inevitably, Gardner at nineteen, with her lust for life, longing for love, and passion for Ireland, fell deeply in love with this Oisin. Looking back, in 1958, she wrote to her then-lover, the southern writer Allen Tate: "I have thought myself in love at least six times since I was eighteen but looking at my life though I don't deny the *in* love-ness of those six or seven I think I only really loved three. My first lover and the only man I had a total relationship before my first marriage and Bob [McCormick]; and you whom I love entirely and finally and with a difference." She added a few months later: "[b]y the way I was 19 when I fell in love with him but 21 when we were lovers."[21] Stressing that Childers had "notorious affairs" (passed over in Young's adulatory biography) and never prudish herself, Mary Manning, gadfly and cat queen, was sure that Gardner was indeed still a virgin in 1935.[22] She was certainly innocent. She made a side trip to Paris, where she was taken in hand by Countess Palffy, who reported to Gardner's parents that the "dear, darling child" was "really *fascinating*," but also "a goose. Perhaps it's her age—perhaps young America. . . . [S]he has taken for the last week to being what one might call featherheaded. Poor kid, I don't blame her, she is really very pretty and attractive."[23] A few weeks later Palffy added: "To my mind she ought to develop into a fascinating *woman*. . . . Far more so than any girl I've seen so far. . . . So much am I interested in her that I have put everything aside to show her different things and as many different kinds of people as possible."[24]

With an expensive Paris evening dress in her trunks, Gardner returned to Boston in the fall, infatuated with Childers and, consequently, more moved by Ireland and the Irish than ever. She steeped herself in Irish folksongs, poetry, myths, but also politics, and was outraged by what came to be called the Arranmore disaster. On Saturday evening, November 9, 1935, nineteen poor Irish died when the boat that was ferrying them back from Scotland to the island of Arranmore hit a rock, for it was dark and foggy and there was no beacon. Only young Patrick Gallagher was rescued; clinging to the boat for fifteen hours, he had long held on to his father and brother only to see them slip into the sea. As there was hardly any work for the young and uneducated poor in rural Ireland, like many others they had gone as cheap labor to Scotland for the season, "tatie hoking" (gathering potatoes). Gardner saved many clippings about this tragedy. IRA adherents recognized its political capital against the backdrop of the

Great Irish Famine, caused by potato blight. Though over eighty years in the past, the famine's dramatic consequences were still felt both economically and emotionally and the British still blamed for culpable neglect or, by some, for downright genocide. The deaths of nineteen potato-picking Irish were made to measure for patriotic clarion calls against the British imperialist oppressors. One clipping says it all: "Yes, the Northern counties, and Fermanagh in particular, are rich in the historic traditions of the Gael. These traditions belong to the whole people of Ulster, irrespective of creed. They will prevail against artificial boundaries—against the might of Imperialism, against all those enemies who would dare to prolong the dismemberment of the nation, and they give reality to the cry we raise against the foreigner, 'Ulster is ours, not theirs.'"[25]

With suchlike political rhetoric reverberating in her impressionable mind, Gardner, once more accompanied by Betty Farley and Mary Manning, returned to Ireland and Childers in the summer of 1936. That year Manning's reclusive childhood friend Samuel Beckett was back from London, again living with his mother. Some ten years older than these Americans abroad, Beckett fell head over heels in love with sparkling, extrovert, vivacious Betty Farley, who, however, was not at all romantically interested: Beckett was much too self-absorbed, somber, and quiet for her taste. Joined, often, by Childers, the four spent much time together, driving, playing tennis, and visiting other members of the Anglo-Irish upper and middle classes.

In Betty Farley's account of one such visit "Bella was asked to pour the tea, an honor in that country, but one that had not been accorded her before. She sat down gracefully at a large table laden with a massive silver tea service surrounded by an array of delicious looking food. Silence reigned. Beth had observed that when an Irishman is shy, he stands straight, and folds his hands in front of him in what appears to be a protective gesture. A large group of men were standing thus on one side of the room. The ladies were seated wearing tentative smiles. . . . Their host, warm hearted man, decided to somehow end the extended silence. He strode across the room bearing a plate. 'And will you have a cookie?' . . . The four of them, Sam, Beth, Bella and lover, broke into uncontrollable laughter. . . . It became apparent that their only recourse was to leave."[26] Gardner also spent much time in less innocent ways. Quick to feel deeply for the oppressed, hurt by mad Ireland itself, propelled by "the excitement and thrill of the revolution, the fact that the Irish had been downtrodden for so long," and inspired by Childers, Gardner hurtled herself into politics.[27] Young's emphasis on Childers's peacemaking, nonrevolutionary stance on Irish politics may be a whitewash for the sake of his memory as Ireland's elected fourth president in 1973—the year in which he died. For Betty Farley found him "angry about his father" and "bristling with revolution"; she remembered the "aura of romance . . . with this revolutionary man" which made him all the more attractive in Gardner's eyes.[28] It seems indeed improbable that Childers would easily have given up on the dream of a united independent Ireland for which his father had given his life, even if de Valera, now in power, was becoming very anti-IRA. With or without Childers's complicity, Gardner was roused to action and became mixed up with the revolutionaries who fought against the injustices done the Irish poor.

Manning's and Farley's Anglo-Irish relatives and friends, whose comfortable existence was threatened by the IRA, were enraged by Gardner's "playing around with the IRA," which later, hyperbolically, became Gardner's "almost toppling the Irish Government."[29] Peabo Gardner was informed and dashed off a telegram filled with paternal wrath, signed, atypically, "Gardner" instead of "Popkin": "CABLEGRAM RECEIVED FROM FARLEYS INDICATED YOU HAVE NOT PLAYED FAIRLY WITH US WE ARE HURT AND MORTIFIED WANT YOU RETURN SOON AS POSSIBLE."[30] Gardner had once more let the family down. Unused to being rebuked by her father, she obeyed, asserting much later that "if I *had* defied them they couldn't have done a thing about it! But in those days parental authority existed."[31] Nothing was further from the truth, however, as she was financially dependent on her father, and so, although she was more entranced by Ireland than ever, the Republic had to make do without her subversive activities in its behalf. For the second year in a row, Gardner had to leave the man she had come to worship, Erskine Childers, in her eyes Ireland's heroic personification. Although they had become much closer, their relationship still had not blossomed into a complete physical love-affair; at twenty, Gardner may have hesitated taking for her first lover a married man, or, conversely, Childers may have been otherwise amorously engaged at the time. The one odd liaison that did occur, later that summer, was between longtime friends Beckett and Manning: Beckett on the rebound from Farley and Manning scared by her hasty marriage to Mark De Wolfe Howe (which would last until his death in 1967) sought comfort in each other's arms.

Ireland and its plight made such an indelible impression upon Gardner that some of her new friends in America were sure "she was very Irish . . . one part of the family strain was Irish."[32] They noted Gardner's "really superb ability to sing genuine Irish songs, not the 'stage-Irish' that Americans know, but 'The Rose of Cuchulain' etc., head tilted back and the eerie Irish sob just under the lilt of the tune. She'd stand on a low table at parties and was transported."[33] One of them was Martin Manulis, who met Gardner in an acting venture that she had set her heart upon after having been ordered back to the States. Four years earlier, at Foxcroft, Gardner had played the role of "Emmy" in Lulu Vollmer's Broadway tragedy *Sun-Up* and had all the girls cry, because "her tears were so convincing."[34] During her last year there, she had starred as princess in A. A. Milne's *Ivory Door* and been president of the Dramatic Club, which put on popular plays like Shaw's *Pygmalion* and Alice Hegan Rice's *Mrs. Wiggs of the Cabbage Patch.*[35] Back from Ireland, Gardner took up acting again, starting out with fundraising plays for the Boston Junior League in which she "invariably was cast as a little boy or a little girl of ten."[36] Dating back to 1901, the Junior League was based on the old aristocratic idea of *noblesse oblige:*

> At its best the Junior League has done a limited but efficient stint of philanthropy, and even more important, has given many rich girls a chaperoned glimpse of how the other half lives. Even at its most snobbish, the Junior League has made society women eager to wait on tables, sell all manner of articles over the counters of bazaars, assist doctors in the clinics of slums, and perform other drudgeries because they are "exclusive"—a voluntary and aristocratic debasement like that of medieval kings who washed the feet of the poor on Maundy Thursday.[37]

Following in her father's footsteps, Gardner also performed in the Harvard Dramatic Club, playing Mrs. McFie in Merton Hodge's romantic comedy of student life *The Wind and Rain,* the *Harvard Crimson* noting, probably put up to it by Gardner herself, that "Isabella Gard[n]er and Bettina Grey are from the Erskine School."[38] There were many more plays, and late in life Gardner remembered that she had "great fun": "I had presence; and I was very good at character comedy. . . . I played the lead woman's part in a play by Mary Manning directed by Whitey Lutz. . . . The caustic lady critic said we were all thoroughly cast to type. We were not bland or pleasant characters. Then Whitey Lutz and I and Bill Otis started the Studio Club and we put on plays there, and readings. It was a rendez vous for artists and writers—Frieda Lawrence came; and Robert Hillyer and Dorothy (now de Santillana) were regulars."[39] The Studio Club was partly funded with Gardner money and, like the Junior League and Harvard Dramatic Club plays, very much an experience for socialites.

Having dabbled successfully in drama, Gardner "wanted to be an actress but it took several false starts and numerous amateur productions" before she landed her first professional part. It was, clearly, not expected of Gardner, as an heiress, though no longer Grade A, to choose a profession at all, but to engage in pleasant and charitable activities, pending marriage. But acting deeply appealed to Gardner's imaginative and feisty spirit: "I suppose acting is a *re*-creation—not of the character as indicated by what the author has said alone but of all that he has not said," she wrote in the mid-1950s to her brother Robert and his wife, Lee. "The actor must (I used to believe and think I still do) fill in all the gaps in the character's life."[40] Gardner felt safe when she acted, losing herself in grand gestures, living, for a magical moment, in a make-believe world, living other people's lives rather than her own as an awkward loner in the Gardner clan. And then, both of her parents had been skilled amateur actors, and the Gardners, Grosvenors, and friends always played charades enthusiastically and competitively at Roque; so acting just might improve her standing with the family. Then, too, the generally left-liberal, bohemian world of actors, the an-tipode of what the Gardners stood for, was an added, powerful attraction, and Gardner did her utmost to blend in:

> There was never any worry about bread or even butter
> although that worried me almost as much as my stutter.
> I drank coffee with the others in drugstores and then went
> back to my room for which I paid a lower rent
> than I could afford and where I was proud
> of the bedbugs, and where I often allowed
> myself an inadequate little Rhine wine.
> ("Not at All What One Is Used To . . . ,"73)

In the summer of 1937 Gardner went to East Hampton, Long Island, to en-roll in the Leighton Rollins School of Acting.[41] Harry Leighton Rollins Jr. had joined the theater after college. At the Repertory Theater of Boston he became general assistant to its director, Henry Jewett. As he later recalled, "I was a fac-totum. Over a period of three years I was at one time or another assistant stage manager, stage manager, assistant production manager, box office attendant, public relations director, and dean of the theater school. This was on the job training of the most effective sort, and I got it for nothing."[42] Moving to New York City in 1926 he met "all the literary folk of that period—all the poets of that golden age—Amy Lowell, E.A. Robinson, Robert Frost, Vachel Lindsay, Robert Hillyer, Edna Millay and many others." He also met many talented but underworked actors. Inspired, he founded one of the earliest summer stock theaters in the United States, in Surry, Maine, where the company, in the appre-ciative words of the British garden writer Marion Cran, was made up "of men and women (just out of Yale, Vassar, such as Joseph Cotten, Van Heflin, Hank Fonda, etc.) ambitious, poor, very pleasant to look upon. . . . Leighton Rollins . . . is a man who follows a star—he knows how to pick people. Only one thing matters to him—the future and security of his dream."[43]

A few years later, Rollins opened his theater school nearer New York, in artsy East Hampton, Long Island. Many wealthy native New Yorkers owned second homes in this picturesque village, assuring Rollins of excellent possibilities for fundraising (at which he was a past master), a regular crop of well-paying pu-pils to balance those who were talented but without much money, and an audi-ence. The Leighton Rollins Studio was based on the large estate of widow Mary Woodhouse, village benefactor and patron of the arts, who first loaned and, later, much to her son's chagrin, gave Rollins the land and its buildings, including its sumptuously elegant manor, "Greycroft," East Hampton's architectural showcase.

Rollins used it "to house his boarding students (numbering about thirty-five a season) presided over by his mother, Mrs. Harry Rollins, whose title was Dean of Residence. The *Greycroft Carriage House* was adapted as the Laboratory Theater for classes and try outs of plays. The major productions were presented at the John Drew Theater, Guild Hall. Rollins' own headquarters were in the *Greycroft Windpump Tower,* a separate structure on the estate, where he held court at a large double knee-hole replica of George Washington's writing desk. The only new building was a dining hall located behind the main house."[44] Tuition for the summer was $200, room and board $18.50 a week, enormous sums at the time, and so Rollins, truly dedicated to young talent, set about and succeeded in finding funds for scholarships.[45] Stewart Stern, who was to write *Rebel without a Cause* and who won an Emmy Award for his television movie *Sybil,* was one of the lucky ones: "I won one of the scholarships and went out to this amazing summer theater. It was run by a man named Leighton Rollins who was mentor to I can't even tell you how many budding actors who really became something, and a man of the highest principle. Boston-born and bred of the old school, and he had a staff that also came out of the old school, the classic theater, people whose names meant something back then and mean nothing now, and body movement way ahead of its time."[46]

A Long Island journalist, Dorothy Quick, also praised him for discovering Sylvia Weld, Barbara Robbins, Van Heflin, and set designer Jonel Jonqulescu, although she did wonder about his engaging Henry Fonda, "because no one thought he could act, . . . perhaps the one instant where Mr. Rollins' remarkable insight for picking talent was at fault." She regarded Rollins as "a far-seeing man with a likeable personality that wins friends for him wherever he goes, . . . a poet, an author and an actor himself, with an addiction to loud tweeds and striking colored shirts."[47]

Martin Manulis, who became famous as producer of TV's daring "Playhouse 90" in the 1950s, started out as Rollins's assistant director and, later, his general manager. He was more critical.[48] He thought Rollins "essentially a dilettante, who had never really had any professional career in the theater to qualify for this. But he was a man who read a lot and who was in general a literate and good person. . . . He always had the sensibility to raise scholarships from rich people for supposedly talented young people who could not afford it. So, although the school had maybe a preponderance of kids from richer families, there was a lot of very poor ones who came on scholarships."[49] One of them was an unemployed Betty Comden, before she partnered with Adolph Green. Comden and Green would alter the face of the Broadway and Hollywood musical with such seminal works as *On the Town* and *Singin' in the Rain*. Another was the British actor Patrick Troughton, arguably the best Dr. Who of the television series of that name, who had enrolled at sixteen at the reputable Embassy School of Acting in Swiss Cottage, London, run by Eileen Thorndike. The British and American schools exchanged their talented actors, and Troughton earned a scholarship to the Rollins Studio.[50]

In 1937 there was a heady mix of amateur and professional players at the studio, and Gardner tried to blend in with the serious, talented scholarship students:

> Most of the kids were very poor and struggling young actors trying to get an education and trying to go to this place for the summer. Belle was certainly part of the group and very popular with everybody. But one time her family were coming down to East Hampton during the summer and they wanted to have a party and Belle wanted to simply invite everybody. She had been very careful, so nobody had any idea what background she had. So now that the yacht was arriving she felt she had to come clean about everything and so she was underplaying it to say: "Now do not be upset when you see my family's boat. It is about as big as the Queen Mary!" And indeed it was, it was a great yacht.[51]

Rollins claimed that more than half of his students and summer staff became successful professionals, and his record is indeed impressive. Of the students of 1937, Ruth Enders (only seventeen at the time) and the New Yorker Lemuel Ayers would go on to Broadway or Hollywood. Ayers had just graduated from Princeton and became the set and costume designer of such Broadway classics as *Kismet* (1963) and *The Pajama Game* (1954). He is best-known for the musical *Kiss Me Kate* (1948), which won him two Tony Awards, one as its producer and one for best costume design—even though, when the production ran short of money, he had had to use heavy-duty curtain fabric for some of the period costumes. And there was Henry Levin, a graduate from the University of Pennsylvania, who would soon, in true wide-ranging East Hampton tradition, work as dialogue coach, actor, stage manager, and director on Broadway. In 1943 Levin left for Hollywood, where he became spectacularly successful as the director of some fifty movies, first with Columbia and later with Fox, working with all their stars, from Myrna Loy, Betty Grable, and Susan Hayward to Pat Boone, Bobby Darin, Dean Martin, and Omar Shariff. His biggest challenge was Errol Flynn, but, according to his schoolmate Maurice Donohue, Levin "could and did control Errol (knew he was afraid of his Mum!)"[52]

Levin's dramatic talents had first been discovered by his Trenton high school drama teacher, Harold Van Kirk. Van Kirk secured scholarships to East Hampton for his gifted high school pupils, when he became one of Leighton Rollins's directors, or got them jobs as members of its staff. He had also spotted Maurice Donohue, "Don," who was, at twenty-seven, two years younger than Levin and who also felt beholden to Van Kirk for his recognition of his gifts, even after he left acting for the Air Corps. Van Kirk also fostered the career of Trenton's Ernest Kovacs, for whom Van Kirk obtained East Hampton scholarships two years in a row. Van Kirk's influence on young Kovacs, who became "best of all those wildly inventive funnymen" in the new medium of television cannot be overestimated.[53] At the request of Kovacs's mother, Harry Holland, yet another of Van Kirk's all-male cast of Trenton protégés—"they were crazy about [Van Kirk] and very admiring of his talent and ability"—promised to take care of her young son amidst all these artistic types.[54]

As for the staff of the Rollins Studio, lean, silver-haired six-foot-two Harold Van Kirk directed, staged plays, gave voice and acting lessons, and served as production manager. William Raymond was, like Manulis, an assistant director. The two women on staff were modern dancer Ingeborg Torrup, who had been in seven shows on Broadway, including as Regan in *King Lear* (1930) and a petite, luscious Roxanne in *Cyrano de Bergerac* (1928); she was in charge of dance and body work. The other was sensible Frances Pole Sacco, who taught at New York's elite Finch School for Girls during the academic year and convinced many of its classy young graduates to attend the Rollins Studio.[55] Divorced from the much older English director and actor Reginald Pole (lover of the artist Beatrice Wood and many others), she was wed to the stunningly good-looking musician John Sacco.

In 1937 most of the actors at the Leighton Rollins Studio were virtually unknown; fame would not come to them until after the war, but it would have been hard to find a more promising group. Gardner formed long-lasting friendships with the most talented among them, excepting Kovacs, who was too young and prankish for her. Her "very close group of friends" included sensible Martin Manulis, hyperactive Maurice Donohue, Henry Levin, Harry Holland, and her soul mate Lem Ayers. "There was an *extraordinarily* gifted group. Martin Manulis (Playhouse 90—etc. etc etc.) Henry Levin, Hollywood director, Betty Comden. Ernie Kovacs, above all my beloved Lemuel Ayers, *great* scene designer—Forrest Thayer—costume designer."[56] The Finch graduates for whom Rollins Studio was simply an exciting summer camp generally left her cold. Her one true woman friend that year was Blanche O'Riorden, to whom she remained devoted all through her life.

The women lived in luxury in gabled Greycroft, had bedrooms with fireplaces and indoor bathing facilities, and were served food so excellent that Harry Holland felt privileged to get leftovers from the cook, who had taken a shine to him. The men, including the staff, stayed in the old barn on cots, with only one cold shower outside for all. In the big house, at four o'clock, tea was served, supervised by Mrs. Rollins, who often invited such potential sponsors as Mrs. Winthrop Gardiner, Mrs. Cortlandt Godwin, or Mrs. Thomas Jefferson Mumford for the young women to meet. Many afternoons, too, Mrs. Woodhouse herself, fashionably hatted and wearing scarves to hide her double chin, presided over tea (always Lapsang souchong) at her mansion just across the lane; all were expected to pay court.

Greycroft was too much like the Boston milieu Gardner was fleeing, and so she vastly favored the company of her literate, liberal male friends, who, like her, preferred white wine to tea. "There were far prettier girls there," Martin Manulis remembered, but Gardner "was a personality, she stood out. Even at that young age, she was intellectual in a sense. . . . I was impressed with her knowledge of literature and her knowledge in particular of poetry, which I knew very little about, and her awareness of what she had read and what she had absorbed."[57] Whereas Lem Ayers appealed to her creative and sensitive side—"they were really birds of a feather"—Gardner found an intellectual companion in multi-talented, wild Irish Maurice Donohue. "He was very bright; he was an impassioned person. We had some local bar in East Hampton we would all frequent. If you came upon them when he and Belle got there first—because we would always sit together, people did not go off into corners—he and Belle were nose to nose, talking about some weighty matters . . . things that were too weighty for most of us at the time."[58] Since her stay in Ireland, politics were high on Gardner's agenda and Donohue, too, was gripped by and incisively au courant with world affairs. Manulis recalled:

> They certainly were liberal Democrats and Belle's family of course was Republican. We were young, we had been educated and we felt that it was wrong for some people to have so much and other people to have nothing. I later married into the very staunch rich Republican Bard family from Illinois. I remember a close friend of theirs—Frank Knox, who during the War became secretary in the Navy—once saying to my wife [Katherine], who said she was very upset about the fact that her leanings were to the other side: "You know, if you are not a communist before you are twenty-one, there is something wrong with your heart. If you remain one after you are twenty-one, there is something wrong with your head." I always thought that was a wonderful thing, because the theater in New York was very heavily, heavily to the left then. Not the big stars, not the Katherine Cornells and the Helen Hayeses and those people, but the big active theaters, working class theater, group theater. . . . People like Belle and my own wife—who was then not my wife—felt that.[59]

It was a magical, heady, innocent time. Intensely responsive to her new friends, who were so much more electrifying than most of the men she had met in

Boston, Gardner lived the romantic life she craved. They talked on the beach into the night or went to New York City, to the old Lincoln Hotel on 8th Avenue between 44th and 45th Streets, where they had coffee for five cents, got innumerable refills, and discussed their future, the atrocities committed by the Loyalists in the Spanish Civil War, or joining the Communist Party. Gardner's sympathy for the party is beyond dispute: she attended its meetings and picketed enthusiastically, upsetting her politically conservative capitalist father. To his immense relief, she drew the line at becoming a card-carrying member, as Gardner threw herself wholeheartedly into her theater work; acting was more urgent than trying to save the world.

From July through September, for the five full-length plays the Rollins Studio mounted, its students learned how to act, to move, to speak, but also how to light the stage, paint sets, or borrow props from patronesses. That year, Gardner was, for instance, assistant stage manager in Lynn Rigg's *Green Grow the Lilacs,* on which Rodgers and Hammerstein later based *Oklahoma!* and had a substantial part as a charwoman in a play directed by Harold Van Kirk:

> I imagined and listed her parents' occupations, no. of siblings, upbringing, husband's first name, age, character and profession (he doesn't appear in the play), her feelings to-ward him, when and why they married. Her politics, her tastes in food, her attitudes to-ward her own children and their number and gender (the author does not say if she has any) her feelings to-ward each character in the play etc. And *her* first name which is not given. In the play she is called Mrs. Woodman or Woody.
>
> I shall never forget how exciting creating that character was. I tried to do the same thing after that but some-how in stock there wasn't time, no director was ever as exciting as Van was on that show and I became lazy and perhaps tricky. But oh what *fun* it was. That particular play (a bad one called *Crime at Blossoms*) was as exciting as writing a poem that comes close to what one intends.
>
> Ridiculous perhaps to work that intensely on a middle-sized part in a bad play but the *working* was so exciting and I can still feel the glow of it.[60]

Mordaunt Sharp's *Crime at Blossoms* was performed in July, 1937, but this letter, written almost twenty years later, still radiates Gardner's genuine seriousness about and deep-seated joy in her work as an actress. In August, to raise funds, the Rollins Studio presented "Stunt Night," comic sketches written and acted by its students, at the stylish, professionally outfitted John Drew Memorial Theater—a gift from Mrs. Woodhouse to East Hampton which seated over three hundred playgoers. A reviewer noted that "the entire program was amusing and greatly enjoyed; but a few numbers were so outstanding that they might have been the work of professionals in the theatre. Isabella Gardner, as the toothless old Irish woman, was priceless; Pauline Kissell, singing 'Parlez Moi d'Amour' in French, was extremely appealing; and Ernest Kovacs, doing the Jersey family and the tramp, brought down the house."[61] In Frances Pole Sacco's production of Aristophanes' comic masterpiece *The Birds*, Gardner, as a citizen of the Birds' kingdom, did an imitation of Eleanor Roosevelt and was "marvelous, because there was the impression that she was pretty scatter-brained. The background was similar, so the speech was right and Belle was re-ally very good at that. And she came in with a knitting bag all full of little babies and was very amusing."[62]

Maurice Donohue regarded Gardner as a "very good actress," but some of her professional friends were more judgmental, Manulis calling her "good enough" particularly in comic parts and Manning finding her "alright, but not brilliant."[63] Considering her upbringing, it is ironical that Gardner was often cast as a maid and, much to her regret, hardly ever as the leading lady. This was partly because she was no classic beauty. Her snub nose and high cheek-bones reminded the writer Harold "Shag" Donohue, Maurice's much young-er brother, slightly of Eleanor Roosevelt (perhaps he saw her in *The Birds*), yet Gardner in her youth was far more good-looking with her symmetrical face, glowing pinkish complexion, golden-red hair, and aquamarine eyes, re-minding others of Renoir's "En la Grenouillère." Many have noted her physi-cal resemblance to her great-great-aunt Mrs. Jack and the likeness is indeed startling, the more so as they were not blood relations. One of Gardner's po-etry workshop students in the 1960s "grew up in Boston, and one of the thrills of meeting Isabella was the sense that Sargent's portrait of her ancestor . . . which I'd seen at the Isabella Stewart Gardner Museum many times in my ado-lescence and young womanhood—had come to life."[64] But in contrast to Mrs. Jack's harmonious small stature and in spite of (or because of) her mother's harping on posture, Gardner was "ungainly; she was always trying to be short-er, because the men were, so she would always walk with her knees bent. If a woman thinks of herself as a beauty, whether she is or not, she walks tall and if the man is down there, he is down there. But she did not have that. The only time I saw that was the early days with [Allen] Tate where she really did look like a ship in full sail."

Gardner's voice was "a marvel. Enormous range of tones—and very melodic in quality."[65] Yet "she did have quite a stammer, which occasionally got con-trolled." Manulis "never knew what controlled it or what stopped it, but on the stage she never had to stammer. In ordinary conversation she would be halting sometimes, it was a difficulty in getting a certain word out. Then she would talk for sentences and be o.k. It never bothered me; it was not that bad, but it was a stammer."[66] Frances Pole Sacco was sure it was "psychological; she would stutter and hesitate. It came from her not quite living up to what her proper

Beacon Hill family would expect of her. She pretended it did not make any difference, but I am sure it did."[67] The impediment kept her in minor roles, but Gardner nevertheless chose to make acting her career, prompted by, Maurice Donohue was sure, her "family life with its need to entertain each other and accommodate so many different personalities, especially in the summers on the family island in Maine. She delighted in doing favorite family charades, and in recalling Cape Cod dialect anecdotes told by Peabo, her father, some based on his managerial or directorial role on the railroad there.... The charades made her an actress."[68] Significant, too, were her precious father's love for acting (and for actresses?); the theater's nonconformist, intense atmosphere, where Gardner could "soar and pounce in conversation," an "until-dawn dazzle and challenge" which she "*adored*"; and, obviously, the high praise she received for her comic roles.[69]

Deeply serious about becoming a professional actress, Gardner jumped at the chance to study at London's Embassy School of Acting in fall 1937 along with Blanche O'Riorden and Lynn Hancock. Comparing it to the Rollins Studio, Manulis praised it as "a much more professional, well-regarded training school for actors; not as sought after as the Royal Academy of Dramatic Arts, but really very good."[70] Led by Eileen Thorndike, who as an actress always stood in the shadow of her sister, Lady Sybil Thorndike, the Embassy School trained such British actors as Rosamund John, Herbert Lom, Daphne Oxenford, Hugh Paddick, Dennis Price, Frank Shelley, and David Waller. It had been based at the Embassy Theatre in Hampstead, London, since 1932, enabling its talented students to play small roles in professional productions, and Thorndike's connections with theater people, combined with those of her knighted sister and actor brother Russell also profited her aspiring actors. Gardner was glad to go to London, with its history, museums, culture, and lively theater tradition. She might stand out as an American in this dynamic metropolis, but she would escape provincial Boston, where she lived in a fishbowl. And London was a springboard to the rest of Europe—most of all, to Ireland. For Ireland, the Irish, and Erskine Childers were still very close to Gardner's heart. At twenty-two, Gardner was ready for her first love affair.

Childers, whose marriage had become a facade maintained for political reasons, might have been involved with other women since Gardner had left the year before, but he had not forgotten his American admirer. At thirty-two, consciously ascending the ladder to a career in national politics, Childers was still very much a raffish romantic, with a penchant for blue suits and expensive cars. Older, literate, and flirtatious, he embodied Gardner's developing taste in men. Surrounded by three American women—his wife, as well as his Bostonian mother and grandmother, who lived close by—Childers embarked on an intense affair with a fourth American. As a single theater student abroad, Gardner was relatively free from prying eyes—even though it sometimes seemed as if London was filled with Bostonians of leisure, there to meet and match—and Childers's work gave him enough freedom to travel and tryst.

A letter to her parents, written from Hyde Park Hotel in fashionable Knightsbridge, vividly depicts Gardner's life as a wealthy young woman abroad, insisting on her independence, keeping her parents at bay, but also a bit homesick:

> *Darling* Mother and Daddy,
>
> Please forgive all this indecision and changing of winds but—we are *definitely* going to move in to-morrow to 134 Piccadilly. . . . The flat is lovely. Quite a big sunny sitting room with a nice coal fire and a lovely colour green covering on a very comfortable sofa and two comfortable chairs. Then a desk and telephone etc. One single bed-room and one big double bed-room and a very nice bath-room with a huge bath.
>
> I will pay about $165.00 a month—which will include break-fast and supper, heat, light, telephone—coal fires—bed-linen valet and maid service etc. In fact the woiks. . . .
>
> Rosa Lewis is becoming a problem. I *wish* I hadn't but I was feeling so lonely and dreary in London the first Sunday we arrived and so were Blanche and Lynn that in the afternoon we went down to see her and took her out to supper. I thought then I probably wouldn't see her again for a month or so. But ever since she has pursued me—in the *kindest way imaginable* but making it terribly diffi-cult for me. I *know* that she only wants me to meet the "best people" and to give me fun and to do the right thing by 'Peabow' and I can't *bear* to hurt her feelings as I'm very fond of her but I can't go down there except once in a *great* while and it's embarrassing to have her telephone me constantly, write me incessantly—send me flowers etc. And one night I was dining with Barbara and Paul at Pru-niers and Bob McCormick (a friend of Antelo's and Artie's) saw me there, he was with his wife, and pretty soon he and his wife left and just as Barbara, Paul and I were about to eat Rosa and Bob McCormick came bearing down on us . . . dragged us out of our seats and back to the Cavendish where she proceeded to tell Paul how she 'ated the 'Inchingbrookes—the Hinchinbrookes being Paul's Aunt and Uncle that didn't go down so well. . . .
>
> I had a sweet note from Mrs. Manning the other day saying she'd enjoyed see-ing me in London . . . and what else do you think she told me. Ruth Childers is going to have twins!! Poor old Erskine—or maybe he's thrilled. But five children seem rather a large menage.
>
> Oh dear how is Green Hill? Is the maple tree on the drive-way over yet? Does everything look beautiful? Is everybody well? I long to know so much about all of you. Dearest Mummy I think it's *rotten* luck that Mrs. Bacon and Mrs. Amory aren't going to be around. You must go often and visit Mrs. Bacon in Washing-ton. And get the Jameses to come down and visit you and Daddy and go to New York more often and give parties and buy pretty clothes and don't play too much

bridge and collect 3 of your friends and take a course with Mrs. Kennedy and ride and read and don't see Mrs. Hamlin *exclusively.*

I hope you're not *too* worried about the Market Daddy. . . . I wish you would sell *every* stock in the family and put it in the bank or a sock or a bond but *not* a stock! The family financier has now made clear her stand.[71]

In contrast to family friends Barbara, Paul, Antelo, and Artie, who were to remain on the periphery of Gardner's life, Robert Hall McCormick III, whom Gardner at this time clearly could not stand, was to play center stage: they were married in 1951. Dropping her aitches, Rosa Lewis was very much a London Cockney, but one who had come far, becoming the owner of the idiosyncratic Cavendish Hotel via King Edward the Seventh's belly and bed. Only those she approved of were allowed to eat or stay at the Cavendish, among them Kaiser Wilhelm of Germany, who, rumor had it, became one of her best customers and grew so fond of her bland cooking that he gave her a picture of himself—which was hung in the men's room during World War I. Other treasured guests were the Duke of Windsor and the Churchills, upper-class artists Ellen Terry, George Bernard Shaw, Isadora Duncan, as well as Isabella Stewart Gardner's great friend John Singer Sargent, who also painted Rosa Lewis. Known as the "Duchess of Jermyn Street," Lewis had a great love for American aristocrats, particularly Bostonians, and Peabo Gardner (though not his straitlaced wife) was a particular favorite of hers. Still going strong at seventy, Lewis was intent on giving his daughter a good time indeed and on furthering her career by introducing her to Ruth Draper, who had been dazzling London—and the world—with her dramatic monologues since 1920. But Lewis was too pushy—and just a tad too unconventional, even for Gardner's taste.

Whether her affair with Childers had already taken off when Gardner wrote this letter in October 1937, a few weeks after her arrival in London, is uncertain, but his wife and five children (the twins were born in November) were no obstacle to their burgeoning romance. Gardner had fallen in love two years earlier and had since idealized this boyishly sweet romantic man, son of a tragic hero, a man irrevocably bound up with Ireland's history. And he was tall, so Gardner need not stoop or bend. It was only to be expected that Childers fell in love with his vivacious, persistent admirer, who shared his passionate interest in Irish politics and love of poetry and the theater. Soon they met whenever and wherever they could, both in Ireland and England, their affair an open secret.

Spending as much of her time as possible with her first true love was Gardner's priority, but when he could not be there, she was bent on leading an exciting social life, exploring London with Blanche O'Riorden and Lynn Hancock. She made new friends outside the American colony, forming a lifelong bond with the self-centered British painter David Rolt—who was to portray her impressionistically, characteristically, if slightly over-sweetly in 1939—and a more intense, though less sustained one with the beautiful, unpredictable Basque Ramon de la Sota, both from venerable families. Christmas is never a time for adulterous lovers, and Gardner spent the holiday with a few friends in the village of Ober-Gürgl in the Austrian Alps, then boasting four hotels. The trip to her small Pension Jenewein, situated high above the tree line, was breathtaking: "At eleven that night we sleighed for two hours way up to the top of the mountain. Ourselves and our luggage were distributed on three sleighs each drawn by a horse and jingling with bells. . . . We went single file. It was the most beautiful fantastic thing I've ever done. Very black night, snow lightly falling." Jenewein was "very small and gemütlich. . . . The proprietor nor the servants speak any more English than we do German, but we smile and roar with laughter all day long. The only bath-tub is in the cellar and there is no hot water in our rooms. The food is delicious—of course we can't order: it is just brought us." Gardner still made herself out to be the well-behaved, dutiful daughter: "We go to bed very early except Xmas Eve when we danced to the 3 piece orchestra at the hotel next door and then went to chapel at mid-night." She did miss her Christmas at Green Hill: "No stocking—no tree—no family breakfast and lunch. . . . I kept imaging at different times of the day what you would be doing."[72]

In London, Eileen Thorndike had identified Gardner's strengths as an actress, but also her weaknesses: "Before we left we each had a conference with Mrs. T. She told me I had a brilliant comedy sense—that my personality was far too big for the room . . . but would be good on the stage—that I must work on my voice."[73] Gardner prepared determinedly for her chosen career, benefiting greatly from the Embassy School of Acting: "Everything we were taught was taught by professional actors and actresses. I worked hard, I learned a lot, and after one play I had a good part in, a famous director (English) said 'You are the perfect adorable silly ass.'"[74] Gardner performed with Thorndike's first-, second-, and third-term students on April 12, 1938 at the Embassy Theatre, playing Dorinda Caswell, a young society gossip sponging on her ex-husband in James Parish's thriller *Distinguished Gathering*.

But the English director did not offer her any roles which would make her financially independent, and in the early summer of 1938, still very much in love with Childers, Gardner sailed home. She knew that Childers was not going to leave his wife and children for her, if only because in Catholic Ireland this would put an end to his role as keeper of the flame and to his thriving political career. Anyway, an ardent affair was probably more appealing to Gardner than becoming his second wife—and stepmother to five children. Later Gardner painted a picture of both herself and Erskine Childers and Ruth Childers with her lover "all co-existing in a gloomy castle . . . sitting mournfully in front of a fire." Though sexually inexperienced when she became involved with him, she came to "delight in his sexual prowess" and did not seem to mind his tales of his successes with other women.[75] In the last year of her life Gardner looked back lovingly:

> He wrote me after his wife's death and my divorce [from Maurice Seymour] asking me to come to Ireland. I did not because of my children and because I knew his life's dream would not become the reality it did were he to marry a twice divorced Protestant. My hand shakes as I write this. . . . I chose to return to America rather than the cottage in Wicklow he urged. I never saw him again, I was 22, but we wrote, not steadily but each year, no year passed. Though he was 33 when I last saw him, Allen [Tate] at 59 reminded me of him, the bones of his face, the high forehead, the eyes, the laugh like a waterfall, a cascade . . . I loved him always. Even my father said not long before he died Erskine should have been your husband—Perhaps I always thought of him as such.[76]

Gardner's parents may have been unaware that their daughter was sleeping with Childers, though rumors must have reached them through their connections with the Mannings, the Osgoods, and the Farleys. Rose Gardner would certainly have disapproved of her daughter's liaison with a married man, and it is unlikely that her husband would have sanctioned it, even if, in accordance with the double standard of those times, he was not the most faithful of men himself and, it was rumored, tended to his sons' sexual education by taking them to London, where Rosa Lewis provided them with compliant partners to introduce them to life's physical pleasures.

Back in America, Gardner enrolled once more in the Rollins Studio. Most of her friends were there: Martin Manulis, Lem Ayers, and Harry Holland, and, from Trenton, Henry Levin and Ernie Kovacs, together with their hawk-faced guru Harold Van Kirk. Ingeborg Torrup and Frances Pole Sacco were still there. The group even had its dash of nobility, much to Anglophile Rollins's satisfaction, as Eileen Thorndike had chosen to send talented red-haired Henry Tuchet-Jesson, later Lord Audley, as her exchange student.[77] Gardner was, again, indifferent to the women students, except for Shirley Osborne, also from a rich family, who became involved with and married Lemuel Ayers, and Helen Machat, a "wonderful woman and a very funny acerbic lady," who wedded Maurice Donohue.[78]

Frances Sacco painted a vivid portrait of Gardner's "essence" as she saw it at East Hampton:

> Sometimes we had dinner at the Seaspray Inn and Belle could always afford to have dinner there if she wanted to. And I walked in and there she was in this beautiful chintzy kind of place and she had ear of corn in her hand and she was going across it with such voracity, with so much hunger, I never saw anybody eat

corn with such absolute delight, with compulsion. It had to be eaten, it had to be eaten, it went back and forth and back and forth. She was very young then, and this mane of yellow hair going back and forth, and I thought, that IS Belle. That is the way she attacked her whole life, and continued to the end. She was ferocious about it. She did not want to lose a minute, a single corn on the cob. She was eating it all, taking it all in, almost with a touch of anger as well as excitement, everything she devoured.[79]

All the Rollins troupe indulged in drink, too; Harry Holland remembered both Gardner and Van Kirk being rather intoxicated on the afternoon of a premiere and having to slap them and sober them up with black coffee. Later, in the repressive atmosphere of the 1950s, the free lifestyle and antics of the theater people annoyed a poisonous group of concerned citizens, who called themselves "The East Hampton Protection Society." They tried to get rid of the summer theater at "their" Guild Hall, regarding it as "a hangout of immoral people and the attractor of people who would not be acceptable in their clubs. The drumbeat grew and grew. Pedestrians were asked to sign anti-Guild Hall petitions." The actor Robert Montgomery identified the immoral element: "You're talking about Jews and fairies, it's as simple as that. That's what should be substituted every time you use the word 'undesirable.'" The petition was rejected.[80] In the late 1930s, however, with exceedingly respectable Mrs. Woodhouse, East Hampton's main benefactor, very protective of Leighton Rollins and his entourage, such bigoted voices were not heard, even if passions smoldered amongst Rollins's heterogeneous WASPs, Jews, Hungarian Catholics, and homo- hetero- and bisexuals. Those, like Martin Manulis and Lemuel Ayers, who did not know which way they were swinging sought out Frances Sacco for advice. Having survived her disastrous early marriage to Reginald Pole, she seemed most experienced in matters of love, and she grudgingly advised them, preferring to concentrate on her work rather than on what she regarded as adolescent heart-to-hearts; she considered the obsessive womanizing of men like Maurice Donohue and Harold Van Kirk equally immature.[81]

Striking, senatorial, with a sonorous voice, ruggedly masculine yet elegant, dressed artistically—sometimes even wearing sandals—Van Kirk mesmerized his students. One of his Trenton pupils told of "his playing a record of a German classical playwright, in German, and tearing up, crying visibly. Oh, he was heavy. . . . He knew his stuff, and I would say he was a hell of a good, strong influence on everybody who worked with him. He pointed out our weaknesses and gave us incentives to do better. No ham bone. No excuses for silly stuff. Do it right."[82] Maurice Donohue agreed that Van Kirk—always called "Van," never Harold—was a man "of extraordinary talents": "He could appeal to the Stanislavski method, but also to Boris Chaliapin's naturalistic way of acting. When you have to play a cripple, you either consult your sub-conscience or you observe cripples and then mimic them until they feel right; Van used both methods. He was extremely observant about distinctive gestures and always gave you the choice of two ways and then showed you what the right way was. He taught voice training, too, and was a master rhetorician. Actors sensed that Van loved them and that he would know when they did it right."[83] Harry Holland thought him "an attractive male," who spoke beautifully, slowly, articulating carefully, and remembered the lovely way he folded his hands.[84]

Van Kirk's background is dramatically obscure. According to Donohue, Van Kirk Senior wanted to visit the 1893 Chicago World's Fair, but his wife allowed him to do so only if he brought back a baby, and so Van Kirk became the adopted son of, as he used to call them, "simple country people."[85] As his obituary gives Hudson, Michigan, July 23, 1893, as his place and date of birth, it is entirely possible that Van Kirk, a consummate liar, fabricated this story because his parents were not glamorous enough for him. Donohue, for one, sincerely believed that Van Kirk "could do everything."[86] He had been a student of Robert Morss Lovett's, knew Harriet Monroe during the first years of her editorship of *Poetry Magazine,* and after graduating from the University of Chicago, had been a preacher, a lawyer, and a teacher at Heidelberg College in Tiffin, Ohio. During World War I, in 1916 and 1917, he was an ambulance driver in France, and it may have been then that he met the famous lesbian actress Eva La Gallienne and became more involved in the theater. In later years a reporter for the *Philadelphia Inquirer,* Donohue knew lots of local gossip, and the rumor was that Van Kirk's first wife was the scandalous daughter of one of the Pittsburgh steel families whose parents paid her a tidy allowance to stay as far away from them as possible. She got married and, in Europe, met and fell for young Casanova Van Kirk, who was peddling medicine at the time, and swapped him for her husband. Tall tales tend to cluster around Van Kirk, and in one "a student at Temple, six foot and handsome," also could not resist Van Kirk's charms and killed herself in despair of winning his eternal love.[87] Certain, if less sensational, is that he became the drama teacher at Trenton High School in New Jersey, married Gertrude Reckless, also well-off, and fathered two children. But the second marriage of Rollins's most charismatic director had soon failed, and he was, in Donohue's words, "very mixed up."[88]

At the beginning of the summer season of 1938 it was clear to all that Van Kirk and Ingeborg Torrup were involved in a torrid affair. But Gardner made a play for him, and he simply traded Torrup in for her younger rival. On the rebound from Erskine Childers, and now a vibrantly sexual woman, Gardner was enthralled: "He would look at you and hold you in his eyes, fix you with his eyes, both the men and women, even though he was heterosexual; he was a Svengali to males and females."[89] Taking his cast into corners, he had soul-to-soul

talks with them, "interlocking and feeding from each other, it was almost can-
nibalistic."[90] It is not hard to understand why Gardner, in her early twenties
and still aroused by her love affair with the unattainable Childers, was smitten
by her inspirational teacher Van Kirk, with his gallant World War I past, his
extensive theater experience, his knowledge of and love for literature, and a
serpentine charm that few could resist. It is equally conceivable that Van Kirk
fell for Gardner's youth and pizzazz, her intelligence and her sensuality. A dalliance in the hothouse atmosphere at East Hampton was only to be expected, but
what shocked the theater community was that Van Kirk and Gardner decided
to get married. When Gardner told Harry Holland, he "was absolutely floored.
But I did not let on that I was floored, so I said 'marvelous' and 'wonderful' and
things like that."[91] Martin Manulis regarded Van Kirk as a dyed-in-the-wool
opportunist and was sure of Van Kirk's prime motive: "Even if Belle had been
totally infatuated with him, which she was, he could have guided it in a slightly
different way. He was the teacher. He encouraged it and wanted very much not
only to have an affair with this rich girl, but to marry her. . . . . I noticed he did
not have gainful employment for the years of their marriage. They did not have
any deprivations and he knew that they would not."[92] Gardner's family was appalled: the groom was twice her age, twice divorced, father of two children, and
a schoolteacher. They "cross-examined him to see if he was a fitting husband,"
considered him a fraud, a charlatan, "an incredible asshole and a thief," but, as
Gardner was of age, could not prevent the wedding.[93] The announcement of
their engagement was curt:

Isabella Gardner Weds in November

Mr. and Mrs. George Peabody Gardner, Jr., of Brookline, announce the engagement of their daughter, Miss Isabella Stewart Gardner, to Harold A. Van
Kirk, of Falssington, Bucks County Pennsylvania.
Miss Gardner made her debut in Boston in 1933. Since that time she has been
much interested in theater and has studied both here and abroad.
Mr. Van Kirk is a graduate of the University of Chicago. He served in the American Ambulance Service with the French Army during the World War. He also
is interested in the theater and for a number of years has been an instructor of
dramatics.
No definite date has been set for the wedding, but it will probably take place
late in November.[94]

Apart from this announcement, Gardner kept no mementos of her engagement
or, for that matter, her wedding to Van Kirk, which took place a few months after
the end of summer stock. Why they married in such a rush is unclear, although

one unreliable account has it that the couple eloped first and that Gardner's parents could only squelch such a scandal by arranging a hasty marriage.[95] As there is no indication either that Gardner was pregnant, Van Kirk, knowing on which side his bread was buttered, must have just swept his heiress off her feet while she was still in thrall. They vowed eternal love in November 1938 in Green Hill, with Gardner wearing a green velvet dress with matching hat. The contrast with her sister's glamorous wedding in August 1934, which had featured repeatedly in both Boston and national newspapers was stark. Kitty's nuptials had been "of great interest to Capital society," her "becoming gown of white taffeta, made on princess lines" much admired, the "white blossoms and lighted tapers against a background of dark feathery palms and ferns" of chic Trinity Church where the wedding took place, extensively described.[96] Gardner's marriage was kept quiet, the bride "quite nervous," and her father, only five years older than the groom, "very emotional," whispering when she left with her new husband, "I hope you are doing the right thing."[97] It was not an auspicious beginning.

Gardner followed Van Kirk to Fallsington, Bucks County, just across the Delaware from Trenton, which (before U.S. Steel built a plant there) was secluded and idyllically pastoral. They rented a farm for sixty dollars a month.[98] Gardner immediately had a difficult part to play—that of mother to Van Kirk's two young children, Anneke and Peter, whom he brought with him. They never really knew their own mother who had left them early on.[99] As she had "a great theatrical gift for becoming the person that fitted her role," Gardner quickly learned the entirely new responsibilities of being wife and mother, tasks for which her life so far had not prepared her.[100] She worked hard to be the ideal homemaker, and in the notebook that she kept during the first years of her marriage to Van Kirk, she diligently scribbled down lists of meats (from oven roast to scrapple), fish, vegetables, fruits, soups, desserts, and starches, and listed weekly possibilities for wholesome dinners, a typical menu consisting of "steak, creamed potatoes, fried onions, beans."[101] Unfortunately, she initially had no idea how to cook anything and so, famously, kept on calling the Gardners' chef long-distance, asking her for instructions. She tried to spend prudently, even keeping accounts during this, her first attempt at playing house. But balancing the budget was not all that difficult, as, thanks to the Gardner money, the Van Kirks could spend some $10,000 annually, a substantial sum if one takes into account that a well-paid accountant in those days earned about a quarter of that amount.[102]

After all the excitement and resultant tension of the past few years, against all expectations, Gardner lived happily, peacefully in Bucks County. In January 1939, begging her "Darling Mother and Daddy" to forgive her for not writing sooner, she explained that she had been busy "studying English History. I'm planning to study it thoroughly from the Norman Conquest through Munich 'peace.' Then Van and I are going to study economics. . . . Everything is fine here. The children are well—I'm still passionately addicted to cooking and Van is always wonderful to be with and love."[103]

In early 1939 Gardner splurged about eight hundred dollars on their postponed honeymoon trip, which took them to all the highlights in a Europe on the brink of war: London, Paris, Athens, Rome, Florence, and then on to Cambridge, England. Van Kirk's notes on their voyage in a communal letter to friends and "Thoughts while en route from Beaulieu to Genoa," both written in March 1939, mention problems with passports and their eleven pieces of luggage ("Packing the night before was nightmarish!"), the quality of hotels (a French one was "plus Anglais que les Anglais, we hated it immediately"), the superiority of Italian second-class trains over French first, and the inimitability of members of the British upper-class: a fellow passenger ("her air of magnificent, self-confident imperiousness—all of which has made Great Britain what it is") or Gardner's painter-friend David Rolt ("his family rather looks down on The Windsors"). On their first night in London, Rolt dined them "*Chez Josef* with wonderful Serbian food and wines, then to see 'They Walk Alone' with Beatrice Lehmann as a mystico-neuro-nymphomaniacal servant girl . . . a grand and grisly performance." Though Van Kirk regularly speaks of "we," his narration is curiously impersonal, his bride mentioned only in passing as in "Belle waiting . . . at Lyons while I got . . . places for us"; and "Belle rested."[104]

In France, on March 24, 1939, Van Kirk saw "war-clouds hover" but, he wrote his friends, "I *simply* don't believe it will rain . . . so little do we believe it that we're away for Greece in the morning . . . Rome and Florence as we come back." But en route from Beaulieu to Genoa, the next day, he noted the oppressive pervasiveness of "black shirts" and "[m]ore black shirts" and they saw "swastika and fasces on all important stations."[105] They did, however, continue on their honeymoon as planned, staying in the extravagant, "extortionate" Hotel Briscol in Genoa with its "great circular staircase up nine stories to *dome*," where they occupied a "beautiful room and bath," but had "dinner almost duetto," because most tourists now shunned Italy. Before dinner, Van Kirk had "Baedekered to Via Garibaldi and . . . found Andreas Doria house . . . lovely." Although newly wedded, Van Kirk often saw the sights on his own while Gardner rested: she was expecting their child. "The doctor in London said our baby was due to arrive about September 27th," she wrote Helen and Maurice Donohue. "He was very cosy and asked me if I had any whims and seemed quite disconsolate when I said no. However, I brought the gleam back in his eye when I remembered my definitely whimsical aversion to even the lightest liquor! . . . I feel fine—none of the traditional 'morning sickness' and no noticeable increase in girth."[106] After Genoa they traveled to Naples, where Van Kirk found the "Neapolitans . . . a degenerate looking lot" and on to Greece, where they took numerous photographs of antiquities and other tourist attractions but hardly any of themselves, before making their way back to Great Britain.[107]

During their few days in London at the trip's beginning, Van Kirk had gone "to Cambridge, to house[-]hunt, with some success. . . . Belle came out with me Sunday—approved."[108] The Van Kirks now settled in Cambridge with Gardner planning to pursue her acting career and Van to enroll at the university. Their house was on the outskirts of town in a quiet, upscale neighborhood; it was large, because Anneke and Peter would join them there. Their time together was idyllic. Gardner studied and read, taking care of Anneke and Peter as well as Van, who "was used to having things done for him."[109] Intent on making a name for herself in the theater, Gardner, six months pregnant, played the part of a—fortunately—podgy American matron in Elmer Rice's burlesque *See Naples and Die* (1929) in a Cambridge Festival Theatre Production and sent one reviewer into raptures: "Belle Gardner gave possibly the best performance of the week as the American tourist. She was the incarnation of all that Mark Twain ever said about the American in Italy."[110]

Pictures from this period show Gardner innocently blissful and radiantly pregnant; some thirty years later, looking back, she referred to 1939 as one of the happiest years of her life. But the dark clouds over Europe could no longer be ignored, and Van Kirk realized that his earlier assessment of the political situation had been far too optimistic. "[H]orrid Mr. Hitler" sent them "home in haste," and the Van Kirks returned to New Jersey.[111] Safely back in America, on September 25, 1939 (only a few weeks after the beginning of World War II in Europe), Gardner nearly died giving birth to their daughter, whom they named Rose, for her mother. At Van Kirk's insistence, Gardner had delivered her baby without anesthetic, which was quite uncommon for upscale mothers in American society at the time and horrified her female friends.

The Van Kirks turned, briefly, into the ideal picture of an American family. They bought a pre-revolutionary stone farmhouse, situated on a hill, near quaint historic Doylestown, Pennsylvania, on the road to New Hope, and restored it beautifully, creating a huge living room, adding a kitchen and a garage. Down the hill, about a hundred tree-lined yards away from the road, they dug an artificial lake that gave the house its name, "Still Pond," after the expression "Only a still pond can reflect the stars." Their theater friends often came up the hill to observe the progress and have lunch outside, made by Belle, served by the household help. No longer teaching, Van Kirk now envisaged himself as a gentleman farmer. He resolved to raise chickens and had the outbuildings reconstructed elaborately at great cost. With Gardner money they bought another farm across the main road, a little farther toward Doylestown, where corn was to be raised for chicken feed. "The farmer who lived there, an irascible, aggrieved, drunken man, stayed on to do the actual farming."[112] They had huge laying houses, thousands of chickens and hatchlings, and a trained poultry man. But the old boozer did not produce enough chicken feed, and the chickens died of hunger and neglect; this angered and saddened the large black woman helping the Van Kirks in the house much more than it did the owners. If Harold Van Kirk loved being a country squire, that did not include participating in, or even supervising, actual farm work and with Gardner as unsuitable as a farmer's wife, this experiment was soon stopped. Their friends would only remember the bucolic beauty of the place with at most some stray picturesque chickens clucking about.

Gardner tried to be a loving mother to both baby Rose and to Anneke and Peter. She took care of her stepchildren's education, prepared nutritious meals, bought them clothes and big presents, took them swimming, and wrote funny, personal poems for them:

> I want to be big—the little girl said—/ and not have to get up when it's comfy in bed
> I want to be big and do as I please / and lie in the grass and look at the trees
> I want to stay in when it's cold outside / and I'll have a little rock horse to ride
> When I go to bed I'll read all night / with no-one to say put out the light
> I'll wear pretty thin dresses on ice cold days / and do my hair in all sorts of ways
> I'll be lazy and lie on the sofa and read / and have all the paper and pencils I need.

And:

> I want to be big—the little boy said—/ And never have to go to bed
> I want to be big and do as I please / and never have to wash my knees
> I want to wade in puddles and wet my feet / and buy all the candy that I can eat
> And jump on the sofa and run thru the halls / and not have to listen to Momma's calls
> When I grow up I won't practice a bit / I'll play all day with my catcher's mitt
> I won't go to school and won't look at clocks / and I'll certainly never change my socks. [113]

"Momma" or "Mommele" bestowed much more time and love on them than their swashbuckling father, who was more interested in the theater, his cars and antiques, and expensive guns, which he ordered from the Stradivarius of gun makers, Harry Pole. But Gardner tired of being handmaiden, full-time exemplary housewife, and mother and started looking for jobs in the theater, in Frances Sacco's view because she "wanted to get away from Van."[114] Only three months after Rose's birth, Peabo Gardner's friends had already written on her behalf to Broadway producers. Others, too, used their connections. "While having dinner at Henry's at 52nd and Madison," Harry Holland "saw Moss Hart pass by, the director and writer and collaborator with George Kaufmann on *The American Way*, which was a massive, patriotic, flag-waving and also popular production playing in Radio City Music Hall. And I said to Belle: 'Are you interested in becoming part of this?' and Belle said: 'Yes.' So, I went up to Moss Hart and interrupted him at dinner—he was dining alone—and said: 'I have this lady here with me and she is interested in the theater and interested in your play.' And Moss Hart said: 'Well, have her come over' and he took her address, but he never, ever called her."[115] Mary Manning tried to help also, writing her friend Orson Welles: "This is to introduce Belle Gardner who has done good work at the Embassy School in London and with the Easthampton people. I think she has real talent. Maybe you'd give her an audition any way? You seem to be waltzing on the crest of the waves! I haven't done anything with plays lately but I have a novel coming out in the Fall. Who hasn't? . . . Sorry to bother you but I do think Belle is worth a trial."[116] Trying to make it as an actress, Gardner spent much time in New York City, with hundreds of other hopefuls beating paths to producers' and agents' offices. While her competitors often had to work at all kinds of jobs to make ends meet, Gardner, trying to fit in as best she could, often played at being poor: "Belle could buy all the taxicabs in New York City but preferred to take the subway, to be with the people," was how Frances Sacco put it.[117] Far too self-conscious to audition, she messed up her tryouts:

> I smoked for hours in producers' anterooms where
> I prayed that interviews I had come there
> to beseech would be denied.
> Usually my prayers were granted and I stayed outside.
> I was a tense impostor, a deliberate dunce,
> in a lobby of honest earnest seekers. Once
> or twice thanks to a letter of introduction I
> got to see the man, but instead of "chin up" and "do or die"
> I effectively slouched and stammered in disorder in order
> to thus escape the chance to read I might be
> offered.
> ("Not at All What One Is Used To . . . ," 73)

Failing to land even a small comic role on Broadway, Gardner turned to summer stock, spending the summers of 1940 and 1941 in Gloucester, Massachusetts,

at Bass Rocks Summer Theatre, established by Henry Levin and Martin Manulis and sponsored, in part, by the Gardners. "I am definitely, D.V., going to
Bass Rocks. Of course I don't know yet what plays they are doing nor how
many weeks I'll work. But probably I'll be on the job from late June till early
Sept.," Gardner wrote her mother.[118] Rose Gardner, worried about her grandchild Rosy's welfare, offered to rent a summerhouse on the North Shore, near
Bass Rocks, where Rosy could also stay, so she would be protected from her
mother's aspirations as an actress. Or, Rose Gardner indicated, she might take
a place in her beloved Nantucket, where Rosy would be most welcome; it was
over a hundred miles from Bass Rocks, but some two hundred miles closer
than isolated Doylestown. Gardner's answer is a confused mixture of trying to
mollify her mother and, simultaneously, making sure that she could do exactly
what she wanted—which was spending the summer with her theater friends,
and emphatically not within easy reach of Rose Gardner.

> You are so sweet to say that if you took a house on the North Shore or in Nan-
> tucket we could have it for a little vacation. But of course if I am working till Sept.
> 5th then Nantucket would be out of the question, as I'd want Rose, Anni and
> Pete near me. . . . Naturally I'd love it if you took a house on the North Shore. If
> you did that I would love to have Rosy go to you and have Molly [Laughlin] take
> care of her. I myself would stay at Moorland because though uncomfortable it is
> convenient for rehearsals and the atmosphere is conducive to concentration and
> hard work. . . . I think Brookline would be a disappointing summer for you. What
> about Honolulu? And when are you coming down here?
>
> I am having a heavenly time. No New York. Just rest, Rosy, voice work, plan-
> ning a flower-garden, and the children! I plan to do some riding soon. There's a
> stable near where I can rent a horse for 1.00 an hour and I may give Anneke les-
> sons at $2.00 per hour.
>
> Everyone is well and we are all so happy. Tell Daddy we are planning to use
> some of Granny's present on trees and shrubs for the place.
>
> I so long for you and Daddy to come down *soon.* So does Van.[119]

Gardner played comic roles at Bass Rocks, among them a garrulous coun-
trywoman, Lulu Pung, in Parker Fennely's *Two Story House,* a performance
the *Boston Herald*'s reviewer deemed "excellent." Another was as the maid in
George Kaufmann and Moss Hart's *George Washington Slept Here,* where an
equally enthusiastic reviewer thought she contributed "to an exceptionally well
acted and smooth performance."[120] And, in typical Gardner fashion, she provided comic relief in Victor Mapes and William Collier's play *The Hottentot*
(1929): "As I started to leave the stage my foot caught in a telephone cord and
the receiver fell off the table. Knowing the next person to enter the scene had

to use the telephone I picked it up and replaced it and started to exit again only to be tripped a second time by the cord and to have everything crashed to the stage a second time. It provided a huge laugh for the audience that was not in the script."[121] In her poem about her acting career, "Not at All What One Is Used To . . . ," dedicated to Frances Sacco, Gardner wrote:

> I did not boggle
> at summer stock, and somewhere north of Boston I had
> at last become a paid member of a company where sad
> to relate I was successfully grotesque in numerous unglamorous
> bit parts (usually dialect for I did not stutter
> in dialect) and I was always differently grotesque, utter—
> ly; but people laughed and / or cried, always saying I was play-
> ing myself, that I was a 'natural.' Through the good offices of a
> well-connected friend I at last read for a producer who was
>   Broadway
> and was given the part of a Cockney maid, afraid
> and eager, who moved and talked in double-time.
> ("Not at All What One Is Used To . . . , 74)

The friend was Martin Manulis, who got Gardner an audition for the part of the addled maid in Noel Coward's *Blithe Spirit,* in which a man and his new wife are haunted by the ghost of his first wife. The play was an instant success on Broadway when it opened in November 1941; in 1945 it was made into a popular film featuring Rex Harrison and Margaret Rutherford.

At the end of 1941, against the somber backdrop of the Japanese attack on Pearl Harbor and America's entering the war, John C. Wilson, in his first project as director, formed a new troupe intending to conquer the Midwest with this light farce. The cast was star-studded and, as was fitting for a Coward play, very British. It featured Estelle Winwood, Dennis King (also British by birth), and Carol Goodner. Though a New Yorker by birth, Goodner had, since her first stage appearance at age four, built a career for herself in London. Valerie Cossart, born in London, with a first stage appearance when she was five, had already played in two Coward productions on Broadway before she joined the cast of *Blithe Spirit.* Suave-looking and wavy-haired, seeming more British than American despite his midwestern origins, Lowell Gilmore had already appeared as supporting actor in a host of successful Broadway productions. Dainty Suzanne Charpentier, with stage name Annabella, married to Hollywood heartthrob Tyrone Power, was French and made her American stage debut as the ethereal titular spirit, her foreign enunciation apparently an asset for a ghost.

Gardner was the least experienced, least professional of the company, and for her to have obtained the coveted role of the funny female domestic in one of the year's top hits was proof of her recognized ability as a comic character actress. Gardner had to transform herself nightly into a red-faced clumsy Cockney maid, and as she had trained in London and played in Cambridge, England, her East End accent was convincing, certainly to an American audience. She also had quite some theater experience as a domestic, and her character's fleet-footed ineptitude was true to type. In an interview, "Junior Leaguer Is Cockney Maid of 'Blithe Spirit,'" Gardner confessed that it was "somewhat strange to be making my formal American debut in my home country after playing in England. . . . It always has been easy for me to do dialect parts and we did every type of play. The war stopped my appearance in London with the Gate Theater Company and I came home to find Broadway quite unresponsive to my talent."[122] The role in *Blithe Spirit* might well turn out to be her springboard to the Great White Way. Van Kirk was sure it would and cabled her on opening night in Chicago on February 17, 1942: "There was a young lady named Belle who acted eccentrically swell but the critics were kind and they said how refined which made her madder than hell. . . . Best of luck darling but I know you have it—Van."[123]

As *Blithe Spirit* toured in the Midwest both the play and Gardner received brilliant notices: "Coward Comedy Is Tops," a reviewer in Detroit wrote; the play was "a treat from another world," "sheer heaven," and Gardner "excellent" as "the unwitting and half-witted agency of all this mix-up."[124] A Pittsburgh critic called her "a pricelessly comic servant"; another thought Gardner "a scream," noting in comparison that "Lowell Gilmore and Valerie Cossart fill their small parts satisfactorily."[125] There were hardly any dissenting voices about the merits of the play, but even those ("It is no less than remarkable that Mr. Coward, oppressed with the state of his income tax and his native land, could take six days off and produce such a play. Few others could and very likely some others would care not to.") applauded the help: "Belle Gardner supplies still more 'straight' fun as the leaping maid."[126] The dean of American drama critics, Ashton Stevens, was positively ecstatic: "Death takes a hilarious holiday from war in 'Blithe Spirit,'" he wrote reviewing an early performance in Chicago. "It is magicianly. If it doesn't take your mind off the front page nothing will. Britons have been knighted for less." He singled out Gardner, a nationally unknown actress in a supporting role, for praise in one of his very first paragraphs: "John C. Wilson has reproduced and redirected this prevailing favorite of the better audiences of London and New York with a cast warranted to be four-square against failure by Dennis King, Annabella, Estelle Winwood and Carol Goodner, to say nothing of Belle Gardner, the custodian of a hurrying, gawky maidservant whose every entrance is a comic earthquake, not to mention some of her exits."[127]

The play had run for a few glorious months in Chicago when Gardner made it to Broadway. From June 29, 1942, onward, she played the part of the bungling servant in the Booth Theater. Her first Broadway appearance was reported by the *New York Times* with both text and an alluring picture.[128] Van Kirk again wired his love and support: "Hang me up and look at me I'm here all the time really to wish you luck and love Van."[129] But the show soon "took a summer rest," and Gardner's contract was terminated after less than a month.[130] Wanting to capitalize on her Broadway debut, she then tried her luck at the movies. But Gene Martel, later a director of horror movies, then in the Paramount Pictures talent department, kept her on a string: "I am returning the notices, which are very impressive. Rest assured, should anything suitable arise for you, I shall be happy to let you know. Please, keep me informed of your activities in the theatre."[131] In October Gardner was on tour again, this time with *Stage Door,* a play by Edna Ferber and George Kaufmann with a plot faintly recalling her own life: its protagonist is a young inexperienced debutante who aspires to be an actress and who is given the lead because of her father's maneuverings and money. But, be it in a supporting role, Gardner was making it on her own, earning forty dollars a week with this gig.[132] Van Kirk's obligatory cable on her opening night was lukewarm—"BEST OF EVERYTHING FOR TONIGHT AS ALWAYS VAN,"—but his daughter's was heartfelt: "DEAR MAMA I HOPE WITH ALL MY HEART THAT YOUR PERFORMANCE WILL BE SWELL LOVE ANNEKE."[133] Again, the show's run was short, perhaps because too many had seen and preferred the 1937 movie version starring Katharine Hepburn.

Gardner was still hot, however, and Lester Shurr, of the Louis Shurr Agency that contracted stars like Bob Hope and Ginger Rogers, sent her "SINCEREST BEST WISHES FOR A TERRIFIC SUCCESS" for her next performance, as the parlor maid in Arthur Pinero's whimsical *The Playgoers,* in which a naïf aristocratic lady, acted by Gloria Swanson, tries to treat her servants to a night at the theater. *The Playgoers* was part of *Three Curtains,* a combination of one-acts in which Swanson, gorgeous star of silent movies, played the lead. The male protagonist was the hunky Czech Jewish actor Francis Lederer, also a silent movie celebrity, who had most recently starred, paradoxically, as a pro-German professor in the propagandistic anti-fascist *Confessions of a Nazi Spy* (1939). One reviewer from Wilmington began by commenting cattily on an "evident lack of preparation and a failure on the part of producers to realize that three unconnected plays and inexcusably extended intermissions tend to tediousness," and ended with "[t]he genteel parlourmaid as presented by Miss Belle Gardner merited a better chance for a continued playing time."[134] Another reviewer from the same town agreed, thinking the supporting cast "generally satisfactory, with Harold J. Kennedy, who also directed, and Belle Gardner outstanding."[135] Obviously, not all reviews were as laudatory, and one about the performance at historic Ford's Theatre in Washington, D.C., merely mentioned Gardner's lending the principals "experienced support."[136] Nevertheless, by the beginning of 1943, about a year since her professional stage debut as the maid in *Blithe Spirit,* Gardner had made quite a name for herself as an excellent comic character actress. She might go much further.

Back in sleepy Doylestown, Van Kirk jealously watched yet another one of his former pupils outshine him: his wife. He always needed to be center stage, but was so no longer in Gardner's eyes. After their first happy year together, after the glow of their initial passion had been spent, Gardner came to take the true measure of her husband in their day-to-day life together. Van Kirk may have been passionate, but he was cold-bloodedly selfish as well. His pupils, whose talents he had discovered and developed, adored him, but they did not have to live with him. Those who did, including his children, realized that for Van Kirk the whole world turned around himself. Those who were not captivated by his wolfish charisma described him as "kind of bizarre and kinky . . . slightly disgraceful," as "a fake and a phony," or even more deadly, as "the supreme actor."[137]

While his interest in guns and fast sports cars may have indicated a death wish, even his friends were certain he toyed with the idea of death just to get attention; few believed that the scar on his cheek was the result of a Heidelberg duel, as Van Kirk maintained. At one of the many parties at the farm, the revelers were startled by a loud pistol shot and found Van Kirk in the bathroom, smoking gun in his hand and a hole in the molding. He explained that he had wanted to kill himself, but had had second thoughts: "I ducked."[138] By firing his weapon anyway he had managed to be in the limelight again. Van Kirk "loved to manipulate and was like a little boy in front of an ants' nest: give a little poke and see what happens. That is that little diabolical thing that Belle hated so much in him. And Van was not to be trusted."[139] Admitting to Van Kirk's "very masculine" charms and his sex appeal, Manulis detected a "sadistic" streak in him and thought that Gardner, who was in his perception "on the masochistic side," came to be "quite frightened of him. He had a wild temper. I do not mean she cowered in the corner, but he certainly ruled the roost. It was her checks that paid for the roost and he ruled it."[140]

After the chicken farm debacle, there was not much to do for the Van Kirks in isolated Doylestown but to read, which they both loved, even if Van Kirk usually lorded it over Gardner on account of what he regarded as his superior intellect; or give parties, to which they invited all their New York and Trenton theater friends. The Ayerses and Manulises (married within two months of each other) would be there, the Donohue brothers, Henry Levin and Harry Holland, but also the Saccos and Brahmin Barbara Van Rensselaer Spalding with her husband, Hobart. At one New Year's Eve party, Harry Holland remembered, every room was lit up and was wired for sound, something dozy

Doylestown had never seen before. The guests had fun, but the children were forgotten in the heat of the merriment, as they often were, and the few mothers among them kept an eye on little children sleeping haphazardly on top of coats or blankets amidst drunken goings-on.

Since her second summer at Bass Rocks Theater, in 1941, Gardner had not been home much because of her theater engagements. She spent most of her time in Chicago with *Blithe Spirit* and stayed with friends in New York City or Washington when she was on tour. Molly Laughlin, Gardner's own former nanny, often acted as her stand-in, taking care of Rosy, Anneke, and Peter; Van Kirk showed hardly any interest in his children. Being away from home pursuing her career as an actress, financially independent, Gardner hardly fit the mold of the typical housebound mother of the 1940s, but the stepchildren she took under her wing for a few years always felt loved by her, and Gardner felt more responsible toward them than did their own father. Anneke, the more communicative of the two, wrote Gardner loving letters all through her thorny life, asking for advice, telling of her day-to-day struggles and successes. A soft touch, Gardner almost always helped her out financially, too, but having been left by her own mother and neglected by her father, Anneke Van Kirk depended on Gardner's genuine love for her as much as on her monetary assistance: "you are the only one I can lean toward . . . and know that that on which I lean will not bend. Poppa's no damn good for anything."[141]

In 1952, aged nineteen, six feet tall and a coastguardsman, Peter (who had just turned seven when his father married Gardner) wrote "Dear Mama: I[t's] not that I hate Papa or anything like that, I[t's] that I don't feel much of anything for him. I don't know, ma[y]be that's worse than anything." Peter ended this six-page letter: "I think of the day in the park with you and Rosy. I think of reading lessons in the window sills in Monument Beacon. The surf and rocks and sun in Bass Rocks. [Ely] Cathedral in England. Anni and the vegetable man with the horse and wagon in England. Apple dumplings (cannon balls). Chocolate sauce on icecream. The Queen Mary and SS Washington. I think of that and so much more."[142] In this same letter Peter asked for a staggering loan of eight thousand dollars for a garage, but if he knew how to push Gardner's buttons, the sentiments, so naïvely put, are sincere. In his early thirties, thanking Gardner for money she had sent him, he wrote: "You are my mother and nothing can change that for me. I don't have any other family—no father as far as I'm con[c]erned. That may sound funny, but as a child you learn to give back as much love as you get. Except for you I never got any. Not really."[143] And in 1965, feeling very protective, he wrote: "It would hurt me to know that you had another disappointment in life. Heaven knows, the first one with Pap was enough to cover a lifetime of hurts. You with your youth and inexperience in life and he because of . . . worldly experience."[144]

Van Kirk's "worldly experience" included affairs with Gardner's friends, among them Lemuel Ayers's wife, Shirley, and Elise Vickers. At the time, Vickers was married to Hugh Morrow, who was a colleague of Maurice Donohue's at the *Philadelphia Inquirer;* later he became one of Nelson A. Rockefeller's most trusted aides. It had been a shotgun wedding. The Morrows "were first cousins once removed. They were still almost children when they married. He was twenty-one. She was fifteen." Her father, whom she always called "that monster," had forced them to marry when he realized they were having sex. According to her son, the journalist Lance Morrow, she charmed by her "vitality and intelligence, her sheer passion for life, her embrace of it"; he described her as a voracious reader, "hectically intense," and "a magnificent actress [who] should have practiced the art professionally."[145] Gardner and Vickers were curiously similar in spirit, but physically unalike: Vickers was "pert and tiny." Many fell for Elise Vickers's charms, Shag Donohue being one of them: "Elise was gorgeous in every way. As the boys would say in Oxford, not a brick was out of place . . . perfectly molded. She was petite and wore high heels and silk stockings before the war and she had what we called potatoes in her heels, holes in her silk stockings." Later, "Elise broke up with Hugh Morrow and there were six kids and he went to the Catholic Church and he got possession of the six kids" because of her loose morality and drinking.[146] Later still, in a warped twist of fate, Vickers married Gardner's third ex-husband, Robert Hall McCormick, just a few months after Gardner had left him.

Gardner had become totally disappointed in Van Kirk because of his violence, his narcissism, his unfaithfulness, his lies. Nevertheless, some fifteen years later, describing one of Rosy's teachers at her boarding school in Sedona, Arizona, she could still see why she had fallen in love with Van Kirk: "Am anxious to meet the teacher, Cliff—that she so adores—who now has a plan to get a group of kids to his house Sundays to discuss Plato over bacon and eggs! I hope he will require them to read what they attempt to discuss! Everything she tells me about him sounds eerily like Van! A type (inevitably fascinating if one is both romantically and creatively inclined) that I'd rather she fell for at 16 than at 20!"[147] In 1960 Gardner realized that Rosy Van Kirk, who created crisis after crisis as soon as she reached her teens, was "frighteningly like Van. But she is young and when I first knew him he was over 40. I refuse to believe that my [R]ose cannot resolve her problems with time and help and luck."[148] Time would prove her wrong.

Barbara Van Rensselaer Spalding, whom Gardner often visited as she lived with her family in New York City, recorded Gardner coming in one day with a gallon of white wine, plunking it down on the kitchen table and saying: "I am leaving Van" because he had been "desperately and brutally unfaithful, laying all her friends" and that she could not stand that anymore.[149] But then, she had another man waiting in the wings.

Chapter Three

"Shapiro Shangri La," 1943–1949

They spoke fractured English fractured Yiddish
and fractured Russian when they did not want
their children to understand. Most husbands
drove down from Chicago fridays but mine
came to me thursdays bringing the squat green
bottles of Chilean white wine which I drank
(he was angry if I forgot to buy cucumbers)
My daughter then five, now in
Bedlam, chased butterflies and thirty years
ago my infant son, now for some years
lost, was happy too.
("That Was Then")

At the end of 1942, only four years after she had fallen madly in love with Van Kirk, Gardner packed up and left him and her stepchildren and went back to Brookline with Rosy, then just three years old. Disturbed because she would never know "how he really felt" and wondering about why, when, and with how many he had betrayed her, Gardner nevertheless hoped he and Elise Vickers, with whom he was still involved, would "find happiness together."[1] Gardner had a part in a Broadway revue, *New Priorities of 1943* (Clifford Fisher's disappointing remake of his successful *Priorities of 1942*), and Molly Laughlin took care of Rosy while her mother stayed in hotels, with the Spaldings or, most happily, with the Ayerses. Shirley Ayers's having slept with her husband did not bother her; in fact, Gardner was grateful as Shirley was willing to testify in court that she had committed adultery with Van Kirk, making it easy for Gardner to divorce him. Whereas most American women in the 1940s were dependent on their husbands' income, making it virtually impossible for them to separate from adulterous or even abusive husbands, Gardner, cushioned by her money, could easily afford to leave Van Kirk. With Rosy she traveled to Reno, America's divorce capital, and spent the required six weeks' residence at an expensive ranch, reading, riding, and waiting for her marriage to be formally dissolved. A free woman once more, she moved with her daughter to Chestnut Street in Chicago, the city where she had starred in *Blithe Spirit.*

Van Kirk lost his wife, daughter, and main source of income, so he went back to teaching and, later, being truly a man of all trades, started dealing in antiques, meanwhile trying to write and sell plays rather unsuccessfully. His third marriage left him a nest egg: feeling guilty, Gardner gave him the valuable Doylestown farm, as it represented to her their loathsome life together. According to Frances Sacco, Gardner had "developed a real hatred for Van Kirk and rightly so," but their infrequent contact over the years was generally civil, partly because Van Kirk did not care about what happened to his daughter, and there were no fights about Rosy's upbringing.[2] Writing some twenty years after Gardner had left him, he told his "Dear Domi," that Peter "tells me you are the only mother he has ever known. . . . You see, he has no mother, except you. Maybe that was part of what the matter was. And I know that you've always done all you could for him and for Anni. And you'll never know the satisfaction it has given me."[3] Van Kirk admitted that he had been "a gross egoist," yet most of his communications remained centered on himself.[4] Late in life, he took months to answer a letter in which Gardner had written him about her father's death and the institutionalization of their then-brain-damaged daughter, apologizing that he had not wanted to think of "'old, unhappy far-off things.'" After expressing his condolences (Peabo Gardner "was fair and kind and good. And I have—am glad—that I kept my word to him in all things, despite lawyer's contrary advice"), Van Kirk wondered whether he should continue to write to his daughter or not, clearly preferring the latter: "It is all so sad. And I can do nothing." To him it was more important that his "Doctor of Law came through recently, and I retired Professor Emeritus from my college." Past eighty, he was saying goodbye: "And I want particularly to thank you for the generous way in which you have helped Anneke and Peter. But then the girl I first saw under the apple tree at East Hampton would do that—she couldn't do otherwise!"[5]

Van Kirk's last wife, Julie, who managed to stay married to him for decades, wrote Gardner considerately in 1974: "There is something I think I want you to know—you are the only woman in his past life he speaks of with affection and happiness. In contrast—some of the bitternesses and even hatreds—heaped on former wives and lovers—with all the water that has passed under the bridges—is appalling. I know—if it were me—I should like the knowledge of this I tell you—he still has some kind of thing for his life with you."[6] Soon after their blissful stay in Great Britain and Rosy's birth, Van Kirk's violence, his cold heart beneath his warm-blooded facade, his womanizing in spite of protestations of love, the pseudointellectualism concealed by his sophistication had lacerated Gardner. Having lost some of her naïveté with respect to men, she had no regrets at walking out on him. Without almost a second thought, however, she also deserted her young stepchildren whom she had showered with love and who had come to regard her as their mother. In light of Van Kirk's callous behavior, Gardner's defection of his family is understandable, yet it shows that she did not comprehend that Anneke and Peter were devastated by her departure and, self-absorbed, was swayed by the intensity of her passions rather than the exigencies of motherhood.

Gardner had first met the photographer Maurice Seymour through her East Hampton friends Maurice and Helen Donohue (Helen was a cousin of Seymour's ex-wife, Faye). In 1940 Seymour and Faye had divorced fairly amicably; they still saw each other often because of their daughter, Sydney, who was two at the time of their divorce. In 1942, Maurice Donohue, who did not own a car, asked well-to-do Seymour to drive him to the airport to pick up "a girl from Boston." Seymour's first impression: "She had long beautiful golden hair, very nice, and the sun was shining, I will never forget it, very beautiful, and I said: 'God, your hair is beautiful, you do it yourself?'"[7] It was "sex and love at first sight" and another version of their first meeting has Seymour pouring a highball over Gardner's hair, Gardner slapping him, and Seymour countering: "I just wanted to see if your red hair was real."[8] Seymour's version of their courtship is sexually whitewashed but no less lively and entertaining for it. It has Gardner calling him about a month later:

> "Mr. Seymour, this is Isabella Gardner." I say: "Isabella Gardner? Gee, that reminds me of somebody," because I had just met her for five minutes. She says: "I am here with a play." I said: "What play?" "We are opening in *Blithe Spirit.*" I said: "I will be glad to see it." She says: "I will leave some tickets for you.". . . She had three words in the show. She was the maid, you know, to bring in the tea or something. To make a long story short, afterwards I went back and I congratulated her and I said: "I hope to see you, goodbye" and I left. . . . Well anyway, after a while she said: "What do you do after the show on Saturday night" or whatever night it was, so that is how little by little we became acquainted. I saw she wanted company and I had no particular person that I was involved with, outside of [movie star] Lizabeth Scott at the time. . . .
>
> Belle interested me more because she was an intelligent person and she was not drinking with me, at the time anyway. . . . Meanwhile this became a habit, night in and night out, after the show and I usually worked late, it did not matter, so that is how our romance started, because she enjoyed being with me, because I

did not demand nothing from her, I did not challenge her, I did not threaten her with anything. She was much more intelligent than I was and I knew it, I mean I enjoyed her intelligence, but I did not challenge her in any way. . . . Anyway, this went on for about three months. The show closes and she tells me she goes back to her husband and tell him she is in love with me. I say: "What!?" She said: "That is what I am going to tell him." I said: "You are crazy. I never heard of such a thing." . . . She comes back about six months later, with a little girl, Rosy, and she says: "I am going to Reno." I: "Reno, what are you going to Reno for?" "I am going to get a divorce." I say: "What!?" She is going to get a divorce. I said: "Are you serious?" She says: "Yes, I am." . . . Then she starts writing me letters, from Reno, all of this and all of that and I enjoyed them. . . . She comes back and she says: "Would you help me find an apartment?" I say: "Well, if I know some people around, that have an apartment, I will be glad to." So I found . . . a very nice apartment, with a maid and all of that and I do not know what she paid and then I began to talk to her, I said: "Well, where do you get all this money?" She says: "Oh, I do not know, I have some sort of a trust." I was not curious really, but it bothered me a little bit. Where does all this come about, all of me, Russian little me? To make a long story short . . . Belle, we got this apartment and all of that, we became friendly and we had an affair, for a while, it was enjoyable."[9]

Maurice Seymour was born Seymour Zeldman, the youngest of six children, in 1902, in the old town of Khotin in Bessarabia, a country on the Black Sea annexed to Russia in 1812. A year after his birth, the infamous Kishinev pogrom took place in Bessarabia. Over three days of rioting almost fifty Jews were killed on the pretext that one had murdered a Christian Russian boy; although it was evident that he had been killed by a relative, anti-Semitic newspapers alleged that he had been murdered by Jews, one paper insinuating that his blood had been used to make matzos. Neither police nor military intervened, and it was widely believed that the pogrom had been instigated by the state. Between 1905 and 1907, in the tumult leading up to the Russian Revolution, anti-Jewish brutality increased, as Jews were associated with both the insurrection, and conversely, the Tsarists. Against this dark backdrop of violence, fear, and political unrest, Zeldman Senior left for the promised land—America. He took his two eldest daughters with him and settled, like many Eastern European Jews, in the ethnic Near West Side of Chicago.[10]

In Khotin, his wife, his daughter Manya, and his three young sons struggled to survive. Zeldman sent some money now and then, but they had to help out, which Seymour did by selling gasoline from house to house. The boys received a solid Jewish education. Seymour "used to go . . . to cheder. Cheder is a little synagogue school for children that stay there until eight o'clock and then they go home with their lanterns and that is what I did. And study the Talmud. The

Talmud is the most biblical book in the entire Jewish religion and I studied it until the age of twelve."[11] Soon, Seymour's sister Manya, not yet twenty, had to shoulder the burden of the Bessarabian household as their mother died of a broken heart—or, more prosaically, of pneumonia. When one of the boys also died, Manya was left with Maurice ("Maury") and Seymour. "At that point the father said: 'Come,' but he had not up to then sent for the rest of them. So they went and they were in Paris about six months, because one of them got the measles."[12] When they finally arrived in Chicago, they moved in with their father and Molly, their eldest sister.

The three young Russian-Jewish immigrants, Manya, Maury, and Seymour, arrived in Chicago in 1920. Seymour remembered speaking four languages in his late teens, none of them English:

> So finally my father put me in a school with children, even though I graduated high school in Russia: I still had to be with a bunch of kids and they used to laugh at me. But they enjoyed me, because I used to play ball with them and they used to call me Babe Ruth and I had no idea who Babe Ruth was. I was a big boy in comparison with them. And then, after a while, the teacher used to call me up to do mathematics and I was good at that, so the kids used to come to me and they all needed my favors, so they liked me and I was very good and that is how I learned how to speak English. [13]

Zeldman Senior was doing well as an umbrella-maker, and Seymour was allowed to attend the Jewish People's Institute, instrumental in the Americanization of many Eastern European immigrants, "a university," to Seymour, "but more or less of foreigners."[14] He learned to appreciate the arts, often went to the Art Institute, and dabbled in aquarelle painting. But his father insisted that he learn a trade, and so he was apprenticed to an Italian photographer. An Eastern European Jew, he took pictures of little Catholic girls in their first communion dresses, earning a mere twelve dollars a week, just enough to buy a bike for work and to eat packed lunches.[15] Then, one day, out of the blue, he got a huge salary increase ("Gee, the man is paying me thirty dollars a week!"), motivating him to put his "complete energy and mind" to taking pictures. Seymour "learned more, was more enthusiastic" and his boss "was so surprised, he said: 'These [pictures] are great, much better than I could do.'"[16] Later, Seymour found out that his father had slipped his boss the money for the raise.

When Gardner met him, Seymour was known as America's foremost photographer of ballet. A genius of light and line, consciously and artfully concentrating on pose, not movement, he made dancers' bodies seem even more beautiful than in real life. "Who, once they have seen it, can ever forget Seymour's glamorous full-figure portrait of ballerina Alexandra Danilova in her

Swan Lake, Act II, costume?" Jack Mitchell, himself a famous photographer, wrote in *Dance* magazine in 1999.[17] Seymour "experienced the greatest satisfaction" in his work when shaping his iconic ballet portraits, but he made good money shooting portraits of famous entertainers and, often, strippers, in his studio.[18] Founded in the late 1920s, the studio was on the top floor of Chicago's landmark St. Clair Hotel. Seymour's introverted older brother, Maury, ran the darkroom, perfecting Seymour's images. Seymour came to be known as the "Photographer to the Stars," and over the years he took sumptuous pictures of everybody who was anybody: Amos and Andy, Harry Belafonte, Tony Bennett, Carol Channing, Tommy Dorsey, Benny Goodman, Frankie Laine, Virginia Mayo, Edith Piaf, Anthony Quinn, Will Rogers, Lizabeth Scott, Laurette Taylor, Natalie Wood; they and many others came to Seymour's studio, as he made them all alluring. Those who wished to be famous also had their pictures taken by Seymour, hoping that his photographic magic would get them noticed by agents, or that one of his many contacts would land them a job. Teen idol James Darren was particularly lucky: Seymour's secretary introduced him to agent Joyce Selznick, who then took the credit for discovering him, getting him a contract at Columbia Pictures.

Seymour was indeed an important macher in the entertainment world, regularly mentioned in Chicago's newspapers, often as a judge in a beauty contest. When she met him, Gardner was not unaware of his status in the theater milieu, but his attraction for her was first and foremost physical. Short and stocky, balding though hairy, Seymour was not Gardner's usual type, but he was very sure of himself; oozing a macho sexuality "like a bull," he turned every meeting, every conversation with an attractive woman into an occasion for flattery, suggestiveness, and caressing, and Gardner was susceptible to flirtatious men.[19] She was keenly attracted to his "titanic energy"; "wild and wonderful" Seymour was exuberant, vital, spontaneous, and generous to boot; life around him was an exciting, ongoing feast.[20] As a truly creative artist, earthy, without a trace of sophistication, Seymour promised to be real, to be everything that Van Kirk was not.

Their initial flirtation was not as one-sided as Seymour has depicted it, but it was Gardner who wanted to turn it into a serious relationship. An archromantic, she rationalized that Seymour was perfect, Van Kirk's antipode. Gardner was ready to entrust herself to Seymour for life. Seymour, though used to female attention, fell hard for Gardner, too. She was a successful actress, funny, and openly sexy at a time when women behaved asexually so as not to be considered promiscuous. He loved her infectious joie de vivre and her raucous laugh and was impressed, though not intimidated, by her intelligence and her wide reading: "She used to love to read and I, the only books I used to read, is chess books . . . . And the people that we used to entertain, used to love me for myself, not because I read Shakespeare, or Nietzsche or Schopenhauer, because I know all about it, but I did not inhale it, like they do. They absorb it to such a degree that, if you are being raped, relax and enjoy it, you know, because Shakespeare said so. I mean to them these things are so important, that nothing else matters. Well, to me nothing: I am a simple guy, a peasant, call me a peasant for short."[21] For him Gardner was "brilliant," the apex of intellectuality.[22] She also provided his entrée into the upper echelon of the American dream, which had been closed to him. Taking studio portraits of debutantes and society women, Seymour had gotten a taste of WASP culture, but as a Jew with a heavy accent and a mere photographer he had always remained an outsider looking in. With a Gardner at his side, he could climb the social ladder and gain acceptance.

But Gardner had even more to win by becoming part of Seymour's milieu. His siblings wholeheartedly welcomed their baby brother's new girlfriend into their midst. Molly took the shiksa under her protective wing, admonishing Seymour "to be careful, she is like a doll, she is fragile," and giving her the warmth Gardner's own "ice-cube" mother lacked.[23] "That Was Then," a poem written in the 1970s, brilliantly evokes the lively intimacy of the Zeldman extended family:

> Molly the matriarch and my mother
> too Molly amply Yiddish mama
> bountiful heart bountiful flesh married
> to tender Ben Blevitsky book-binder
> and Bolshevik, not Communist though he
> thought he was and paid his Party dues.
> He pressed on me, a bemused fellow traveller
> The Daily Worker which I occasionally
> scanned. Aside from Ben's misguided fealty
> to a party that betrayed his each, his
> every dream, he taught the Shicksa wisdom,
> ancient Hebraic, of the heart and pulse.
> This Shicksa loved him all his life.
> ("That Was Then," 121)

It was a new universe. Molly and Ben's teenage daughter, Riva, met Gardner's brother George at their house, "shortly after he returned to civilian life after being in the Navy during World War II. My mother made her usual large dinner and afterwards commented," Riva recalled, "that it seemed strange to see such a rich man wearing clothes that were too small for him. He was dressed in a tweed suit and the trousers were above the shoes, and to my mom that was a sign of poverty, wearing clothes that did not fit. She did not understand the reverse snobbery of that time, that if you had money, you did not care what length your trousers were—and they wore them short purposely."[24] Emotions ran high and loud, and Gardner loved this intensity, so different from the well-behaved frigidity of her New England family. The Zeldman clan, which included cousins, friends, former wives or husbands, stepchildren, and cousins many times removed was close on a "fundamentally human level... chicken soup and chopped liver."[25] Seymour was her passport into this world.

Gardner, who had fallen head over heels in love with Seymour, would not live a lie and left Van Kirk within months of their first chance meeting. "Belle was incapable of living with one person, when she was in love with another.... It had to be total commitment."[26] With three-year-old Rosy she moved into the apartment Seymour had found for them in downtown Chicago. Soon, they were living together openly, unmarried, a practice frowned upon in the 1940s, even in Gardner and Seymour's unconventional circle of singers, theater people, and movie stars. Seymour's sisters certainly felt they were living in sin. And despite all her rebelliousness, Gardner was still too much of a Boston Brahmin to cohabit with confidence. Regardless of her adultery with Childers and failed marriage to Van Kirk, she still swore by the commitment entailed. She wanted to wipe clean the slate of her former loves and, wedded to Seymour, life would be eternally blissful. She set about convincing him:

> I used to go bowling, I used to play chess, I used to do everything but read the Book of the Month Club. So she used to go to the Book of the Month Club, I used to do other things, till one day, after a while she insisted that we get more serious about our relationship. I said: "Ok, well what is it?" She says: "I am not married, you are not married." I said: "What are we going to gain by being married?" "Well if you want to raise a child and all of that." I said: "Well, that is sensible," so . . . we discussed it back and forth and we said: "Alright, we will get married."[27]

Peabo Gardner was not so sure. "He put on the guy from Turkey, the little guy, the investigator to see whether I am going with Belle for any reason of the money or anything."[28] The report was positive. Unlike gold digger Van Kirk, Seymour was earning good money at the time and had no intention of living off Gardner. He had far too much fun working and, besides, was too proud and controlling to let a wife hold the purse strings. But the serious question of his Jewishness remained. Nelson Aldrich has argued that for the old money class "anti-Semitism is the most salient manifestation of their 'family' fears and loathing. . . . If Jews are an obsession with the WASP Old Rich, and they are, it is not because they spell the destruction of things Old Money holds dear but because the WASP Old Rich half-suspect that Jews take better care, can afford to take better care, of the patrimony than they can."[29] As a first-generation immigrant who had gained middle-class economic status, Seymour certainly did not pose such a threat, but his being a Jew of low birth and position made him totally unsuitable as a husband in the Gardners' eyes. Only some ten years earlier, Sam Zemurray (known as "Sam the Banana Man"), another self-made Jew from Bessarabia, had traveled to Boston for a meeting of United Fruit, one of the world's most controversial multinationals, in which the Gardners were major shareholders. Then "the toptable [had] professed not to understand a word he was saying because of his Russian accent," for "Boston Wasps didn't take to Jews in business, or anywhere, really."[30] Gardner's friend Barbara Van Rensselaer Spalding, whose parents also were very proper Bostonians, "never saw a Jew, much less a black in [her] life, because you did not invite a Jew into your dining room."[31]

So, sturdy rustic Russian-Jewish Seymour was summoned to dinner at Green Hill, the apex of WASP aristocracy—enough to put the fear in anyone. He was divorced and older, and the parental reception was expected to be icy. But Seymour, self-assured, all passion, all emotion, melted them with ease. When he arrived for inspection

> I was dressed like this, nothing fancy, but her mamma had made dinner, a luncheon for us, for the family. The entire family was there and she says: "I want Seymour to sit next to me." . . . So I sat with her and I even remember what she had: she had chicken a la king. Chicken a la king was her favorite. She says: "I made the cook cook it special for you." So she gave me a portion and she says: "Bring him another portion, he is a Russian guy, he eats." And I would eat it, I enjoyed myself. And then she says: "I am going to take you for an automobile ride." . . . Then later on I spoke to Peabo. Peabo says: "You want to hear the story, now that you took a ride in mamma's car, I will tell you the story. Mamma told me she was buying a little baby car, very cheap. I said: 'Go ahead, you do not need my permission.' So she spent thirteen thousand dollars!" In those days . . . thirteen thousand is like a hundred thousand. Well, anyway, Peabo says: "She came back and she says she has paid thirteen thousand." "Thirteen thousand," he said, "well, what am I going to do, argue?" He was a very nice man. He is the kind of man that you cannot help but embracing him, you know, men or women. He is a great guy. I loved him.[32]

The love was mutual and outlasted Gardner's adoration of Seymour; when Peabo died in 1976, he left Seymour money in his will. Gardner's younger brother John, though chary of information because he found it painful to talk about his sister's thorny life, was sure his "father had a very good relationship with Seymour. And my mother had a pretty good relationship with him. Of all the four husbands, he was the one whom her brothers and sisters felt the closest to. . . .

[H]e is such a genuine human being in a great many ways, very outgoing, sense of humor, and a rough diamond . . . a kind, generous man."[33]

Although from completely different worlds, Peabo and Seymour, manly men, agreed on proper behavior for their women. Seymour thought Gardner misbehaved when she embraced him in the presence of her father and a business associate at the beginning of their courtship, and he was still angry at Gardner's refusal to pray with her father and him at Roque almost fifty years after the event: "They have a path to this place where they said a prayer every Sunday. And he says: 'Come on, Seymour and Belle, let us go.' Belle says: 'No, I do not want to go.' I say: 'What have you got to lose? Now, you heard, your father wants you to go.' . . . We started a big fight."[34] In both cases, Gardner was showing her loyalty to Seymour and his Jewish background vis-à-vis her WASP parent, but Seymour saw her as a disobedient wife and daughter.

The parental blessing given, a wedding was planned. Another ceremony at Green Hill, barely four years after Gardner's marriage to Van Kirk, was unsuitable, and the couple decided to get married in Los Angeles. Peabo Gardner's only sister, Catherine Gardner Mayes, lived close by, and George, who was stationed on the West Coast in the wartime navy, had leave on his sister's wedding day. Two worlds touched.

> So George says: "Why do not you have aunt Catherine rent with a bishop, to marry you. . . . I said: "Well, as long as we are going to have a bishop, I am being Jewish, how about having a rabbi?" So Belle says: "That is a good idea, let us get a rabbi." And THAT was the problem, because no rabbi will marry you if you are marrying a gentile girl, unless you have a reformed rabbi. So I called up every rabbi in Los Angeles. Nobody wanted to do it, but one guy suggested: "Why do not you call up the funeral parlor, a certain rabbi there that might do it." So I called up that guy at a funeral parlor. He says: "Yeah, I will do it for twenty-five dollars." I said: "Alright, you got a deal." So he came and he married us off.[35]

On January 4, 1944, the *Chicago Daily Tribune* published a lovely picture Seymour had taken of Gardner and an announcement of her marriage, reporting that "after a month's sojourn in Mexico, Mr. Seymour and his bride will be at home in Chicago."[36] Gardner's second honeymoon was modest, but there were many parties, one thrown by Gardner's dear friend Lem Ayers, already one of Broadway's glitterati. The Zeldman family had a big Chicago gathering, and those who were not invited felt sorely passed over, foremost among them Seymour's daughter, Sydney. Only six at the time, Sydney Zeldman was already captivated by her father's second wife, who had set out to win the heart of this new stepchild. Before their marriage, Gardner and Seymour, together with Rosy, had moved into a two-bedroom apartment with one bath and a sun parlor on 222 East Pearson Street, and though not awarded by the court to her father, Sydney passed most of her time there: "that just sort of became my second home, because that is where all the activity was." Rosy was slightly younger than Sydney, and they became very close, Sydney spending "more time with Belle and Rosy than I did with my father during that whole period" and Sydney "always felt totally comfortable there and welcome."[37] She was enchanted by the aura of avant-garde glamour that Gardner brought to her life. The apartment on Pearson Street was "contemporary . . . just wonderfully redone. An older building, a walk-up, it was grey stone, old, and we always had the nicest furnishings, wonderful paintings. The basement of this building became our playroom and she had a Van Gogh, the woman sitting in a chair, and that was just so fantastic, to put a painting in the playroom. And she used astonishing colors with grays, really ahead of her time. . . . Rosy and I would go try on Belle's dresses; she had beautiful silk dresses, her clothes were glamorous. . . . And then she would use fresh herbs or ground pepper when in those days people did not. It seemed to me she was more progressive, more European in her style. Having more money might have made the difference, because my mother was very poor, living on a really tight budget and so the contrast was very stark to me."[38]

The maid kept a watchful eye on the children, because Gardner was not home much, spending her days with friends, in libraries or bookshops. But she was no longer working; her acting career had ground to a halt, just when it had seemed about to take wing. She had acted with stars like Betty Comden, Francis Lederer, Gloria Swanson, and Estelle Winwood and had gotten brilliant reviews as a character actress. Martin Manulis was sure that, given her potential and possibilities, Gardner, had she been truly dedicated, might have gone far as a comedienne. Frances Sacco, who devoted her life to the theater, agreed that Gardner had talent and the right connections, but in her opinion she did not make it on the stage, because—like Leighton Rollins's rich female summer students from Finch—being on the boards was a pastime, not an avocation for her. Sacco was too severe, for Gardner did take her work seriously, but the man she was with now was the center around which her entire life gravitated. And although Seymour had fallen in love with Gardner when she was an actress, he was too much a man of his times, and too dominant, to want his wife to have an independent career. Having money of her own, Gardner could delegate the everyday humdrum household responsibilities to her housekeeper, but in spirit she became what Seymour desired, an extension of himself and "a Jewish hausfrau," if an unconventional one.[39] (Seymour's third wife, Helena Dudas, would emulate Gardner. She auditioned for Frances Sacco's husband, then music director at the Paper Mill Playhouse, who was bowled over by this "absolutely glorious young woman, who sang like a dream. . . And by Jove, she comes along and becomes Seymour's next wife after Belle. She gave up her career, ZING, just like that!"[40] Dudas was twenty-three and a musical comedy star, playing the role of Nancy in the musical *Annie Get Your Gun* in Chicago, when Seymour, twice her age, married her. "She is the one who made that marriage work. . . . She just gave herself up. She did not make life that much easier for him, or more pleasant really, but [gave up] her career: she became a mother."[41])

In America, Seymour, who had studied the Talmud as a boy in Bessarabian Russia, swore off religion and adapted to the "commercial" American way of life, but his cultural orientation remained resolutely immigrant Eastern European Jewish.[42] The Zeldman family formed part of the Chicago Russian Jewish community and Seymour, though a self-styled ignoramus, "used to buddy" with intellectuals like "Oscar Tarkov and [psychiatrist Louis] Cholden: all of us, we used to be together, friends"; others were Chicago newspaper columnist Sydney Harris (like Cholden and Tarkov, high school friends of Saul Bellow's who, however, never belonged to the Seymours' inner circle) and Victor Weisskopf.[43] The Zeldman tribe and their friends were all close-knit: there were Seymour's brother and business associate, Maury, with his wife, Sonya; his sister Manya, who was a Yiddish actress, and her best friend, Sulya, the mother of Louis Cholden's wife, Myra, who became one of Gardner's best friends; and earth mother Molly, her husband, Ben, and their teenage daughter, Riva. Gardner, the tall, pale, pink shiksa in their midst learned "to cook kugel / and fix gefillte fish" ("That Was Then," 120). Favored by his sisters, Seymour was at the core of this loving family. They were sometimes shocked by his strippers and nightclubbing but at the same time attracted by the exotic excitement he brought them. "He was not considered to be someone who would do anything that was ordinary. Whatever he did was out of the ordinary anyway as far as they were concerned. He was the baby brother who could do whatever he wanted."[44] His studio was a place "where people went to meet each other . . . [and] became sort of the focal point for all the life."[45]

Seymour had rented the entire top floor of the St. Clair Hotel: "I used to have a studio on the third floor, 312, and I used to live in 311. Then, when the radio studio upstairs was disbanded on account of some sort of a fire, I looked up and I saw all these little nooks in cork, so I figured that it made good darkrooms."[46] Soon after opening his studio, Seymour got his lucky break. Some of his pictures were exhibited in the windows of the National Bank, and Freeman Gosden and Charles Correll (Amos and Andy, the leading radio stars of their day) strolled past, saw them, and decided then and there to have their publicity pictures taken by Maurice Seymour, catapulting him to the position of Chicago's celebrity photographer.

Daniel Jones, later the photography curator at Harvard University, came to work for Seymour in 1947 and had "the very happiest time in my whole life, other than some early childhood years."[47] He sketched a vivid picture of how he came to be part of Seymour's wondrously free entourage after his regimented years at St. Mark's, Harvard, and the navy.

I met George Gardner at St. Mark's school as a teenager and we met up again in the United States Navy in the Pacific, in World War II, where we found ourselves both members of the same admiral staff in a cruiser division and we were roommates and got to know each other extremely well.... He had a sister whom I had heard hours about, because on a ship in the war there is not much to do except talk, so we talked and talked and he told me all about his wonderful sister Belle.... What happened in 1946 was that George went to Chicago to see his sister and they were just about to take off to go to Mexico City, where the Ballet Russe de Monte Carlo was for a month, or six weeks, and they were going to drive in this great big black touring car of Seymour's, with all of the belongings in the back of the car. Imagine driving to Mexico City and this is 1946, but they did. They said: "Come on George, come on along." So he went. And the routine was after the performance Seymour would invite the troupe out to a restaurant in the country and they would be there under the stars and they would have food and some wine and relax. There George met and fell hopelessly in love with a young ballerina named Tania Stepanova, and she simply swept him off his feet. He followed her around the world, wherever she went, there were roses and roses and roses and roses.... She did not speak much English, but she was a perfectly charming, wonderful person and they were obviously very much in love. They were married in the spring of 1947, which was the year I finally graduated from Harvard, after having left for six years, and George asked me to be an usher in his wedding. It was at a party before the wedding that I found myself sitting next to Belle, whom I had never met. And Seymour was there and proceeded to do all the Russian dances with Tania and Tania's mother.... He brought some photographs with him, these beautiful photographs of the Ballet Russe. Now this is before strobe: they were all shot with incandescent light and they were just exquisite. And I must have had sufficient champagne to screw up my courage and be absolutely foolhardy enough to say: "Listen Seymour, I want to work for you.... This is not going to cost you anything: we can do it under the GI Bill."... I had six years at St. Mark's school, four years at Harvard, five years of the navy at sea, I was sick of it, I wanted to do what I wanted to do, and for one year, I wanted to work with Seymour.... I spent the most extraordinary year in my whole life."[48]

Jones entered the world of show business photography, which was completely alien to a puritanical New Englander. For Seymour did not just photograph the big names but caught extravaganzas such as roller skating shows and nightclub acts by the thousands. A man who had trained white cockatoos to act as a fire department crew made an indelible impression: "One of them would strike a match and light something and it would start to burn, whereupon the others would scream and yell; then one would ring the bell and another one would pull out a hose and the third one would crank a thing and it would squirt water and put out the fire."[49] In Chicago, only some fifteen years after Al Capone's conviction, it was still impossible to do well in show business without connections to the mob, and Seymour, successful, was no exception. Seymour's world was, in the end, too surreal for Jones. Entering it "was just like snipping his suspenders and floating up like a balloon," but he also found it unsettling, shifty, "too treacherous a world, too desperate a world":[50]

> That hotel where Seymour was, was the headquarters for some of the operations of the mob. And one of the mob's operations is betting and there was a fellow named Eddie Stern, that lived there and Eddie, you would see Eddie and you would not know he was not, you know, a businessman. Eddie ran a place over in a loft building on North Park Street, which you take to be a factory. You go in through one gate, and then another gate, and then finally when you were upstairs, there were all these people, all these people on the telephones, and they were taking bets and quoting odds on race tracks all over the country, and Eddie was in charge of the baseball games.[51]

Seymour's connections with Stern and other mobster colleagues, nearly going back to Capone, were close. If a member of the mob opened a new restaurant, Seymour would be asked to take a picture "for the postcards of the mob."[52] "He would open the shutter of the lens and have you go around with a light and you keep moving and you paint everything with light. It might take you twenty minutes to go all around the room and you create the image by painting the surfaces with light."[53] Jones had never seen anybody do that before and had never "watched anybody work who shot really, really beautiful nude photographs of beautiful women. God, they were just gorgeous, the light, here was a genius of light."[54] Seymour delivered these pictures to the mob and took their family photographs as well. In return, he would receive a slip of paper with the name of a horse in a rigged race, bet and win.

Seymour was the undisputed master of lighting in theatrical photography of his day. All kinds of would-be celebrities, from showgirls to society girls, from mobsters to politicians, lined up for his lens, but he remains best known for his ballet pictures, selections of which were published in *Seymour on Ballet* (1947) and *Ballet Portraits* (1952). Seymour's anecdote of how he became the photographic historian of the Ballet Russe de Monte Carlo and, as a consequence, of America's ballet renaissance in the 1930s and 1940s, is, like many of his stories, perhaps too good to be quite true:

> The De Basil Company [the original Ballet Russe de Monte Carlo] came here in 1929 or 1930 and they opened up at the old opera house in Chicago and they opened up with Scheherazade. I will never forget it. And [Yurek] Shabelevsky was

the main slave in Scheherazade and he could only speak Russian, he comes from a Slavic country where he never heard any other language but Russian. So [Colonel Wasily De Basil] introduced me to Shabelevsky, to give him instructions. Anyway, I at that time had lots of hair. I was walking around during intermission, in the lobby of the Opera House and here comes by Colonel De Basil. He was a big tall dry colonel. He says: "What are you doing?" I say: "Why, what do you want to know?" He says: "What is your profession?" I say: "Why do you want to know?" He says: "I want to know because you look like artistic." I say: "What do you mean by that?" He says: "Are you a photographer?" I say: "Yes." Then I got interested because how does he know I am a photographer? I said: "Well, what is it that you want to know?" "I want you to take pictures of the entire company." Just like that. I said: "Alright." I say: "When do you want to do it?" "After the performance the wardrobe woman will bring you the costumes and you are going to work all night." Just like that. And he, backstage, instructed the wardrobe woman and that is what they did and from then on I started taking pictures, of the ballet, just like that.[55]

Daniel Jones recalled that when the Ballet Russe came to town "I never got an hour of sleep for a week, because the troupe would come up after the show and until breakfast, shoot, shoot, shoot, shoot, shoot, and everything on eight by ten inch negatives, but no flash, all incandescent. And [Seymour] would holler and yell and scream and shout at these people and go up to someone: 'Oh no, do what I tell you!' He was demonic, but he got the results and they loved it. Of course they were all talking Russian, which I did not understand. So, I would go and develop all these negatives, in these great big wooden cypress tank baths, just wearing my t-shirt and dungarees."[56] In the cavernous processing area, Jones had to wear rubbers over his shoes; otherwise the chemicals would eat through the leather. The studio, with one great stage and smaller portrait areas on the side, dressing rooms and a makeup room, was filthy, but Seymour's clients did not seem to care. For Seymour got results in his own way. He gave women more bust and male dancers bananas to put in their tights. When he took a photograph of a ballerina with her leg extended, she had to put it on a stepladder, later to be painted out. He invented and set up all kinds of mechanical controls, so that he could shift great banks of light, individually, directly from his camera. Then he would compose the picture but would not be interested in exposure time or even focusing; to him the right expression was all that mattered. "And he would just go into this wild trance with a sitter and make this person do all kinds of things, kissing and kicking and kissing and kicking, and out of thirty pictures there would be one that was right on and ordered year after year after year."[57]

The kind of portraits Seymour created with passion rather than technique needed a lot of work. This was done by Maurice, an immensely skilled retoucher.

Sweet, shy Maurice was the unseen partner in the studio; Seymour, its loud, ebullient figurehead. The studio's name—the Maurice Seymour Studio—was a combination of the Zeldman brothers' first names, but the studio's patrons never even saw Maurice and started calling Seymour by what they thought was his first name: Maurice. The real Maurice was never overly fond of his pushy younger brother, but whatever love there may have been between them was lost when Seymour legally changed his name to Maurice Seymour, thereby appropriating both his elder brother's and the studio's name. "Maurice made light of it, but it so riled [his wife] Sonya that it was the beginning of a terrible time in both Sonya and Maury's lives and marriage.... Sonya was very bitter about the name for many years."[58] She blamed Gardner for this unseemly action, hinting that Gardner thought the name Zeldman too Jewish. In effect, flamboyant Seymour stole his self-effacing brother's limelight, and retouched him out of his professional life: Maurice is hardly mentioned in his narratives of his career as a photographer. To be sure, *Ballet: 101 Photographs by Maurice Seymour* is dedicated to "My dear brother" whose "help was invaluable in preparing the material for this book," but the "dear brother" remains anonymous.[59]

Seymour was always working, but to the couple's friends, his life with Gardner seemed to be one big party. Soon after Gardner became involved with Seymour, she met Myra and her husband, Louis Cholden. They would be bosom buddies in Chicago, and Myra (with Helen Donohue, both Jewish) was to remain Gardner's intimate friend till she died. The daughter of Manya's best friend, Sulya, Myra had known the Zeldman family for most of her life. Seymour played poker with her father and belonged, in her view, to a different generation. When she was sixteen Seymour made a pass at her, which she rebuffed, thinking him "a dirty old man." She refused to speak to him for a long time. "And then I was visiting my parents in Union Pier and I met Belle and we never separated from that moment. So I had to become friends with Seymour again."[60] Naturally, Myra already knew Helen and Maurice Donohue quite well. Maurice's brother Shag was also very much around; he ran a bookshop in Chicago. Besides, Gardner and Myra had common friends in Hugh and Elise (Vickers) Morrow; in the early 1940s, when he was in the service, Hugh had lived with the Choldens in their one-room basement apartment "until he did not take the dog out during the day when we were gone for work and so we asked him to leave."[61] (The muddle with the dog did not mess up their friendship.) Later, when they knew Gardner, the Choldens lived in a dirt-poor section of town, amidst bars, above a doctor's office on Lake Street, with streetcars and the El thundering past their windows. Myra earned some money as a social worker, while Louis specialized in psychiatry. When he got a part-time job as an industrial physician, Myra remembered, "he ran out and got a book on first aid and the first sentence he read was 'What to do till the doctor comes' and he realized he was the doctor. That was frightening, but we had free rent. He would be at call; at night they would ring a bell and down he would come. And so, after a while, all the people in the neighborhood used to come at night whenever there was an emergency. And he never turned anybody down, like the policeman who came and said: 'Hey, put the light on it, doc,' which meant that he had gonorrhea and that was the way to cure it."[62]

All the women, Gardner included, doted on him. Myra's (and soon Gardner's) friend Anabel Holland, who studied at the Art Institute and was roped in by Seymour to paint black-and-white backdrops for his pictures in the studio, fell completely under Cholden's spell, thinking he was "the nucleus around which everything revolved, a truly charismatic personality and brilliant—that goes with it of course. He was an eager analytical explorer of life and people, unharnassed: he enhanced everything around him."[63] Myra, somewhat nonplussed at the effect her husband had on those around him, allowed that he was "very natural, there was no pretense about him," he was the soul of any gathering, "wild," always willing to do things, from dancing with the women to playing chess with Seymour or Tarkov. She admitted, though, that she was the gregarious one, the one who always wanted to go out, and that he may have just livened parties up in order not to be bored. Multitalented, Cholden played the bass professionally at sharp nightclubs for good money, but his main concern was medicine. He was seemingly so natural at both that he had to offer proof of his bona fides: he convinced his bandmates by dissecting a cat at the club, his medical colleagues by staging a jam session. An all-around experimental psychiatrist and a lucid speaker and writer, he was invited by Karl Menninger to join him in Topeka, Kansas, in the early 1950s. Cholden soon became the leading expert on the psychological impact of vision loss, as well as one of the first who seriously studied the value of LSD in psychotherapy. But that came later; in Chicago, not yet thirty, he was cherished for his caring soul, "the courtesy and courage" of his heart, and his "life-spirit robust past compare" ("Zei Gesund," 51, 50).

The Seymours' life-spirit was robust, too, and with Gardner as the "connective tissue" they had a ball: "it was a little like the moveable feast."[64] Although Myra always abhorred Seymour's attitude toward women—"they were either good lays or lesbians or whores; they were whores or lesbians if he did not like them"—she tolerated him because he was Gardner's husband. Moreover, they "had wonderful times together. He was old as far as we were concerned, but we even forgave that. He was the only one who had money, the only one who had a car, the only one who was not struggling. He would take us to dinner, because we could not, possibly. We would go to clubs and the four of us were always together. . . . In a sense we still thought of ourselves as children."[65] Seymour was always picking up the tab for everybody—probably with an unobtrusive infusion of Gardner's money. (Gardner told Anabel Holland that she had $15,000 annually; around that time Saul Bellow earned $2,500 per year at the University of Minnesota in Minneapolis.)

Almost every Thursday night, Cholden's night off, the Seymours would throw theater parties. Whatever troupe with old Gardner friends and colleagues was playing in Chicago dropped by 222 East Pearson Street for an after-performance party. Accompanied by the cast of *The Glass Menagerie,* as well as Texas theater producer Margaret Jones, Tennessee Williams came by clad in his sailor suit (he went out on the prowl afterward). It was the end of 1944, at the dawn of his fame, just before the play was picked up by a Broadway theater. Myra and Williams danced: "I was very slender and he was very slender and we were two light-feet."[66] Seymour's dancers from the Ballet Russe (after posing) were regulars when in town; all the cast members of the popular musical revue *Pins and Needles,* produced by the International Ladies Garment Workers' Union Players, partied at Pearson Street; tough-guy movie actor Richard Widmark, then starring in Elmer Rice's *Dream Girl,* was the Seymours' guest, as was red-haired folksinger Susan Reed; now and then even a medium would come down to earth and relax. "We always had those great parties, a lot of drinking, a lot of smoking, but no playing around. One Hollywood actor was found in the bed seducing somebody or other, and he was never invited back. . . . Everybody just had a good time."[67]

Not everybody: one night José Ferrer broke down the door, because his wife, Uta Hagen, was there with her costar Paul Robeson, with whom she was having an affair. Hagen played Desdemona to Robeson's Othello, while Ferrer was Iago in one of the most successful performances of Shakespeare ever on Broadway. In real life it was Ferrer who was green-eyed with jealousy; the play's varied themes of racism, love, and betrayal played out with a warp. Touring, *Othello* was the subject of much controversy anyhow, as some audience members did not accept a white woman and a black man having physical contact on stage. As Robeson also had communist sympathies, high drama followed him wherever he went. At the Seymours', though, he felt at home. "Paul Robeson was a liberal man, a man's man, you know what I mean? And I [Seymour] used to take him to dinner and have a few drinks and joke and kid around and tell dirty stories and everything was alright."[68] He played chess with Seymour and sang to the children, but Robeson's meeting a Bessarabian-Russian Jew aroused much FBI suspicion, and agents grilled Seymour for hours about his contacts with Robeson.[69]

Gardner's East Hampton theater friend Harry Holland (who thought her "utterly romantic, utterly erotic, utterly poetic") often came by during cocktail hour and was "in awe" because Seymour put on his elegant smoking jacket and stylish slippers but felt harassed by Countess Palffy. She came in one afternoon, put down her many shopping bags, exclaiming: "I am ready for a drink and I swear to you right now, I am giving up drinking, smoking and fornicating tomorrow." Holland was surprised to hear these words from the mouth of a stately countess, but appalled when she mentioned she had two gorgeous daughters and wondered if he were interested.[70] Generally, though, cocktail hours and evening gatherings were more innocent. A new friend, Patricia Haskell, met the Seymours in February 1948: "These people came in announced by a stocky man with a bald center pate who said: 'I am Picasso' with a very Russian accent and at that point I was not sure whether he was or was not. He was followed by a woman who was considerably taller than he and then by a man who was perhaps his height, who turned out to be Daniel [Jones]."[71] Haskell hit it off with them, and from then on, at least three times a week, the Seymours took her along with some of their other friends to Ric Riccardo's legendary restaurant and gallery, where they ate his famous green buttered noodles. Shag Donohue "was just fascinated." "It was like the Sardi's after openings. Chicago art and movie people would meet there and it was Seymour's show and Belle's. They held court there and I was introduced to people. They were all in the arts, not so much politics, because Chicago politics was the good old Irish Catholic Democratic corrupt mayor [Edward Joseph] Kelly."[72] After Riccardo's, they would all return to East Pearson Street and play games. "Because Belle was an actress and a good one," Patricia Haskell thought, she "did an absolutely wonderful charade." Another game, with which they were "absolutely obsessed" was "Essence":

> One player had to leave the room and the people left had to settle on a person living or dead. When the player returned, he or she would go around the circle and would ask the others: "What is the essence of your person in architecture?"... We would spend from eleven or twelve at night till four in the morning on "Essence." And you had to have an unending period of time and unending patience. Belle was the only person who could have got, as she did once, with only three people playing the game, Harriet Beecher Stowe in two questions. She had an intensely associative, intuitive understanding of both the people who were giving the essences, and the implications of those essences. Two questions was incredible; it is a VERY difficult game....
>
> Seymour was less patient with the game. Not just because of the language, I think he wanted a little more action. But we also danced, you see. During those times when Louis Cholden was with us, we put on records, "Give me a pigfoot and a bottle of beer" from Bessie Smith and a few others and have a wonderful time.[73]

Seymour's niece Riva Blevitsky was thrilled to gain a new, radiant aunt with splendid, clinging, soft dresses, Blue Carnation perfume, and a novel way of cooking, who moved in an exciting, sophisticated world with famous actors and actresses. "It was a meeting that changed my life. . . . She became my role model and mentor, as well as my aunt and friend."[74] Gardner took a serious interest in Riva's education and gave her book lists and books to read, among them *An Intelligent Woman's Guide to Socialism and Capitalism* (1928) by George Bernard Shaw, and, through a friend, a copy of D. H. Lawrence's *Lady Chatterley's Lover* (1928)—banned in America until 1959—which was, aptly, about the love affair of a working-class man and an aristocratic woman. To the envy of her friends, Riva, feeling terribly grown-up, was allowed to attend the parties at which Gardner shone:

> It was a salon-type party that she ran. There was a party every Saturday. There was a man named Buddy Lester . . . [who] worked at the studio with Seymour. He really liked Belle and he became engaged to this lovely woman. He brought her over one Saturday night and Belle was just her usual self; there were always people, it was always conversations and games we were playing, charades and all these different games. . . . Buddy was there with his future wife and then they left. Ten minutes later the doorbell rang. He came back, very, very upset. He wanted to talk to Belle; he called her out into the hall. His girl-friend was crushed and in tears, hysterical, because she was sure that Belle did not like her. I guess she did not take any extra time with this woman and Buddy had told her how wonderful Belle was and how everybody loved her. I am sure he really thought she was their best friend; it was that kind of thing. Everyone felt this: she was THEIR best friend. This woman came away feeling that Belle hated her and . . . that was how people reacted: if you thought she did not like you, you were crushed.[75]

Gardner was devoted to her ardent husband who was, like her, Dionysian in nature. She loved being sheltered by her newfound, down-to-earth family and simultaneously leading an unconventional life; she had the best of both worlds. Its acme was reached when she bore Seymour a son, Daniel, on March 11, 1945. The year before she had suffered a miscarriage and then informed Helen Dono-hue that her doctor had warned her that it would be "difficult to *stay* pregnant, which is not a happy outlook. I do want to have at least one child of Seymour's. And here I thought I'd be dazzling Seymour with my health and activity during the 9 months! I know I'm not built right for easy delivery but I thought I could at least *carry* the child o.k. Goodness knows I felt wonderfully strong and did anything I chose when I carried Rosy." She begged Helen to "ask Elise *please* not to mention my miscarriage to Van. No-one knew I was pregnant so there's no need to know this."[76] Once more expecting, Gardner was practically forbidden to travel by her doctor, but she pined to see Helen "to talk about something besides recipes and how well the Russians are doing, God love them." She was scared "for after the war. I fear a wave of reaction and race prejudice. Anti Semitic feeling is growing and there are too many in high places who will subtly stir up the muddled feelings of returning service men and I think there are evil times ahead unless each of us who is aware can do his part to elect and ensure a liberal Congress."[77] This time Gardner carried her baby full-term, and Seymour smothered his wife in roses and served champagne to celebrate Daniel's birth; the Choldens were with them in the hospital, and actress Laurette Taylor came to visit. Daniel, possessing the exuberance of both Gardner and Seymour, was the delight of everyone, of every age. Haskell thought him "the most giving of children, . . . a charmer beyond belief . . . the golden child of all times. . . . Myra said to me—at that time Myra had two children—'I love my children and others love theirs, but we always think of Daniel as the golden child.' He was an extraordinary little boy."[78]

The end-of-war years 1944 to 1946 were among the happiest of Gardner's life. During the day she might "read two or three books and hold what she had read, she was terribly darn bright in that way," at night she "would tuck little Daniel in." She "would lullaby him with that Irish song, 'the Rose of Tralee,'" and later, she would be the focal point of lively gatherings with some of the most dazzling people in Chicago, adoring relatives and faithful friends.[79] Summers were the best of times. Like many Jewish Chicagoans, the Zeldman families would rent a number of cabins in Union Pier, Michigan, a lakeside town about ninety miles from Chicago; in this "Shapiro / Shangri La" the women and children were free from the sweltering Chicago heat for a few weeks:

> Simcha little Rosy littler Daniel
> and the Shicksa we were all of us joy—
> full then in Shapiro Shangri La when
> we were young and laughing. On the lake beach
> the women waded and gossiped. The men,
> supine on the hot sand sucked in the sun
> through every work and city tired pore
> and on the blithe beach played chess needling each
> other, "singing" they called it. The Shicksa
> swam and her daughter, round pink Rosy made
> castles out of sand and when the big rough
> boys' unseeing feet crushed her battlements
> she cried.
> ("That Was Then," 120–21)

Seymour arrived on Thursdays with Gardner's white wine (there were no liquor stores at Union Pier) and would gorge on cucumber slices on Wonderbread. The relaxed women swam, talked, cooked, and tended their exuberant children and tired husbands, who would play chess and talk politics, Gardner and a few other women joining them. Myra and Louis Cholden were there, Helen Dono-hue came from Philadelphia with her children—her daughter Deborah ("Deb-bie") becoming Rosy's particular friend, their other playmate being Seymour's daughter, Sydney. Chicago friends Daniel Jones, Pat Haskell, Buddy Lester, Os-car and Edith Tarkov, and longtime friends of Seymour's Victor Weisskopf and small John Sarkissian all would come over. Those were halcyon days.

Idyllic, too, was their brief vacation with George in Mexico in 1946, where they danced the Mexican hat dance, dined with the Ballet Russe, and George Gardner fell in love with ballet star Tania Stepanova—even though Seymour had wanted to couple him to another ballerina, as he disliked Stepanova's duck's feet. Before they left, George had tried to convince pretty, innocent Ana-bel Holland to accompany them, but she had refused, somewhat wary of the Seymours' endless partying. She was not sure of her feelings for George either, although she was sorry for him because as the Gardners' oldest son his career in the world of finance was prescribed; had there been a choice, he told her once, he might have studied history, but the finger of the family was upon him. Marrying outside Brahmin society was to be his one step off the beaten path.

Melting into Seymour's milieu, Gardner expanded her limiting Boston back-ground; she learned some Hebrew and kitchen Yiddish, cooked, bonded, be-longed, and was loved. Simultaneously, she enriched Seymour's world with her passionate intensity and balanced his street smarts with her cultural sophistica-tion. Anti-Semitism, both outspoken and hidden, was always a subject for heat-ed discussion among the Zeldmans and their relatives and friends. They argued political questions with fervor, but, inexplicably, the reality of World War II and the horrors of the Holocaust hardly touched this Jewish enclave. "It did not en-ter into our conversation, into our daily lives and interchanges," Myra remem-bered. "We were involved with Roosevelt and the war and so I remember, when the St. Louis which was carrying German-Jewish refugees from Nazi Germany seeking asylum was turned back on President Roosevelt's orders, that made headlines for a few days and we were furious, but . . . it disappeared into our involvement in our own lives."[80] Indeed, even for those who were at the front in Europe, like Blanche O'Riorden's physician husband, William McDermott, and who "had read and heard of such horrors . . . the reality was a staggering blow."[81] Tarkov's friend Saul Bellow found himself "too busy becoming a nov-elist to take note of what was happening in the forties," to his own brooding bafflement in later years.[82] Gardner had a Jewish husband, her brothers George and John in the navy, and friends like Henry Jesson and Maurice Donohue, a famous war reporter, also serving, but she was too preoccupied with her own everyday life to let the atrocities committed on the other side of the ocean, the destruction of the European Jews, sink in. With Seymour, Gardner was on cloud nine.

But not even Gardner, "the most romantic of romantics," could stay on such a high forever.[83] Daily worries began to make capillary cracks in the Seymours' triumphant happiness. Danny had a narrow escape when a maid turned out to be less trustworthy than Gardner had assumed; she got into the gin and left a glass out with what Danny thought was water so he drank it. Moreover, even considering that the Seymours were absurdly generous, their household bills went through the roof when another maid siphoned off large sums. On her own, Gardner did not do much better. Typically vague, she had their carpets cleaned, forgot by whom, and had to take out an advertisement in the Chicago newspapers in order to get them back. She loved her children and stepchildren (and her niece Riva), cared for them, and catered to their needs, from braces to books, but thought that her profound affection alone would help them grow up; after all, she had craved such love from her mother. But as she had always been protected by her family, Gardner did not teach the children that they might one day suffer the consequences of their acts.

Rosy got short shrift. After having been abruptly severed from her father and her half-siblings, Peter and Anneke, at the tender age of three, Rosy now had to take a backseat to crown prince Daniel, worshipped by Seymour as his heir and adored by all. Daniel Jones, who often babysat, "could never make any contact with Rosy. I don't know anybody that ever could, except for Seymour's daughter by his first wife, Sydney. . . . Rosy never was with it, and it was as if she just was not tuned in. Belle never noticed it, or paid any attention to it. Seymour did, but did not talk about it."[84] Anabel Holland, who sacrificed her career as a painter for her offspring, alleged that Gardner, so sensitive to the needs of strangers, did not understand her own children. When Rosy was inconsolable because she had lost her favorite doll, "George," Gardner wondered what the fuss was about: she would get her a new one, would not she? And the children were dragged everywhere, lived, in Holland's eyes, in a house that was "like a hotel . . . like a circus."[85] It is (too) easy to blame her mother for Gardner's shortcomings as a parent; unusually cold and usually absent, Rose Gardner had not been a role model in any sense, but Gardner's laissez-faire attitude also resulted from the fact that her children did not come first in her life and affections; she was ruled by her desires.

By 1948 Seymour's proverbial "great hands," at the time when the "performance-oriented' Wasp approach to lovemaking [was]: 'getting it up, getting it out, getting it off,'" had become routine and the marital bed boring.[86] Gardner and Seymour were no longer embarrassing and exciting Riva by constantly stopping to cuddle and kiss in the streets, no longer making love via a special telephone line to his studio; they were now either shouting at each other demoniacally or not speaking to each other at all. Not sexually magnetized anymore, Gardner grew apart from her husband the better she got to know him, though she would always treasure the warm Jewish universe he symbolized for her. Whereas before she had succumbed with all her heart to his macho posturing, seeing it as an expression of his obsession with and devotion to her, she now chafed under his constant need for control and the attendant jealousy of everyone she saw and everything she did without him. For Gardner was more and more creating a life that was separate from Seymour. As an artist, Seymour's sensibility was entirely visual. Not proficient in English, he did not share Gardner's love affair with language and books. He preferred to play chess or go skating or bowling. For spiritual companionship, she spent her time with fellow book-lovers like Myra Cholden and Anabel Holland: "We were the only people she knew who were up to scratch with respect to reading and literature, because for us it was normal to be acquainted with all literatures from all times. I mean, if she was referring to a certain episode from *Madame Bovary,* we knew what was going on. We were omnivorous readers."[87] Other intellectual companions were Seymour's old friend John Sarkissian, bookshop owner and writer Shag Donohue, and prolific journalist, essayist, and drama critic Sydney Harris, who had recently started his column "Strictly Personal," which was to be syndicated in some two hundred newspapers for decades.

Surrounded by friends also devoted to literature, Gardner was inspired to write poetry again: "I *deliberately* avoided reading *any* contemporary poetry. I knew that one day I'd get back to it but I was still afraid of glib facility, and I, above all, did not want to be influenced by *any*one. And one day I wrote a poem. And then another and another."[88] The children found little pieces of paper with cryptic references to pulsing hearts, lost phoenixes, or gluttonous shrews they could make neither head nor tail of. But Seymour could see that poetry and literature were taking Gardner away from him and became even more suspicious of her motives when their friend Sam Freifeld—also one of the Tuley high school boys, then an expert at shoplifting books and now an attorney—"brought Oscar Williams to our apartment. Oscar (at Freifeld's request) read the 3 or 4 poems and told me I *must* keep writing. Oscar was present when the milkman came to my porch. He said *there* is a poem. And I did write *The Milkman.* Oscar had many 'faults' but he helped *many* people and if it were not for his insistent encouragement I doubt if I would have persisted. But I did."[89]

Williams was about Seymour's age, and his background was similar. He was born Oscar Kaplan, a Jew, in Russia. His family fled, like the Zeldmans, because they feared persecution and pogroms and came to Brooklyn's Jewish quarter in 1907 when Williams was seven years old. In his teens, he submitted his poems to magazines under his own name, but they were all rejected. After he resubmitted them under the pen name Oscar Williams, they were published. He therefore "took on a new world for himself."[90] He told Richard Eberhart that "he had what is called an illumination, a psychological or even psychotic episode, where he stopped his car, and pulled his car off to the side of the road, and stood there entranced . . . and decided that he would change his life and that he would devote the rest of his life to poetry, his own poetry, and the poetry of others. . . . Then he went up to New York and he literally changed every facet of his life and in the next twenty years he became the primary, or the best anthologist of poetry that we ever had."[91] From then on, Williams kept his Jewish origins hidden from everyone, and he was known in the literary community for his anti-Semitic utterances.

His main goal was to become one of America's major poets—"'The poet is the prophet of society. . . . He leads the race. After all, it was the poets who created love!'"—and everyone and everything had to make way for this dream. He often gave more space to his own poems than to those of, for instance, William Carlos Williams, in his best-selling, influential anthologies such as *The Little Treasury Poetry Series,* which was widely used in high schools and colleges in the 1950s and 1960s.[92] He carefully created a literary persona, complete with bow tie and jacket. Nobody knew of his double identity, not even his son, Strephon, who was sent to a militaristic boarding school when he was six and was allowed to visit his parents, Williams and painter-poet Gene Derwood, for a few weeks every year. "Strephon had never been a member of the family. There was no family; only artists." (Most of Williams's friends never knew he had a son until after his death in 1965.) Living in their cocoon of paranoiac duplicity and monomaniac ambition—"Both my parents were great deceivers"—, Williams and Derwood sooner or later quarreled with all and sundry.[93] The tributes to Williams at his memorial were all backhanded. Here is an example by Eberhart:

> Oscar Williams, who was somebody else,
> Is somebody else again, having passed death.
> He knew life as a spiritual breath.
> He knew the spirit greater than the flesh.
> Now that he is dead, in death's poetry,
> He cannot see where we can see to see.[94]

Conrad Aiken wrote that "there were times when we thought Oscar was irrepressible and when we thought his motives and methods were obscure; but we know now that he was irreplaceable, and a true and devoted servant to the poets and poetry of his time. He was an extraordinary man, and I think we all loved him more than we knew."[95] Earlier, in 1957, Karl Shapiro had called Williams "the most unprincipled" of all the people he had ever met in his life—"[e]veryone knows this about him"—and he was therefore disturbed by Gardner's loyalty to this egomaniac.[96]

Gardner, who started her memorial tribute with an epitaph Williams had written himself: "Here Oscar lies, / Here Oscar lies, / No enemies" with double entendre clearly intended, did fight bitterly with Williams in the 1950s, but found "his interest in my verse, his affirmation, advice, exhortations, and warnings ... of infinite help."[97] Indeed, Williams had been astonishingly altruistic in his initial contacts with Gardner, commenting on her first poems and trying to get them placed. As early as January 29, 1949, he wrote:

> You are very foolish in thinking I should never want to bother with you. I have great confidence in you and in your ability. In fact I have been planning to use your poem "Of Mercy" in *A Little Treasury of the Human Spirit,* but I haven't mentioned it because the book is so far in the distance—it may not be published until 1952—I have just started working on it. . . .
>
> I find I do not have copies of "Summer Soldier" and "Luncheon Party." It might be a good idea if you would send these two, together with "Triolet" to SRL [*Saturday Review of Literature*], as you suggest. I am not on good terms with the poetry editor of this publication, Mr. W. R. Ben[é]t, who imagines that I have treated him abominably by leaving him out of all my anthologies (and the other Ben[é]ts as well).
>
> If I do not place your poems with the magazines I have mentioned [*Poetry* and *Atlantic Monthly*] I should like to try some of the smaller but fairly decent poetry magazines (always a good place to appear in), such as *Contemporary Poetry, Tiger's Eye,* etc. All this will take time, but YOU MUST CONTINUE WRITING, turning out the poems.[98]

A few months later he added: "I have your lovely letters and your lovelier poems: I was not mistaken: you are a real poet. I expect to be through Chicago the 1st week in August, and I am ever so grateful for your invitation, for I will be able to go over your poems with you personally. Love Oscar. Regards to Seymour."[99]

Such encouragement was music to Gardner's ears, and she eagerly anticipated their meeting, as she felt that "the writing would perhaps make up for the lack of rapport with Seymour."[100] Their marriage had started to founder in 1947, when Daniel was not even two, but both Gardner and Seymour tried to make it work, and they went into analysis, which was "enormously big among intellectuals in Chicago. Everybody was in analysis. It was almost like playing a game, so you were always talking about everything and all your subconscious wishes and whatever. This was bliss to Belle."[101] Gardner would spend her life in and out of analysis, but most of the analysts were no match for her: she seduced them with words and soon had them eating out of her hand, telling her exactly what she wanted to hear. In her heart, Gardner may not have wanted to learn from her analysis, but that one of her doctors started writing his own poetry during their sessions and that another abetted her drinking reflects poorly on these practitioners, the more so as analysis was very expensive. Gardner did not have to pay for it out of her annual allowance, as medical expenses were extra; they had to be approved "by Boston" to be sure, but that was a piece of cake. Seymour did not fare much better with his analysis and thought Gardner's "whole gang was psychiatrically dizzy"; he "was just more concrete," and he never succeeded in explaining to his sisters what he was doing in analysis.[102]

With their marriage in deep trouble, in an act of faith they bought a two-family house on 5318 Woodlawn Avenue in Hyde Park, which Gardner decorated in "perfect taste. The house was carpeted in very thick light gray wool shag. One's first impulse was to take off one's shoes. The sensuous quality of the rug was set off by rather simple and stark Swedish modern dining and living room furniture. Daniel had a built-in bunk bed that had been designed for him. There was a floor to ceiling photo of the ballerina, Alexandra Danilova, at the head of the stairs . . . it was Belle who insisted that Seymour put it up."[103] The sensuous surroundings clashed with the spiritual and physical frigidity of their union. On the brink of their divorce, Gardner analyzed their relationship in a long letter to Riva:

> The basic difficulty between Seymour and me has always been the lack of any kind of companionship mentally and spiritually. For this reason I should not have married him and it is his misfortune as well as my own that I discounted the importance of that factor. His violent jealousy and extreme possessiveness made him behave cruelly and humiliate me constantly. For the first three or four years I was enough in love so that I could take it, but in the last two or three years, when I was no longer in love, it became unbearable and I became lonely and desperate for human warmth and understanding.
>
> You may wonder why I ceased to be in love with him a couple to three years ago and I suppose it is because there was really nothing to sustain that love. I suppose that it was not really love in the proper and mature sense of the word, but a kind of passion that was essentially without substance. I tried terribly hard. A kind of crisis came in our relationship around last Christmas when Seymour's totally unfounded jealousy of Sydney Harris made him abusive, mentally, to me. I have been unhappy and lonely for the last two years and was fearful that I was beginning to lose control and needed help and I was desperately anxious for our sakes and above all for the children to save our marriage. So we both agreed to go to analysts.
>
> As my analysis progressed, it became crystal clear to me, the analyst made it clear to me, that Seymour was a neurotic choice, that I had unconsciously chosen a man, Van also, who would fulfill my neurotic need for punishment. The analyst

felt that only a complete change in my personality and in Seymour's could save our marriage. I worked very hard at the end. I gave up drinking wine, which was painless for me. I withdrew from most of my friends and I devoted myself to the job of saving our marriage. Seymour tried very hard, too, but he is older than I and his personality is more rigid, his insecurity more complex and more deeply rooted and his whole behavior pattern is that of a child of ten. It is hard to live with someone who is utterly illogical and unpredictable and his constant rapid switches from violent hatred of me to extreme adoration, the constant demands for individual attention and affection which were insatiable. . . . I did succeed for a while, but it was exhausting and nerve-wrecking even then.

He resented my reading, my writing, my opinions, my friendships. Mind you, I am far from blameless in this situation. I need to keep a part of my spiritual self *to myself* and Seymour felt that intuitively and minded terribly. I have had a need for affection and mental companionship and communication with others . . . . I could not communicate in that way with him. I like to be alone by myself. I didn't much like to be alone with him. He sensed that and it is not hard to understand how painful that knowledge can be. However, I can honestly say that I have been a good wife and mother and I dreaded this end to our life which for a while was very, very happy. At least the illusion of real happiness.[104]

In hindsight, Gardner had some points. Until his death, Seymour remained like a willful child who wanted to dominate his siblings, wives, and children as he did his customers. And Gardner during these Chicago years was not a problem drinker. She drank more white wine than Seymour thought wise, but to him, "coming from the Jewish background he grew up in, *any* drinking beyond a glass of wine in a whole evening would seem like too much. Until the current generation, Jews were very light social drinkers. An alcoholic was really quite rare compared with other social groups."[105]

Much worse than her drinking, to Seymour's mind, was her thirst for intellectual companionship. "He was so jealous, I could not lift a book," Gardner told biographer Jean Gould.[106] Matters came to a head when Oscar Williams visited. "Seymour insulted him and made a scene in a restaurant, just as he had done with Syd Harris. This was sort of the crowning blow as it again was irrational, and above all, I felt it was a real act of hostility to me, as Williams was helping me with my poetry."[107] Although Gardner hotly denied having had sex with Williams, Seymour saw that she was physically, as well as mentally and spiritually, attuned to other men. So he badgered his friends, interrogating them about her behavior, till his chessmate Oscar Tarkov squealed on Gardner: she had committed adultery with mousy John Sarkissian. Most of their friends could not believe it; Daniel Jones, usually the most discreet of men, compared their coupling to "a Pekinese mounting a great Dane."[108] Seymour's worst nightmare had come true. By cuckolding him, Gardner had dealt him a blow where it hurt most, and he was livid, the more so as, adding insult to injury, she had had sex with one of his good friends. Forty years later, in his account of their separation, Seymour tried to salvage his pride:

> I called up Johnny Sarkissian, little Johnny. . . . I say: "Johnny, will you do me favor, hop a cab and come on over?" He says: "It is two in the morning." I said: "Get dressed and come on over; it is important." And he came over and I said: "Johnny, tell the truth, there is nothing going to happen to you. What happened?" He says: "I came home from the book club and she had a few drinks, she grabbed me and she insisted on making love and I just could not control and I made love to her and she is a lousy lay." That is what he told me, so finally I said: "Johnny, will you sign that thing? Sign right there." The following day, we told Belle. She says: "I cannot believe it, I cannot believe it." I say: "You do not have to believe a thing, Isabella." I called up Peabo and I said: "Peabo, do me a favor, send me a check for $15,000 immediately." See, we bought a house together. She put up fifteen and I put fifteen. I says: "Send me a check for my part of the house: Belle just did this to me." He says: "I cannot believe it." I say: "Yes, the lawyer has the papers and everything else." The following day I had the check. That is Peabo.[109]

In fact, their divorce was much more drawn out and acrimonious and Seymour threatened with violence and blackmail. In October 1949, as soon as she knew that Seymour had Sarkissian's affidavit confessing that he had slept with her, Gardner fled East with Daniel and Rosy, first staying with Lemuel and Shirley Ayers in New York and later with her family in Brookline. She was afraid that Seymour would sue her for adultery and drinking and thus gain custody of Daniel under Illinois law. Battle lines were drawn among their friends who had partied so harmoniously. Tarkov was in Seymour's camp, but Maurice and Helen Donohue helped Gardner pack up and leave stealthily, for which Seymour never forgave them. When he threatened to put Sarkissian on the stand, psychiatrist Cholden was prepared to swear that Sarkissian was a neurotic and therefore to be doubted, which earned the Choldens Seymour's lifelong hostility, too. Gardner broke with the Tarkovs. Many years later Edith, fearful of "further pain and rejection," wrote her what amounted to a consecrative love letter:

> I have always remembered your very being—your atmosphere; your tenseness I could understand only so much later; your walk, your voice, your lyrical presence. You always had the soul of the poet, of course; and, at the time we knew you, your artistry was tragically and beautifully expressed in your intense life. I can still see you stand on your stairs, on the veranda in Hyde Park, calling the

children to come home, with unwonted lavished lovely voice. It was one of the moments I shall always see—like you, once, made me see a moment when you heard a Brahms concerto in the winter, when it was snowing. Enough. I knew I could not control this letter. But—perhaps—you remember me and understand.[110]

Once more, Gardner's too-idealistic expectations of a relationship had imploded, once more the semistill waters of marriage had proved alien to her spirit. For her, the failure of their marriage had been a fait accompli since Oscar Williams's visit, if not before, and there is no doubt that she acted on her physical desires, although John Sarkissian never meant more to her than a—puny—sex object. Being a woman, however, she was condemned harshly for her escapade; her youngest brother, Robert, accusing her of being provocative, and her censorious friend Anabel Holland putting her down as "the female equivalent of a womanizer."[111] Seymour had not wanted a separation both for Daniel's sake and his own and had gone to great lengths, including a stab at analysis so foreign to his mind, to try and keep them together. Gardner's extramarital adventure shocked Seymour into realizing the true state of their relationship. In his eighties, he reflected: "I do not think I was intelligent enough for her," but he also perceived that Gardner "was a romantic soul that did not understand herself. She really did not. If she could only live part of her fantasies, she would have been the happiest woman on earth, but she tried to absorb all the fantasies. She could not separate them."[112] Although a philanderer when single, in the end he believed in the sanctity of marriage, and it is unlikely that he, too, strayed, even though Gardner had accused him of trying to seduce Helen Donohue at Union Pier. Humiliated, out of sheer rage and spite and armed with Sarkissian's confession, Seymour set out to cash in on Gardner's betrayal, feeling that her fling entitled him to a good chunk of the Gardner riches as well as custody of Daniel. Bolstered by Cholden's offer of his expert psychiatric testimony against Sarkissian, Gardner stood firm, maintaining, unconvincingly, that she "would not be able to support the children if I gave [Seymour] what he first demanded" and would have to work. Her counterbid was "that Seymour could have Daniel two months or six weeks during the summer and that he could have his share of the house in cash . . . . provided I have custody and may live with Daniel where I choose" and have "the final say on education." She thought Seymour should contribute to his son's education and laid claim to the contents of the Woodlawn house "with the exception of the television set." She knew she was "hurting Seymour" and that "[i]t is harder for him, because he will miss Daniel terribly and he did not want the divorce."[113]

The battle went on for months, but in the end they settled more or less on the terms Gardner had offered. They met in Indiana, Seymour admitted, because Gardner "was afraid to bring Daniel to Chicago, that I will take him away from her. I was not that kind of guy, but for some reason or other she must have thought I was a gangster."[114] Gardner's infidelity was not mentioned, and the ostensible motive for their divorce was Seymour's cruelty. The Chicago society pages had a field day. Adorned by a fabulous Maurice Seymour picture of Gardner reading, the *Chicago Daily Tribune* noted on February 16, 1950, that Gardner charged Seymour "pushed her from a chair Jan. 1, 1949, causing an injury. Last Oct. 13 . . . Seymour dug his finger nails into her arm, severely injuring her. She asks support for herself and their son Daniel, 4."[115] A few days later, now with a suitably subdued picture not by Seymour, the paper announced that the divorce was granted: "She testified he struck her on several occasions following petty quarrels."[116] As had happened with Van Kirk, and contrary to contemporary custom, Gardner received no alimony. Seymour paid a meager fifty dollars a month in child support, even though he could easily have afforded to pay more as his business was thriving.[117]

Only in her mid-thirties, Gardner felt that with two botched marriages and children from different husbands she had failed miserably. She had once more let her family down, too, and soon returned to the Midwest, to the Woodlawn house in Chicago, far from her parents' disapproving eyes. The children slipped through the cracks, the more so as Seymour did not try to alleviate some of their pain but instead "tried to capitalize on every situation that he saw as helping his image as the cuckolded husband."[118] To his mind, he had "raised Rosy as much as I could control her" and been more of a father to her than Van Kirk, but now, to spite Gardner, he refused to see his stepdaughter ever again.[119] At ten Rosy had been deserted by two fathers, impressing upon her that she was not worthy of their love, and she now hid even deeper in her shell of indifference, detachment, and apathy. And though one of Gardner's reasons for wanting to live in Chicago had been closeness to Seymour for Dan's sake, Seymour soon left for New York City after a quarrel with Maury and founded a Maurice Seymour Studio there. (Maury kept the Chicago Maurice Seymour Studio and in a curious if understandable move, his wife, Sonya, still aggrieved by Seymour's earlier name change, compounded the confusion and "took her whole family into court and had their names changed: Maurice Zeldman became Maurice Seymour."[120]) So dream-child Daniel, at four, became flotsam on the waves of his parents' emotional ebb and flow. Sydney, Seymour's daughter, was a victim, too: her world "just collapsed." She remembered "one day coming and looking for Rosy after school and she was not there and my father said: 'Do you know where she is?' And I said: 'No.' And then I got a letter from Rosy shortly after that and she was living in Brookline."[121] Sydney and Rosy were so traumatized that they "both vowed that . . . no matter how terrible the marriage was, we were going to stay married."[122] (Sydney Zeldman Fingold celebrated her fiftieth wedding anniversary in 2008.)

The Zeldman family, though shaken by the storms that racked the Seymours, remained a stable beacon for both the children and Gardner. They realized that the wreckage of their marriage was not solely Gardner's fault, and most of them refused to take sides, which drew Seymour's ire. When Riva dared to take care of the children at Gardner's request after the divorce, Seymour took her to task in "the worst way that anybody ever talked to me. It was terrible," giving her a taste of the irrational anger Gardner had had to deal with.[123] Gardner still regarded Seymour's sisters as "her real family," often declaring that Molly and Ben Blevitsky were "her parents" as well as Riva's. Both continued to support and love her, although Ben "disapproved of her as a mother. He was very puritanical and he found her life to be filled with excesses."[124]

The Gardner family, knowing that their daughter and sister idealized her husbands and was therefore doomed to be disappointed, were sensible, too, and did not blame Seymour alone for the break-up. He remained dear to George, as Seymour had introduced him to his Tania. Robert, too, had grown fond of Seymour. He had often stayed at the Seymours as his future wife, Lee, lived in Chicago. Besides, Robert, who was to become one of America's foremost filmmakers, recognized Seymour's brilliance as a photographer. But when he wanted to visit Seymour six years after the divorce, Gardner demurred:

> In some ways (the possibility of early death for me) I think it good that he feel comfortable with some member of my family. But I hope you are not sentimental about him to the point where you do not recognize that however (apparently) rancor-less he is *now*—he did abuse me vilely and publicly for a long time. . . .
>
> Though there is much in him to affirm and much in the early years of our marriage to remember happily, the happy years of our marriage took an *incredible* amount of giving (emotionally and spiritually) on my part and he *is* a vindictive, immature, and in many ways *brutal* person. Even his sisters to whom I still am fairly close have always recognized this. I can't forgive him his cruelty to Rosy, though I can understand it—nor his neglect of his daughter Sydney. . . . I was unfaithful to him with only one person and that was done through despair and disgust because he accused me times without number of the most fantastic infidelities. . . .
>
> I suppose the most poignant gap between us was one of ethics. His being strictly a gangster code which like all codes has its virtues I will concede. . . . Whatever evil and pain we have inflicted on one another is in the past.[125]

But by taking Daniel from his Jewish father and family, Gardner "had betrayed the very soul of that society."[12]

Chapter Four

"Writing Poetry," 1950–1954

Is one game that no-one quits while he or she's ahead. The
stakes are steep. Among the chips are love fame life and
sanity. The game's risk is that winning one chip often means the
forfeit of another but despite the penalties there is a surfeit
of players.
("Writing Poetry")

The tumultuous years with Seymour had made Gardner yearn for tranquility: "I am interested in no-one. . . . I do not want to act again. I want to write and
to look after my children peacefully," she wrote Riva.[1] It would have been hard
for Gardner to work her way back into the world of acting anyway. Lem Ayers
and Martin Manulis, both flourishing in show business, remained devoted to
her, and Gardner had retained her connections with many stars through the
merry gatherings at Pearson Street, but she had left the stage in 1943. Broadway
had forgotten all about Gardner's mayfly appearance as a supporting actress.
Moreover, with two children to raise, Gardner had no time to dive into the energy-
sucking theater world. Having shucked her troublesome, jealous husband, and
supported by her annual family income, Gardner was free to concentrate on her
poetry.

Her painter cousin Billy Congdon rejoiced with her: "Yes—what a blessed
freedom for you—for the writer in you."[2] Because of their similar sensibilities,
Gardner was the only one in the intertwined Gardner, Grosvenor, Congdon
families who did not blame "the cousin of [her] heart" for having chosen to be
a painter instead of a businessman and for living abroad instead of close to his
parents and siblings.[3] Congdon was restless and traveled from country to country in Europe, Africa, and Asia, not only because he needed the visual impact

and stimulus of different cities and landscapes for his paintings, but also because he wanted to put an ocean between himself and his New England background, fleeing in particular from his Pharasaical father who had battered him and his older brother when they were small boys: "We screamed and screamed. It must have been terrible for my poor mother. . . . [F]or a man to descend to that level of hatred is death; it is a way of killing his child."[4] Congdon left, too, because he was gay, which, in America, could land you in prison, while the American Psychiatric Association listed homosexuality as a mental disorder. Gardner alone did not judge Congdon for his sexual orientation; even Robert, who in his mid-twenties as a budding artist also had become very close to Congdon, condemned him for his secretive, complicated relationships, which often involved much younger or uneducated toy boys. After Congdon had fallen for a student from Phillips Exeter Academy in New Hampshire, Robert wrote of his "unsavory dalliance with the young Exonian," and grumbled about Congdon's victims, his "personal arrogance" and "unmitigated selfishness."[5] Gardner bristled, arguing that Congdon was as much a casualty as his younger lover. Begging Robert to forgive her "if I seem to *immorally moralize*," she asked him to "[r]emember that [Congdon] bravely attempted therapy, and with problems far more difficult than ours. It did not work. He is now over 40—he cannot now by any act of his will or ours become 'adjusted' in our sense of that word. He makes his life and his art in terms of his present being *as he must*." She thought her brother "harsh in . . . judgment," although she did agree with him that Congdon was selfish: "Both his generosity *and* his selfishness are extreme. Many artists with his intensity of creative gift share this paradox."[6] Gardner was again defending herself as much as her cousin when a few weeks later she added: "I think there is a change that *is* possible, which would come about in his work and his life if he spiritually grows to the extent where he out-grows the demands of sex and aggressive possessive emotion."[7]

Now that Gardner had also chosen to be an artist, the two, though continents apart, were closer than ever before. "Impossible such an identity at such a distance," Congdon explained in 1990, long after he had converted to Catholicism, in his characteristic metaphysical-religious way, "if it were not that Belle *is* my painting and my painting *is* her poetry . . . . The identity of our history which includes of course the gift that God put in us. The relationship was in the creative gift, which *was* the relationship."[8] Knowing that Gardner understood him and was loyal, Congdon confided in her in letters he sent from all over the world, simultaneously and consciously writing a painter's travel diary, for most of his letters picture the colors and shapes of the places where he lived. From Cuba, with Fulgencio Batista still in power, he wrote in 1955: "Havana has a beauty, as you enter by ship—narrow, the old fort on one side and the glittering white city on the other, as you coast past parks and palms and boulevards. I always love the trick of dimensions, scale of ship and city, how even a freighter dwarfs the city but Venice knew how to accent the verticals so that the city does not fall away as you enter it by sea. But once inside, Havana is a hell—... every vulgarity of the U.S. is paraded pandered and played for you. ... It is the same false booming that you see wherever the giant '[B]rother' has clamped his standards and his industry on [what] can only remain jokingly the 'banana republics.'"[9] If he was easily carried away by his impressions and often drunk on his own words, and if his egocentrism, manifest in these letters, is indeed excessive, in between references to his real and spiritual journeys, his executed and planned paintings, he did, now and then, make room for Gardner's travails as an aspiring poet. Gardner was much more generous and sensitive to his ego, needs, and feelings than he to hers: Congdon used her as his artistic and personal sounding board, withholding little:

> Oh—there was something about that Arab boy's wear-tear in the fly of his trousers, and as I was passing in the noon crowd I could see his prick, the damp soft folds of his prick end, the balls behind folded together; dormant as the inner folds of an artichoke but explodable at any raging preposterous moment swelling and barred to fire to spurt and to recede again into sweet damp petal folds, into the dead bird feeling (did you ever hold one in your hand?),—and all peekable through the tear in his noon trousers. I am trusting St. Augustine to keep me from liking the subject overmuch.[10]

Congdon was very much lost, not only as a forlorn, self-exiled homosexual painter, but also because as a volunteer ambulance driver during World War II, he had witnessed death beyond comprehension, having been one of the first to enter the concentration camp Bergen-Belsen, which had shocked him into an ever-present awareness of evil. Trying to maintain a precarious balance between "joy-pain, sex-love, work, talk, etc. etc.," desperately seeking answers that neither his liaisons, alcohol, pills, nor even his painting could give him, Congdon was nevertheless savvy enough to plug his work to Gardner in order to get her friends to buy his art, sometimes through devious schemes in which he tried to circumvent the percentage due to his agent and patron, Betty Parsons.[11] These attempts at underhand business deals made Gardner mad at Congdon, but she always forgave him. She bought much of his best work, and not only in the 1950s, when he had numerous one-man shows at Betty Parsons's Gallery, a feature in *Life* magazine, and exhibited at the Whitney Museum and the Phillips Gallery in Washington and was bracketed with Jackson Pollock and Mark Rothko as an action painter (though, paradoxically, a figurative one). She continued to buy his work in the 1960s, after he had converted to Catholicism and temporarily took up unfashionably religious themes.

Their artistic careers ran parallel, because Gardner also reached the height of her fame in the 1950s. When she left Seymour, Gardner had written fewer than twenty poems and published not a single one. She knew she wanted to write, but although she felt sustained by Oscar Williams, she had no confidence in her ability as a poet. Williams was trying to place her work, but it was not until 1950 that *American Mercury* published her "Triolet," an example of Gardner's command of rare poetic forms.[12] Soon after, in the winter of 1951, her ironic but rather slight "Folkways," in which she demythologizes heroism ("Was Galahad hired, / Artemis laid? / Was Hercules tired? / Ajax afraid?" (141)) appeared in the sardonic little magazine *Furioso;* and that year's fall issue contained her poem for Leighton Rollins, "Homo Gratia Artis," which Gardner drowned on purpose in mythological, biblical, literary and theatrical references: "Victim-father son bride-mother / You are Abel and his brother / Eden Persepolis and Hell / Raskolnikoff and Philomel" (33).[13]

Gardner was living in the Chicago Woodlawn house, which was now hers alone. Teeming with white immigrants from Europe and black ones from the South, an industrial center with a class structure more nouveau riche and less static than Boston's, Chicago was the intermediary between America's East and West, a symbol of the country's transformation from old money to new. Effervescent Chicago was also a main train junction and frequent transfer point at the heart of the Midwest, and many poets, painters, musicians, and actors stopped over, enlivening its spirited cultural community. Before she had set foot in Chicago for the first time with *Blithe Spirit,* the city had meant to her "the often beautiful bawling of Sandburg, Farrell's Studs Lonigan, the shrieking slashed throats of pigs, the mooning moos of stunned huge cattle, the St. Valentine's Day massacre, the assassination of [mayor] Cermak, the Haymarket Riot, *and* Poetry Magazine." But when she moved to Chicago to be with Seymour, she found "an aliveness, a rawness, a reaching in the very air that one is not aware of in the East. I was no wistful exile but an a[f]icionada."[14] Looking back from Minneapolis in 1963, Gardner elaborated:

> I *do* think Chicago has a curious facility for heightening one's feelings and sensibilities. Rousing, exacerbating et cetera. The climate of *feeling* is strong.... Oh I was taken by the town.... Chicago was cigars, cuspidors, booze. In my fashion I'd been genteel. Chicago was corny and gutsy and all the two bit phonies were 'real people.' I fell in love in Chicago. He was Russian and Jewish and Real and I was not Russian or Jewish and did not quite believe I was real.... Near North Side—a son born and circumcised. Playgrounds not quite integrated.... Late-night talk about Kafka—Dostoevsky—recordings of Josh White, The Almanac Players. Chess games with Paul Robeson.... All our friends poor except us. We were fake poor.[15]

In the late 1940s and 1950s, Gardner still was at home in the city, treasuring the friends she had made in its Jewish community as well as the literate ones whom she had gotten to know during her many visits to places like the Main Street bookstore, Shag Donohue's smaller specialist shop, and Book-of-the-Month Club. The intellectual climate in Chicago was bracing, in large measure thanks to the University of Chicago and its innovative president, Robert Maynard Hutchins. He had realized the importance of lifelong learning early on, and in 1952 Maurice Donohue, Gardner's bosom-friend, became dean of "the University College, which embraced Home Study, Radio & Television, Trade Union, Degree, Non-Credit, and—for a while—Business Programs . . . . The principal jewel in our crown was The Basic Program of Liberal Education for Adults."[16] For this program, based on his insistence on serious reading as essential to a truly human existence—though sneeringly ridiculed by some as a sop for bored housewives—Donohue recruited a kaleidoscopic set of intellectual stars, making him "one of the most important leaders in American adult education in this century."[17]

After having covered the Arab-Israeli War for the *Philadelphia Inquirer* in 1948, Donohue had "had a nervous breakdown, because he was so upset as word was truly in now about the Holocaust," yet was always available when Gardner wanted to discuss poetry, politics, or philosophy.[18] Although he was a Don Juan (even before his marriage to Helen was on the rocks, when she fell in love with Jack Butler, one of his University of Chicago colleagues), Donohue and Gardner were never attracted amorously to each other. They were too much alike in their intellectual passions; besides Donohue was mentally so maniacally energetic as to be exhausting if you were around him constantly.[19] Deserted by Helen and unable to live alone, Donohue got wedded to a young, adoring wife, Virginia. When they also broke up, he embarked on a series of marriages, ending up after a long courtship in the 1970s with his sixth wife, upper-class Sylvia Slade, who in the 1950s was still wedded to Shag, his younger brother.

Also incapable of living without love, Gardner was now drawn to the world of literature and had come to worship another intellectual journalist, Maurice English. Like Donohue, English was Irish-Catholic and a few years older than Gardner. The youngest of seven children, he grew up in Chicago and graduated magna cum laude from Harvard in 1933. English began his career as a reporter, was a foreign correspondent for years, and during World War II worked for NBC's radio news department and was Italy's *Voice of America*. After the war, he wrote and edited for a number of newspapers and magazines, published poetry, and dreamed of editing a midwestern metropolitan journal modeled after the *New Yorker*. He returned to Chicago to start his magazine and spent the early 1950s lobbying, finding sponsors and advertisers, as he himself had very little capital. Many women, among them the poet Ruth Herschberger, author of a neglected, witty feminist classic, *Adam's Rib* (1948), were buzzing around him, but English fell in love with Gardner, admiring her for her poetry and for her liberal political bent. Gardner, for her part, treasured his Irish parentage and his erudition as a radical change from Seymour's unsophisticated tastes. They became immersed in each other, and Gardner was all set to strike up another fiery affair even though English was married to a Rumanian immigrant, Fanita, and had two children. Fanita had spent her youth in Istanbul and had studied psychology in Paris, but her literary interest was "zero, . . . a major bone of contention" for the couple. Nevertheless, she slaved to help her husband found his magazine and to take care of their children and, in the spirit of the age, had subordinated her interests to his. They were poor, and she felt exhausted, drained, and angry and was irritated by English's and Gardner's "mutual admiration society." No admirer of her husband's inamorata, Fanita English found her "very glamorous and attractive," adding "cachet to any situation," but was angered by the fact that Gardner "with all that money, prestige and time" was not "socially useful," and far too "dramatic," even "narcissistic."[20] Laboring in the background to keep her shaky marriage together, Fanita was legitimately jealous, for Gardner and English were wrapped up in each other and their literary careers.

Gardner had not yet met a man who could withstand her charms and expected that English would happily make love with her, but as English had been brought up by priests and nuns and was a "most moral man," their relationship remained platonic, to Gardner's deep regret.[21] She ended her lament "Lines to a Seagreen Lover," dedicated to Maurice English: "I wish my love had lain with me / Not on the sand beside the sea / But under my ailanthus tree" (25). Twenty years later, on the brink of divorcing Fanita, English was sure he had always been a good husband and tried to prove this to her by insisting that he had not even slept with Gardner. It was only in the late 1970s, when English was rereading "Lines to a Seagreen Lover," that he acknowledged that "it was reminiscent of the many occasions of passionate feeling I let go by in my life. It is hard to undo one's upbringing, and not to pay the price for not undoing it."[22] By that time Fanita English was fed up and "wish[ed] that they had had an affair," so that her husband could have gotten Gardner out of his system.[23]

Gardner was so sure of the strength of their mutual attraction that when Erskine Childers asked her to marry him after the death of his first wife, Ruth, in early 1950, she refused, not only because she felt that his marrying a twice-divorced Bostonian would ruin his political career or because she was worried about schlepping her children with her to Ireland, but also because she was certain that English would leave his wife for her. Still romantic after her two disastrous marriages, Gardner remained optimistically naïve with respect to matters of the heart, still believed that love conquers all, and was fully prepared to follow English to the ends of the earth. But English, though enthralled by Gardner, was much more realistic and did not consider upsetting his life for mere love; a deeply intimate mental relationship was all he had to offer Gardner. Without sex to sustain her love, Gardner's passion for English petered out, and she settled on being his friend, including Fanita and the couple's children, Deirdre and Brian, in her affection. But Fanita, knowing that Gardner had wanted her husband and resentful of her financial independence and freedom, was never won over. She was convinced that Gardner "did not realize who she was," which made her see herself as a victim rather than a predator.[24]

Sensing that her relationship with English was going nowhere, Gardner leapt at an opportunity for diversion offered by her brother Robert. Although they had not been close as children because of the age difference of ten years, Robert Gardner, caught in the closed Boston Brahmin world, looked up to his big sister, who had succeeded in her small rebellions against it. Her career as an actress, her marriage to a Jewish photographer, but, above all, her deep love of language, literature, and art set her apart from the family and attracted Robert. Late in life he reminisced: "She really kind of saved my life. I mean, we were at opposite sides of the family, except for one sister who was older than she, and yet tight as could be. We were just very united, united in a way that meant we responded to and felt things in much the same way. We thought about such things as politics, which were never discussed at home over dinner at Green Hill. And she gave me a take on life from which I have both suffered and enjoyed but mostly enjoyed and I thank her for that."[25]

In his midtwenties, Robert was at a crossroad in his life. For a while, he had followed the path laid out for him. Like his older brothers, George and John, he had duly attended St. Mark's School, where Wystan Auden's long disquisition on the American hot dog had made more of an impression on him than his discourse on literature. Again like his brothers, he was drafted into the navy during World War II. He did not see active duty but was sent to Harvard as an officer candidate: "It was an odd world in which a war was still going and our lives as students never really started. Whatever I learned in those semesters was entirely accidental and certainly did my country no good whatever." His one feat in these "inglorious days" when he worked at "becoming an officer opting for the Marines for no reason other than to be different" was his appearance in *The Proof of the Pudding* show at the Hasty Pudding Theatrical Society with his roommate Jack Lemmon, who starred under a pseudonym because he was on academic probation. When World War II came to an end, Robert decided to stay on at Harvard, choosing civilian life as "points earned as a swab in boot camp let me out of the service. I was to be glad of this when the Korean War would have meant going into that catastrophe." After graduating from Harvard and "a brief flirtation" with medical school, he did conservation work in Turkey, learning during his travels "that I knew nothing and that I had little time to lose correcting that appalling truth."[26]

In 1949 Robert moved to Seattle to teach art history, which he had learned on the job in Turkey, married his Chicago lover, Lee, and became friends with the poet Theodore Roethke and the painter Mark Tobey. He started reading widely and discovered how the visual and literary arts helped him gain greater understanding of himself and humanity. A book by anthropologist Ruth Benedict, *Patterns of Culture* (1934), which described in vivid detail three "primitive" societies, prompted Robert to make a film about the Kwakiutl Indians, whom Benedict pictured as the most intensely rivalrous conspicuous consumers among the three. And he involved his admired sibling in this adventure: "She was my sister and she was an actress. . . . I cast her as an Indian princess in love with a Canadian traveling salesman who was selling the idea of visiting noble Redskins in their quaint villages. Now, that was wild then. It is not so wild anymore [in 2007]."[27] Robert, Lee, and Isabella Gardner left for the Kwakiutl village of Fort Rupert in British Columbia, Canada, and lived on a houseboat, the *Tanda*. Gardner played her part as a poor, opportunist, promiscuous princess, but the feature film never got made. They had a glorious time, though, and as there were attractive men like filmmaker Sidney Peterson on the crew, Gardner stopped pining for the unattainable Maurice English.[28] A few years later she admitted: "I 'carried on' . . . like a banshee about my 'seagreen lover' . . . but now I cannot imagine that I did though I like and respect him."[29]

Back in Chicago, Gardner briefly but wholly enjoyed the freedom to do what she desired most: reading and writing, unhindered by disturbing emotions or raging libido. Warmly shielded by her friends the Choldens, the two Donohue families, and now the Englishes (or at least Maurice), in close touch with Sydney Harris and Sam Freifeld, with promising literary contacts through Oscar Williams, Gardner focused on language, literature, and literati. Wallace Fowlie, the great French scholar and translator of Baudelaire, Rimbaud, and Mauriac, lived in a Woodlawn apartment nearby and became her dear friend (as he was, as a celibate Catholic, of libidinous Henry Miller and Anaïs Nin). And when T. S. Eliot, the vested authority in poetry and literary criticism was in Chicago, Gardner, banking on her background, seized the opportunity to meet with him. Eliot thought "it would be a pleasure to meet a daughter of Peabo Gardner" and accepted her invitation.[30]

Gardner's piercingly evocative sexual poem "The Milkman" shows that the (autobiographical) narrator's attempts to keep her lust at bay were doomed from the start. "The door was bolted and the windows of my porch / were screened to keep invaders out, the mesh of rust- / proof wire sieved the elements. Did my throat parch / then I sat at my table there and ate with lust / most chaste, the raw red apples; juice, flesh, rind and core." But when the milkman's "boots besieged my private yard" and he "mounted / my backstairs," / . . . / "I had to slide the bolt; and thus I was the robber / of my porch" (37). Respectable women did not have superficial sexual flings in the 1950s, but it was as unthinkable for Gardner to live without the love of a man, and in accordance with the mores of the time that meant another husband. Sex played an important part, but Gardner was equally in need of warmth, protection, and intellectual compatibility. Above all, her new husband would have to support her calling as a poet. This time she set about choosing her spouse carefully, and as her impulsive, overpowering feelings for Van Kirk and Seymour had brought her far more pain than joy, she did not allow her emotions to take the upper hand.

On June 20, 1950, the *Chicago Tribune* noted: "R. H. McCormick III Sued by Wife for Desertion."[31] Robert Hall McCormick III had married Helen Bersbach in 1937, and it was on their honeymoon to England, that Gardner, then studying with Eileen Thorndike, had met and disliked the couple. This had not been her first encounter with McCormick, for they had always moved in the same circles. He was a scion of the McCormick dynasty whose enormous fortune was based on inventing, perfecting, manufacturing, and marketing the mechanical grain reaper, which ushered in the era of modern agriculture in America. The family was among the wealthiest in America, and although Bob McCormick insisted that he was "of the poorer strain," being a descendant of Leander McCormick rather than of his more famous brother Cyrus, he belonged to Chicago's First Families and was more than comfortably well-off.[32] Leander McCormick had extensive real estate holdings in Chicago, and his offspring, Bob McCormick's father included, concentrated on real estate rather than reapers. Bob's parents took care that their children received a proper education in the right social strata: his two elder sisters, just a few years older than Gardner, had gone to Foxcroft, and Bob McCormick himself, born in 1914, had gone to St. Mark's, where he mingled with the Gardners, Grosvenors, Lowells, and Peabodys. He then attended Yale, as his father had done. The family usually summered in Bar Harbor, Maine, where rich industrialists had started building mansion-sized summer "cottages" in the 1870s. Often called the "Newport of the North," Bar Harbor in the 1930s was frequented by the Rockefellers, the Morgans, and other movers and shakers of the day.

While at Foxcroft, Gardner visited Bar Harbor as a guest of Kate Davis Pulitzer (descendant of the media-magnate Joseph Pulitzer), at the time McCormick's girlfriend. Gardner made an impression: "We were certainly aware of each other."[33] The society pages recorded McCormick's subsequent involvement with Pauline Palmer, of the Chicago Palmers, and other suitable partners, as well as his marriage to Bersbach, the granddaughter of Judge Theodore Brentano (famous for having branded tipping illegal and un-American) on

September 11, 1937, when they both were in their early twenties: "The warm colors nature uses so lavishly in autumn formed the color scheme for the wedding of Miss Helen Bersbach and Robert Hall McCormick III, which took place yesterday afternoon in Winnetka. . . . The bride, tall and stunning, with titian hair, was a picture in a white satin gown trimmed with Brussels lace that had been worn by the bridegroom's mother."[34] The couple had two daughters, Deborah and Barbara, in quick succession, and a son, Robert Hall McCormick IV, a few years later. World War II intervened, and McCormick went into the army with eagerness as the war provided "relief from my marriage." Far too immature when they married, the two had been miserable. When McCormick returned from the war, he was drinking more heavily than before. He left his wife in 1947. Liberated, he started attending AA meetings.

Always interested in architecture and real estate, he became vice president of the McCormick Management Corporation, which his father, Robert Hall McCormick II, headed. Bob McCormick was aware of the global trends in architecture and an early and ardent admirer of the work of the pioneering master of modern architecture, Ludwig Mies van der Rohe. A refugee from Nazi Germany, Mies had settled in Chicago and been installed there as the dean of architecture at the Armour Institute, now known as the Illinois Institute of Technology. At that point, Mies had completed some twenty buildings. His subsequent work for ITT's campus was relatively modest, but once World War II was over and war-related construction restrictions were lifted, the glass-and-steel constructions of which Mies had dreamed might become reality. But Mies needed patrons who believed enough to invest in his genius.

McCormick was working with young, flamboyant millionaire developer Herbert Greenwald, and they, Maurice Donohue maintained, "exhumed Mies who existed mainly on paper and imposed him on the world."[35] Mies had designs ready for the Chicago towers, and McCormick and Greenwald were instrumental in getting them built. On April 8, 1949, Bob McCormick's father announced plans for the Lake Shore Drive buildings, the *Chicago Daily Tribune* reporting that "Twin Co-op Apartments Are Planned" at an estimated cost of some six million dollars, a huge investment for a precarious undertaking. Herbert Greenwald tried to whet the interest of potential buyers by extolling the apartments' amenities: they were to be "equipped with radiant ceiling hot water heating, with thermostats for individual unit temperature control. . . . Underground parking will be provided for 100 cars in the basements and subbasements of the building. Each building will have a master television antenna. A television set may be installed in any apartment within an hour." Architecturally revolutionary, the exterior of these towers was to be entirely of glass and steel and "devoid of ornamentation," but the *Tribune*'s readers were assured that the "floor to ceiling windows will have . . . 60 inch upper windows reversible for interior washing." The article ended: "Robert Hall McCormick Jr. is sales agent. ... The north part of the land is owned by the McCormick Management corporation. The south section, given to Northwestern University in 1944 by Col. Robert R. McCormick, editor and publisher of THE CHICAGO TRIBUNE has been optioned by the sponsors of the project."[36] Late December that year, the formal groundbreaking ceremony took place, launched by "the arrival of 'Santa Claus' by helicopter to present a six foot model of the proposed structures" at 860 Lake Shore Drive. In attendance were Mies van der Rohe, McCormick Senior, and Bob McCormick, who had already assigned more than half of the units to enthusiastic buyers.

Half a year later, Gardner saw the notice of McCormick's impending divorce in her daily paper and wrote him a consoling note. They got together and found that their shared social backgrounds and unhappiness in their earlier impulsive marriages made for an easy understanding. Politically, too, they saw eye to eye. Whereas McCormick's distant relative Robert R. McCormick, "The Colonel of Chicago," was rabidly right-wing and had consistently falsified liberal positions in his *Tribune,* Bob McCormick, like Gardner, went against the family grain and was a liberal Democrat. Finally, Gardner was sure she had found a man who did not covet her money, as Van Kirk had done, and was, in contrast to Seymour, intellectually compatible. Very tall and handsome in a patrician way, McCormick had impeccable manners, and Betty Farley and other friends called him "Garbo," because he looked like a male version of the inscrutable Swedish film star. What more could Gardner wish for in a man? It is true, McCormick was not sexually sparkling, but his shy reserve was a relief after Seymour's obsessive possessiveness. He was introvert and taciturn, but those traits, too, gave him the edge after the screaming and yelling to which Seymour had subjected her during their last years together. McCormick was "like home."[37]

McCormick was also sure that this time he had chosen well. Although Gardner was never perfectly groomed, as something was always awry, her upper-class bearing and charm were indisputable, and she fit seamlessly into the world of the Chicago aristocracy. At the same time, McCormick was glad to notice, "she did not play the arrogant Boston Gardner game."[38] Gardner's interest in modern art—spurred by, but not confined to, Congdon—matched McCormick's, and although he was far more knowledgeable in architecture, her open-minded yet critical sensitivity to new structural designs was uncommon. Both having been burned by their overly intense earlier marriages, they decided within months of their renewed relationship, stirred by sense, not sensibility, that they were made for each other. "We had similar backgrounds, we seemed to like the same things and I thought I understood her," McCormick explained in 1989. "We were both stunned by the collapses of our previous marriages and I thought I was able to take on a marriage and thought I knew what I was doing."[39] Gardner shelved her plans to go to Europe and visit Congdon and instead made arrangements for spring nuptials.

"Don't you think Daddy will be pleased?" Gardner asked her youngest sister, Rose, telling her of their wedding plans.[40] The family was indeed delighted; on her third try Gardner finally seemed ready to return to the conventional Gardner fold. This time, they were ready to broadcast their daughter's engagement to the world, and this wedding received more coverage than her first or second. In March 1951, the *Chicago Tribune*—the writer being under the erroneous impression that Gardner had divorced Seymour only a few weeks earlier—announced the "[s]urprising news" of her engagement to McCormick III, "member of one of Chicago's most prominent families."[41] A few weeks later, though, the paper carped that "[o]nly members of the families will attend the quiet ceremony, which will take place in Gordon Chapel of Old South church, Boston, and the luncheon the bride's parents. . . will give afterward at home. . . . Mrs. Seymour's daughter, Rose Van Kirk, 11, and son, Daniel Seymour, 6, will not go east for the ceremony. However, their mother and new step-father will return here within two weeks to make their home in Chicago."[42] McCormick and Gardner exchanged vows on April 20, 1951. Gardner's parents hosted the wedding, and several of her siblings attended; both of McCormick's parents were also present, though they had been divorced for years. They were thankful that their son, who had disgraced his family with his severe alcoholism, was now reformed (he had not touched a drop in years) and doing well in the family business; his marrying a Boston Gardner marked his comeback as a responsible McCormick. Their marriage was to be a new beginning for both of them, and McCormick remembered, "they were all very pleased and hopeful."[43]

A few family members and friends, however, were not too thrilled with Gardner's choice. Robert found McCormick "stiff and humorless" and, because of his alcoholic past, "pulled together in a precarious way."[44] McCormick was Seymour's polar opposite, and Robert feared his vulnerable sister had tipped the scales against her heart, in favor of her head; he could not imagine Gardner flourishing in a marriage of convenience, devoid of passion. Anabel Holland found McCormick "too damaged from his years of drinking . . . like a small figurine, smashed up and patched together again," but her less hypercritical friend Myra Cholden said, "he was alright, he was nice and formal, very polite, but . . . too Waspy."[45] Careful and controlled, McCormick preferred to be in the background, in the shadow of his captivating wife. It was hard for him to open up and reveal his innermost self, but beneath his self-protective armor he was as vulnerable as Gardner, not the "cold fish" Robert Gardner took him for. Maurice and Helen Donohue were the couple closest to the McCormicks in the 1950s, and Maurice credited Bob with being "as near as you can get in this world to a saint."[46] Congdon also described him as "a saint, and yet—? I could not perhaps touch him, reach him."[47]

The third-time bride and her upstanding groom honeymooned briefly in Mexico before taking up their daily lives in Chicago. They lived in Gardner's Woodlawn house but planned to build a new home in Elmhurst, hoping it would be ready in the fall of 1951. Designed by Mies van der Rohe, the house was to be a horizontal one-story slice of his glass-and-steel towers. McCormick intended their house to be the prototype for architecturally innovative, reasonably priced family housing and wanted it to be constructed of simple, affordable materials. The house, with ceiling-to-floor single-pane windows would have no air-conditioning; its floor would be concrete and covered with cork. The kitchen was to be modest, the rooms connected, separated by moveable partitions. Once the house was finished, McCormick expected to find the financial backing to build numerous Mies row houses.[48] While their house was being built, the McCormicks moved from the Woodlawn house to an apartment in the Lake Shore Drive towers. Gardner easily changed to decorating in modern design. Living in the Towers, related to the developers and married to its sales-agent proved to be somewhat awkward. "[T]he one who was a big pain in the ass was Mies van der Rohe, because he had determined that everybody who lived in that building had to have the same curtains. It was one of the first glass buildings ever and no one had any experience with this. So people would move in and then they began putting their curtains up and then he would say 'NO'. . . And the acoustics were terrible: noises would go from the first floor to the twentieth floor."[49]

As if to mark her transformation from irreverent rebel to dutiful daughter, Gardner burned her entire past correspondence in "a long overdue bonfire."[50] Effortlessly, she became one of the Rockefellers of Chicago, as the McCormicks were known, but unlike her mother and elder sister, she refused to let her life be determined by her milieu. She took up only duties absolutely necessary to a woman of her class, avoiding committee and charity work if possible—although giving generously—but hosted dinner parties for her husband's business friends and architectural associates. Herbert Greenwald and his wife, Lee, Mies van der Rohe, as well as Mies's Bauhaus colleagues Walter Gropius and Marcel Breuer (when in town) were welcome and charmed guests: "Belle was very good with them."[51]

Explaining to Ted Roethke why she could not organize a lecture tour for him in spite of her social standing, Gardner understated: "My husband and I have no social life involving McCormicks or other of that ilk, we have no station-wagon-country-club-life—our friends are mostly U[niversity] of C[hicago] people, but we live quietly. The poets here, [Henry] Rago, [Reuel] Denney, [Elder] Olson, Ruth Herschberger etc. are our friends, and we would love to give a party for you. . . . I belong to no Women's Clubs and have no entrée—Divorced twice, a one-time professional actress, a one-time fairly 'engaged' radical, now a deliberately isolated (socially) being—I am not in a position to arrange dates or programs for any one."[52]

Anyway, Gardner was far too busy to take up extra duties. Her career as a poet had gotten off to a flying start just a few months after she had married McCormick. Then Karl Shapiro, Pulitzer Prize winner and editor of *Poetry*, had written to her: "I am excited by these. Please stop by the office some day."[53] This not only signaled Isabella Gardner's first acceptance by that prestigious magazine of verse, but also marked the beginning of her intense editorial association with it. To be accepted by the magazine that was regarded as "that mythical dreamland for young poets" and which T. S. Eliot had called an "American Institution" marked her coming of age as a poet.[54] "After tremulously telephoning for an appointment," Gardner found herself in the "private dusty burrow" of the *Poetry* offices, where Shapiro, who thought she "was a fine poet and felt that he had discovered her . . . asked her if she would be interested in reading for the magazine."[55] Gardner was "*terrified*," protesting her "ignorance . . . self-imposed non-reading of most contemporary poets, . . . [and] lack of college education."[56]

Why indeed did Shapiro ask this fledgling poet and housewife to decide all by herself which of the over three hundred poems the magazine received on average every week to return and which to submit to him for final judgment? In the second part of his autobiography, *Reports of My Death* (1990), and in interviews, Shapiro has protested that the fact that Gardner was a "Boston Brahmin beauty heiress poet" and Mrs. Robert Hall McCormick III to boot—or, in her own words "Mrs. Rich Bitch poet"—had nothing to do with his request.[57] But Shapiro was not quite truthful, for the precarious financial situation of the magazine preyed continuously on his mind, and he knew full well that with Gardner on board, *Poetry* could feasibly tap into new sources of old money. Besides, it seemed to him she would feel at home with the Bryn Mawr and Vassar socialites who performed *Poetry*'s secretarial duties for free. Then, too, he was well aware that she had great publicity value: for figuring in a cigarette commercial Gardner was offered $1,000 (two months of Shapiro's salary), as well as "a free trip to N.Y.—an evening dress and $50 for a minute on television and another $50 every time they used the T.V. thing. Mrs. Robt. Hall McCormick III of Chicago routine." Gardner declined "in view of lung cancer and other less tangible reasons."[58]

Though suspicious of Shapiro's reasons for asking her, Gardner wished so ardently to be involved with poets and *Poetry* that she agreed to become, without pay, its first poetry reader. Realizing Gardner's advertising potential, the magazine's new publicity director immediately sent out a press release, informing editors of society pages of the blue-blooded pedigree of the magazine's new volunteer. She felt "deceived and betrayed" and decided to quit.[59] By summarily firing his publicity director—which landed him in trouble with *Poetry*'s board of trustees—Shapiro managed to convince her to stay on. But, then, he knew that he "had struck gold."[60]

If Shapiro had hoped that Gardner would become a patroness to *Poetry,* as her godmother, Isabella Stewart Gardner, had been to Henry James and John Singer Sargent, he was not to be disappointed. A month after her acceptance, she had already convinced McCormick to offer the use of the brand-new Mies van der Rohe buildings on Lake Shore Drive for a benefit for *Poetry* "to conduct tours of the premi[s]es, have a cocktail party or anything else we wished."[61] A few years later, when *Poetry* was homeless, McCormick offered the magazine, rent-free, "either the Roanoke Building or the McCormick Building, and you can feel that those are available as soon as you want them, just give me a little notice so that I can get the space fixed up for you."[62] Moreover, as Shapiro had hoped, the McCormicks gave generously to *Poetry* and got their relatives and friends to donate as well, while Gardner helped raise considerable sums of money by organizing readings by public personalities.

Gardner's work as its first reader benefited *Poetry* even more, if less tangibly. Even after moving to the new Mies van der Rohe house in suburban Elmhurst in the summer of 1953 when it was finally ready, she came in religiously every day of the week, six hours a day, to work her way through "the mountain of manuscripts."[63] After years of searching, Gardner had finally found her true vocation. Poetry had become so essential to her being that she was willing to be "an angel stuck in [a] broom closet" and spend most of her day in its service.[64] Returning to writing, Gardner threw off the masks she had worn as an actress, when she had hidden behind lines written by others; now, much more vulnerably, she presented her own to the public.

She metamorphosed from a party-queen dwelling with her gregarious, tempestuous husband Seymour in a warm, slightly murky subterranean world, into an almost unnaturally disciplined worker bee living with her reclusive, calm husband McCormick as part of Chicago's upper-class in a glass house. The *Chicago Daily News* wondered if the Elmhurst dwelling was the "Dream House of Tomorrow," but the house's "stark steel beams, stone and glass" were clearly much too bare and experimental for the paper's conservative taste.[65] And a number of aspiring poets, invited for tea and a poetry reading, thought that despite "the opulence of its natural setting which invaded the interior through every windowed wall, the house seemed too small for [Gardner]," while its "few brick corners could barely contain the vibrant canvases done by her artist-cousin Billy Congdon."[66]

In the world of poets and poetry, Gardner thrived personally and professionally. If Shapiro greatly exaggerated the impact of his considerable charms on Gardner in *Reports of My Death*—she "loved him all her life and would have been happy to be his wife if he had asked"—she certainly fell under his spell.[67] A far cry from the pugnacious persona he presented to the world in collections of his essays such as *Beyond Criticism* (1953) or *In Defense of Ignorance* (1960), Shapiro was, in fact, "a warm, wonderful, sweet man," as poet-critic Robert Phillips found, who had been "scared to meet him; I thought he was a head-chopper."[68] Passionately polemic and constantly contradicting himself in his criticism over the years—swinging, for instance, from love for T. S. Eliot, to "swapping the tsetse," to admiration—Shapiro was consistent only in his touchstones for poetry: intuition, emotion, romanticism, vision, personality, originality, and joy.[69] At a time when the self-styled objectively impersonal intellectual moderns virtually monopolized the literary and poetic scene, Shapiro believed that poets are "enormously emotional animals" and found in Gardner a kindred spirit, also apparent in their shared love of D. H. Lawrence, Dylan Thomas, and Rainer Maria Rilke.[70]

The *Poetry* offices became Gardner's home; she took her slippers along and diligently waded through mind-cluttering masses of manuscripts even though only a small percent was worth reading. Shapiro was not a manager, but a poet among poets, and the atmosphere at *Poetry* was open, congenial, and clubby. Business matters and finances were necessary evils, the board of trustees the common enemy, and lunches long and bibulous. The only fly in the ointment, perhaps, was the African American poet Margaret Danner, a former student of Shapiro's and since 1951 editorial assistant at *Poetry,* whose later much anthologized series of four poems, "Far from Africa," was published in the magazine that same year. Being the only black in an all-white office must have been hard for Danner, but she got everybody's hackles up, from secretary Sue Neil to Gardner and Shapiro, who recalled:

> She was the first black person on the magazine. There was something about her that was disturbing; she was herself a little mentally disturbed. . . . She had published, but she was not as good a poet as Gwendolyn Brooks. I am trying to remember why I did not ask Gwendolyn to be on the staff. . . . I used to go to the South Side and give readings to black groups and that is probably how I met Danner. I published something of hers and she was a reader. Being a reader she had to be subservient to Belle: Belle was the main reader and what Margaret Danner was supposed to do was to weed out the poems that were obviously impossible, like stuff by illiterates, or the kind of thing that gets in newspapers about your grandmother, or something. I think they might have had clashes about stuff, but I never really knew.[71]

The only one who got along with her was Henry Rago, who promoted her to assistant editor when he succeeded Shapiro.

Gardner spent much more time working for the magazine than did its editor, as Shapiro, in order to provide for his wife, Evalyn, and their children, Kathie, Jake, and Liz, often held down three jobs simultaneously. In addition, Shapiro, though keeping final editorial say, spent nearly a third of his time teaching and writing. Gardner proved such a diligently independent reader that Shapiro, in "his big carpeted office," was soon "staring out of the window into Lake Michigan and feeling foolish and in a sense out of work."[72] In early 1952 he reported to the trustees that Gardner was a "major addition to the volunteer staff," adding that she preferred "to perform the duties of first reader of the manuscripts anonymously; consequently her name has never appeared on the masthead of the magazine."[73] But in July 1952 Gardner was mentioned as assistant and in April 1953 as associate editor; by that time she apparently knew her value to the magazine and no longer feared being misused as a moneyed decoy.

Shapiro "relied on her opinion and her taste very much and . . . never questioned her," usually following her suggestions for publication.[74] Usually, but not always. When Lee submitted a poem, Gardner warned her sister-in-law: "If I *love* it and Karl is just *dubious* we would have to turn it down," which Shapiro proceeded to do.[75] Whereas in this case Shapiro was probably right, he was less sensitive than Gardner with respect to a number of promising poets. It was mainly thanks to her that Philip Booth, John Logan, and Galway Kinnell came to publish in *Poetry* when they started out. The latter, for one, submitted large batches of poems that Shapiro, in spite of Gardner's advocacy, turned down, indiscriminately using, as was his custom, printed rejection slips. This might have thoroughly discouraged Kinnell had not Gardner written him long letters, commenting extensively and positively on his work, and repeatedly encouraging him to submit work. Finally, in December 1953, he broke through with "The Wolves" and from then onward appeared more or less regularly, although Shapiro never really recognized his talent.

Gardner's relationship with John Logan was similarly nurturing. In January 1953 he wrote to Gardner that he was "sad that you will not publish my second-rate poems because unfortunately that is probably the only kind I am now writing. But it is a joy to know that if I find the strength and the time to do something better you are willing at *Poetry* to help find an audience. . . . I am very pleased that you like my shorter lyrics . . . because I love to write them and though publishers are interested in the longer more dramatic things it is hard to touch them with the lyrics."[76] One of the two poems that made up Logan's first appearance in the magazine two months later was the lyric "Spring Chill," which, however, paled beside his ecstatic, exalted "Mother Cabrini's Bones."[77] At the start of their acquaintance, Logan, eight years Gardner's junior, was just a young poet, struggling to take care of his fragile wife and swarm of children; in fact Gardner wished he would reserve his fire for his poetry instead of his wife, whom he—a converted Catholic—got pregnant serially. She was "disturbed by his unhappy and compulsive preoccupation with 'getting thar fustest with the mostest,'" but considered him "extremely gifted. . . sensitive, deeply troubled, not smug or arrogant, but 'driven.'"[78] Logan taught at nearby Notre Dame in South Bend, Indiana, and they met in Chicago or Elmhurst. At first, although much better educated (with a bachelor's in biology, a master's in English, and graduate work in philosophy at Georgetown and Notre Dame), Logan was somewhat in awe of Gardner, because she was both a published poet and *Poetry*'s first reader, but soon they traded poems equally. Their aims in poetry were uncannily similar, both expressing yearning for joining, for love rather than lust. Gardner searched all her life and in her poetry "for the specific and particular recognition of one human being by another—the response by eye and voice and touch of two solitudes," while Logan called poetry "a reaching of the poet through his language, a way of touching others and bringing them together in a shared experience."[79] An intense musicality was the hallmark of Gardner's work, and Logan described poetry as "a ballet for the ear."[80] They were kindred souls.

Desiring his aspiring fellow Irish-American poet-friends to share Gardner's "kindness" and "careful criticism" as well as hoping to get them published, Logan often mentioned their work in his letters to her.[81] No such promotion was necessary in Kinnell's case, but she needed convincing with respect to Paul Carroll, whose attempts to peddle his work were unsubtle: "you may print [the Arcady poem]. . . . I want you to have it; however, I am not at all interested in third-rate critical rejections from Karl or Henry Rago. Forgive me if this does smack of arrogance. I am Irish."[82] Carroll's work finally appeared in *Poetry*'s March 1955 issue with "Un Voyage à Cythère," a surprisingly controlled classicist poem in view of his backing of the Beats a few years later.[83] It was his only poem to appear during Gardner's years with *Poetry*, but, as with Logan and Kinnell, her detailed and reassuring reactions to his submissions fostered his latent talent and made him a lifelong and devoted, if troublesome, friend.

Others who were enriched by Gardner's appreciative criticism of their work included new writers as different as the powerful, poised New England poet Philip Booth ("she gave me some of the earliest, warmest responses") and rough Beat poet Gregory Corso ("Thank you for a beautiful helpful letter. 'Mental muscle'—yes, how right you are"), as well as established ones like Richard Eberhart ("I'm glad you liked the poem. . . . Karl didn't think it had my idiom [should readers become too accustomed to an idiom?]") and Theodore Roethke ("Here are some different final versions—of the sequence you liked. . . . I always will cherish your phrase about their being 'the very voice of love.'")[84] These explicit acknowledgments come from sprawling, simultaneously literary and intensely personal letters that Gardner received from these poets to whose submissions she reacted so extensively, impassionedly, and encouragingly.

Consequently, they continued to submit, as did poets like Reuel Denney, Ruth Herschberger, and Barbara Howes, all of whose work Gardner actively solicited. Denney, cowriter of the most widely read book on American society, *The Lonely Crowd* (1950), and Ruth Herschberger became friends, although Herschberger found Gardner bourgeoise, which did not keep her from discussing her love affair with Conrad Aiken in graphic detail over lunch. Herschberger was Richard Eberhart's relative, eking out a meager existence by typing, and Eberhart and Gardner often conspired to help her out. Eberhart, who was "very keen" on Gardner's poetry, had known her off and on since the 1930s as he had taught her younger brothers, John and Robert, at St. Mark's.[85] "She came to the school to see them and that is where I first met her. I got very much interested in her, because she was a very attractive and lively person. She must have invited me to go to her parents' house and I remember how impressed I was with . . . the garage. Maybe there was some negative aspect to my feeling, because her father had at least six or seven cars, and I thought that was really. . . [laughter]. And then you heard all these stories about Mr. Gardner owning about a third of the whole of Boston; he had all kinds of local real estate."[86] Eberhart recalled Gardner's "lush and sweeping gesture as [she] entered a room bearing a noble bottle of wine" and his letters to "Bellissima" are interspersed with longing remarks such as "I w'd love you for your beauty alone."[87] With Howes, too, there was a Boston connection, as she had been adopted into a well-to-do Massachusetts family and reared chiefly in Chestnut Hill, where she had also attended Beaver County Day School.

Gardner's reading of poets' work often consisted in her listing of lines she particularly enjoyed and her reasons why. Sometimes, therefore, she seems merely gushing, but it was part of her diplomatic critical strategy to concentrate on what was good, adding just a few suggestions for improvement, for which she usually apologized profusely. Nevertheless, if she was sure a poem was substandard, she would point that out clearly, for she thought nothing "more hideously degrading than to compromise one's integrity and an artist's integrity by praising out of 'pity,'"—although she admitted she would usually find "one thing to praise."[88]

Shapiro hardly ever took such unselfish pains with poems by others, generally restricting himself to endorsing Gardner's choices for the magazine, or, now and then, to vetoing them. Neither did he ask for work from admired poets, trusting the mail to bring in more than enough submissions. He made an exception, though, for *Poetry*'s fat fortieth-anniversary issue, published in 1952, which consisted of solicited poems only. Gardner also invited contributions for this occasion, sometimes using her family connections, as in writing to T. S. Eliot, who unfortunately had "absolutely nothing in the desk which I could offer" and who refused to act as a judge for the best poem in the anniversary issue, as "he didn't want to be put in the position of judging his contemporaries in a competition."[89] Ezra Pound, whom Gardner also approached, did not appear either, but the editors could be justly proud of a double special issue amounting "to an anthology of the latest poems of many of the foremost living poets," among them Elizabeth Bishop, E. E. Cummings, Robert Graves, Randall Jarrell, Archibald MacLeish, Marianne Moore, Theodore Roethke, Wallace Stevens, and William Carlos Williams.[90]

Another special issue, on Dylan Thomas, took the joint exertions of *Poetry*'s editor, two acting editors, and Gardner as associate editor to finally come into being. It is hard to overestimate Dylan Thomas's influence on the American literary scene of the time. A romantic poet with a dramatically powerful voice containing a subtle Welsh lilt, uninhibited, usually drunk, Thomas fitted all low-, middle-, and highbrow expectations of what a true poet should be. His captivating public readings in the United States in the early 1950s brought him great acclaim—Elizabeth Bishop thought that "hearing Thomas read was a highlight of her Washington year" as poetry consultant to the Library of Congress—and his celebrity status may have led to an overestimation of his stature as a poet; nevertheless, Shapiro, Logan, Gardner, Oscar Williams, and many others admired his magical musicality, sensuality, and paradoxically obscure openness.[91] It was Gardner's idea to launch this issue as a spin-off of Thomas's profitable benefit lecture for *Poetry* in the spring of 1952.

But as early as January 1953, Shapiro called it a "rather abortive plan."[92] Instead of submitting, as promised, new poems to *Poetry*, Thomas had "borrowed" Shapiro's two copies of D. H. Lawrence's *Collected Poems* and reneged on reviewing a rhyming dictionary, which he had also taken. Irritated, Shapiro wrote to R. M. MacGregor at Thomas's American publisher, New Directions: "I wish I knew who was actually in charge. Oscar [Williams] is one of the impressarios but apparently there is a man in England, various publishers and friends. It takes a lot of people to take care of Thomas."[93] MacGregor explained the complicated situation with respect to Thomas's agents, some of whom were not on speaking terms with one another, and tried to temper Shapiro's annoyance: "I expect that there is no point in trying to trace the two copies of D. H. Lawrence's COLLECTED POEMS. If you have ever seen Mr. Thomas looking for his other shoe of a morning, you will realize that his attitudes towards impedimenta are not exactly acquisitive."[94] Mollified, *Poetry*'s staff invited Thomas for another lecture in the autumn, perhaps hoping to acquire new work, but this was not to be. On November 5, 1953, Shapiro, in Rome on a six-month Guggenheim grant, received a letter from acting editor Nicholas Joost: "apparently Dylan Thomas is critically ill in New York and is not expected to pull through. . . . We just managed to get back our cards, announcing the lecture, which were out at the University Press."[95] Thomas died four days later.

About six months after Gardner's first meeting with Shapiro, he knew he had roped in "an extremely competent and . . . highly talented person"; Gardner had become a fully participating member of the *Poetry* team.[96] Her unremunerated work was valued the more when small but barrel-chested, belligerent Shag Donohue, who had been appointed *Poetry*'s business manager in May 1952, was fired after only three months, because, as Shapiro wrote to Wallace Fowlie (then an advisory editor for *Poetry*), the magazine was in a "quite desperate situation financially."[97] Shag Donohue, however, was convinced Shapiro threw him out "because he thought I was bizarre. He found a bottle of whisky in a drawer. Karl is a wonderful person and I love him, but he was under the gun of being serious."[98]

At home with McCormick, their children, and their friends, Gardner blossomed. For the first time in her life, emotional peaks or abysses were absent; living with McCormick on a plateau of quiet contented camaraderie, Gardner was absorbed by her work, rather than by dramatic disturbances and was amazingly productive, certainly considering her almost full-time volunteer work for *Poetry*. In June 1952, T. S. Eliot had assured Gardner he would "always be interested to see more of [your work.] The poems which Mr. Donohue showed me made a definite impression."[99] Shag Donohue explained at length:

T. S. Eliot is making a tour of the United States and he is coming to the University of Chicago. Because he is a practical publishing man he is going to go to [my] bookstore that is selling more Faber and Faber books than anybody else. So, I am sitting behind my desk at the bookstore and I know Eliot is going to come. And here comes this man in Chesterfield and the black bowler and the umbrella. T. S. Eliot! He comes down our stairs and he says: "Mr. Donohue?" and I say: "Yes." And he takes off his hat, I pull back my hand. He says: "My name is Eliot." I say: "Yes." He says: "T. S.," and I say: "Yes." Now, in the American army or in all the American armed forces, T. S. meant tough shit, so, too bad, too fucking bad. . . .

Three days later I see him at Belle's and I say: "I wish we had had more chance to talk about things. I am not very good at these parties." He said: "Maybe I am not, either. Here is the number of my secretary that the university has given me and we go and have lunch." It is 1950, Jenny was born October 14th. There were steps in our apartment, Sylvia could not leave for three weeks, and it was our first time out. She wore a beautiful dress, low-cut cleavage, pearls, and we went to the Windermere, where Eliot was staying, and we had a wonderful lunch. He could not take his eyes off her. . . . He turned to me and said: "You and I are going to have double martinis." And from there, I asked him about Ezra Pound—and I did not know about Eliot's anti-Semitism at the time—and he said Pound was brilliant when it came to prose and poetry and cookie when it came to politics.

Belle heard about Eliot's visit to my store and about our lunch. The next party, a week later, she said: "Shag, T. S. Eliot went to Harvard with my father and for weeks I have known that he was going to visit here and be my guest and for weeks I am saying: 'I am going to show him my poetry.' And I have not. Would you please write him a letter enclosing some of my poems and do not tell him that I have asked you to do this? Just tell him, because you do like my poetry?" I said: "I think your poetry is wonderful." So I dutifully wrote the letter, saying: . . . "Enclosed are some first poems, unpublished by my dear friend Isabella Gardner, who asked me to show them to you, but also asked me not to tell you I am showing them to you. So please do not tell her that I have told you." . . . He played along with the gag in his reply and said: "If I were editing *Poetry Magazine,* I would publish at least two of these poems." . . . When I get Eliot's letter, I show it to Belle, and she says: "That is okay, Shag. Oscar Williams has accepted some of my poetry. He is getting it published, so we do not need T. S. Eliot." I am a businessman, right, and I thought that was a little tough. Oscar Williams! As far as I knew, he was a small little twerp, who lived off other people because he was an anthologist; his own poetry was terrible. I did not say anything to Belle, but my feeling was: if T. S. Eliot likes two of her poems and suggests that she send them to [*Poetry*], saying that T. S. Eliot suggested that I, Isabella Gardner, send you my poetry, Holy Mother Mary of God, who wants Oscar Williams![100]

McCormick was away on business during the day, and in the evenings he went regularly to AA meetings, yet during their first years the McCormicks, including Daniel and Rose, spent much quiet family time together. Bob McCormick was a loving father to the children, although he, like most everyone, was partial to Danny and later confessed he "should have cared for Rose more."[101] Danny became very attached to him, and Rose, too, came to call McCormick, her third father in a little over ten years, "Pop." From the beginning, though, Rose, an adolescent with a troubled past, complicated their lives; during their first summer together, Rose went to camp but showed up back home the very next day. Her behavior, which became increasingly difficult, was reinforced by her best friend, Maurice and Helen Donohue's disturbed daughter Deborah. Rosy did exactly as she pleased, lied and played truant, and her behavior became the main bone of contention during the McCormick marriage. Gardner accused her husband of misunderstanding Rosy, of interfering, and told him her daughter "was none of [his] business."[102] Danny was beloved, bright, charming, and alive, chasing glowworms in the dark, drawing, singing, making up prayers and songs:

> My son is five years old and tonight he sang this song to me.
> He said, it's a loud song, Mother, block up your ears a little, he

said wait I must get my voice ready first. Then tunelessly
but with a bursting beat he chanted from his room enormously,

> strangers in my name
> strangers all around me
> strangers all over the world
> strangers running on stars.

("A Loud Song," 70)

Daniel went to his father for most of each summer and the majority of week-ends when Seymour still lived in Chicago.

Gardner tried to juggle the multiplicities of her life. When she told her fellow poet Carolyn Kizer, who was some ten years her junior and then living in Seattle, that "out of deference to my husband, I do not write in the evenings or on weekends," Kizer was flabbergasted. "My God, what else IS there?" "That is when women write! It was hard for women in the 1950s, very hard. Women poets got very little attention from men, other than that men wanted to go to bed with them, but they were not taken seriously intellectually."[103] While Gardner had rebelled against her fate as a society wife by putting her wish to become a writer first, she had internalized many of the values of her era. She endorsed Robert Graves's saying that "no woman poet has been true poet and born and mothered children" and although she often wished she had more time to write, she never explicitly questioned her role of "nurturing and cherishing and soothing and stimulating of the human beings whose lives have touched mine; and whose needs I *cannot* deny. . . . The women . . . poets I know of who write truly and well are chickless and cockless. I cannot so be."[104] To her brother Robert she wrote in 1954:

I thoroughly enjoy cooking lusciously (if sloppily) for company here—and lovingly and deliciously for Sunday brunches for Bob and me—otherwise I happily tell Mary what to cook and how; and *season* it. I make beds reluctantly on her days out. I pay the kids on her days out to wash the dishes. I sometimes dust the books and always fix the flowers which I love, and hang up, pick up and send out Bob's clothes. That's *all*. Except for name-tapes, shopping, dentists, doctors, paying bills, budgeting, cub-scouts, P.T.A., weeding, raking leaves, corresponding and editing. Clothing, hair, face and figure get short shrift. Friends get shortchanged. But there just cannot *be* a female Dick Eberhart! And a woman writing or painting or whatever *must* choose and with me its *Bob and children* and then *writing*. After that everyone and everything else. If writing sometimes comes first it is not *conscious* choice but a *factor* that colours everything. The reason of course that there are no female Dick Eberharts is that there are no *male* Betty Eberharts! I don't think I'd like it if there were.[105]

As a woman with her own income who could afford live-in help, it was far easier for Gardner to find time to write than for most women with children, but as she spent hours at the *Poetry* office each day, she, too, had to write her poems in the lost hours. Those that she managed to write were snapped up. *Poetry* published a batch of her poems every few issues, although Shapiro did not print everything she submitted, centering on those poems that best showed her voice, such as "The Milkman"; the frightening "The Panic Vine" ("quickens on the spine with the rise / and fall of every breath; and blooms inside the eyes" [35]); or the autobiographical "This Neighborhood," written after she had left Seymour: "Apart / at last and yet a part afire a-cold / Unfeathered but impassioned in the bone / Like dying Ivan I am on the wing / Articulate alight aloud alone" (129). Very different types of periodicals presented her work to their readers: lively little magazines like *Accent* as well as *Botteghe Oscure* in Italy catered to wayward literature lovers; the literary quarterlies *Kenyon Review* and *Partisan Review* and *Sewanee Review* were studied in the academic world; and the *New Yorker* and the *Atlantic Monthly* pleased a generally well educated readership. Placing her poems so easily gave Gardner much-needed confidence in her work, and her friends helped bolster it. From Bennington College in Vermont, Wallace Fowlie wrote that he "would say again: yes, you are a poet, you have already created poems. A sense of experience and a mastery of form are both here in these pages. Very soon now you should have enough to make a volume. That you must do. It is time to see your poems collected and presented as a work."[106]

Gardner followed his advice and in the spring of 1953 sent about thirty poems to Kitty's friend Dorothy de Santillana at Houghton Mifflin, asking her if they were interested in bringing out a book of her poetry. Paul Brooks, its editor in chief, answered in July: "I have enjoyed these poems more than I have the work of almost any contemporary poet that I have read—though I should add that my reading in modern poetry is not as wide as it should be. . . . [T]here is great satisfaction in reading contemporary verse that is at once so warm and exciting and—praise God—intelligible." He wanted Gardner to add ten good poems to the twenty-five he thought ready for book publication.[107]

Gardner's life seemed sorted out, and most of her Boston relatives were jubilant, which piqued Congdon: "Everyone in the family now says how fine Belle is, how much they admire you etc. and I could not help inserting now and then, that this is not the time to appreciate you, now that your life is ironed out to their satisfaction, but before, when you perhaps had need of their support and love."[108] Gardner was then closer to Congdon and Robert than to George. McCormick remembered that George remained her "favorite" because of their shared childhood and that they still had "funny jokes and baby talk, their own sort of little language, A. A. Milne and so on," but as the oldest son, George was far too preoccupied with the family business to have time for his sister.[109] In November 1953, on the eve of United Fruit's involvement in the CIA-organized coup in Guatemala, which overthrew President Jacobo Arbenz, George was elected a company director, next to his work as an investment banker with Paine, Webber, Jackson and Curtis, one of the largest brokerage firms in the country. And he became United Fruit's chairman at the age of forty-one in 1958. "No bunch of bananas was better connected," Chapman wrote in his history of the company.[110] Gardner "sneered at" Kitty's social life in Paris and her obsession with clothes, yet asked her elder sister for an extensive account of her presence at a dinner and dance in London for a young Queen Elizabeth, where she had been jetted by the ambassador to NATO: "Both Queens [the Queen-Mother was also present] wore white, and had the garter across their bosoms—In the Queen's case it is not nearly as ample as I'd feared from pictures. . . . Churchill when he arrived at dinner demanded of a young man present to take him at *once* to see the Ballroom—to the person's astonishment as he, the P.M., cared nothing for Ballrooms—However, he naturally complied and once away from the others the P.M. said 'Forgot to do up my trousers'—whereupon he did!"[111] Gardner did not have much in common with her youngest "sweet, dear, warm" sister, Rose, either and tried to avoid her mother, McCormick said, who made no secret of her disappointment with Gardner because of her first two marriages. Peabo still "was the most wonderful thing in the world" to Gardner, but with him she could not discuss literature, the arts, politics, philosophy, her thoughts and inner life.

With Congdon and Robert she could, dashing off long disjointed letters, pouring out her thoughts, often ending after pages of postscripts that she realized that she had gone on at inadmissible length and that a postcard in reply would suffice. A much-abbreviated version of her fourteen-page letter to Robert and Lee, written from her Mies house in Elmhurst on September 10, 1953, just after her return from Roque is typical in its meandering, mixing the personal and the public, poetry, and politics:

> Fortunately the cream, the cod, and the kindness of Roque and of you combined put me in good health and good humour otherwise I would be quite distraught by now. My dear sweet Bob met us at the train with the news that Lyn, our maid, was leaving. He declared Sunday our day of arrival my official birthday and had gotten a woman from 'the building' to come and cook a turkey and had, himself, filled every pot, jar and vase with flowers from the garden! There was a cake and there were presents and we had a lovely family party.
>
> Lyn, it appears, had joined . . . a church on the south side, had found a girl to share a room with and hoped to get a clerical job. She told Bob she was too fond of me and the kids to see us again. Day before yesterday I got a telephone bill with

$76 worth of toll calls to Indianapolis, her hometown—of course I had to pay
and of course I can't collect and wouldn't if I could. But how *sad* this frequent
terrible lag in human relations, particularly race relations—where the white (no
matter how warm, candid and unprejudiced) is still the enemy—is in negro lingo
that marvelous and terrible word *Ofay* which many negroes use without realizing that it was coined by their sophisticated brethren and is, of course, pig Latin
for *foe.* Anyway dear Lyn has gone. Since I got home I have done a huge wash,
ironed, cooked, cleaned a much neglected house, taken the kids riding, bought
them school supplies, gotten them started in school, read *90* manuscripts—at
least 300 poems—Karl hadn't time to read, paid bills, [waxed?] furniture, dusted
books etc. . . . Bob was wonderful and advertised for help in the Sunday paper. A
lady arrived to-day but is used to being a *waitress,* won't wash or iron, doesn't like
it because we go out so little etc. If *only* I was still on Woodlawn Ave. I could get
help for a few hours a day but here (though I love it) that is impossible. I suppose
I *can* be wife, mother, poet, cook, laundress and *human*—but not for long and
something will probably suffer! Or everything.

Have been re-reading the poems I showed you and wish you liked *Of Flesh
and Bone* (LATER Sept. 28. Found this tucked in a drawer and will go on with
it.) and *Southwest of True North* better as I feel they are among my best. Karl likes
of Flesh and Bone better than anything I've done and asked if I'd let him send it
to Botteghe for me and print in *Poetry* if they send it back. Dick Eberhart wrote
me to ask me for some poems for New World Writing V but as *Accent* took *The
Sloth* and *Reveille for a Rockinghorse Poet* I've only S.W. of True North and your
favorite *Mindful of the Forest* and three old ones to send him.

Oscar Williams' publishers wrote me that he had taken my Cock a' Hoop (Lee's
favorite) for *A Pocket Book Of Modern Verse,* which excited me very much.

I want very much to discuss with you point by point and carefully Of Flesh and
Bone because I think I can defend and show as right and essential what you ob-
jected to but you haven't a copy of the poem and it would take a few pages. . . .

Bob and I have been living very quietly and contentedly. . . . The snobbish
"waitress" left declaring us too "rustic." We now have a very nice Italian woman, about fifty called Mary [Facio?]. She tolerates my trying to talk Italian with
her (six months Berlitz School) and alto-gether she is a pleasant person to have
around.[112]

As Karl Shapiro had left for Europe but remained *Poetry*'s editor abroad,
Gardner continued her daily conversations with him by mail, discussing not
only *Poetry* business, but also their life and work. They had become very close.
As an intuitive critic of poetry, Gardner was in almost total agreement with
Shapiro's just-published *Beyond Criticism,* the first of his books in which he
takes a sharp stand against the objective criticism that Eliot had advocated and

which had conquered the American academic world. In praising this book and his new *Poems 1940–1953*, she quoted extensively as was her wont, implicitly unfolding her own poetics:

> I remember Keats' phrase "The fellow-ship with essence" which is the Einfüh-lung you mention. Psychiatrists call it "the oceanic complex!" at least mine did when I described my intense feeling of it.
>
> It would be a delight to me and exceedingly boring for you if I were to con-tinue for pages quoting your own words but [*Beyond Criticism*] is akin to poetry and as you say "the accurate quotation of poetry is equivalent to a point of evi-dence."
>
> In my much underlined copy I have occasionally put a question mark in the margin. Is a poem just as much "a false reality" to a mystic? I agree that "the mys-tical is the opposite of the creative process." I suppose that Hopkins for instance was not a mystic while he was writing a poem? I would almost say that to the mystic who is also a poet a poem is just as much a reality as any other *phenom-enon* (miracle, magic-stigmata-Lucifer etc.)—perhaps I'm saying what you did but twisting it.
>
> On page 46—I am not sure that I agree about the inevitable bedlam of more than one level of meaning. I'm hostile to the prevalent and facile use of the phrase—I suspect it is used often to clothe the naked nothing of a poem but to eschew such a technique (or rather *eventuality*) entirely could sometimes mean throwing the baby out with the bath-water?
>
> Some-times, I think, *facets* of meaning, (rather than levels) polish, bevel and set off the jewel of the "integrity of meaning", refracting, isolating, both comple-menting and complimenting.
>
> Page 25—I think it must (not *should*, but must inevitably) matter to the art-ist whether the civilization he lives in is compulsory or voluntary, because I do not think that personality and spirit are free to grow under a totalitarian re-gime where the artist by "the human imperatives of sympathy" could not permit himself to survive intact. . . . I am thinking of course of contemporary despo-tisms—Russia to-day could permit no Tolstois and Dostoevsky wouldn't leave prison alive. . . .
>
> As I read and re-read your poems I am struck, almost as by a blow, by the tender, yet hard as a *core*, exquisitely made, full of grace, yet raw as a bared nerve perfection of most of your poems. It does not surprise me that during the ten years I've refused to read contemporary poetry I could not resist reading yours though I never allowed myself to *really* read them. I read them almost as an al-coholic might sneak drinks, smuggling into my consciousness a vague awareness of a few poems of yours, Hopkins, Eliot, Auden, Spender, MacLeish; and going back occasionally to Yeats and Frost, and I sneaked a look at Pound. Until four

years ago I'd read Dante and Chaucer but I'd never heard (consciously that is) of Marianne Moore, Wallace Stevens, Bishop, [Richard] Wilbur, Roethke, Leonie Adams, [Peter]Viereck—anyone you care to name! . . .

Your recent poem about the brothel . . . is the only poem of yours I've ever read that I reject with my feelings and with my reason, such as it is. Somehow it does not seem to be your poem. There are marvelous lines that are entirely you and then that last line "She asked in iron tones are you a Jew?" seems out of the essential context of the poem as written. It is not convincing, and not painful. It is nearly funny. Perhaps if the whore made some colloquial crack about circumcision it would be better? I don't know. And I am presumptuous to say anything.[113]

This is again a very characteristic (shortened) Gardner letter: she spills her thoughts and feelings onto the page, admires, quotes, and enumerates, but is, in spite of her protestations about "my reason, such as it is," sure of her values in poetry: poems have to be well-made, multifaceted as well as permeated with the "fellow-ship with essence."

At this time, Gardner was no longer flirting with communism, although she remained a left-liberal all her life. The Washington McCarthy hearings horrified her:

[T]he atmosphere of near-farce adds to the horror. I am more than ever thankful that we don't have a T.V.—I would be afraid of becoming even more emotionally involved. Hating McCarthy can become a full time pre-occupation hindering not him but ourselves. Roethke sent me a poem about it a few months ago (not submitted to *Poetry*!) brutal, and boiling with hatred—*not* a good *poem*—he (R) *became* that which he hated, but he said it all out loud and I imagine it helped him to do so. Mine is a sullen mulish kind of resentment. . . .

Politics, in the immediate sense, cannot be permitted to occupy too much space in the imagination, the thinking—the energy. Such seems a dead end creatively or an exhausted means to-ward the end. That is why, I think, there is so little *apparent* reaction to McCarthy etc.—among many poets. Of course there are poets of all ages who are and always have been entirely a-political. But not many, and not good.

There seem to be two trends among the not-so-good young poets (young in years, rather than career). Either they are blown glass-ily fragile, stylized, fluting on archaic Recorders, pastoral, Pans without *panic*, or lust. Or they mewl, puke, vomit, spew. Every image is turgid with blood, excrement, bile, bloat and corruption—and all so *labored,* so ponderous, and so hopeless.[114]

It is odd to find Gardner so detached, in particular as her friends and former colleagues (Anneke's husband Woody Guthrie, Paul Robeson, Orson Welles) were blacklisted. Poetry had clearly become much more important than politics—and Gardner was weary of political poetry. Nevertheless, in September 1957, when Arkansas governor Orval Faubus tried to prevent by force nine African American children from entering the white Central High School in Little Rock, Gardner was moved to write the highly crafted poignant poem "Little Rock, Arkansas 1957": "Their valor iron in their ironed clothes / they walk politely in their polished shoes / down ambushed halls to classrooms sown with mines / to learn their lesson" (59). And years later, Gardner wrote nursery rhymes against Vietnam ("Sing a song of slaughter / A pocketful of bombs / Four and twenty children / Baked in their homes" [146]), but she never collected these unsophisticated verses in book form.[115]

With Shapiro in Europe, *Poetry* organized a fundraising champagne party in the French Renaissance family home of Ellen Stevenson on September 29, 1953. *Poetry*'s headquarters were in a circular tower room—once Stevenson's boudoir—and in what Nicholas Joost, acting editor, called "the black hole [where]. . . . Miss Isabella Gardner . . . reads every manuscript submitted to the publication."[116] The party for nearly four hundred guests raised $2,700, only half of the magazine's goal. Gardner could not contribute more than her time, as McCormick was having job problems. This did not mean they had to economize on the necessities of life in Elmhurst or even on the household help, but Gardner was just a little bit more careful than usual with her money for art or charities; for once, she was not at the beck and call of Congdon, whom she usually sponsored by buying his pricey paintings whenever he needed money. McCormick praised his wife for her frugality. She spent extravagantly on cab rides only, for Gardner, still skittish, drove just the one road from home to the *Poetry* offices. (Even the one road taken sometimes posed problems, as when Gardner, returning home from Chicago, unlocked the car with a little more trouble than usual and drove off, only to be shocked into awareness by an enormous barking dog in the back of what was obviously not her vehicle.) There was money, too, for a three-week holiday with Bob in Mexico in February 1954, their first holiday without children, but on their return Gardner was buried under a pile of *Poetry* manuscripts.

With Shapiro feeling misplaced in Rome, Gardner now became embroiled, too, in the magazine's business and financial problems. She accompanied Nick Joost on visits to possible donors, lending cachet as Mrs. Robert Hall McCormick III, and read with him and Maurice Donohue on the radio the evening of the magazine's forty-first anniversary, very nervous in spite of her drama training. Although she did not care much for *Poetry*'s critical section, she tried, in vain, to get Allen Tate to review Roethke's *The Waking*, which won the Pulitzer Prize in 1953; considering Tate's penchant for classicist intellectuality, he was probably not the best choice for a critique of Roethke's musical, intuitive poetry. Hardly any time was left for Gardner's own writing, and

in her correspondence she worried about not having produced any new poems since Shapiro's departure.

In all, though, Gardner felt "full and peaceful and alert," and particularly
after their brief trip to Mexico, "[v]ery happy."[117] Rose, "a tough one" in Mc-
Cormick's uncharacteristically harsh view, had not been doing well in Elmhurst after all, and her decision to attend a small progressive Arizona boarding
school with a strong anthropological curriculum, Verde Valley School, was a
joyful turn of events, although the McCormicks went through the motions of
"testing to make sure by saying we want her at home etc. etc."[118] Rose's departure in the fall of 1954 would mean far less hassle, fewer fights, and much more
time for Gardner's work, for Danny remained loving, easygoing, and adaptable.
Gardner's home life was stable for once, her exertions for *Poetry* recognized,
and her poems admired, yet she went back into analysis, she confided to Robert, "because of nervousness in regard to reading aloud publicly—radio etc.—
Apparently I still have a problem of guilt to mother—i.e. my happiness and
success destroys her etc—but the sessions helped."[119] Gardner had given her
first reading ever of her own poems for Indiana University's extension program
in South Bend in February 1954. Logan invited her "for supper. You mentioned
that you have a couple of children, so probably our five would not scare you."[120]
Gardner was much more panicky about the reading, however. Paul Carroll remembered both her splendid performance and her spectacular appearance in
a green, velvety dress, with her hair up as if she were at a debutante cotillion,
for a stunned lower-middle-class audience.[121] Despite her misgivings, Gardner
had read in such a memorable, dramatic manner that she was the only one of
the poets in the series who was asked back the next year.

In her small study in Elmhurst, Gardner always made time for her many
correspondents, among whom Billy Congdon and Robert, as well as the poets
Lee Anderson, Edward Dahlberg, Richard Eberhart, John Logan, and, when he
was away, Karl Shapiro predominated. One of Robert's first attempts at writing poetry she critiqued succinctly: "*Your Capacity of Man* is very neatly done,
and except for the last stanza which wobbles, unified. I agree it is 'belabored of
image' but there is not a messy multiplicity, I like a consistent use of one motif
through-out a poem. There is nothing flabby about your lines."[122] Analyzing
the work of family and friends at times became a substitute for struggling with
her own poems, but the careful attention she bestowed on others was often reciprocated, and though Gardner hardly ever yielded to their suggestions, they
were usually helpful in that they confirmed her in her own convictions, for she
was as certain of what was good in her work as she was uncertain and insecure
about its reception. In an angry letter she never sent to Oscar Williams, Gardner explained: "I can't use the last lines you suggested for *Seagreen Lover*. First
of all they don't work for me. That is: it is not *my way of saying*. Also I can't bear

the idea of using another poet's words in a poem of mine. Never have, never will!"[123]

She need not have worried. Although she described herself as a "kindergarten poet," Gardner received high praise for the poems she sent her correspondents.[124] Roethke admired "the wonderful complexity of emotion" in Gardner's long poem of alienation "Southwest of True North," recognizing it for "a true poetry of exasperation."[125] Congdon thought this and other recent poems "all life, and inevitable, never self-conscious. They are trenchant and tough. You have been through a lot, but because, now, you have, in your living achieved as much, your anger becomes image." He was touched most by the "very, very beautiful 'Of Flesh and Bone,'" one of Gardner's poems in which she tries to stave off death: "I vowed that eyeless earless loinless lonely, / I would refuse to die; / that even if only / one sense was left me, touch or smell or taste, I would choose to live" (31).[126] Gardner's lyrical "Lines to a Seagreen Lover" reminded Logan of his beloved Rilke, and he wrote enviously: "to be able to do so much with these small old words."[127] Houghton Mifflin cabled on May 28, 1954: "WE DEFINITELY WANT TO PUBLISH AND LOOK FORWARD TO DISCUSSING BOTH ARRANGEMENTS AND ARRANGEMENT WHEN YOU ARE HERE."[128] Gardner had arrived as a poet.

Life in Elmhurst rolled on smoothly, even as the McCormicks—generous, loyal friends—became involved in the problems of others and tried to solve them. Anneke Van Kirk knew that Woody Guthrie was suffering from Huntington's chorea, a debilitating and fatal hereditary disease that rendered him erratic and violent and made their life together a disaster. Still, they decided to have a child, and Lorina Lynn Guthrie was born in April 1954. But "filthy with guilt," Anneke soon divorced Guthrie because the strain of minding him as well as the baby became too much.[129] Harold Van Kirk took no interest in his daughter or grandchild, but Gardner tried to help with advice and money. Anneke was too mixed-up at the time to take care of Lorina and farmed her out while she tried to earn some money in New York, only to spend her time falling in love with one unsuitable man after another. The situation came to a head when a Japanese lover suggested she follow him to his home country without her child and Anneke consented. She wrote Gardner she would feel untold relief if someone took care of Lorina, for the "love I have for her isn't the love a mother has for her child. It is an unstable and emotional conglomeration of feeling . . . like Poppa gave me."[130] Two different families had looked after Lorina while Anneke was trying to put her life back on track: the Ganters (parents of Anneke's best friend, Louise) and the Koeths, with whom Lorina had already spent more time than with her mother. After much turmoil, Mrs. Hela Koeth sent Gardner a distraught yet sensible letter: "[N]o one but us seemed to think of the baby. A. thought of her lover, Mrs. Ganter of the money, Louise of her feelings (I know she loves the baby) and you (forgive me!) of sparing Anneke[']s feelings—and no one wanted to do anything about it." Sure that Anneke "really didn't feel towards [Lorina] as a mother should," Koeth informed Gardner that although she and her husband were already in their fifties, they wanted to adopt the child. [131] Gardner supported their decision and sent the Koeths a large sum of money, which they put in the bank for emergencies.

Congdon turned to Gardner, too, when he got into trouble. McCormick thought he "was the most important person in Belle's life" at this time, as both now lived a life "gratia artis," by the grace of art, their temperaments, thoughts, and works echoing one another. McCormick was far less tolerant of Congdon's self-centeredness and disapproved of his parading his lovers (among them a Venetian gondolier called Gianni), when he came to stay with them in country-club-conservative Elmhurst. Gardner was hurt, however, when at the very last moment Congdon decided not to come to Chicago (and Elmhurst) in February 1954, where she had arranged a major exhibition of his paintings together with those of John Heliker. She forgave him within days and singled out for praise his Venice painting "Red Piazza," whereupon Congdon, wondering "if Mr. McCarthy will brand me for a C[ommunist] for so titling it," offered the oil to her for a song.[132] And when, during one of his last visits to America, Congdon got into trouble with the New York police because of his homosexual activities, it was Gardner whom he called upon for help and Gardner who flew to support him with money, lawyers, and love; he never thought of asking his siblings, let alone his disapproving parents: "I was in a terrible situation legally . . . a terrifying situation and Belle was there then. . . . [S]he gave me the possibility of surviving. And luckily it turned out well and I ran back to Europe."[133] Just before he flew back, he thanked McCormick for "so generously releasing your Belle to come to my help in New York—She was a great boon and boost to me—and now all is over, and I am rather bewildered as I emerge from the pills, and out again into the new-found freedom."[134]

The oldest son of Gardner's friends the German aristocrats Otto and Lulix von Simson (Otto von Simson, an art historian, was Jewish but he converted to Catholicism just before the outbreak of World War II; drafted, he managed to flee to America on his military pass and was later offered a job by Robert Hutchins on the Committee of Social Thought) became involved in an ugly hazing incident, and again the McCormicks offered solace and secured legal services. As John Logan's behavior was growing ever more unpredictable, and he became a problem drinker, Gardner saved him from falling apart by paying for his analysis, also because therapy opened up new avenues for his poetry and criticism, which came to include Freudian and Jungian concepts. Paul Carroll, too, was unstable, and Gardner also helped him, although she never became as close to him as to Logan and was never won over to his poetry; her support remained restricted to a financial injection now and then.

The McCormicks' roles as loyal friends to artists and patrons of the arts were also apparent from their involvement in Maurice English's *Chicago Magazine*, the first issue of which appeared on February 26, 1954. Bob McCormick and Ellen Stevenson were among the magazine's directors as both were main sponsors. The day before, Sue Neil, *Poetry*'s high-spirited secretary, wrote Shapiro: "I'm having lunch with Maurice English today. He is bringing along some copies of CHICAGO!!! It goes on the newsstands tomorrow.... Mrs. S. [Stevenson] saw proofs on the Art Center story and thinks it is wonderful. Everyone who was completely disgusted with this project six months ago is now most enthusiastic, and waiting with outstretched claws for the long anticipated first issue."[135] According to the *Tribune*, the first-day sales of the magazine "reflect[ing] all facets of life in Chicago" were "brisk."[136] Gardner wrote an essay about *Poetry*, pleading with Chicagoans to support their other magazine, but "Postillion for Pegasus" was never published because *Chicago Magazine* itself folded after a short-lived run for lack of advertisers, leaving Maurice English to look for a new job, which he soon found as an editor at the University of Chicago Press. Fanita English, looking back in anger on years of wasted effort, claimed that the McCormicks gave "peanuts" to support her husband's venture, but McCormick saved the bound issues of *Chicago Magazine* to remind him of a failed business venture in which he had lost substantial money at a period in his life when, being out of a job, he could ill afford it.

In June 1954 at *Poetry* there was a falling-out between Karl Shapiro and Ellen Stevenson, and Stevenson resigned in fury. Gardner thought her "an incredibly vain and destructive woman [who] withers whatever she grasps." Stevenson had "threatened to put the magazine into receivership and take over lock stock and barrel" and "undermined and by-passed Karl at every turn." Gardner felt "*terribly* sorry for her but she is totally lacking in human understanding and everything she has 'helped' has been for the greater glory of Ellen. Kiss of death."[137] Oscar Williams had been ensconced in an empty room next to the *Poetry* offices, biding his time for a chance to take over from Shapiro. Gardner had written him an indignant letter just before the blowup:

> I have been told, and it has hurt me to hear it, that you spoke critically of *Poetry* and its editor to Ellen Stevenson. You are certainly entitled to disapprove of the contents of the magazine but it is hard to understand why you did not first express these opinions to me or to Karl? . . . Karl has no bias, no coterie affiliation, no raison d'être as editor except to select the best. . . . *You, specifically,* have been urged to send poems. You send none. You have been asked to review. . . you decline. . . . I imagine you refused to edit an issue because we can't afford to pay you properly. . . . Speaking of money I hear that you told Ellen you thought Karl was *overpaid*! A man with three children must feed them. Or do you think poets shouldn't have children? I should think you of all people

would feel that the editor of *Poetry* should make somewhere nearly as much as a brick-layer![138]

She never sent the letter, however, feeling sorry for Williams as his wife had died in agony of stomach cancer just a few months earlier, knowing that he had to return to his lonely cold-water apartment in New York City.

Gardner's summer had been tranquil, though: she had weeded her beets and carrots in Elmhurst, stayed at the quiet colonial beach village Cotuit on Cape Cod with Rosy (Daniel was with his father), and gone to Boston for a brief visit with her parents and siblings, including Kitty, who was visiting from Paris. She lunched there with Paul Brooks to sign her book contract and discussed the manuscript with one of Houghton Mifflin's editors, wonderful Gerta Kennedy—daughter-in-law to Edith who had guided Gardner's reading when she was a post-debutante. Advised by wily Williams, Gardner had decided to call her book *Birthdays from the Ocean*, comprising the first line of her signature poem about the near-impossibility to communicate, "That 'Craning of the Neck,'" while each poem was also a birth, the Atlantic Ocean Gardner's "*mother and my redemption, my purgation, my element. I am in the arms of the mother I never had, the ocean is Eros to me also. Not the soupy balm of the Pacific, but the glorious bite of the Atlantic.*"[139] Logan thought it "a splendid title," capturing the "unalloyed joy and song of a child and the primitive generative power, partly mysterious and partly ordered, of the ancient sea. It has a charming naivete yet, in its suggestion of sources of renewed life (and the need for them), a kind of ominousness that ricochets in the mind."[140]

Gardner's stay at her beloved Roque in September 1954, however, "was a mistake," she told Robert:

> I was not in temper for it—and the amount of work and organization to get Rosy off to school was gargantuan. I contributed "nothing to nobody." I wish I had—to Mother and Daddy especially, but this old cow is *dry*—and was ungenerous. Few moos in the last year—and not much milk. No butter or cream to churn a poem or nourish those I love. Perhaps the book's a calf? Poet friends tell me they dried as their first book came out, and as [psychiatrist] Kraus says—(I'm back with him for what I hope will be a short and final assault on my remaining conflict) it is the perilous joy of writing and of succeeding that frightens me and temporarily paralyses me. Idiotically because of Mother. . . . He reminded me yesterday that I was far from the first and only child whose mother did not love them. Absurd that I should still mind so much.[141]

Congdon did not understand Gardner's conflict. "Usually success removes the conflict. . . . The meat of your poetry certainly betrays no such lingerings, or confusion—but seems to me to have gained the peak wherein you can really help and be friend to your mother without remaining with her . . . [in the] childish trap. A danger of analysis I think is in falling in love with the technique, as tho' the maturity it revealed to us were not enough—and instead of . . . being mature we run back along the track of analysis."[142]

After the breakup with Stevenson, the magazine moved to new quarters in the attic of the Newberry Library, and Gardner complained in late 1954 that it was "miserably cold in these offices—no heat up on this fifth floor except for 2 futile radiators plugged into electrical outlet—drafty windows above the desks etc—but as I told you—no rent!" She went on to say that "Karl has a fine job at Berkeley and leaves to everyone's distress, in late January."[143] For Shapiro had had enough of *Poetry*'s politics, was vexed by constant obstruction from the board of trustees, and had started looking for a new job. In October 1954 he wrote Sue Neil that he had "talked to Ellen Stevenson the other day, believe it or not, about some of her property which we apparently transported in great haste. Ellen seems to think that we have some of her Dylan Thomas manuscripts. But Belle and I today went through the Thomas papers and discovered none of Ellen's. Do you have any recollection of the Thomas manuscripts belonging to Ellen ever being in the office, in the exhibit case, or do you recall Ellen taking them home? Any information will be appreciated by us and the F.B.I."[144] Departing in January 1955 for a temporary lectureship at Berkeley, he appointed Rago as acting editor, but, as had been the case when he was in Rome, reserved all final editorial decisions for himself.

For a while, correspondence from California to Chicago concentrated on Shapiro's asking Rago's and Gardner's advice on his prospective successor, on enclosed poems, and on young West Coast poets like Michael McClure: "I think he is talented and may be something of a discovery. However, I want you and Belle to help me decide."[145] Another topic was the celebratory-turned-commemorative Thomas issue, almost three years after Gardner had first broached the idea. It had dwindled to "a good, honest, busy, living issue of the magazine, with Dylan Thomas's name prominent on the cover." At this time, the editors were only sure of a Thomas photograph, an elegy especially written for *Poetry* by Edith Sitwell, Gardner's—but not Stevenson's—Thomas worksheets, and a prose piece promised by Shapiro. If the unpublished Thomas manuscripts yielded some good new Thomas poems, and if Roy Campbell, one of Thomas's friends, delivered a high-class article, the issue, padded with fifteen pages of poetry by others, might just avoid becoming merely a "souvenir brochure."[146] It finally appeared under Rago's editorship in November 1955, two months after both Shapiro and Gardner had officially resigned. Sitwell's "Elegy for Dylan Thomas," which out-Thomased even the five previously unpublished poems from 1933 by the Bard himself, opened its poetry section.[147] The highlight of the issue was Shapiro's Laurentian essay "Dylan Thomas," in which he described Thomas's death as "the cause of the most singular demonstration of suffering in recent literary history." Shapiro particularly admired the poet because he "did the impossible in modern poetry. He made a jump to an audience which, we have been taught to believe, does not exist."[148] Where Shapiro saw Thomas as "a male Edna St. Vincent Millay, or perhaps a Charlie Chaplin," Roy Campbell considered him "very manly, a[th]letic, and a great runner, though there was something wrong with his reflexes and he never learned to fight, which was a great pity in one so extremely aggressive and pugnacious."[149] The eight pages dedicated to Thomas's worksheets may have been worth their weight in gold to the Thomas aficionado, but did not add much to the surprisingly varied, exciting quality of this special issue.

Gardner had actually spent her last day at the *Poetry* office excerpting "a meager 10 or 12 pages" from her seventy Thomas worksheets. She "felt no real pangs at leaving *Poetry*. I think I stayed too long but had promised Karl to. Henry [Rago] was friendly but obviously panting to get rid of me. I shall miss only the contact with working poets. The coming upon and encouraging of talent."[150] In one of the very few letters Gardner ever typed, written in September 1955 to Shapiro, she was more explicit about her departure:

> I came back from my heavenly weeks in Edgartown prepared to work through the month of August but Henry's anxiety to get me out of the office was almost funny. I didn't mind in the least as you can imagine, but he was far from friendly in any genuine sense of that word. I scraped my things together, dumped my old red slippers in the wastebasket and scrammed. I tried to say that I had enjoyed "working" with him, that I would love to drop in at the office once in a while for coffee and talk; but he didn't even say "please do" or words to that effect. I can think of nothing I[']ve done to offend him, though I know he articulately resented letters I got from poet friends etc. . . .
>
> You say Henry is the "best man available for the job." I do not agree. . . . [T]here are at least a dozen poets, young and promising, or older and distinguished who are certainly "available" in the sense that they would joyfully undertake to edit Poetry for two years at a crack. Cal Lowell? Roethke? Maybe not Wilbur because he has children. Donald Hall? I don't think that to qualify as available the poet needs must be a Chicagoan. You were not. And if a Chicagoan is desirable (and I do not feel this is true) then Reuel Denney is . . . warmer, more gifted, and more imaginative.[151]

In her letters to others, Gardner remained loyal to Rago and a few weeks later wrote Eberhart that she was "*sure* he'll do well." She explained that she had "wanted to [leave] for more than a year but stayed on because Karl asked me to wait until he also could resign."[152] It "was suggested in a sub rosa sort of way," she continued, "that I edit with a capital E when Karl was to leave but I am *both* inadequate (grossly) and unwilling."[153] But there was never any really serious thought of making Gardner editor. In an interview in 1990, Shapiro emphasized that it "probably was because the magazine had sort of half criticism and half poetry . . . . and I can see that I would not have asked her because of that gap in that part of her interest." In fact in 1954 Shapiro had delivered avuncular advice, discouraging Gardner from branching out into criticism: "I liked your paper. It makes sense and is well written. But all the same I felt a little pang of regret that you should be drawn into the life of making pronouncements. . . . Actually, you could be a good critic, but who would even dream of criticism who has the poetic talent for getting past criticism?"[154] He himself had "felt inept at the handling of criticism, so that I hired . . . people like Wallace Fowlie . . . and Hugh Kenner . . . I needed someone as criticism editor."[155]

In spite of this and all his many public statements against criticism, Shapiro, in truth, was a lively, prolific critic, if an inconsistent and idiosyncratic one, who would get wholeheartedly involved in critical skirmishes. Gardner, on the other hand, for all her sensitive, precise reading of her contemporaries' poems and her great ability to spot their weaknesses and strengths, could not have cared less about the differences between fighting factions such as the New Critics and the Chicago School of Critics. Also, for all her acuity with respect to new poems and poets, Gardner disliked taking final editorial decisions: "Nick [Joost] just came in and tells me I must choose single-handed six pages of poetry by Dec. 30th. I hate to do so without your o.k. especially as there's so little that['s] good."[156] Given that *Poetry* continuously teetered on the brink of insolvency, the magazine needed a manager, taking care of administrative problems, finances, and fundraising. If Shapiro himself was not a good manager by any standards, Gardner, perhaps because of her Boston Brahmin upbringing, trust fund, and Bohemian nature, was totally incompetent in that respect, so in spite of her immense contribution to the renewed fame of *Poetry* during Shapiro's editorship, she certainly could not have become a second Harriet Monroe, even had she wanted to.

But Gardner no longer wished to be involved in the magazine. She could not get along with Rago, a serious, conservative Catholic theologian, who wrote very abstract poetry and "used to brag about the fact that his family, who were funeral directors, were the ones who buried the Capone gang, whenever they shot each other."[157] Shapiro "didn't particularly care for his poetry" either and comparing Rago, "pedantic. . . . non-emotional . . . essentially a professor," to Gardner, he stressed that his successor accepted "poems for the magazine that I never would, that had a great deal of classical literary background; they were . . . literary things. Whereas Belle's poetry . . . is quite personal and even though she keeps her emotions in check, there is an awful lot of emotion sort of boiling under the surface."[158] It is no wonder that Gardner and Rago, poles apart, wished to sever their connection as soon as possible. But Gardner's main reason for leaving was that without Shapiro, *Poetry* had lost its main attraction. In "Postillion for Pegasus," one of the few pieces of criticism Gardner ever wrote, she lauded him as "a wonderful editor to ride postillion to. He . . . has charity, clarity, acute judgment and courage. His respect for other human beings engaged him to his own cost where a lesser man, editor and poet might have withdrawn from engagement."[159]

Chapter Five

"On the Wing," 1955–1958

Birds in a vulnerable land
where there is sea to salt the sand
I rut, and roost, and rot, and sing,
occasionally on the wing.
("Southwest of True North")

Starting out, in 1951, as an insecure, unknown poet without the literary connections she craved, Gardner, thanks to her indefatigable dedication to the
nation's most famous poetry magazine, had moved to the center of a large
literary circle and had made lifelong literary friends. Working for *Poetry* had
greatly increased her self-confidence and boosted her career, but after four
years of volunteering, she was weary. Since she had become Shapiro's help-
mate, some 40,000 poems had passed through her hands, and she was feeling
stale. Galway Kinnell, who himself had sent a considerable number of these
poems over the years, understood: "I am sorry for *Poetry*'s sake that you have
left it. And it must be a loss to Henry Rago. But for your own sake I suspect it
is for the good. Too much reading of one's contemporaries is never an advantage."[1] Others were similarly appreciative. Philip Booth had "heard the very
bad thing that you are leaving Poetry this fall" and felt "lonely . . . knowing
that you are leaving who always read my poems best."[2] John Logan was "sorry
you are leaving *Poetry*. The magazine needs your taste. But I suppose it has
taken too much of your blood"; while the magazine's foreign editor, Wallace Fowlie, had found her "support especially tangible during the interval
between the two regimes."[3] Richard Eberhart wished "it had come about that
you, as excellent poet, had followed in Harriet's footsteps" and wrote to Rago:

"I regret the resignation of Belle Gardner, who threw a lot of force, fire, and imagination into the works."[4]

In his first issue, Henry Rago briefly thanked Gardner: "It is a sadness to announce the resignation of Isabella Gardner, who will be missed by countless contributors as the wise and helpful associate editor she has been."[5] About a year later, Shapiro touched on his editorship of *Poetry* in his correspondence with Gardner: "I feel hostile to [Rago] at this point. He's been quite the big shot. I'm a dilly at picking people for jobs: Ellen, Stanley [Pargellis] and Henry. . . . Still, POETRY is good. I always liked it better when I wasn't on it. Not meant as a remark about your job. You did the bulk of the work for years."[6] Julia Bartholomay, a subscriber to *Poetry* from her childhood in the 1930s onward, had joined the board in the 1970s and become its president. She had served with editors Daryl Hine, John Frederick Nims, and Joseph Parisi and regarded the Shapiro era "as a vital, exciting one . . . . one of its most productive, yet challenging periods" and Gardner as "a more knowledgeable and intuitive critic" than Shapiro. She did think, though, "there was a need for a Henry Rago. . . . [H]is editorship greatly increased private and public support and put the magazine on a more stable financial basis."[7] Under Shapiro *Poetry*'s finances had indeed hit "rock bottom," as Billy Collins wrote in his introduction to *Dear Editor: A History of* Poetry *in Letters* (2002); he dismisses Shapiro's reign as "one of the stormiest editorships," but he gives Rago much credit for imaginative special issues that had in fact been planned by Shapiro's team.[8] In 1989 Shapiro, in long retrospect, thought "Belle was right about Rago as editor. It should have been somebody else. He over-edited. Belle, who was not given to unpleasantries, called him Ragout."[9]

Gardner herself, helped by analysis, was "a reasonably round and solid apple now and can settle for a blister on the skin and the vestige of a worm at the core. I am blessed with a curiously resilient autonomous kind of jubilance about just being and seeing that has been constant even in bleakest times and is certainly a fact now (with the added plus of a loving marriage)."[10] She mourned her temporary creative aridity, for at the close of 1954 Gardner was so nervous about her forthcoming book that she spent much of her time hounding Houghton Mifflin about galleys, publicity, book jackets, and the like, her imperious manner, which had become more prominent over the years, reducing at least one of its employees to tears. As always, she read a lot (John Ciardi's translation of Dante's *Inferno*, the Bible, the Swiss historian Jacob Burkhardt, and her "usual sedative dose of detective stories") but the only poem she wrote in months was the songlike "Canzonetta" inspired by Robert and Lee's five-year-old son, Stewart: "Strut your stride / Raising praising choosing losing never hide- / ing, heeled by the hope that hounds your hunting / Sound your horn Astound your dawn and Ride"(72).[11] She read and cherished E. E. Cummings's love poems and read and commented on Gregory Corso's; she read French with a woman who taught at Elmhurst College and translated Villon; she had a frantic Christmas with Rose (home from boarding school), Daniel, and Bob's son, and an alcoholic New Year's Eve at the Maurice Donohues', but these activities and festivities masked her apprehensive anticipation of the first reactions to the galleys of her book.

One of her first blurbs came from an unexpected quarter. Aristocratic, angular Dame Edith Sitwell swept bejeweled and turbaned through America on one of her dramatic poetry-reading tours, alighted in Chicago in February 1955 and was carried away by Gardner's poetry and personality; according to the *Chicago Tribune* looking "like a medieval carving . . . [Sitwell] leaned forward in her chair with a warm friendly glow in her voice and manner as she described Isabella Gardner as a most talented young woman poet."[12] A month later, the *New York Times* quoted Sitwell's blurb for Gardner's forthcoming book: "I believe Isabella Gardner to be a very distinguished poet . . . . I can think of no young woman of our time whose poetry shows so much promise—indeed, achievement." (Sitwell was then recording for Caedmon, the *Times* noted, when "a small frown appeared on her face because the room next to the recording studio got noisy. The engineer furiously drew up a sign and hung it outside the door. It read: 'Danger. Keep Out. Poet Reading.'")[13] Sitwell gave Gardner "new strength and IMPETUS."[14] Also, just before *Birthdays from the Ocean* came out, Shapiro took a moment to recall how far Gardner, who had "depended so on Karl's judgment," had come since their first meeting:[15]

> The way you have mastered your style is something to impress anyone. In a sense, you can coast on your control now. Not forever but for a time. One thing writers have to guard against is change! You can't disrupt yourself or your readers; you can only lead them, lead yourself, to the gentle turn. I'm also very happy about Sitwell's opinion of you. It couldn't be otherwise but you have a kind of fierce shrinking-violetness in you. It is part of your charm and beauty. You are so lucky to have matured as a person before publishing your work: you are beginning in perfection. I have a kind of fear almost that you will become too well known. Partly it is your presence that will carry you where even poetry can't. You are that strange mixture of pure talent and compelling presence (personality) that makes for fame. I could envy you if I didn't wish so much for you.[16]

As if this were not enough, William Carlos Williams sent Houghton Mifflin, unasked, a "token of [his] admiration" after reading her poems: "I have been much moved by them and surprised that I have not long since been acquainted with this writer. . . . The poems seem to me most remarkable because of what they reveal of the character of the author, her straightforwardness and the un-flinching character of her mind. Her use of rhyme is something to be proud of. I wish her all success and shall back her henceforth in whatever she undertakes. My curiosity over what she will do next is thoroughly aroused."[17]

Delmore Schwartz, who was at the time a *Partisan Review* editor and had not yet succumbed to alcoholism and madness, wrote an official blurb: "Many of Miss Gardner's poems make me wish that I had written them, a feeling which must be the most intimate form of admiration, and one which other poets surely will have." He added: "I'm afraid this may have a little note of the pompous in it, but the truth is that I don't get too much practice in expressing admiration."[18] Eberhart's blurb described Gardner as a "wild tiger lily .... conjuror.... true poet . . . regenerator of the exact, possessor and passer of wisdom in sensory signs"; Gardner thanked him: it "put some of the tiger back in this drooping lily."[19] With all these accolades under her belt before *Birthdays*'s official publication date of March 25, 1955, Gardner had no reason to be drooping.

More praise came in from family and friends, who had received advance copies. William Congdon loved her "dear vulnerability"; Oscar Williams congratulated Houghton Mifflin on publishing Gardner's "sharp metaphysical lyricism, facet-bright ambiguity, philosophic insights, a love of words and an understanding of the human condition"; Mary Manning was surprised into uncharacteristic high praise as she had never "been so impressed by a first book of poems."[20] T. S. Eliot sent his Harvard chum Peabo "[c]ongratulations on Isabella's poems, which HM sent me. There is some very good stuff here."[21] Gardner's parents were finally proud of their daughter and decided to show it by throwing her a tea and cocktail party on Green Hill on publication day for which they invited over a hundred and fifty people, a mixed bag of Boston Brahmins and business friends (the Aldriches, Coolidges, Curtises, Delanos, Eliots, Jameses, Paines, and Whitneys), Peabo's old friends who had made it in the literary scene (poet Archibald MacLeish at Harvard and editor Edward Weeks at the *Atlantic Monthly*), old Boston friends of Gardner's (Betty Farley and her husband, Charles Stockton; Robert Kennedy and his wife, Gerta; Mary Manning and her husband, Mark De Wolfe Howe) and literary ones (Conrad Aiken, Richard Eberhart, Wallace Fowlie, Donald Hall, Nicholas Joost, Violet Lang, Robert Lowell and Elizabeth Hardwick, Oscar Williams). Gardner had somewhat mixed feelings about the celebration, wondering whether she would seem ostentatious as she had imagined one with other poets and close family friends, without business and literary lions, but was grateful that her parents wanted to share their pleasure in her achievement.

Upon her return to Elmhurst, Gardner gave Robert an account of her hectic celebratory days East. She had a reading in Cambridge that he had organized for her, and she remembered taking "the edge of panic off my nervousness with two or three cocktails at just the right time" and so enjoying her parents' party in Brookline after all, even with their mother rather ill, though bearing up. She then left for New York, where she had cocktails with the Sitwells ("Poor Sir Osbert! What a gallant desperate ruin! I left in 1/2 an hour—I couldn't stand it") and dinner with Joseph Bennett, Delmore Schwartz, and Oscar Williams ("Oscar spent an hour vilifying Karl . . . and went on to attack . . . every one who has praised me . . . [W]hat a battleground his soul must be"). The next day, Tuesday, she saw her old friend Barbara Ransom Jopson for lunch and had dinner with Shirley and Lem Ayers ("Lem has a unique . . . kind of anemia and he feels dreadfully all the time"); on Wednesday she saw Williams for cocktails at noon ("I wished I hadn't") and Shag Donohue for lunch ("He's doing better than anyone though unhappily divorced . . . separated from his children, and jobless. But he has realized he's alcoholic and hasn't had a drink for 6 months"); Anabel Holland and Myra and Lou Cholden flew in from Washington in the afternoon ("Anabel just over a nervous break-down. Milly Levin joined us at 5—desperate and drinking too much because she is in love with Maurice Donohue . . . who she sees about twice a year.") The last day, Thursday, she had breakfast at the Algonquin with Anneke, who was accompanied by a writer friend with a large manuscript ("He is 6 ft 5, negro, blue-eyed, long-headed, black kinky hair—beautiful face and quite a beautiful person."); they then visited Lorina, Gardner paid Anneke's debts and boarded the train back to Chicago. She was nearly in a state of collapse on arrival but survived an autograph party where she sold almost a hundred books and then was the honoree at an intimate party organized by Helen Donohue, where she was touched to receive gifts representing a bell from all present. After all these festivities, Gardner was glad to get home, tend her bulbs and rake leaves.[22]

She was on tenterhooks, waiting for reviews to appear. The first one, by Josephine Jacobsen, lauded *Birthdays from the Ocean* as "gusty, tart, feminine, . . . high-spirited . . . and . . . successful" but disappointed Gardner, as Jacobsen mainly caught the bright casing of her melodic poems and missed the desolation and death underpinning most of the book.[23] Taking personally this review by a poet from his hometown of Baltimore, Karl Shapiro flew off the handle: "I was shocked about Josephine Jacobsen's review. It sounds stupid. She must be jealous, although I would never think of her that way. In any case she is a desperate personality, raging at the moment because her son, who is about 18, is getting married. She has lived an intense high-society-old-Catholic-Maryland-family-life and has always been frustrated because of her own poetry, which has never gotten out of Baltimore."[24] Admittedly, Karl was as desperate (and Evalyn more so) as his Fulbright at Berkeley was coming to an end. Seattle had put out feelers, but "following in Ted's [Roethke] footsteps is not an appetizing prospect. He crucifies himself for the students." He was therefore thinking of moving to nearby University of California at Davis, which had offered him a job, though at $6,300 only. Meanwhile, at Berkeley, it was "wonderful to say to a bunch of kids that Eliot and Pound are the enemies of human nature and spontaneity and progress."[25]

In the *New York Times* Selden Rodman extolled Gardner's voice as "the most original" among books by Merrill Moore (the psychiatrist who had written more than 50,000 sonnets in between patients), Elder Olson, Lyon Phelps, and others, but thought her "verbal agility . . . tiring."[26] Forgetting that for a first book of poetry rating a review in the *New York Times* was an achievement in itself, Gardner was in sackcloth and ashes, but her shining knight Shapiro ran to the rescue once more: "Selden is another disappointed poet and although he is extremely honest, his views are limited by his belief that poetry is just another form of politics."[27] Roethke was angry, too, Kizer reported and quoted him as calling Gardner the "most promising woman poet writing in English."[28] Her friends agreed: in *Chicago Magazine* Galway Kinnell extolled Gardner's "lyric brightness" and "powerful writing," though he signaled a weakness in holding a longer poem together; and Wallace Fowlie praised without stint this "work of significance, of achievement in the art of poetry" standing "securely by itself" and pinpointed "the ancient theme of exile" that pervades Gardner's poetry.[29] In a review in the mainstream *Saturday Review of Literature,* Edith Sitwell reaffirmed her opinion of Gardner as "a very accomplished natural poet": "There is no flopping, no untidily hanging about, none of that unfortunate mincing and teetering that is to be found in so many poems written by women."[30] Gardner was grateful for Kinnell's review and was of the same mind with respect to her failure to sustain longer poems: "I think it is my (a *feminine*??) lack of intellectual muscle that defeats me."[31] Congdon disagreed: "[I]t takes plenty of intellectual energy to gather and seize and spear it the way you do," adding a day later with his usual self-assurance: "Anything *complete* is sustainment. What more do you want? Quantity? Yours are quick and short. Mine are quick and short. But they are eternal."[32]

Over the months an unprecedented number of rave reviews about a first book of poems appeared all over America: in literary quarterlies from New York's *Partisan* to southern *Sewanee,* in little magazines from New York's *Voices* to the *New Orleans Poetry Journal,* and in newspapers from Boston to San Francisco; sometimes solo, more often in combination with reviews of other poets. In Gardner's Chicago, John Frederick Nims bracketed Gardner with Randall Jarrell, who was known as a (war) poet and incisive critic. But Jarrell got much the worst of it, for though Nims was sure his *Selected Poems* would be "one of the year's most highly touted volumes of poetry," admiration for Jarrell's work remained to him "a mystery into which I hope some day to be initiated";

Gardner's book on the other hand seemed to him "the finest work by a new poet that I have seen in many years."[33] Like Lowell, Jarrell was constantly trying to prove to the world that he was the number one poet among his male compeers and to be bested by a mere woman, a novice, called for serious measures. One put-down was not enough; using his rapier sharp critical intelligence in two negative reviews, he put Gardner to the sword in *Harper's Magazine* and delivered the final blow in the *Yale Review*. Quoting "mean ole Randall Jarrell" in *Harper's*—the "poems have enough personal charm to make you forget their influences and self-consciousness but not enough to make you forget that they are never, quite, good poems"—Gardner surrendered at the first strike: "He's probably right."[34]

From Davis, Shapiro wrote to commiserate: "Randall is always on the watch for a new target. He is famous for this and has taken a pot shot at every new and old poet. . . . He's whammed Stevens, M Moore etc and eventually changed his mind. . . . You know your own worth and you must never be shaken by such things. Poetry is a jungle but most of the lions and tigers have rubber teeth."[35] Jarrell's were sharp. Baring them in the *Yale Review,* he began by calling Gardner a "fresh, individual, irregularly appealing poet" but then bit deeply: she "almost never, as yet, manages to write good poems"; her world is "a costume-party for which she has just breathlessly overdressed herself, and these poems are her stray, tinselly, gold-leafy entrance into it."[36] Disbelieving the praise that had been heaped upon her by other critics, Gardner was undone by Jarrell's attacks and felt "naked in my own eyes and grotesque and ashamed."[37] She realized she was sinking in "a repulsively egotistical morass" but would not be comforted and mentioned Jarrell almost obsessively in her correspondence.[38]

Yet she had a wonderful summer with her Rose and Barbara Jopson and her daughter in Edgartown on Martha's Vineyard. At Verde Valley School, Rose had literally been counting the days to be with her mother again; her homesickness evident in poor grades. She did not fit in well and was lonely, writing her "queridos padres": "Five more class days and 14 more days; oh joy, joy, joy! . . . The flowers are coming out on the prickly pears now, great yellow ones with scarlet hearts. Every day is getting more beautiful, but I'd rather be home."[39] After Edgartown, where Gardner's "beautiful bountiful womanful child" was "gold in the sun and bold in the dazzling water" ("At a Summer Hotel," 69), Elmhurst in August was dull for Rose until Dan came back from Seymour, though "aggressive and swaggery" as usual after one of his visits with his father—but at any rate he had a father who cared.[40] "It is good to be with [Bob] again," Gardner wrote Robert. "He is almost ready to start building some houses and has just been offered a big job renting space for a new office bldg which a N.Y. firm is building here. I hope it works out as he has been strapped financially and if it happens and if he can sell the space it will mean both prestige and money."[41]

Gardner family problems engaged her. Her brother John and his wife, Susan, had a very ill baby but displayed typical New England reticence: "Poor Jacobus. He is as lonely as anyone I know. More so perhaps because he does not acknowledge this to himself."[42] Because Kitty was coming to visit, Gardner frantically rushed around buying silky sheets, snowy blankets, fancy imported foods, and proper cups, saucers, and wineglasses, but to her delighted surprise they enjoyed each other. Robert and Lee asked Gardner to take care of their children in the event of their deaths, but, though honored, Gardner presaged that they would outlive her by decades. "Of course I worry often and acutely about what my demise wd. mean for Rose and Dan. Their fathers would not permit Bob to bring them up and though Bob would want to it would be dreadfully difficult for him sans me. I of course fiercely want them to stay *together*. I think Van and Seymour would be happy (or could be 'convinced') that it would be wise for them to be 'raised' by you and Lee, or George and Tania."[43] Gardner had sent Van a copy of *Birthdays from the Ocean,* and he had politely acknowledged it: "Ma'am, I'm very proud to have known you.... I know what it means, none better than I. What a pity Yeats is not with us now."[44]

She wrote Congdon that another former lover, Erskine Childers, had rejected her poetry, and her cousin was sure that "the man (his past rel. to your 'devotion''worship') cannot accept the challenge—Few artists can, [a] man from a woman."[45] Women artists and career women in general were viewed with suspicion at midcentury. A woman's American dream was supposed to be a suburban kitchen with the latest household appliances, and "Father Knows Best" was one of the most popular TV shows. In 1955 Adlai Stevenson told the graduating class of Smith College that they should participate in political life by becoming wives and mothers—his ex-wife Ellen Stevenson disagreed—and a year later *Life Magazine* published interviews with distinguished male psychiatrists who argued that female ambition was at the root of mental illness in wives, emotional upsets in their husbands, and homosexuality in boys. Around this time, too, the famous theologian William Lynch, spiritual advisor of Allen Tate and his wife Caroline Gordon, warned Gordon that "[m]arriage must be an adult relationship ... between a man who maturely commands and a woman who maturely obeys," implying that the main reason for the failure of their marriage was her inability to submit.[46] Likewise, Gardner's spiritual advisor, the psychiatrist Kraus, stated categorically that women belonged to their men, and men to themselves.

The men of letters clustered around literary magazines such as *Kenyon Review* and *Partisan Review* and ran the show at the major universities, dispensing jobs and grants to one another. Paramount, perhaps, among the male critics, was John Crowe Ransom, founding editor of the *Kenyon Review*, which by foregrounding the text and by emphasizing contemporary and American writers had changed the way in which poetry and prose were received, but in his belief that most women were intellectually inferior to men, Ransom spoke for his times. In his (in)famous essay "The Poet as Woman," he had argued that a woman is "[l]ess pliant, safer as a biological organism" than a man and as such "indifferent to intellectuality." Among women poets only Marianne Moore he thought "[n]ot deficient in [intellect]."[47]

Ransom could make or break literary careers, but he was comparatively circumspect. Much worse was Gardner's tireless correspondent Edward Dahlberg, autobiographical novelist, poet, and mystic critic. Their correspondence had started in the course of Gardner's work for *Poetry*, when she had tried to mediate between Dahlberg and Conrad Aiken after Dahlberg had attacked Aiken's *Ushant* (1952) in a vicious ad hominem way and Shapiro had tried in vain to calm both. (Aiken never forgave Shapiro for defending his decision to publish the review, nor Gardner for defending Shapiro.)[48] When Gardner left *Poetry*, she was pleased to have found in Dahlberg a correspondent who had published six books, who was a friend of Herbert Read's, and who was gratified to receive her long literary letters and responded in kind. With only one book published, Gardner took on the role of Dahlberg's eager pupil, tolerating his verbal abuse in an almost masochistic manner. When Gardner once dared to disagree with Dahlberg, firm adherent of the male superiority principle, he warned her that neither "you, nor any female, will ever rule me." A few days later, he graciously added that Gardner might "not even realize that you endeavor to rule me, and I am a male, and [in] spite of great feeling for you, I cannot countenance that."[49] Dahlberg was a paranoid misogynist and tireless attacker of communists and "pederasts," but his outbursts are more extreme versions of generally held male sentiments at midcentury. Although she had fought against her predestined fate as a second Kitty and was bossy rather than subservient in character, Gardner was also a woman of her time. She endorsed Robert Graves's saying that "no woman poet has been true poet and born and mothered children" and accepted her role of "nurturing and cherishing and soothing and stimulating of the human beings whose lives have touched mine; and whose needs I *cannot* deny. . . . The women . . . poets I know of who write truly and well are chickless and cockless. I cannot so be."[50]

In the fall of 1955, in spite of Jarrell, Gardner professed to have "a sound and even eager feeling of well-being. Bob is well and working on new projects, Dan is well and a successful and happy 6th grader. Rosy is well and at last alertly involved at school. . . . And now that I'm not at *Poetry* I go in [to Chicago] but once a week and spend hours at the library where I at least make scratches on a pad of paper. Bob and I go out very little and see very few people."[51] As she had more time to think, however, doubts about being a suburban housewife were creeping in. Her gay confidant Congdon, artist, outsider, and loner who had never had a long-term live-in relationship, counseled her about her marriage and art: "*Feeling* your work, I can't help but feel, whether your husband and you like it or not, that your real reality is in that work—Not that it could be what it is without Bob, but (1) the work should have all precedence—(2) it's sin to have guilty feelings about God's presence in you. Bob will have to love you more and need you less."[52] Bob McCormick was, in fact, a far less demanding husband than most at the time; certainly less so than Seymour had been. He had not begrudged Gardner her many hours at *Poetry,* although he thought her work there was to the detriment of her own writing. But as Gardner's fame grew, he came to mind the poets and hangers-on who swooped down on his Elmhurst house, "weeping in their beers."[53] Because of his former alcoholism, Gardner usually did not drink in the evenings when they were home alone, but when there were visitors, Bob would be the only sober one. Her fellow poets and friends (among them Conrad Aiken, Lee Anderson, John Berryman, Elizabeth Bishop, Paul Carroll, Ruth Herschberger, John Logan, Karl Shapiro, and James Wright) all drank immoderately; it was almost a mark of true poets. After a few years of sobriety with Bob, Gardner started tippling again. When her brother Robert took her to task for overindulging during a hectic short trip East (when she had spent time with Anneke Van Kirk, her old friends Shirley Ayers, Henry Levin, and Bob and Gerta Kennedy, given a reading with Archibald MacLeish, signed books at Houghton Mifflin's, met with Paul Brooks and Dorothy de Santillana, and had breakfasted, lunched, or supped with parents and siblings) Gardner apologized:

> While on this trip I did as always drink every day twice what I normally do which is stupid but seems necessary. . . . I know by now that I am in no danger of being alcoholic. I do "use" it regularly. I went to see Kraus on my return from Boston. . . . I told him exactly what I drank on the trip (and all my feelings) and told him my daily 6 or 7 drinks here which he has always known of and he again assured me they cannot injure my health nor my psyche. These judgments are based on his intimate knowledge of me and his appraisal of my appearance and his knowledge that my marriage is deeply satisfying and successful as are my relations with my children etc. . . . .
>
> Truthfully I am soberly happier in myself than I have ever been and even though I gripe about this rather hobbling period in my writing . . . I am quite certain inside that good things will be coming.[54]

Birthdays from the Ocean was hugely successful for a first book of poetry; it sold out and went into its second printing within six months. Elizabeth Bishop had assured Gardner in October 1955 that she need not feel concerned that Marianne Moore did not seem to like her poetry (she "is often apt to make moral judgments, or fasten on something really unimportant and go by that. You can see it in the astounding and peculiar way her mind works in her own poems"), but she had grumbled fretfully to Houghton Mifflin because she had not received Gardner's book, while Gardner had her *Poems: North and South*.[55] In March 1956 Bishop wrote Gardner's publisher that she was "the best new poet in some time, or at any rate the best I've seen. . . . The most satisfactory thing about reading her poetry is that one feels there is intelligence behind it— real brains—brains and a sympathetic, sincere (a tired old word, but the right one), nature."[56] She connected to Gardner's feeling for geography, love of birds, and keen observation of the natural world: "as Delmore S. [Schwartz] says—I wish I'd written 'the buffalo is robe and dust.'"[57]

Gardner was equally impressed by Bishop. "Am distressed that Auden rather than Bishop won the prize," she told Robert on the occasion of W. H. Auden's *Shield of Achilles* winning the National Book Award for 1956. She did not mention that she also had been nominated for *Birthdays*—the remaining five contestants being John Ciardi, Donald Hall, Randall Jarrell, Adrienne Rich, and William Carlos Williams. Logan jested: "There is more motion / In one Birthday from the Ocean / Than in all the noddin / Of W. Homer Auden."[58] Gardner had every reason to be proud. In June 1955 the *New York Times* had listed *Birthdays* among "100 of the Year's Outstanding Books" with three other books of poetry: Auden's *Shield of Achilles,* Stephen Spender's *Collected Poems,* and Lyon Phelps's verse drama *The Gospel Witch*.[59] Jarrell's *Selected Poems* was not mentioned. In December, *Birthdays* was one of eight books of poetry among the year's 250 best. New were Bishop's *North and South*, Robert Graves's *Collected Poems,* Tristam Coffin's and Jarrell's *Selected Poems,* as well as the Johnson edition of Emily Dickinson's *Poems;* among the mainly male, middle-aged, arrived poets, Gardner was the only female newcomer.[60]

Elizabeth Bishop won the Pulitzer Prize for 1956 and was "awfully pleased" that Gardner had been quick to congratulate her but confessed to feeling "rather embarrassed by this business: surely it's never been given to anyone for such a miserable quantity of work before. It was rather nice to receive it here, though, I must confess, because it is so well-known and now I don't have to convince my Brazilian friends personally anymore that I really do write poetry sometimes!"[61] A year later, on one of her trips back to America, Bishop and her lover, Brazilian socialite and architect Lota de Macedo Soares, visited the McCormicks at Elmhurst: "We did have a lovely breakfast with you; Lota enjoyed meeting you so much, and I am horrified when I think how condescendingly I asked the inhabitant of a Mies v der R house if she was at all interested in modern architecture!"[62]

By this time, Gardner's skin-deep euphoria had evaporated, for death had intruded. In June 1955 apropos of reviews of *Birthdays,* she had stated that the "'sadness' that is there is because I so celebrate and love the world I see, hear, touch and taste. It is perhaps the lacrimae rerum that is surely part of all art—even the most baroque and my style is often (?) baroque. Some people are offended by the stated recognition on my part of the skull behind the roses but I celebrate the roses while acknowledging the skull."[63] Gardner had always been obsessed by death, but her life had not yet been affected by the loss of loved ones. An aunt and her maternal grandmother had died, but these deaths had touched her only indirectly. But in August 1955 her beloved Lem Ayers died of cancer at forty; Shirley had hidden the terminal nature of his disease from him and all their friends. For him, Gardner wrote "In Memory of Lemuel Ayers, Scene Designer," an elegy in the Skeltonic manner ideally suited to the ironic joker Ayers had been: "I that indulgently / am still allowed to be / address these lines to the / 'Late Lemuel Ayers' who / did not elect to do / his dying young" (52). In January 1956, Kitty's eldest son, Jimmy, just twenty-one, died gruesomely in a fire at a ski lodge. Gardner had come to admire her elder sister who, having pulled through debilitating illnesses in her youth and being locked in a loveless marriage to an ill husband, now had to survive the worst tragedy in her life—which she did, held up by the stays of convention.

A few months later Gardner went to Arizona to see Rose act in *Our Town.* Twenty years before, Gardner had starred in a summer stock production directed by Rosy's father, with Thornton Wilder himself as the stage manager. Gardner drenched Bob's handkerchief. On the same trip she went to Los Angeles and visited her aunt Catherine Mayes, Reginald Pole, and Martin and Katherine Manulis in Hollywood. She also saw Myra and Lou Cholden, who were now living in southern California, where Lou was experimenting with LSD as a cure for psychiatric disorders. "Lou and Aldous Huxley are inseparable," Gardner informed Robert and told him of Lou's forthcoming television documentary "Out of Darkness" in which he brought a catatonic woman back to light and speech.[64] But soon after, disaster struck when their car, with Myra at the wheel and their children in the back, crashed. Lou threw himself across his wife to shield her and sustained fatal injuries. Gardner flew out for the funeral and, back in Elmhurst, immediately sent off some honest, heartfelt advice to the widow: "Remember that your grief for some time to come will get tougher, not easier. . . . *Practically*—get some-one to get you black-bordered cards without yr. name engraved. You will find that thanking people for notes and wires will *help.* A part-time job in a month or so . . . will help. Eat all you can."[65] (Then, typically, Gardner addressed the letter to a wrong number, received it back, got testy with the postman for what she regarded as the post office's ineptitude, and sent it off again with addenda.)

Gardner was surrounded by death that year. Other friends, though not as close, died young: wild, charming, ever-changing writer Violet Lang of Hodgkin's disease; and Lou Cholden's classmate at Tuley High, Chicago wunderkind Isaac Rosenfeld, of a heart attack. "As Lou said, when I last saw him—'The witches are flying,'" Gardner quoted.[66] Dark clouds had begun to gather. Rose was miserable in Arizona, pining for a Mexican boy (known for preying on lonely Americanas) she had met during one of her school trips, trying her hand at acting and writing, but getting poor grades and, in all probability, experimenting with sex and drugs. Helen had left Maurice Donohue, and he was marrying Virginia on the rebound. Gardner predicted their marriage would not last but was relieved that he was sober on their wedding day and, in the end, had asked Bob and not his ex-wife's lover, Jack Butler, to be his best man. Helen married Jack after *his* divorce, but Helen and Maurice's troubled daughter Deborah took thirty-seven aspirins in the aftermath of the wedding: "The whole business is a dreadful tragic muddle."[67]

The summer of 1956 brought no relief. Gardner and Rosy shared a cottage in Wellfleet with Lulix von Simson and her children (Gardner paying two-thirds of the rent), but as she was the only one driving a car, however badly, she was at the beck and call of all, which irritated and exhausted her. For once, not even the Atlantic could restore her. Swimming naked had lost its appeal as Gardner was being stalked; she did not report the culprit to the Wellfleet police as they did not look kindly on the nudist frolics of the town's artistic summer colony. These months were wasted as far as writing was concerned, so she read widely and deeply (Blake, Rilke's *Duino Elegies,* Li Po, and Kierkegaard) and let fly long letters to all her friends. Much of her energy went into promoting the work of Anneke's middle-class black writer friend, Smith Oliver, whom she believed to be an extraordinary talent with a fabulous ear for dialogue, though as yet a rough diamond.[68] She sent his stories and plays to Conrad Aiken, Saul Bellow, Princess Caetani at *Botteghe Oscure,* Lillian Hellman, Elizabeth Hardwick and Robert Lowell, Mary Manning at the Poets Theatre in Cambridge, and Karl and Evalyn Shapiro.

Writing from Union Pier (which Evalyn detested for its lack of privacy and where Seymour and Dan as well as Helen and Jack Butler also summered), the Shapiros proved critical. Evalyn believed that "to an absolute critic an evaluation is done in cold blood," and doubted if Gardner, so struck by Oliver's personality, could "see his *writing*?"[69] Karl considered Oliver's work too pale and polished: "The thing I dislike deeply about the Jewish writer or the Negro writer or the Catholic writer etc. is that it all ends in an appeal. It should be the opposite—it should be 'I don't give a damn—I am what I am—take it or leave it'. . . . The American Negro is at the beginning of something—horrible or wonderful—whatever—but nobody is going to listen to him intellectualize! Jesus!"[70] In Gardner's response, she went overboard, comparing Oliver to Cervantes and Swift. She noted that the Poets Theatre did not want to produce his plays because his use of the word "nigger" would make their white audiences wince, while black actors threw up their hands in horror because he wrote about the snobberies of the middle-class southern black:

> He is writing as a *man* about *men* and the men he knows best are coloured. . . . He is speaking *to* mortals *of* mortals—*of particular* mortals of course and necessarily, but essentially Unamuno's "man of flesh and bone" not just *a* or *the* coloured man. . . . [N]either in anger nor in love does he draw a colour line in a polemical way. Perhaps this is basically what disturbs readers of every colour. Perhaps the white reader *wants* to be hated and the Negro perhaps cannot endure scorn and indignation from another Negro, *nor* understanding. He *wants* to be a cause not a fallible man and therefore resents Oliver's seeing him as a man.[71]

As a Jew, Shapiro was stung into defending himself in a provocative letter in which he tried to counter Gardner's belief that all true literature transcends racism and politics:

> Smith may not be crude *enough*. If I were Smith I would think (as he does) that publishing and producing is a White business. No Negro writer will ever be any good until he gives up that split personality. I don't know one good Negro writer in the English language. Name one. Wright, another Margaret Cunningham [Danner]. Ellison. Hughes. All bellboys and boot-polishers. I wish I could be a Negro just long enough to create a Negro audience for one poem or story or play. It would be the first time, except for the spirituals. "There goes Richard Wright," says the American Jewish writer with a Jewish-poetic beard, at the Deux Magots, or however you spell them. Afraid to come back to New York. Belle, it doesn't matter about Broadway and all that. It doesn't matter about Smith making the Negr[oes] come to him. AND IT DOESN'T MATTER WHETHER THE WHITES AND THE HEBREWS COME TO HIM OR NOT. I wouldn't trade one chorus of Satchmo's for [all] the so-called Negro literature ever printed. . . .
>
> This isn't purely academic. It is the same as the Jewish writer's problem. Whenever I am mentioned in a Jewish anthology or encyclopedia, the idea is that I have been accepted by non-Jews: therefore I am acceptable. The meaning of this psychology is that there are no standards for the Jewish writer today except outside standards. But my ambition is to be accepted by Jewish standards or, if

they are non-existent, to create them. The Negro like the Jew despises the one who gives in. And the Negro writer, when there is one, will not give in but be the more Negro for all that. . . . [T]o the American black man there is no language but English, *but he doesn't have to speak it Properly!* The more improperly the better.

On the other hand I distrust Primitivism: the Palm Wine Drinkard etc. I love the primitive when it's real and it's almost never anything but Grandma Moses and Henry Luce publicity and Haiti. . . . Putting it over on another "race" isn't much of a bull's eye. Putting it over your own bunch is the real jackpot.[72]

Gardner agreed in part:

I love Satchmo too. It is *easy* to. He's pure and hot and black. . . . Smith Oliver presents everyone who reads him with a problem—not the least of which is *embarrassment*. . . . He *is* a hybrid. . . . He *cannot* and *should* not be a Satchmo of writing because he *is* not. It would be arrant fakery. He is the end result of aristocratic white mated to black with white genes preponderant and brought up in an anti-'nigger' (black African) lower middle class respectable snobbery toward poor white and deep black. . . . [H]e cannot be expected or wanted to think purely as a Black man anymore than my son Dan . . . can or should be expected to think and feel solely and purely as a Jew. I know how you feel about the hybrid but that it seems to me *is* the crucial theme to-day—not the blackness or the Hebrew-ness or the Celt-ness but the brew.[73]

Evalyn rated another letter in which Gardner protested that her compassion for Oliver's raceless and jobless state was separate from her critical judgment: "I am, believe me, tough minded when it comes to writing." She rejected Evalyn's suggestion to try prose herself: "I haven't the courage to screw to the sticking point of hurting people and I see no way out of that in prose. The abstractions of poetry are less wounding."[74] Gardner had been trying to fuse her love for poetry and drama by writing a verse play, but she abandoned the attempt after months of work.

Shapiro was "a little upset" by their correspondence. In September he apologized from Lincoln, Nebraska, where he had taken up the editorship of the *Prairie Schooner,* which had been publishing mainly fiction:

The sense of my position was really that I couldn't judge the stuff to my own satisfaction. This disturbs me for a personal reason—that I now have to read lots of fiction and be intelligent and perceptive about it. I certainly agree about the hybrid as a crucial theme for Negroes or Jews or moderns in general. Your view of Oliver's work is better than mine for that reason—that is, my tendency is to think of the issues as black-and-white and not brown or gray. That must be an unconscious motivation of a pure Jew who intellectually refutes racial difference. I withdraw my stupid remark about Satchmo. I wish I had your insight about this whole business.[75]

In a gesture of reconciliation, he solicited one of Oliver's stories for his first *Schooner* issue and, with true eagerness, poetry from Gardner. Gardner buried the hatchet but continued to harass other friends in Oliver's behalf, arguing rudely with Elizabeth Hardwick, for one, who was dead against him. (Lowell thought Oliver was promising.)

In all, the summer of 1956 had been arduous with no bright spots—not even Gardner's first meeting with Allen Tate, who did not make much of an impression: "Poor Tate has an ulcer. We spoke fondly of you and Evalyn."[76] Gardner was "so happy to be home and with Bob again" that she did not mind that their Italian housekeeper had left. Myra, in need of comfort, came to visit with her children. After her departure Gardner kept her abreast of the ongoing misadventures of Maurice and Helen's Deborah, from cutting classes to switching schools without her parents' knowledge. Her Rosy, at least, was doing well enough at Valley Verde School, she had told herself, so she was shocked when, after Rosy had eaten somebody's ice cream, the democratic student council, knowing that she had visited a psychiatrist in the past, drew up a resolution "saying she should be punished by social probation *unless* her misdeed was caused by 'mental illness.'"[77] Gardner was up in arms at this cruel stigmatization and persuaded the school to put her on probation. Soon after, on a school trip to Mexico, Rosy met her Mexican boyfriend without permission and was sent home. Gardner now worried her daughter would not be allowed to graduate, let alone, with her meager marks, get into a good college. Banned to Elmhurst, Rosy roamed Chicago with Deborah, hanging out and picking up men, yet Gardner remained sure that her daughter was a "babe in the woods" compared to Debbie (who was two years younger), although she now agreed with Bob that the relationship was destructive to both friends. As usual, Kraus only reinforced Gardner's shortcomings: "I asked him if there was anything I was doing 'wrong' or not in regard to her and he said 'not one thing.' He said her admiration and feeling for me was both a great compliment and a responsibility."[78] To Gardner's joy, Rosy (whom she described as "nonconformist," while Dan was "conventional") was willing to be analyzed, was allowed to graduate after all, and was to attend Bradford, a small, structured, all-women's junior college in the fall.

Jolted by the deaths of her friends, Gardner was writing again: "Mea Culpa," a narrative poem chastising an arrogantly careless heart surgeon, arriving late while "expected by the families / of the dying, who pay his monstrous fee / and fare, to be God's Almighty's cousin" (63); an elegy for Lou Cholden, "Zei Ge-sund" ("In the preposterous sunlight / we watched them wincingly lower you / into your formal April grave" (50)); and, for Myra, its companion piece, one of Gardner's most anthologized and misinterpreted poems, "The Widow's Yard." In a perfectly mastered and therefore unobtrusive, natural seven-syllable line, this poem confronts her main subject: the impossible necessity to communi-cate. The autobiographical speaker cannot reach out to her newly widowed neighbor and therefore talks about a seemingly safe subject, snails, unfeelingly mentioning their mating habits: their consummation is so slow "in coming that love begun / at dawn may end in fatal sun" (48). The widow retaliates and talks about the slime-secreted openings in their shells, "those little doors which sing / she said, when they are boiled. / She smiled at me when I recoiled" (49). Myra Cholden also misunderstood, and Gardner begged their friend Anabel Holland to explain that "'I'—in my cowardice and non-experience 'recoil' from her courage and realism and that her 'smiling' forgives me and is the measure of her greatness."[79]

Robert, with whom she, as always, shared drafts, disliked these less baroque, yet highly polished poems and did not see that "The Widow's Yard" was about the "touch of two solitudes."[80] Gardner wondered testily how her brother could imagine that "The Widow's Yard" was about snails and suggested she would no longer expose him to her poetry, only to apologize a few days later: "I know that my poetry is going through a phase of change and that it disappoints some people. I am for the time being stripping away the skills and scallops—it is a necessary process and I think eventually I will re-integrate."[81] But Robert, deep in analysis and unsparingly critical of himself and others, could not "accept the testimony of insentient grubs as poetic insight to the condition of my human-ity" and accused Gardner of having "anthropomorphized a snail into a disfig-urement of man." On his moral high horse, he charged her with expecting "an uncompromising alliance and loyalty," needing to be "continually replenished, continually affirmed," and regarding any criticism as "unfaithfulness and apos-tasy."[82] It took Gardner a while to recover from this blow dealt her by her be-loved brother, but she came back, assuring him he was all wrong, for Kraus had shown her that "I can and do *love* but I cannot accept love. I can abet others' success but I cannot *endure* success."[83]

Gardner did have a decidedly ambivalent attitude toward success in life and art: wanting desperately to do well, but messing up when succeeding (as in her debutante days) or discrediting her achievements and focusing on her "fail-ures" (as with *Birthdays*). She had gone back to therapy with Kraus in January 1957 and seemed to trust him unconditionally, because he affirmed everything she did or said, however contradictory:

He did *wonders* for me before. I was *able* to write and finish the book and more important I was able to love a man who is kind and gentle and honorable. But the success of the book threw me. I pretended I minded the bad reviews but it was the good ones that fixed me . . . good! . . . I try in every way I know to make Dr. Kraus think ill of me[;] I implore him to see my fraudulence and wickedness—he says my fraudulence is in pretending I want love when 'a thimbleful can make you vomit.' . . . My drinking, which is increasingly less, Kraus says is a red herring. That I use it to persuade people all's not well with me (not to earn pity but to avert envy). To keep Bob at arms length. Bob and I are *wonderfully* close but occasionally there is that faint odor of sneaked gin to announce that I am *not* all that he thinks I am! So that I will spare him from total commitment and possible loss. . . . I have nurtured and projected the image of a child rejected by her mother because that was more tolerable than the guilt . . . . to Kitty because of her illness and because she was [sent] 'away' . . . for two (or more?) winters in my childhood.

"This may not make a great deal of sense," Gardner allowed, and when Robert did not reply immediately to this confused effusion, she followed it up with another outburst.[84] Kraus's therapy of supportive noninterference was typical of his psychiatric age, but from this reportage, it seems as if both doctor and patient were denying Gardner's growing dependency on alcohol; he was, at any rate, not addressing the emergent problem.

When almost sixty, Gardner confessed to George that she had "drunk too much since the age of 19 when I found that my 'shyness'—my *fear* of people, the strangle in my voice could be eased by booze."[85] Compared to the drinking habits of most of her male literary friends, however, Gardner was, in her early forties, still a moderate drinker. When inebriated, she became dramatic and imperious, flirtatious and vague, but because she was a woman she was censured more severely than her male colleagues, who true to the stereotype of the inspirited poet could get away with boorish behavior. After a visit by Gardner to the Shapiros in Lincoln, Nebraska, Evalyn worried because Karl had been drinking far too much and "stalked about naked . . . [and] frightened us all."[86] Karl himself "felt sheepish about being 'out' last Thursday. I'm not used to good drink, that's about the size of it. I imagine you take as dim a view of this kind of thing as Evalyn does, though I don't. I enjoy everything, almost everything, that happens."[87] In a very frank but deeply depressed letter written the same day, Evalyn analyzed her relationship with Karl: "I like to see him think, and hear him and watch him. When he drinks, he falls apart, and then he has to recover. He can't write as he doesn't remember. *How*, Belle dear, *how* can it help him? It is a backward game. . . . And how long can *I* pretend to be forgiving? I say forgiving, for while infidelities don't touch me they touch the corest core of our whole world. . . . What is at bottom is that obviously I only exist with Karl, truly, and when I can't communicate with him. . . I'm lost."[88] Caring about both Shapiros, Gardner told Karl to slow down on liquor and infidelities and save his marriage. Karl retorted: "It's the only preachy letter anyone has ever written me except my father, who is a babbitty old soul and doesn't know better. . . . I'm writing mainly so you won't think I'm sore at you. My inclination was not to write to you for about ten years."[89] If one may judge from *Edsel* (1971), his autobiographical novel about this period, Shapiro did not change his spots. But the marital breakup was averted for a while and, helped by "loans" from Gardner, the Shapiros could even pay their dentist bills. Earlier, Gardner had helped pay their mortgage but made clear that they were not beholden.

Shapiro then asked Gardner for a contribution for another alcoholic poet, Theodore Roethke, who needed a staggering three hundred dollars per week for intensive analysis "for God knows how long! As you probably know, I am dead against psychoanalysis and the squandering of large fortunes on that sort of hit-and-miss medicine; but there seems to be no other solution to Ted's difficulties."[90] Ever-generous, Gardner also fostered Kinnell's career by offering to have his first book-length manuscript (which he had sent to her for comment and which was sloppy, full of crossings-out, retyping, and addenda) retyped: "Let me, if you will, make that a present to you. A token of faith." She was willing to approach publishers for him, but warned: "I urged H. M. Co to print Philip Booth's book and they turned it down only to have it win the Lamont prize."[91] She also critiqued his poems with care, and writing from Nice, France, Kinnell was "moved by your letter, Belle, not only by its faith in me, but also by the energy and unselfishness which are characteristic of you."[92] Two months later, Kinnell found that he had lost Gardner's correspondence and asked her to spend a few minutes arranging his poems into a presentable manuscript. There Gardner drew the line; the definitive order of his poems should be his decision, she told him, then relented and made suggestions, which he treated, like her mail, in a rather cavalier fashion.

Gardner also believed in John Logan's talent and gave much attention to his work. Logan enclosed poems, reviews, and short stories in his many letters, asking Gardner for comment, which she gave in conscientious detail. Logan was "deeply grateful" for her "heart-full, honest and hard to do remarks" on his Rimbaud poem. "To be read and helped so well is the most important kind of response to the blood-giving of the poet as you know."[93] He also inundated Gardner with mediocre manuscripts by his friends and students, which she bravely read but often dismissed out of hand—exactly as Logan needed, because he wanted Gardner's confirmation of his own judgment. Gardner wrote for him to publishers, sent him books, and sent his first book, *A Cycle for Mother*

Cabrini (1955) to literary lions such as Edith Sitwell, hoping to make him better-known internationally. Logan's mother had died when he was just one month old, and he came to see Gardner as a mother-confessor ("I want my nose wiped and my tears dried, and it is hard to be of any use to others"), discussing with her his religious ecstasies and doubts, the births of his children (nine by 1958), and the growing problems in his marriage as he became mentally unstable: "I very much wish you would tell me . . . what your experience has been of the effects of psychoanalysis on creativity. I know Rilke refused to be analyzed as he feared it would kill his gift." Gardner answered that a surreal poem like "The Panic Vine" ("the analytic wind / the dazzling showers of the thundering sun bird blood / the grey goose feather and the white mare-mother's cud" [35]) was written during a period of sessions with Kraus but that she preferred the ones written after analysis. Logan was "glad you don't think my gift will be hurt by a completed analysis" and ended up as Kraus's patient, with Gardner's financial assistance.[94]

Gardner nurtured her fellow poets with her innate generosity, while she made do with less attentive support. Oscar Williams had proven invaluable at the beginning of her career, but he had become more and more morose as Gardner became famous and he did not. During their daily cooperation at *Poetry*'s office, Shapiro had also been instrumental in boosting Gardner's confidence in her gifts as a poet and an editor, but she hardly ever acted on the occasional specific suggestion he made; and if she did, she regretted it. Her third mentor was Edward Dahlberg. Although he had a high opinion of his work, Logan had refused to engage in correspondence with Dahlberg, knowing that he "would get oracular and tyrant father, like Pound. I still hurt over Pound's telling me not to write again until I had read all the books on the stupid list of his."[95] He was right. Dahlberg sent Gardner numerous lists of books she had to read, in one letter alone mentioning, among many others, "[f]irst volume of Strabo in Loeb. First volume of Diodorus of Siculus, Loeb. Complete poems of Christopher Smart, Harvard University Press. . . . William Gilchrist's Life of William Blake. Biographia Literaria, Coleridge. . . . Jane Harrison's Prolegomena to the Study of Greek religion. . . . Columbus Four Voyages, edited by Navarette."[96] In another he exhorted her to "shun modern books. Go back to Beginnings; ritual will heal a line, a stanza, your whole head; you need symbols, Isis, Hathor, Typhon, the Kabala for your image and vision. Go to school with some Master, Ovid, Plutarch, Livy, Tacitus, and you will then find the river back to your own identity."[97] He had "not the least doubt" that Gardner was "a congenital poet," but wished she "would *please* read the books I suggested to you" (quickly adding such naturalists as Bartram, Buffon, Darwin, and Muir) and was livid when Gardner did not obey his commands promptly.[98] In his own work Dahlberg paraded his learning in endless classical, biblical, and mythological allusions, and he was disappointed in Gardner's newer, more narrative style, hating to see a pupil escape from his grasp: "I do not like the poem on the doctor in the airplane ['Mea Culpa']. I loathe this machine anyway."[99] He also disliked Gardner's love letter to her husband, "Letter from Slough Pond" ("I couple with the ripples of the fresh / pond water I am rolled by the roiling sea. / Love, in our wide bed, do you lie lonely?" [60]): "Of course I respect your tender feelings, but you must, dear Isabella, find symbols for your feelings. . . . Alas, feeling alone, without ritual and myth, will not be art. . . . I fervently wish that you would buy only those books that are essential to your productive nature. We must not love books or people promiscuously; you give your heart too readily, a defect of Dido, Medea, and all the women men have ached for with or without avail."[100]

Dahlberg was almost alone in his aversion to the more open direction Gardner's poetry was taking, for most of her literary contemporaries were complimentary. Lowell, who himself was experimenting with free verse and off rhymes, "like[d] a lot the way you get good prose into poems," and called Gardner "an awfully polished workman. . . . I marvel particularly at the snails with its wonderful hidden couplets and diamond-like on your toes description."[101] His friend Philip Booth thought her elegy "Zei Gesund" "a stunner, all the weave of form and warp of emotion in one tough fabric that shrouds the human being being human that this guy so obviously was"; while Carolyn Kizer, who was writing a survey of trends in American poetry, found Gardner "wonderful. You and Garrigue are the best girls (speaking in a strictly literary sense; in a personal sense I'm sure there's no comparison!) to my way of thinking."[102] Later Kizer wrote James Wright that in the section "The Hotshots" of her survey she had "set up dialectics," comparing Berryman's "fierce masculine rhetoric" to Gardner's "unrhetorical femininity."[103] And Theodore Roethke (once again hospitalized for mental illness) told Gardner that he had used her poems in a seminar in Rome and that the "Italian kids said they liked you better than Marianne Moore."[104]

Gardner gave readings all over the country, was asked to record her poems, to submit to the *Hudson Review, New Mexico Quarterly, Texas Quarterly,* and other magazines. Clearly, she had found her perch as a poet in the male-dominated literary world of the late 1950s; and she was living a busy, fulfilling life as a wife and mother at the center of a wide spectrum of artists, writers, and the Chicago intelligentsia and moneyed elite. Yet all was not well. Fate struck a cruel blow when Barbara Ransom Jopson, whom Gardner had known "dearly well" since they were at Foxcroft together, died painfully of emphysema at the end of 1957. The deaths of three of her best friends (Ayers, Cholden, and now Ransom Jopson, all her age) left Gardner "in a black depression."[105] An obsessive fear of death had always haunted her life and poetry. As a very young child, she had talked with her brother George about the nothingness after death; at Foxcroft she had written about "the agony of losing life"; and over one-third of the poems in *Birthdays from the Ocean* had death as their theme.[106] When young, the "noun death and the verb to die were exiled from my / vocabulary," but Gardner could no longer deny "the releasing / of the I" ("Of Flesh and Bone," 31–32).

"Why do so *many* of us crack, dear Edward," Gardner cried out to Dahlberg at the beginning of 1958. "Both Ted Roethke and Cal Lowell ill now. I love Cal. He is a *caring* person. I suppose it is ambivalence that destroys us all."[107] A few weeks later she added: "We [poets] all seem to walk wires of one sort or another and must needs be acrobatic even when the abyss is in the mind. Please continue to be my friend even though I may betray your belief in my abused muse."[108] Gardner's depression only increased: "[l]ittle energy is left over and though well loved and well fed I despair," she wrote Dahlberg in the early summer of 1958. She told him of her two former marriages and her children, of her stepchildren, Anneke, Peter, and Sydney, and that she was more often in touch with them than their own fathers, and of Bob's three children, whom they saw often at Elmhurst. Apologizing for not having written in quite some time, Gardner explained that Dahlberg's admiring, exhortative letters with their long lists of obligatory reading had made her feel fraudulent. She had hoped to have enough poems for a second book by 1960 but had only thirteen good new ones since the publication of *Birthdays from the Ocean*: "My accedia for the last three years has been such (and *continues*) that I cannot write nor even read." She burst out in uncharacteristic desperation: "Edward I wish you could help me. I'm afraid no-one can."[109] This letter shocked Dahlberg out of his customary egocentrism into trying to help Gardner instead of making her over into his ideal woman poet. "I am very troubled about your mood. . . . You speak of aging which deeply saddens me. I have a strong impression of you rather than a delicate knowledge of your face, and I remember you as vibrant and a woman in all your powers." Adding remarks about books she should have gotten, quotations from letters by Emily Dickinson, references to Sir Thomas Browne, Herbert Read, John Ruskin, William Carlos Williams, and others for good measure, he ended his letter: "I earnestly hope you will heed me: go off somewhere, for a while, anyway, to perceive what it is that is diminishing the light you need, and quenching the heart, which is a Vesta in every tender woman."[110]

"On Looking in the Looking Glass," Gardner, now over forty, saw her "small embattled eyes dispute a face / that middle-aging sags and creases. / . . . / And now in an instant's blink my stare / seizes in your beleaguered glare / the pristine gaze the blown-glass stance / of your once / total innocence" (54). Asking what she had to show for herself at middle age, Gardner saw that nothing much remained. Her political ideals had fallen more or less by the wayside, Ireland had been but a dream; acting had proven a short drama, and she was not using her great talent for writing poetry as she was suffering from writer's block. Three of her most beloved coevals had died. She had married the wrong men twice and though her present husband was kind, loving, and generous, their relationship was not the passionate one that for Gardner betokened true love. Was this it?

(Above) Rose Grosvenor Gardner with Belle, Kitty, and George, c. 1917. Courtesy Daniel Jones.

(Opposite top) The only known picture of Isabella Stewart Gardner, "Mrs. Jack," and her godchild and namesake. Courtesy Daniel Jones.

(Opposite bottom) Belle and her beloved brother George, taken at Green Hill, c.1920. Courtesy Daniel Jones.

(*Above*) Members of the Leighton Rollins School of Acting working on the beach, c. 1937. Harold Van Kirk is lounging Adonis-like on the right, and Gardner is reading with Lynn Hancock. The woman with the headscarf probably is Mildred Cohen, who first married Henry Levin and later, after a long adulterous affair, Maurice Donohue. Courtesy Maurice Donohue.

(*Opposite top*) The extended Gardner family posing in front of Green Hill, late 1920s. Isabella is in the top row on the right. Courtesy Daniel Jones.

(*Opposite bottom*) Gardner, her parents and siblings at Green Hill, early 1930s. From left: Isabella, George, Rose Grosvenor Gardner, George Peabody Gardner, Kitty, Robert, Rose, and John. Courtesy Daniel Jones.

(*Above*) Gardner with Rosy and Danny, c. 1945. Courtesy Daniel Jones.

(*Opposite top*) Gardner with Rosy on her lap, Anneke and Peter Van Kirk playing, and nurse Molly Laughlin watching, c. 1941. Courtesy Raoul Van Kirk.

(*Opposite bottom*) Gardner and Rosy mirroring one another, c. 1941. Courtesy Maurice Donohue.

(*Above*) Cartoon depicting Seymour photographing a stripper in his Chicago Studio, 1940. Included by Daniel Seymour in *A Loud Song*.

(*Opposite top*) "Not at All What One Is Used To": Gardner with fellow actors. Probably early 1940s. Courtesy Raoul Van Kirk.

(*Opposite bottom*) Marrying Seymour in Los Angeles, 1944. Seymour is to Gardner's right, her brother George, handsome in his uniform, to her left, and next to him is aunt Catherine Gardner Mayes (?). The "bishop" seems to have his doubts. Courtesy Maurice Donohue.

Gardner with Seymour, George, and his beloved Tania Stepanova in Chicago c. 1946. Courtesy Daniel Jones.

Gardner glamorously photographed by Maurice Seymour, c. 1944. Courtesy Raoul Van Kirk.

(*Top*) Gardner in Maurice Donohue's apartment, "the barrack," at the University of Chicago, 1950. Courtesy Maurice Donohue.

(*Bottom*) Gardner on the beach with anthologist Oscar Williams, here without his usual bow tie, c. 1950. Courtesy Daniel Jones.

(Above) Gardner, late 1950s, photographed by her brother Robert. Courtesy Robert Gardner.

(Opposite top) Gardner with Robert and Lee Gardner on the houseboat *The Tanda*, British Columbia, 1950, during the making of the Kwakiutl movie. Courtesy Daniel Jones.

(Opposite bottom) Gardner as Kwakiutl princess, British Columbia, 1950. Courtesy Washington University Libraries.

(Above) The Tates at home, c. 1964. Courtesy Washington University Libraries.

(Opposite top) Handsome, talented, and wealthy: Daniel Seymour in his early twenties in the 1960s.

(Opposite bottom) In Minneapolis, with Tate wearing his Confederate vest, December 1961. Back row: Pat Stange and John Clark. Middle row: Joe Montgomery, Biddy Brown, and Bobby Clark. Bottom row: Hunt Brown, Allen Tate, Isabella Gardner Tate. Courtesy Biddy Brown.

(*Above*) Gardner, late 1960s. The man sitting next to her probably is Louis Tytell. Courtesy Washington University Libraries.

(*Opposite top*) "The Four of Us and the Monkey": Louis MacNeice; his lover, Mary Wimbush, with monkey; and the Tates, Hampton Court, Great Britain, 1962. Courtesy Washington University Libraries.

(*Opposite bottom*) With Marianne Moore in her signature tricorn hat at MacDowell in 1967. Standing in the background is Rosemarie Beck. Courtesy Daniel Jones.

(Above) Gardner in the early 1970s, her face ravaged, even before the tragedies that overtook her children. Included by Daniel Seymour in his *A Loud Song.*

(Opposite top) Queen of the Chelsea, early 1970s. Photo by Layle Silbert.

(Opposite bottom) Gardner (in the background) and her children partying at the Chelsea, c. 1970. Courtesy Raoul Van Kirk.

(*Above*) Gardner and Billy Congdon at his show in Italy in 1981. Courtesy of the William G. Congdon Foundation.

(*Opposite top*) Gardner with Gill and Vera Gold's baby in Ojai, c. 1972. Courtesy Vera Gold.

(*Opposite bottom*) In 2007 the Isabella Stewart Gardner Museum in Boston organized an evening around "The Other Isabella," where biography and poetry were interwoven to tell the story of the poet, rather than the patroness. Courtesy Isabella Stewart Gardner Museum.

The Other Isabella

ISABELLA
STEWART GARDNER
MUSEUM

Chapter Six

"Courting Lovers," 1958–1961

Wing fin and wrist bend wishfully
to cadences of summer noon
and courting lovers cast their bait
into the laden air of love.

The deft rod waits the still stream stirs
and mute gills tremble to the lure,
the lovers' taut hands listen to
soft nimble arias of love.

A ridden hawk screams like a cat
as hook is caught as mouth is reamed
as reeling lovers play their catch
through foaming areas of love.
("The Compleat Anglers")

As usual, Gardner had made plans to stay at Wellfleet from the middle of June till the end of August, having her children and friends stay with her, while Bob remained in Chicago, working. At chic but informal, artistic Cape Cod, mingling with Conrad Aiken, Arthur Schlesinger, Edmund Wilson, and other regulars for cocktails, and swimming in her beloved Atlantic Ocean, Gardner was in her element—provided her writing went well. Other prominent summer guests at Wellfleet were her friends Francis Biddle, who had been Franklin Roosevelt's attorney general, and his wife, aspiring poet Katherine Garrison Chapin. In their turn they were close friends of the southern writer Allen Tate, poet par excellence and professor at the University of Minnesota in Minneapolis, who was teaching summer school at Harvard that year. Tate was a true man of letters. His nine books of poetry had appeared to an admiring if select audience since 1923; he had published biographies of three southern luminaries and a novel about the antebellum South (*The Fathers*, 1938), and was a first-class combative literary essayist, one of the high priests of the reigning New Criticism.[1] He was mentor to many young writers, among them Gardner's nemesis Randall Jarrell; her cousin Robert Lowell, who as a student, fleeing from his puritan home and Harvard, had pitched his tent on Tate's unreconstructed lawn in Tennessee to worship at the feet of his master; and her great friend Karl Shapiro, whom Tate had "knighted . . . as a Member of the Establishment" by getting him, when he was only in his early thirties, the prestigious Consultantship in Poetry at the Library of Congress—according to Shapiro at least in part because even if he was a Jew, he had "been born . . . below the Mason-Dixon line," and "Jews made good Southerners."[2] E. E. Cummings, T. S. Eliot, Merrill Moore, John Crowe Ransom, Robert Penn Warren, and the more specifically southern writers Andrew Lytle and Donald Davidson were among his close friends. Tate knew everybody who was anybody and was a force to be reckoned with in the highbrow literary world.

Allen Tate was born in Kentucky in 1899, the son of a businessman, but he often improved on his ancestry by emphasizing his mother's more noble Virginia stock while in truth he was a southern aristocrat by the widest stretch of the imagination only. Born with such an enormous head that his parents wondered whether he had water on the brain, Tate turned out to be smart after all. While his mother was possessive, his father was both emotionally and geographically distant; he often lived apart from his wife, who considered herself socially superior to her undependable, violent husband, who proved her point when he went bankrupt when Tate was in his teens. By that time Tate had become a promising violinist, but when he auditioned with Ysaÿe, the master's response was to ask him if there was something else he could do, which was the end of that dream.[3] Accompanied at first by his mother, Tate then attended Vanderbilt University in Nashville, where he met his mentor, John Crowe Ransom, and became part of the literary group who called themselves the Fugitives. He championed Eliot's impersonal poetry as exemplified in *The Waste Land* (1922), recognizing that behind the mask of objectivity and reason the onslaught of passion and feeling could be held in check. Indeed, emotional to the core himself, Tate always condemned outward displays of feeling by others both in life and in poetry. The (supposed) order and virtues of the traditional South gave Tate a much-needed refuge from personal chaos for much of his life, and even in northern Minneapolis he wore his Confederate vest proudly and provocatively for special occasions. When the South started to fail him, he found an additional refuge in Catholicism, to which he converted in 1950, encouraged by his wife, novelist Caroline Gordon.[4]

Gordon was also from Kentucky and had married Tate in 1925, five months pregnant with their daughter Nancy. Although Tate was the love of Gordon's life, the marriage was rocky from the beginning and not helped by Tate's congenital philandering, Gordon's often-violent rages, or their drinking. They divorced in 1945, but remarried soon after. In 1947 Gordon became a Catholic, her faith sustaining her through the inevitable deterioration of their relationship, and in Princeton, in August 1956, the bomb burst again. Gordon gave her lawyer proof of Tate's cruel behavior:

> In August, 1956 Mrs. Cyrus Radford came to spend the night here at the urgent invitation of both of us. At that time I did not drive a car. My husband had promised to drive Mrs. Radford back to her home. . . . He left here at three o'clock in the afternoon, saying he was going to the library. Mrs. Radford arrived around four. . . . I kept wondering what had become of my husband and making every excuse I could think of to cover up his absence. Finally I went out into the kitchen at seven o'clock and found a special delivery letter, lying on the floor. In it he said he was leaving me. He had set a trap for a rat the day before and he left the rat struggling in the trap with its back broken. I am afraid of rats. We listened to it struggle all night and when it got light I called an old Negro man who has worked for us for years and he came and killed the poor thing.[5]

They legally separated, but their lives had been intertwined for better and worse for over thirty years, and Gordon again forgave but did not forget. They corresponded continuously, reaffirming their love for each other, which, it seemed, could survive everything but their living together.[6]

In 1958 Tate was safely ensconced as a well-paid tenured professor at the University of Minnesota in Minneapolis. Within the hard-drinking English department Tate was not only admired for his prominent place in the literary world, he was loved for his brilliance and genial personality, his always-exciting gossip, and his talent for warming the cold and boring Minnesota winters with his amorous adventures. Living apart from his wife, Tate was chasing women with more abandon than ever before. "There were so many women passing in and out of Allen's life, that if you were away for a month, you would have missed some of them," his friend and lawyer John Goetz gloated.[7] Of late, there had been an Italian countess, who had followed Tate to Minneapolis and was being spied upon by a faculty wife, who had surrendered more or less simultaneously.[8] There had been Natasha Spender, Stephen Spender's wife, and literary lovers like Elizabeth Hardwick, who then married Tate's intellectual son Robert Lowell, and most recently, the ardent poet Jean Garrigue. It is improbable that these women fell for Tate's physical charms: his huge head on a slight body can have been catnip to cartoonists only. His spiel was to tell every female that she was the most beautiful woman in the room, and this overture by a suave, charismatic man of many talents worked so amazingly well that one young wife started wondering what was wrong with her, as Tate had never made a pass; Tate quickly comforted her, assuring her that he felt about her like a daughter.[9] He was, in general, far more interested in chase and conquest than in the particular women he bedded and as insensitive to their feelings as he had been to his wife's—whom he blamed for his affairs and criticized for her justified jealous rages.

It was in June 1958, when he was deeply involved with Jean Garrigue, that Katherine Biddle invited Tate for lunch, adding as a selling point that Isabella Gardner would also be there. Since their first meeting, when Tate had been preoccupied with his ulcer (and probably another woman), Gardner and Tate had exchanged a few professional letters. In late 1957 she had sent him her "Widow's Yard" for comment, and though Tate had been "put off a little by an irrelevant association with Marianne Moore's endless bestiaries" which bored him no end, he greatly admired the natural, precise language of Gardner's snail poem.[10] Plans to meet on the lecture circuit fell through, and it was not until July 12, 1958, that they met at the Biddles on the Cape and immediately embarked on an impassioned love affair. (Tate dropped Garrigue, but neglected to tell her.) Within two weeks of their meeting, together they visited Robert and Lee, who lived in Cambridge where Tate was teaching, told them tales of their undying love, and asked them to act as postillions d'amour:

> I am so sorry that Allen and I have burdened you with the fact of our feeling for one another. I had not wanted to afflict you with complicity.
>
> I cannot expect you to understand but I know I can count on your affection.
>
> I am afraid I did not even attempt to deny or resist my love for Allen. It has been a matter of the acceptance of a fact and in terms of that fact and the other realities and obligations of my life I shall do my best from day to day.
>
> Allen is the only man I've ever known and loved *for whom* I feel reverence and admiration and dependence as well as the most acute and profound love and tenderness.
>
> If it were possible I would spend the rest of my life with him, whether or not we were married, in any part of the world, in any circumstances. But it is impossible and it is unthinkable. However I shall do everything in my power compatible with my unalterable and dear obligations to be with him. . . .
>
> You'll see Allen Thursday. Give him steak and potatoes! And milk! And your affection.[11]

Gardner's total capitulation to and absolute idealization of her new lover were excessive even for her, but perhaps understandable in the light of her midlife depression caused by a fear of aging, and aggravated by the realization that she was living in a rut and had achieved none of her dreams. Her meeting with Tate at this very low point in her life showed her that new beginnings and grand passions were still possible, even at forty-two. She wrote Dahlberg that she had been "miraculously restored to the joy and fullness of sentient being this summer" and told him not to worry if he did not hear from her for a month or so, as she was "no longer 'on Job's muckheap.'"[12] It did not take long for Gardner to convince herself that she had chosen Bob for his gentleness and conventionality, fleeing from her violent and turbulent marriage to Seymour, but that he was joyless and indifferent to her concerns and needs, although she admitted that he had been good to her and her children. For years, she now reasoned, their relationship had been arid and her sensibilities stunted, but with Tate she felt "absolute commitment for the first time in [her] life" and "for the first time able to love wholly and relinquish self—relinquish in the sense that heretofore I have held on fiercely to an uncommitted core."[13]

Gardner was not the only one smitten. That summer, commuting between Cambridge and the Cape, Tate sent her love letters telling her that she was overwhelmingly important to him, his ever-fixed mark, the love of his life, the only woman forever, his future. Meanwhile, in his letters to his "Darling" wife in Princeton, Tate told Gordon that as her husband he had to dominate their social life and that he was committed to Minnesota, but that he was willing to consider having her share his life there after his sabbatical for the academic year 1958–1959. He had asked his close friend Brainard Cheney in Tennessee to advise him on getting back together with Caroline. Cheney had become a member of the Catholic Church through the sponsorship of Allen and Caroline Tate and his answer was therefore a clear yes, although he warned that "both have got to work at it. . . . It is not an accident of history that Christ was crucified on a phallic symbol."[14] Tate was not only trying to decide between women, but also where to spend his sabbatical. Before his fiery affair with Gardner, he had planned on spending it on a Fulbright grant in England, but Gordon had been much against this as she would not be able to accompany him. Tate had decided more or less not to go, but reconsidered when Gardner came into the picture. Love-struck, he came up with a brilliant idea which he put forward for the consideration of John Clark, chairman of the English department: he would pretend to be in Europe, while in reality he would stay holed up somewhere near Chicago, close to Gardner. Clark told him in no uncertain terms that this was an ill-considered plan if only because he would have no money to live on, and Tate gave in to common sense.

To one of his many confidants in Minneapolis (each believing he or she was the only one in the know), Pat Knowlton Stange, Tate proudly told of his eternal love for his "Titian beauty": a wonderfully fitting description for Gardner, who was peach-complexioned, red-haired, full-bosomed, and tall.[15] On September 23, 1958, he sailed for Great Britain on the *Mauretania* on a year's Fulbright. Written on that very first day of their long separation, Tate's love letter (of almost thirty passionate pages) reiterates again and again his longing and everlasting love for his precious one, his darling, his sweetheart Isabella, and speaks of his divorcing Gordon and marrying her as soon as she thinks it proper and of bringing her to complete fulfillment as a woman and a poet, meaning (Tate hastily added) that Gardner and her poetry were one. For the past five years, he assured her, he had lived in despair and now he was reaching for her like a drowning man. Once landed in Great Britain, he wrote her at least once daily, asking for photographs and perfumed letters, telling her he was so totally hers that even the slightest flirtation now was impossible for him. When he stayed at the Spenders' at their invitation, Tate assured Gardner she need not be upset, as his affair with Natasha was five years in the past and they no longer cared for each other; in fact, he had told an immensely sympathetic Natasha in confidence about his feelings for her. (Gardner was consumed by jealousy nevertheless.) Loving her utterly, to distraction, what kept him going, he wrote Gardner, was the thought of seeing her again in December and January, when he was jetting back for an extensive and lucrative lecture tour. They also hoped it might be possible for Gardner to visit Kitty in Paris in April 1959 and that they could meet each other there and in Italy. His love for her, he insisted, was different from anything he had ever felt before and not, as some might think, the same old record, but new, wild, strange, inevitable, and he would never play any other music again.

Meanwhile he met David Cecil, in charge of his Oxford stay, and Louis MacNeice and his wife, Hedli, and could not resist opening his heart to them about his new love—in confidence, of course. After scuttling back and forth between Oxford and London, Tate temporarily settled in the guest room in New College in Oxford, and although he had "never seen anything so dingy this side of a Southern country hotel" he was pleased to find that his valet was called Charles Dickens.[16] He was angry because the Fulbright committee had not organized any regular lectures for him in Oxford, conveniently forgetting that until the last moment Fulbright had not known if and when he would arrive. He was lonely, and from Minneapolis his old southern friend and colleague Samuel Monk tried to rustle up some Oxford friends for him. Tate had asked him for advice with respect to his possible divorce, too, but Monk was sensible enough not to get caught up in that hornets' nest, knowing from way back of Gordon's penchant for violence and of Tate's Casanovanic leanings.

Even to the suspicious reader it is apparent from these letters that Tate was truly in love with Gardner. However, he was also easily swayed, and hedging his bets. On September 30, he told "His Own Darling" Gardner that he could breathe again now that he had received one of her letters and "Darling" Gordon that he had been a daily communicant at Mass and that they should leave their future in the hands of Christ; on October 5 he asked Gordon for her love and support, telling her he was praying for her every day, and wrote two letters to Gardner in the most amatory terms. His letters to Gordon were far more Catholic and far less fiery and frequent than those to Gardner, but when she did not answer them right back, he was frantic with worry, perhaps understandably so as over the summer she had threatened suicide, causing him to go and see her at her home in Princeton. On October 21 he assured Gardner that his lawyers had the papers for the divorce drawn up, but he worried about his finances as, after payment of Gordon's alimony and mortgage, they would have only six thousand dollars or so to live on; for he refused to live on Gardner's money, insisting on paying all necessary expenses, including her stockings and underwear. Two days later, however, he begged Gordon to meet him halfway toward a reconciliation. Then he told the Biddles, in between many morsels of literary gossip, that he was divorcing Gordon, adding that he was very much in love with Gardner. It is hard to follow the tortuous turns of Tate's mind, but in all it seems that he was set on marrying Gardner but did not want the bomb to burst until he was back in America over the Christmas holidays. Taking courage, Monk tried to warn him off, pointing to both the disparity of sixteen years in age and Gardner's children, who would be an even greater obstacle to happiness.

For Gardner the fall of 1958 was sheer hell. In spite of all Tate's protestations of love, his record was not confidence-inspiring, and he was far away: would he be truer to her than to all of his other women? It took a while for Tate's first letter to reach her, and she was in deep despair when she did not hear from him; this happened more than once, as her mail was withheld when she forgot to pay for the box she had rented. Then, the McCormicks had read Rose's journals, which she had left lying about, and found that Rose at nineteen was far less innocent than Gardner had thought: she had had sexual encounters for over a year. Appalled, Gardner sent Rosy back into analysis, paid for by the family, only to have her daughter turn on her because of her marital history, even though she had as yet no idea of the latest developments. Gardner had to conduct her long-distance affair clandestinely and behave with Bob as if nothing had changed. She cringed from lovemaking with him, blaming her sexual apathy on her anxieties about her daughter. These redoubled when Rose ran away in November without leaving an address. She was soon found living with a graduate student on Chicago's South Side, but Gardner was so preoccupied with her own love life that she left Rose to fend for herself. Bob, meanwhile, had made a very good real estate deal and celebrated by buying a Mercedes, which Gardner begrudged him, and all the more when they were in an accident and Gardner struck the dash, bruising her face. With Gardner withdrawing from him mentally and physically, Bob later thought he "should have noticed that something was wrong with the whole marriage, but I did not realize. I thought we had a happy marriage."[17] In hindsight, he also reasoned that with her growing fame Gardner became as interested in the poetry scene as in poetry itself. Gardner, he said, came to make a choice between poets and nonpoets and "I was supportive and everything, but I clearly was not a poet."[18] As Paul Carroll described it, McCormick "was not interested in poetry, and . . . was polite, patrician and remote. . . . He did not know what to say. There we would be, getting all carried away about Dylan Thomas, and he just was not interested."[19]

Although the poet-lovers had spent, off and on, less than one illicit month together, Gardner had convinced herself that Tate was worth her breaking up her marriage and submitting her children to yet another separation. In keeping the affair from her husband, Gardner was obeying Kraus, whom she was seeing once more because of her severe depression at being without her beloved. He again told her what she wanted to hear: that following her heart was best for her mental health. With Tate in Great Britain, Gardner was so wretched that she had stopped writing poetry and even reading altogether. Her brother Robert initially was no help at all, as he had intimated that Gardner was sexually profligate, which hurt her into defending herself: "The fact that in *seven* years no-one (except Cowan!) has made a gesture in my direction and I have spent 5 summers alone and frequent weeks during the year *and* lunched and worked with men would seem to indicate that my manner and personality are not erotically provocative."[20] She asked him for support instead of judgment and Robert wrote a loving letter that brightened her up:

> It is enough to have seen one love die, but to lose a second—and then to stare at your first child's wretchedness, while your youngest is spirited away and then, woe of woes, to be alone with yourself and your own sharp knife of insight—I cannot see how you can bear it. Remember—always—that I am constantly thinking of you, ready to take you in and care for [you] as much as I am able. Let me be your watchman, your spirit's guard. You fill me with devotion and I will try to make it available whenever and however you need it. . . . Allen, I am certain, loves you and honors you. Bob—poor man—cannot, in spite of you, Rosie is young and muscular—Dan I am seeing with happiness tomorrow.[21]

Next to Robert, Dahlberg was the only one Gardner had confided in early on; as he was far away in Mallorca, he was not part of the American literary grapevine. Dahlberg knew she was in love with an older, married American poet who was in England, but Gardner had named no names. When Dahlberg guessed it was Tate (not a difficult deduction) Gardner was touched by his intuition. She was grateful, too, because in his many letters Dahlberg urged her to leave Bob as soon as possible, reasoning that she needed a man who would treasure her as the poet she was, adding that her departure would be better for her children, too. "Marriage is rough weather, and the mariner must quit the leaky boat if the other shore is not to be reached," he exhorted, wondering how she ever could have given her "body to a man who could never have comprehended your flesh, since the head, the heart and the verse are you, which he could never accept" and ordering her to annul "this philistine wedlock."[22] Opportunely forgetting that Dahlberg was hardly the right person to give personal advice, as his own life was a mess (he had, for instance, not seen his children in years), Gardner read what she desperately wanted to see: abandoning Bob would be to the benefit of all concerned and help her work. She knew full well she was hurting her husband and son but now rationalized that she had let her head dictate her heart in marrying Bob: "I *knew* I did not love him, but he *did* love me *in so far as he was capable.* To that extent I was 'well fed and well-loved'—not as you and I and Allen understand it and desire it but within the framework of my husband's capacities and limitations. My mistake was in marrying him. As we all know. He cannot be blamed for what he could not help."[23]

Cousin Lowell, loving malicious gossip, was spreading the word as early as mid-October: "Everyone is talking about Belle Gardner and Allen Tate and no one knows anything for certain, though there was great fear in Wellfleet that Belle's husband would hear something. Allen's at Oxford and Belle's planning a trip to Europe in April which includes England. Coincidence? but no one knows. Belle was here last night. I do wish she were brighter and more sophisticated. One sinks into the wet sand of her good works, good will and enthusiasm for young poets, fresh and already trailing heavy gray clouds of ennui and oblivion."[24] "I think Tate's plotting to divorce Caroline and marry Belle Gardner," he told Elizabeth Bishop a few weeks later, "but breathe a word of this to no one."[25] By the end of November 1958, Tate had indeed instigated divorce proceedings, hoping to cut the knot forever during his stay in America over Christmas. He wrote Lowell that he was "calmer and more sure of myself than I've felt in years."[26] Gordon now only rated an occasional businesslike letter addressed to "Dear Caroline" and she had as yet no idea of his involvement with Gardner, but she did not take Tate's bombshell lying down; marshaling spiritual authorities, she informed him that upon the recommendation of several priests she had to oppose the divorce. She added that their living apart by Tate's wish was evidence of her love for him and that her financial situation was dire.

With two women emotionally dependent on him, Tate returned to America in early December for the Christmas holidays and Gardner, with whom he had agreed upon a complicated arrangement of assignations across the country, following a strenuous lecture tour which he had undertaken to earn money for their planned European jaunt in the spring of 1959. By this time, Gardner had told the ever-kind and courteous McCormick of her affair and, he remembered some thirty years later, his world fell apart: "I just packed my suitcase and left. I did not want anything, just the house plans to Elmhurst, but I left everything to Belle. This was the end."[27] In fact, McCormick had to stay around for a few weeks, until he had found new accommodations, but divorce proceedings were started immediately. He began looking elsewhere for solace and seemed to find it right away with Elise Vickers, who, long after her fling with Gardner's first husband, now was infatuated with her third.[28] McCormick was truly concerned about Dan and Rosy, though, whose devoted father he had been for years, from visiting Rosy at Verde Valley School in Arizona to escorting her to Bradford for "Dad's Day," from taking Dan fishing to driving him to Brooks in Massachusetts to start school (while Gardner was trysting with Tate), quarreling with Gardner about her unwillingness to ever discipline them. Gardner, however, reasoned that he was not their birthfather, and McCormick noticed that as soon as they separated "Dan was being kept from me."[29] Rosy, at nineteen, went her own way and remained in and out of Bob's life whenever she wanted (often when she needed money), but Dan, a lonely half-Jewish adolescent in a WASP boarding school, was cut off from his fond stepfather's love and Bob from his; this hurt both to the core.

Fanita English believed Gardner had neglected Daniel, whom she described as a "poor little rich boy . . . who got a blunt deal." In English's stern view, Gardner had little natural sense of her children; although she was upset by their problems and crises, she was helpless and did not support them. A transactional analyst in later life, English emphasized that her husband, Maurice English, had been as insensitive to their children, and theorized that as artists they had to make an (unconscious) choice between the creative drive and children, and chose art—an assumption which, in her view, is borne out by the miserable childhood years of the offspring of many artists.[30] Tall, red-haired, and spoiled, Rose admired her glamorous, successful mother and wanted to emulate her but failed every time. When he read a first draft of the almost psychotic "Nightmare," written when Gardner was in analysis, Karl Shapiro wondered whether Gardner was speaking of herself or her daughter: "The dreamer rips the red curls / in handfuls from that hateful head and hurls / the hairy gobbets at those manic eyes / The leerer dreadfully diminishes in size / She shrinks and shrinks into a little child. / The screaming dreamer beats the dwindling child" (47). Gardner herself admitted to Myra Cholden that their weaknesses—the romanticizing, the refusal to see reality, the sloth—were very similar, although inflated in Rose's case. Unfortunately, Rose did not have her mother's counterbalancing strengths. She tried writing and acting but did not have Gardner's talents; and Rosy had Gardner's erotic drive but not her sex appeal. Having failed at all her ventures, with no idea what to do with her life, Rose decided to just wait for her money, which she would come into in two years. Daniel's talents were more like his father's, and he found himself in drawing and photography. Curly-haired, dark, good-looking, and sensitive, Daniel as a young teenager was very popular with girls; both Kathy Shapiro and Deirdre English were enchanted with him. But when Tate appeared on the scene, his life changed for the worse.

Gardner's unfaithfulness made Bob McCormick question marrying for love. He had thought this marriage, which he had entered into with head and heart and during which he had been generous and kind with love and support of both Gardner and her children (and had not touched a drop of alcohol) would last. Yet, soon after his divorce from Gardner, he married Elise Vickers. Her son, the journalist Lance Morrow, wrote that she took from Bob, whom he "idol-ized," "a sort of proprietary sense of the city. . . . She enrolled at the Committee on Social Thought at the University of Chicago. She tried to lose that old shame of leaving school when she was fifteen. She took courses with Saul Bellow and read Thucydides and Kant."[31] That union did not last either and McCormick married again, this time for life, but he remained convinced in all sincerity that there should either be a school for marriage or that marriages should be ar-ranged and entered without hopes for total fulfillment. Thirty years and two marriages later, McCormick was still hurt by Gardner's betrayal and his loss of Dan and deeply angry in his quiet way that in her divorce case against him Gardner had used her black eyes, caused by the car accident, as evidence of his violence.

Gardner's telling Bob, his almost immediate departure, and her subsequent divorce action were suddenly too close for comfort for Tate. He complained to Katherine Biddle that although his "dear one" had great strength and courage, he wanted her to slow down a little and described her as a bit spoiled, as used to getting what she wanted. Tate's own plans and promises for a January divorce were disrupted as, impelled by her love for him and backed by Church and lawyers, Gordon was opposing the divorce with all her might. Accusing Tate of hearing voices and having hallucinations, she suggested in a madly distressed letter (which she never sent) that Tate was in the throes of one of his paranoid seizures when he filed for divorce, adding that his renown was his undoing, be-cause everybody (even priests in the confessional) chose to believe his lies.

Tate, having been with Gardner intermittently over the holidays, was again completely captivated. He left for Leeds, where he was to spend the second se-mester of his sabbatical, asserting that "it began to happen and I knew at once what it meant, that first week-end *chez* Biddle last summer—actually at the lunch table, where Isabella was diagonally across from me. So be it. She is mine and my fate for the rest of my life."[32] Gardner moved to a hotel in Cambridge near her parents, whom she had told about her lover Tate and her divorce plans, which they had taken surprisingly well. Gardner knew their holidays had sealed them together, and being apart again was "brutally unnatural." She felt like a monster who had "gory tasks to perform" in cutting loose from Bob and telling Daniel and her troubled and unstable Rose, feeling guilty also because they would be exposed to scandal, and Bob might slide back into alcoholism.[33]

While her whole being was focused on Tate, Gardner met with Beat poets Allen Ginsberg and Gregory Corso at a reading; the latter, she reported to Dahlberg "was quite drunk and bleated and baahed about his 'love' for me whom he does not know! . . . He and Ginsberg read a poem or two apiece and they just *aren't* any good really."[34] (She realized that Corso was a "poor little boy" who needed a mother, a role she was to play unwillingly when Rose took up with him at the Hotel Chelsea in New York in the 1970s.) Gardner remained so depressed and distracted that contrary to her nature she neglected her friends, and Karl Shapiro and Paul Carroll (who did not know of her affair although gossip was beginning to spread) became quite worried, although they were going through troublesome times themselves. Shapiro was struggling with Evalyn and his manuscript of *In Defense of Ignorance* and in effect was saying farewell to both his wife and academic criticism. Carroll, as poetry editor of Chicago University's *Chicago Review,* had (with editor Irving Rosenthal) battled the board, which suppressed the *Review*'s winter 1959 issue for obscene writing, and was founding the short-lived but trailblazing periodical *Big Table,* best known for its publication of the Beat poets.

Gardner had by now confided in self-absorbed Logan, who put aside his disappointment at not being on the editorial board of *Big Table* to ask if he could help. Suffering, perhaps psychosomatically, from bursitis, Gardner used Dahlberg, who continuously confirmed her as a poet and reaffirmed her love for Tate, as a sounding board. In the winter of 1958 he had moved to New York City, and Gardner had met him and his wife, Rlene, in Tate's company. Dahlberg now became proprietary toward Tate, too, who sensibly kept his epistolatory distance. Gardner put up with his presumptuous, persistent, dictatorial letters (join Tate immediately no matter what, he directed her), patiently defending herself and explaining her actions. Yet, because of his support, it is only in her letters to him that her gloominess sporadically lightened enough for her to remark on people other than Tate and herself. She sent him money, angry that Tillie Olsen (of whom she had never heard) had gotten a grant instead of Dahlberg; and she defended Karl Shapiro against Dahlberg's ongoing attacks in the wake of the *Ushant* affair.

Gardner and Eberhart read together over the Christmas holidays and Eberhart was proud that Tate—as he thought—had come to hear him read. Eberhart himself was as wrapped up in Gardner as ever: "You are beautiful. I enjoyed listening to you but more looking at you. . . . To make it even plainer about you and poetry: I wanted to compliment them both. I love your work and loved hearing it but confess that since you are the first one I have read with for years I couldn't pay full attention as my mind was always wandering around in itself and its own poems. I wasn't entirely objective. Even when looking at you I was not thinking only of your beauty but of feelings I had for you in earlier times."[35]

At the end of January, Tate returned to Great Britain for his semester in bleak, dreary, foggy Leeds. He hardly had written since 1955, but now had time, as there were far fewer friends than in the Oxford-London area. Abjectly lonely and forlorn without Gardner, he counted the hours till she called, the weeks and days until he could see her again, and even flew over for a week in February as he could not wait until Gardner joined him in April. Interspersed with erotic passages, he gave Gardner day-by-day accounts of the state of his finances as well as his poor health as he suffered from hoarseness, bronchitis, ulcers, abscessed teeth, and, often, insomnia. If Gordon continued to oppose the divorce, a divorce and marriage might work in Mexico, or, perhaps, while he and Gardner were in Europe in the spring, he hoped. He admitted that if he had not fallen irrevocably in love with her, he would have drifted forever, starting a new, uncommitted affair every two years or so, and getting out of it with the excuse that he could not marry, but Gardner had saved him from all that. That the Gardners were to be his new in-laws and that therefore Cal Lowell (and Elizabeth Hardwick!) would become related by marriage he thought titillating. The Lowells knew by now, and Tate was glad that they had been very supportive but fearful that Elizabeth would write for the *New Yorker* a thinly disguised story about their soap opera love affair with Mademoiselle Jardinière and Monsieur Tête (or, better, Teste, he joked) as its main characters. Gardner wrote him that she thought Lowell a magnificent poet, but she did not care for his *Life Studies,* which had just come out: "The book is a brave one and a necessary step for him just now. It is the book *after* this one that I long to see because the present incipient one will have cleared him and prepared him."[36]

Now that Bob McCormick had been told, the lovers were spreading the news about their relationship: Tate to young Arthur Mizener and his wife as well as to Eliot in Europe, Gardner to Wallace Fowlie and the Shapiros. Karl was stunned by the news of their forthcoming marriage. He wrote to Tate: "Belle is the closest friend we have had for many years, a person so rich in sympathy and affection that we have always depended on her. . . . I have felt tremendous admiration for you ever since we first met; it is liking and admiration in one, all mixed up with your gentility, your high sense of responsibility, and especially your impulsiveness—as that seems to me a virtue. But I was really astonished when I heard the news of you and Belle, because I had had you in different compartments in my mind and it took me weeks to assimilate you both in the same compartment."[37]

In Princeton, in March, Gordon was distraught and exasperated, for since Tate had filed for divorce in November his one communication with her had been to send a bad check, which only added to the financial muddle created by the Tates' having a joint checking account from which he drew at will. Gordon optimistically but tiredly assumed that Tate was following his usual pattern—that he had promised to marry but would not, plus she had heard from mutual friends that he was not going to go through with the divorce. While she blackened him as morally and financially irresponsible and irrational, she hoped against hope that he would return to her yet again. She was not all wrong, as at about the same time Tate confessed to his old and close friend "brother" Andrew Lytle that he had hoped that the divorce threat would shock Gordon into a reunion, but this may have been one of Tate's fabrications, as only two weeks later he admitted to Lytle that he would like to remarry.[38] He was annoyed at Dahlberg, though, who (initially encouraged by Gardner) intended to dedicate his forthcoming work in *Big Table 1* to both, linking their names publicly, though on opposite pages. Gossip was rife, and Tate was afraid the double dedication would hurt his wife: "I am still deeply attached to her and the life I had with her for thirty-five years. This does not mean any qualification or limitation of my utter devotion and commitment to Isabella. At my age I cannot begin a new life with a *tabula rasa;* it is rather more like a palim[p]sest, with a new text upon the old."[39]

Before meeting Tate in Europe, Gardner first went with Dan to Arizona for her third divorce, which was granted on April 3, 1959. Dan went back to school, and Gardner flew to London, where she and her lover were to meet her parents. In March, Allen, ever the southern gentleman, had written Peabo formally of his love for his daughter: "We have many obstacles to surmount, but I have no doubt of the issue. I owe it to myself to say to you that my deepest wish is to marry Isabella the moment we are both free."[40] Tate realized the comic oddness of his situation in a letter to Katherine Biddle: "But figure to yourself, Madam, the spectacle of an undivorced man making a declaration of honorable intentions to the father of an undivorced woman, the father not being much older than the ambiguously placed petitioner."[41] They had a busy month in Europe, with both giving readings. Gardner had one with William Merwin in London and one for the BBC, and Tate read or lectured there, too, as well as in Italy (Venice, Florence, Rome) and in Greece (Saloniki and Athens) before they returned to Great Britain via Paris, where Gardner stayed with Kitty, and Tate, discreetly, in a hotel nearby. Plans had been made for meetings with, among numerous others, the Eliots, the Cecil Day Lewises, Herbert Read, and Edith Sitwell. Eliot had to cancel their first meeting and apologized, for he remembered Gardner very well from Chicago and thought her "charming." He remarked to Tate that she "has a poetic idiom of her own: I have been looking forward to seeing more of her work. . . . Meanwhile, all our wishes for your happiness."[42]

Gardner and Tate lived and loved openly and the grapevine buzzed. During one of his manic states Lowell took it upon himself to call Caroline Gordon at 7:00 a.m. on April 30 to tell her about Tate's infatuation with Gardner, calling his cousin an "evil scarlet woman" and asking Gordon to rescue Tate, who to Lowell's manic mind was fancying himself as Lord Byron, from the clutches of his Countess Guiccioli, Isabella Gardner. Gordon called her friend, the poet Léonie Adams, who called her friend Katherine Biddle, who, in her turn, sent Tate in England a letter about this development. Gardner, humiliated and frantic, was certain that Gordon would now oppose the divorce with renewed energy. Though she felt betrayed, she tried to understand Lowell, writing to her youngest brother: "The thing is, I guess, that he wants Allen and Caroline to be to-gether because they were kind of mother and father to him and when he gets sick he needs that image but when he is 'well' he loves Allen in a more *real* way and knows his unhappiness, and *is* fond of me and so is, when well, *for us*."[43] Hardwick apologized for her husband to Tate, her former lover: she was "distressed . . . to learn that Cal's outrageous behavior is a really serious deterrent to Caroline and that it makes the whole thing more difficult. Of course, Caroline is merely using this for her own ends and I have no sympathy whatever with her or with Cal on the matter. . . . I feel a deep loyalty and commitment to him, and yet at the same time I don't know exactly what sort of bearable status quo I can establish with him. In any case I told him I envied you and Belle and I do; that made him very angry. By that I meant that I think you will have a good marriage and be a great joy and consolation to each other."[44]

In contrast to Hardwick and Gardner, Tate did not fear practical consequences from Lowell's "treachery"; indeed, Lowell's action precipitated an earlier divorce than expected.[45] But then, as usual, Tate vacillated and wrote to Lytle on May 25 that if Gordon had wanted him back for her sake instead of the Church's he would have taken "a very different view," adding that the "Lowell vulgarity reached its height when he told C. that the lady wasn't very rich—that I could look around and do better."[46] Only four days later he begged Gordon not to oppose the divorce, lying about his liaisons: "I lived for nearly four years without becoming involved with another woman, but I have become involved; and there's no use in not facing it."[47] Gordon scoffed, saying his "pattern may have changed but he proposed marriage to another woman this winter while 'engaged' to Mrs. McCormick."[48] (Gordon may have meant Natasha Spender, but it is very unlikely that even Tate would have proposed to her when she was married to Spender and he was enthralled by Gardner.) Frenzied, Gordon seesawed between separation and divorce—"I gave him a divorce once before and he was back on my door-step within two weeks"—but caved in at the end of May.[49] When Tate received the astounding news that Gordon was no longer contesting the divorce, he wrote Katherine Biddle jubilantly, praising Gardner:

"Isabella has had a very rough time, but through it all she has never wavered. Her courage and singleness of purpose have brought *me* through. You can imagine what havoc an hysterical and demanding woman might have caused in eleven months of uncertainty."[50]

The emotional roller-coaster aside, literary and academic life went on as usual. While Robert Lowell was hospitalized at MacLean's, his *Life Studies* was receiving rave reviews in Great Britain, Gardner wrote to her brother on May 20. The lovers had met her old friend the painter David Rolt and the Eliots, who had been married a little over a year and "held hands all through dinner save when T. S. E. had to make a gesture," Louis MacNeice and his wife, Hedli, whom Gardner disliked, and, often, Edith Sitwell, earlier her houseguest at Elmhurst.[51] Sam Monk reported the latest gossip from the Minneapolis English department: everyone was still drinking heavily; Pat Knowlton Stange was leaving her universally loathed husband, Robert; Frank Butler's new wife was nice enough; and Elizabeth (Bid) Brown, who detested her husband, Huntington, had been in an accident.[52] Paul Carroll, then in analysis, wrote his admired friend James Wright, who had "flipped," that this seemed "to be the occupational hazard of the poet," predicting accurately that Wright would become great friends with Gardner in Minneapolis.[53]

Carroll himself was embroiled in an obscenity trial about *Big Table 1* but actually quite upbeat about it, as he had gotten writers such as Jacques Barzun, John Ciardi, and Lionel Trilling to vouch for the magazine; this led to lots of publicity, and circulation was high. *Big Table 2* was a "honey of an issue," and Dahlberg's haunting autobiographical excerpt from *Because I Was Flesh* its best bit. He had returned Jack Kerouac's "windy self-advertisements" but told Gardner he would love to publish her poem on the death of Barbara Ransom Jopson " . . . And Thou No Breath at All?" in *Big Table 3:* "Please rest assured, Isabella, that issue will feature neither beat / square / or crime. All I want is the best writing I can get. . . . You know I love that particular poem: so much yr very voice."[54] But a few months later he reneged:

> After a great deal of thought and changes of mind I have decided that it would not be right to print yr fine "And thou no breath at all . . ." in Big Table 3. The superb formal violence of yr elegy would, I am afraid, seem conspicuously in "a room by itself" in terms of the other poems. I did not think you would want this. Moreover, the atmosphere of this issue is violent, angry, a kind of sharp but poignant bitterness against The Fathers. I did not think you would feel at home; I did not think it would be good for yr literary reputation to appear in such company. . . .
>
> I missed you at the TSE reading. I came, sullen, suspicious that I would only see the ghost of a great poet, certain that Eliot would not read poetry but would,

instead, be a kind of civilized cartoon, Xtn, cultured, urbane. . . . I was abashed: I heard a great poet. . . .

Ragooo, as you would suspect, was pompous, hopelessly the d[e]ferential guest who eats below the salt but must nag his host into attention. . . . Purgatory must be a musty suburban library filled with only the poems of H Rago, which the penitent must memorize forever.[55]

Gardner answered that "she would not want to appear in such an atmosphere as you describe," wondering how he expected "a magazine full of bilious paranoid bleatings of little black sheep who have lost their Maw to be of interest to any one but themselves."[56] She made an exception, though, for the excerpt of Dahlberg's *Because I Was Flesh,* which she read misty-eyed: "It is magnificent and heart-breaking and heroically beautifully written."[57]

Carolyn Kizer wrote Gardner about her magazine, *Poetry Northwest.*[58] For its second issue she had secured two poems by Maxime Kumin, "who seems to me to be greatly talented (who writes me that she met you and was terrified!—I report indiscreetly, but I'd want to know if I terrified somebody!—which I don't understand; I wonder if she meant over-awed, which I might understand, and might have been, myself, if I hadn't been so busy hugging you with delight.)" As Kizer's own poetry had been turned down by many, she asked Gardner for a letter of reference, hoping that this might convince Indiana University Press to publish her.[59] The University of Chicago Press meanwhile tried to get Gardner to have her next book of poetry issued by them, and Lee Anderson asked her to read for his new venture, the Yale Series of Recorded Poets.

Back in America, Gardner packed her things, put the Elmhurst house up for sale, and then left for Wellfleet with Daniel. Tate taught again at the Harvard summer school, led by Henry Kissinger, and included Lytle's load, as his "brother" had fallen ill, but managed to spend most of the week with Gardner on the Cape. However, with his divorce scheduled for August 18, 1959, Tate again balked, as is clear from a much-quoted letter, again to Lytle: "As the time for the divorce approaches I get more and more depressed. It may take place in the next ten days or so. I have allowed myself, in the vacuum of the past years, to drift into a commitment to a very fine woman, Isabella Gardner (formerly Mrs. McCormick), but am not sure that I ought to marry her. What it comes down to is this: I cannot live with Caroline but I am not sure it would be fair to Isabella to marry her as long as C. is living; and I suspect that she will outlive me. Or, put otherwise, I doubt that I can be committed to another woman in marriage while Caroline is alive."[60] But plans for a small wedding on August 27 in Wellfleet, with guests to include the Lytles, most of Gardner's five siblings, the Denneys, and, of course, the Biddles were made. Spending his last night as a new bachelor at the Biddles, Tate found Francis Biddle's best wishes together with an edition of Casanova's memoirs on his pillow. Tate limericked: "Poor Francis and Katherine Biddle / Were kept for a year on the griddle, / Pretending these lovers / Weren't under the covers, / By the law of the Excluded Middle."[61] Lee Anderson, Cleanth Brooks, Edward Dahlberg, the Eberharts, the Lowells, the MacNeices, John Crowe Ransom, Herbert Read, Robert Penn Warren, and many others sent congratulations, southern critic Robert Daniel couching his in verse: "A fugitive poet named Tate / at baiting the Yankees was great / Till a Boston-bred Belle / Changed his fine rebel yell / To 'Yankee, don't wait, let's mate.'"[62]

Tate duly informed his former wife: "I foresaw that it would be said I was marrying Isabella for her money. I will not try to answer this beyond what I now tell you: she has very little money, just enough to support her children and keep them in school." This was rather a flight of fancy, as Gardner's annual income from her family trust was slightly higher than Tate's salary, and, perennially strapped, he realized full well the advantages of her small fortune. His subsequent remark to Gordon did, however, have the ring of truth: "we shall always be together in a sense that nobody but you and me can understand. And I shall so try to live as to deserve seeing you in the next life."[63] It is doubtful that Gordon, although very religious, was comforted by these promises for their common future in the next life; and certain that Gardner, his new bride, would have been inconsolable had she read Tate's words to his ex-wife.

Looking for a house to buy, the Tates settled for a while in the Oak Grove Hotel in Minneapolis, where Allen Tate had stayed often in the years since his appointment at the University of Minnesota in 1951. They soon found a big, three-story house on Irving Avenue with mostly English department neighbors and within walking distance of Lake of the Isles and Kenwood Park, for only twenty thousand dollars, which Gardner paid. Robert received a house-proud, glowing description of this mock-Tudor edifice with bay windows, a far cry from the cool achromatic steel-and-stone austerity of her Mies van der Rohe original in Elmhurst. The Irving Avenue house had fireplaces everywhere, bookcases all around the living room and in Tate's big study, warm wooden floors or soft wall-to-wall carpeting, curtains in reddish orange and walls from pink beige to apricot white, apart from Rose's and Dan's rooms; they chose different color schemes. The living room was keyed to a painting by Congdon of the Greek island Santorin; the dining room had a Congdon painting of winter in Connecticut and a deep copper shelf in the bay window with plants. A Kwakiutl mask hung in the hall, which further boasted an antique mirror and English table. The house's main advantage, in Tate's view, was that it had a tunnel to the garage, so that in the icy Minneapolis winters, during which he usually was the first in the English department to wear a face mask, he did not have to go outside to get his car. Gardner was "enjoying polishing silver and brass and making everything look its best. . . . We are fatuously proud of it all and bore our friends by touring them round and making them look at everything."[64] With love and optimism she was again remaking herself and adapting herself to her husband's tastes and interests; her new role was to be a faculty wife.

In December 1959, just after Thanksgiving, which they celebrated with Rose at the Stanges (who were still together) with a turkey defrosted partially on the central heating in their hotel room, they moved into their house. A selection of Gardner's poems translated into Italian by Alfredo Rizzardi, *Un' Altra Infanzia,* had just come out, which Tate, in a letter to Katherine Biddle, described as "very nice indeed." Briefly he mentioned his upcoming sixtieth-birthday celebration for fifty people, which would introduce them as a couple to the Minneapolis academic community.[65] There were many parties those first months, which Tate relished, but Gardner sighed with relief when they simmered down, although their social life remained full as they often had people over for cocktails, while Gardner cooked for guests at least once a week, and they were often asked out to dinner. Gardner much preferred being à deux, listening to music or playing chess at which she usually won.

Gardner described Tate as an "angel" and "the most tender loving understanding sensitive and giving person" she had ever known.[66] They made a striking couple. She was "so much bigger than he was. He was so very skinny, very elegant and a very well-bred sort of man and she was this large butterfly with that red hair piled on top of her head; she was blowsy. And she was very physically attracted, hugging and kissing and embracing this man. She ADORED this guy, this little shrunken person. . . . You felt that if she tripped and fell on him, he would be finished."[67] But her nightmarish year had taken its toll, and she lacked energy. And from the very beginning of her marriage to Tate, Gardner's children made trouble. Rose was becoming so much of a problem that Elise Vickers McCormick called Gardner, complaining that Rose was disturbed but that Bob felt so guilty toward her that he gave her money and had her lodge with them whenever she wished. For good measure, Elise had Gardner know that Bob McCormick never wanted to hear her name again but followed this up with a letter in which she praised Gardner for being gifted and glamorous, and another one in which she said that Bob McCormick had married her on the rebound from Gardner. Rose had become involved with a married man, Johnny "Dino" Campbell, an amateur African American performer in nightclubs, who was after her trust fund, which she was to receive in September 1960. Congdon thought Rose was psychotic and should be committed, but Gardner was convinced that Rose's seeing a psychiatrist four times a week would make her see some sense.

Due to the upheavals of the past year, Gardner had not written one single poem, she confessed to Katherine Biddle, while praising Katherine's modest poems in *The Other Journey* (1959) so faintly as to be damning. Her real enthusiasm for John Logan's poetry spoke from a letter in which she also mentioned that she would not have time for poetry until the following summer: "The poems are *marvellous*. All. I like them better than anything of yours I've ever seen. As does Allen. In poems as good as these one does not need to rake through them for *the* moving line, *the* stabbing image. You should be proud."[68] Feelings ran high about *Big Table 2* and particularly about the Yage letters by William Burroughs, which, Tate wrote its editor, he found "offensive not only for their obscenity, but for their ludicrous pretensions to serious treatment of a serious nature. . . . The personality of these letters is, by internal evidence, warped and sick, and the irrestistible inference is that the homosexuality and drug-addiction of their author explain the sickness."[69] He, too, admired Dahlberg's work in *Big Table,* even if, unlike Gardner, he thought it unnecessary to constantly shore up Dahlberg's feelings. Dahlberg grumbled: "Tell Allen that when I hear from him I'll believe in God, and that otherwise I have nothing to sustain me but metaphysics and my own sweet defects, sweet or bitter, what is the difference."[70] But if Tate was not inclined to enter into close correspondence with Dahlberg, whose notoriously acrimonious, bitter, and paranoid missives only Herbert Read and Gardner could stomach over years, the Tates helped him extensively during their marriage.

The Tates were soon regarded as a literary team, Reed Whittemore, for instance, asking both to submit for his new *Carleton Miscellany* ("I personally am particularly pleased about the marriage because now I can in one letter write and ask for poems or other contributions") and Logan pleading with them to give a benefit reading.[71] Gardner's "The Looking Glass" and "Nightmare" had been published in *Sewanee Review*'s 1959 autumn issue, which was devoted to Tate, who had been its transformative editor briefly in the 1940s, in honor of his sixtieth birthday. The issue had been over a year in the making, and its editor, Monroe Spears, confused by Tate's complicated amorous adventures, had thought of canceling it because of the personal nature of many of the essays. With contributions by old friends like Richard Blackmur, Cleanth Brooks, Donald Davidson, T. S. Eliot, Katherine Anne Porter, and his mentor, John Crowe Ransom—whose contribution he was most moved by—the issue pleased Tate no end: "They are all talking about somebody else disguised as Tate. It has given me deep satisfaction and consternation."[72]

The Tates took a Christmas holiday in Florida, but it went badly because of Rose's antics and Tate's impatience with her. By January 1960 they had set the dizzying pattern of their married life, which consisted of lots of (literary) houseguests, parties, readings, and travel. Besides Tate's teaching schedule (which he did not take too seriously), their calendar for the first half of 1960 included a housewarming "at which about 60 people appeared and milled around like a herd of bison"; a reading by Gardner and Lowell in Chicago; visits by first Herbert Read, then Robert Penn Warren, then Conrad and Mary Aiken; a stay at Foxcroft as Gardner had persuaded "Miss Charlotte" to invite Tate to read; and a longish trip to Washington, D. C., for Tate's Institute of Contemporary Art meeting, which meant alcoholic get-togethers with the Biddles, the Lowells, Gardner's old friends the Spaldings, Herbert Read, and the man-loving southern writer Katherine Anne Porter, then seventy years old, who was waiting for her decades-younger Sicilian lover dressed in a long pink skirt, pink blouse, and pink sash: "we—Isabella, Cal, and I—called on Katherine Anne at her house just before lunch. All pink inside. John Prince told us about a young man who was taken to see her, and when he left he exclaimed, 'oh, you beautiful, you famous woman!'" They tottered to the train. Then Rose Gardner stayed over and Tate thought her "great fun."[73] They had weekend guests from Chicago and, scarcely drawing a breath, traveled to Lexington, Kentucky, where Tate was to receive a honorary doctorate:

> I [Tate] had been in my hotel room about an hour (bent on a brief nap) when the telephone roused me, and an aged voice said, "This is your cousin Edward Tate." I haven't lived in Ky. since 1916; so Cousin Edward meant nothing to me. I went down to the lobby. Cousin Edward, aged 81, was accompanied by his wife, who turned out to be "Cousin Belle," aged 78, the DAR smalltown club-woman type. Cousin Edward explained how we were "kin"—a little tenuous, I thought, about fourth cousin—and Cousin Belle, when these amenities were disposed of, got down to the business of the visit—which was to ask if I minded having my picture hung in the court house in Winchester, the county seat of Clark County, my natal spot. . . . Well,—what high-brow American poet has ever had his picture exhibited in a court house. This goes far beyond a honorary degree, and I told the President of the University, who agreed with me.[74]

After Lexington it was Tennessee for ten days and, finally, the summer in Wellfleet.

Besides the social whirl, the Tates spent much time on literary activities, but far more often in behalf of friends and protégés than on their own poetry. Both Tates were dedicated to fostering the community of letters, but helping others was often a flight from facing their own blank pages. After the sudden death that year of the Irish poet-diplomat Denis Devlin, Tate edited Devlin's *Selected Poems* with Red Warren and set up a Devlin fund. Much of his time, too, was spent, in vain, on trying to get a name professorship for Andrew Lytle at Vanderbilt University in Nashville. Tate published his *Poems* (1960) which contained no new poems since the magnificent modernist but outmoded "The Buried Lake," written seven years earlier as part of a cycle of poems in terza rima, one of the most difficult verse forms in English; consequently it received few reviews. New was his essay "A Southern Mode of the Imagination" in which he once more illustrated the inner tensions between community and alienation in the literature of the modern South. And he was targeted by big money: Hollywood was, for a short while at least, interested in his 1939 novel *The Fathers.*

Gardner continued her extensive correspondence with Paul Carroll, Edward Dahlberg, and John Logan, buoying them up, commenting on their work and assisting wherever possible. She praised Logan for having "made a tremendous leap" in his poetry and promoted his work wherever she went. At his request, she commented on a manuscript by Dennis Schmitz which she read and reread but thought drearily competent, tiresome, and too obviously influenced by Eliot: "He says *the* thing in the right way and the reader (I, at least) nods and nods and goes to sleep. I don't feel that ragged edge. . . . Just tell him I read him carefully (God knows I did) and if he were my student I'd suggest he impale himself on some short lyrics."[75] Logan asked for contributions for his new magazine *Choice,* and Gardner sent him " . . . And Thou No Breath at All?"[76] The new *Minnesota Review* asked for a submission, too, and was honored when she sent them "A Loud Song, Mother," "The Man of Faith," and "The Searchlight" for its first issue, but these three, too, were poems from the drawer. To the University of Chicago, which wanted to issue her second book, she admitted having only twenty new poems, none recent as she had not written a poem since she had met Tate. She was "low-hearted about it . . . not depressed because I am so happy with Allen but its been so long that I've lost confidence and am literally frightened of an attempt."[77] Nevertheless, after considerable hesitation, she fell in with their proposal to bring out a slim volume. Asked whom she thought would comment favorably on her work, Gardner mentioned Eliot, Ransom, Delmore Schwartz, Shapiro, Sitwell, and Wallace Stevens, most of whom had publicly stated their admiration.

The Tates' life resembled a Hollywood romance. Lowell conceded to Eliot that "Allen's doing nothing whatever but looks better than he has for twenty years" and commented to Tate on "the glad pageantry of your recent life"; he had heard "that Tate certainly is in love with his wife." He did a complete about-face in admitting to Bishop that the Tates "are best at home and you really feel Belle saved Allen's life from the long inspired nightmare of Caroline"; but he predictably could not forego bitching: "She's slow, imperious, though not to Allen, and sane—no crazy agrarian axe to grind."[78] (Gardner's sister-in-law, Lee, declared Lowell's "offish" attitude to both Gardner and her brother Robert "a Brahmin competitiveness which, I have observed over the years of living here, has a meanness and deadly coldness of seasoned excellence within the class. Outside, who cares, but inside it still works."[79]) Herbert Read wrote that "I don't need to wish you happiness—you so obviously possess it," but as early as March 1960, Tate was complaining bitterly about Rose and Daniel.[80] Robert Gardner wrote from Cambridge that Dan was in danger of being thrown out of Brooks. Rose was not going to school; she was still involved with Dino and was dancing in nightclubs. She had dyed her hair a brassy blonde and dressed to match "without thought or care for art or discipline. Doubtless somehow or other all my fault," Gardner wrote Logan, "but I wish I could help her."[81]

For the first time in years, now that he was married to money, Tate did not have to teach summer school and could work on his poetry at Wellfleet. Yet neither Tate nor Gardner were writing, and though Tate had been barren for years, this now bothered him so much that they left Cape Cod earlier than planned; too many cocktails and friends had made them fritter their time away. Tate feared that his reputation was waning and upbraided *Poetry* for not reviewing his *Poems*. Its acting editor, John Frederick Nims, reassured him, invited the Tates for *Poetry*'s champagne party with W. H. Auden as guest of honor on November 19, Tate's sixty-first birthday, and solicited a poem by Tate—which he failed to deliver. Gardner was offended: why had not Nims invited her to submit also? Nims smoothed her ruffled feathers by vowing she belonged to the *Poetry* family and therefore had a standing invitation, but when months later she wrote him she had writer's block, he must have wondered what all the fuss had been about. Barbara Howes, fellow Bostonian, mother, and poet, had also written to see new poems and in passing had expressed disappointment at recent work by Donald Justice ("pretty thin") and W. D. Snodgrass ("I find him soaking in self-pity").[82] Gardner agreed with Howes about Snodgrass and put in a plug for her favorite young poets:

> Do read Galway Kinnell (H.M.Co.) if you haven't. He is very good. Much better than Justice or Starbuck, or Snodgrass or Ann[e] Sexton. And Logan gets better all the time. . . . I think Reuel Denney is one of the best poets of our generation. . . . I brought him to Conrad Aiken's attention and Conrad is including several of Reuel's in his anthology. Not *one* of mine! . . . Karl Shapiro says he (Karl) wanted to include me when he and [Louis] Untermeyer worked to-gether but I gather he was out-voted, and still is. All this really doesn't matter to me as I feel rather fraudulent as 'poet.' My one and only book got too much attention (good and bad) and I've not followed it with anything. My children aren't home and I can't seem to dare to write so I'm reading her textbooks to a blind graduate student and directing a one act play for some public health nurses.

But Gardner remained "literally paralysed about writing," and literary promoting and politicking were her poor, if absorbing substitutes.[83]

As the Beats, partly through Paul Carroll's *Big Table*, became more prominent, Tate became more opposed; they beleaguered his carefully constructed literary empire. When Gardner, deeply admiring of Tate's brilliance and status, then took it upon herself to tell Carroll of their disapproval of the Beats and his publishing them so extensively in his magazine, Carroll showed his deep exasperation:

> We are at loggerheads, apparently, about what is genuine and valuable among the new USA poets. Disagreement is natural and doesn't hurt: what does hurt is the assumption behind your tone of voice, dear Isabella, that, somehow, I am hypocritical and lack, as your husband so smugly and pretentiously wrote, "editorial integrity." . . . I refuse to think that just because Allen Ginsberg, for example, is an exhibitionist and in many ways a psychotic and vulgar man, I refuse to think that this makes him a bad poet, when, in truth, my sensibility tells me that some of his verse has moved me deeply and, on occasion, moved me to tears. Nor will I allow Ginsberg's dislike and lack of appreciation of my own verse and suspicion of me as a man because I can get out a magazine without having to beg from mother or foundation or university or publishing house: I will not allow this to cloud my judgment of his own work. On the other hand, I do not print Bill Merwin because he has been crowned with laurel and is considered by many to be the most accomplished poet of his generation. I print Merwin and Ginsberg because I believe the poems of theirs I have chosen are good poems. It is as simple as that. I leave literary politics to your husband and to Ginsberg and to whomever gets his kicks out of playing such a crafty and cheap game.[84]

Gardner knew Tate had gone too far and explained that she had been "very much opposed [to] his writing you as he did. I think it needlessly cruel and gratuitous." Nevertheless, she could not

> see what is so *new* about "the new American poets"? Olson is far from new. Harold Norse is no better than he was eight years ago when his outpourings inundated Poetry Magazine and drove Karl and me to distraction. Frank O'Hara I like much better but he's been around in magazines for *years,* so has Koch. And there is nothing really new about the poetry itself. It is old fashioned and dates back to the early twenties. . . .
>
> Maybe I am old, cold and numb but most of the poems strike me as nose-thumbing scribbles on a latrine wall—and far less poetic than "Kilroy was here." They seem designed to epater. Most of them far from moving me to tears do not even cause a frisson. Actually a poem that causes a frisson is far *more poem* than one that moves to tears. One *might* weep at "The little toy soldier was covered with dust" or Millay if one is 14 and a girl but does one *weep* at Dante, Chaucer,

Shakespeare, Donne, Marvell, Skelton, Milton, Keats, Coleridge and so on right down to Eliot, Stevens, Auden, Crane, Williams, Ransom, Tate, Lowell, Shapiro? One shudders, one is *moved* in one's bowels (I don't mean that literally!) one laughs—one *recognises* what one had not seen or consciously known before. There is no *humor* in these people. . . . And the imagery seems to me such common property among "the new poets" that it is both barren and monotonous. They repeat not only themselves but each other. I happen to think that you are better than that.[85]

Carroll was grateful for Gardner's answer, "so warm, considerate, yet firm in your opinions and feelings . . . so you": "I feel a certain envy of your great, good capacity to give in a friendship and become so genuinely involved in a friend to the degree that not only will you praise and commend, when these have been merited, but you will take the time to probe some blind-spot or blemish in a friend which you think hinders him from moving easily in the freedom which is himself."[86]

Gardner, who saw herself as an "older sister" to Carroll, still thought him "led astray and dazzled" by the Beats, as she told their mutual friend Logan. She was far more disappointed, though, she said, by Shapiro's *In Defense of Ignorance* (1960), a full-scale attack on modernism and his literary forefathers (and thus also her husband), which included a paean to Henry Miller: "I love Karl but I do not understand the Henry Miller kick or his frantic repetitive railing against Eliot. His comments on the 'conspiracy' to give Pound the Bollingen are simply untrue. I too have *immense* respect for Karl, and love, and admiration, but I don't like this book and he knows it." She protested too much when adding: "My judgment is of no consequence, but my 'judgment' has not been affected by my marriage to Allen and I agree with Allen (and with you) that 'parts of the book' are 'pretty crack-potty.'"[87] Yet, Shapiro's opinions in *In Defense of Ignorance,* except for his championing of Henry Miller as "The Greatest Living Author" (written when he was "very drunk" and of which he was "very proud") were close to Gardner's own subjective, sensitive, and sensible reading of poetry and similar to the opinions he had put forward during their time together at *Poetry.*[88] He was bothered by Gardner's allegation that he had "damned Allen by implication" in his book: "Illogically, I admire and look up to Allen *and* his work, though when the chips are down I have to stand against much of what he believes in."[89] Naturally, this did not mollify Gardner, who wrote him another irate letter. Still championing *In Defense of Ignorance,* which had withered on the vine and had not enjoyed the smashing success among the reading public for which he had hoped, Shapiro then declared their "silly estrangement" over and ended his letter by hitting out at their common whipping boy Rago: "I could kick myself for not making John [Nims] the editor of Poetry. Some imp of perversity made me choose Henry, who, it seems, turns out to be the worst stuffed shirt and pompous ass I could have picked out. I refuse to send Henry any poems of mine but I will to Nims."[90]

Tate was weary of academic politics, for a change, and asked alcoholic department head John Clark for a sabbatical during the spring semester of 1961. Considering his age and reputation, he was at a crossroads of his career and wanted to finish his Dantesque terza rima cycle, which he had begun in 1952; it would be "the main effort of my life" in Europe, where, Tate emphasized (with little self-knowledge), he worked better as there "are fewer temptations to indulge in extraverted activities and I am of necessity thrown in upon myself."[91] He was helping Gardner put together the manuscript for the Chicago Press, as Gardner wrote to Logan, asking him to also assist: "Allen and I have been through all the poems I have on hand rather carefully—but we have not attempted to establish an order."[92] She used that "frail" book, which was to be called *The Looking Glass*, as an excuse to get out of Barbara Howes's proposal for a writing pact in which each of them promised to send the other a poem: "I just can't."[93] Since she had fallen in love with Tate, she had not produced a single poem, had not even tried. Having met and married a poet and critic who had promised to fulfill her as woman and poet, Gardner must have hoped that their union would bear poetic fruit; instead, so far, having this classical intellectual and one of the acknowledged fathers of the stern New Criticism looking over her shoulder undermined her already meager self-confidence. To his taste, her poetry, though brilliant in form, music, and execution, often ironic with metaphysical touches, was nevertheless too different from the male, modernist canon and far too openly expressive of feelings of abandonment, alienation, and death. During these first happy years together, however, Gardner did not acknowledge this and instead served as adoring wife, muse, and handmaiden to her husband's writing.

Readers' reports for *The Looking Glass* were coming in. Roger Hancock noted its "careful and tight organization": starting with the merciless self-scrutiny of "Nightmare" and "On Looking in the Looking Glass," Gardner went on to explore in distanced autobiographical poems the deaths of her close friends, vacation experiences and simmering summer scenes, children, and love, and closing the circle with two poems on self-expression: "Not at All What One Is Used To . . ." and "Writing Poetry." Hancock noted the experimentation in verse forms used to express different moods and subjects, from the recollective musical alliterative "Summer Remembered" to "Part of the Darkness" about a lumbering, garbage-scrounging, domesticated bear, with outrageously long unlyrical lines. The subtleties of the poems might escape the untrained reader, Hancock warned, but, he concluded, "the value of the poetry and the author's established position make the work an important one."[94]

Elder Olson, the Neo-Aristotelian Chicago critic and poet, thought it "a good, sound work in which the writer makes a clean break with the period of her writing which is represented in BIRTHDAYS FROM THE OCEAN, and moves towards the establishment of a new method and the discovery of new subject-matter. As a consequence, the general effect is perhaps neither so brilliant nor so precise as that of her first book; there are, however, important compensations, for this volume has much more variety of invention and technique, and is less mannered and derivat[ive] than the first."[95] His critical opponent for many years, John Crowe Ransom, perused the manuscript with characteristic thoroughness. At his third reading he rated quite a few poems, among them the elegies, as "tremendous" poems and in his final judgment, the volume was "a proper item for publication." In fact, Ransom admired in spite of himself, for Gardner did not fit in the Eliot tradition of poetry:

> Her taste and style have little consciousness of the tradition of poetry in our language, which had its formal peaks in the lyrics of the seventeenth century, or in the subtle surfaces of the eighteenth century. The boldest innovator among modern poets is T. S. Eliot, but his judgment is always conscious of the past. . . .
>
> One kind of poet now includes those (like Eliot and Yeats) who show many degrees and shadings of the old and the new; often show them in the same poem. They are assured of their readers and their secure place. But we have a large group of good poets who decline to look back of 1900. With them poetry has become again a new art, having its being in contemporary life and character; and that is a development which had to come, and which we cannot but accept. We watch it closely, and gratefully, when it is at its best.[96]

On the basis of the readers' reports, the University of Chicago Press was happy to bring out *The Looking Glass* and even expected to be able to combine it with an English edition, about which Tate, according to Gardner, was "very enthusiastic . . and what with many 'friends in court' in London I think it would almost certainly be feasible."[97] But both Cecil Day Lewis at Chatto and Windus and T. S. Eliot at Faber and Faber turned *The Looking Glass* down. Day Lewis felt "they were rather disappointing after those in her first book, which I greatly admired," and Eliot was apologetic, remembering "being much interested by a volume of her earlier poems some years ago," but explained that Faber and Faber preferred bringing out American authors with multivolumes and that he was no longer involved in editorial decisions. [98]

Plans for Tate's sabbatical were solidifying. The Tates were to leave for Boston (to see Gardner's relatives, including the Lowells) at the end of March 1961, then to spend some days in New York City, and sail for Europe in April; first to London (with invitations from Eliot, Louis MacNeice, Herbert Read, Edith Sitwell, Stephen Spender), then to Paris (to see Kitty), and from the end of April to mid-June to Italy, "for work" (but also visits to William Congdon, novelist Harry Brewster, the writer Iris Origo, Henry Rago and his wife, Juliette, and many, many others). They intended to spend the summer, as before, at convivial Wellfleet. So much for Tate's plan to avoid the lure of gregariousness.

In Minneapolis, meanwhile, the Tates' daily lives were similarly booked. Tate could do practically no wrong, both because of his charisma and brilliance and because he was in the thick of America's literary circuit and thus Minneapolis's ticket to contact with literary luminaries and vicarious fame. Most faculty members did not realize that Gardner was a poet in her own right, with her own literary circle; she was expected and therefore seen to be Tate's housekeeper and hostess. As Robert Stange recalled in 1989: "I would not have thought of her as having a real literary career. Perhaps we underestimated her, because we tended to think of her as sort of incidental, and I always assumed that she would not have had any position on *Poetry Magazine* if she had not been rich."[99] Gardner tried to be the perfect faculty wife and cooked, took care of the house, did volunteer work, and hosted parties, but the role did not come naturally to her. Having her own money had meant that she—within the constraints of her times—lived her own life. Neither during her nonconformist first two marriages nor her socially mainstream third marriage had she slavishly followed her husbands' wishes or the mores of the social communities in which she found herself. Now, however, she desired to be entirely wrapped up in Tate and his life in Minneapolis and was consequently far more compliant than ever before.

Still, the small and ultimately provincial academic community in Minneapolis had to get used to Gardner's outlandish taste in drinks, such as cranberry juice or Campari, and her liking for long flowing robes, very much outside the dress code of the late 1950s and early 1960s. Nevertheless, it was a truth universally acknowledged that the Tates gave great parties. After Tate's death, in 1980, Gordon O'Brien, still a very young staff member in the early 1960s, felt compelled to write Gardner from Minneapolis about "your home on Irving South, your blazing hearth and groaning board, around which there was formed the one true cosmopolitan center, the one true intellectual exchange (so far as I was ever able to discover) of all the upper midwest. And it was made possible by a remarkable combination of the generosity and fame of the host and hostess.... I don't suppose we deserved it, our lack of desert being attested to by the fact that we have never come by another one."[100] The parties were memorable because of the celebrities who attended (from W. H. Auden to Robert Frost), not only because of both Tates' qualities as hosts, but also because their house was warm and inviting and food and drink inexhaustible, as Gardner's added income made it possible for them to entertain lavishly. Town-and-gown Minneapolis, then, enthusiastically accepted their hospitality. The faculty acknowledged that Gardner had saved Tate from gallivanting about, drinking far too much, and, generally, living a dissolute life.[101] Still, Tate's old friends in the English department did not really like Gardner; as a financially independent and worldly Boston Brahmin she remained too different from faculty wives like John Berryman's young third wife, Kate Donahue Berryman, whom the Tates dubbed "Saint Kate" as she time and again meekly put up with her husband's impossible conduct. But she was kind, and among the faculty wives only she and outsiders like uninhibited Pat Stange and eccentric, independent Bid Brown truly valued Gardner as a person. Young James Wright, who was soon to be dismissed for drunken and disorderly behavior, was her only real friend among the male faculty.

In the wider world, American politics were fascinating with Richard Nixon and John F. Kennedy battling for the presidency. The Tates registered and voted for Kennedy, as, like Barbara Howes ("Nixon has never stuck to anything except his policy of running with the pack"), they regarded Nixon as "dangerous."[102] In between visits to Washington for the Kennedy inauguration and readings by Tate in Chicago (with parties by Maglet Myrhum and Helen Donohue Butler), Gardner tried to get Rose back on track. Rose had already been supporting Dino for the past several years, but intended to give him five thousand dollars, on receipt of her capital, ostensibly to help him get a divorce. Peabo came over from Boston to Minneapolis to dissuade her, but in vain. Gardner wrote Myra Cholden that she was in despair as Rose had produced crisis after crisis since she was fifteen: "I think that the reason she has not become pregnant or been beaten up and raped in a back alley is that she is basically narcissistic and not in the least masochistic. She does not suffer from conscience or guilt." She was sure that Rose's chronic lying was congenital, like Van's, but her heart bled for Rose as her daughter seemed to use Dino to fill the void of her empty personality. A woman of her times, Gardner was sure that if "he were a proper man he would not permit her to 'keep' him."[103] A few weeks later, again dealing with her daughter, Gardner remembered her own escapades: "At twenty-one to travel with one's love, one's lover is not something I can in my heart disapprove of. I can't as her mother condone it, but it is thoroughly understandable." But Gardner, four times married herself, was afraid Rose would marry Dino, have a child, and then break up with him, and she wondered what "possibility of a solid marriage to anyone else" she then would have. Thinking, for once, like a proper Gardner (and, perhaps, of Seymour), she wished she "could make [Rose] understand that one can fall in love more than once; that the racial, money, status, education etc. differences will in time make him bitterly hostile to her."[104] To Katherine Biddle, Tate dismissed Rose as having "'a psychopathic personality' in the sense that she doesn't know simple right from simple wrong."[105]

Other relationships were troubled also. The latest gossip from Chicago, funneled by Elise Vickers McCormick ("who persists in writing me," Gardner wrote Myra) was that Maurice Donohue, divorced from Virginia, "a solid brass bitch," wanted to remarry her, although she was involved with a "top echelon Hoodlum" and his own love affair with Milly Levin had been going on for twelve years.[106] And in March 1961 Elizabeth Hardwick sought to divorce Lowell, who was hospitalized once more, and asked Tate to help her get a grant from the Academy of Arts and Letters. Two months later, though, the Lowells were "very much back together and both [felt] as if we had been tossed in blankets."[107] Dahlberg and his Rlene were separating (Herbert Read wondered: "Poor girl, I don't know how she stood it for so long"), and Gardner played matchmaker by bringing him into contact with Patricia Haskell—but the Dahlbergs also reunited.[108]

The Tates, however, were blissful, Gardner proclaiming to all that Tate was an angel, while he told his southern and Minneapolis friends that he had a wonderful time and had never enjoyed Europe so much, even though he had given eight lectures in a month. That "[a]ll but two had been flops" did not dampen his excellent spirits, nor was he overly annoyed by the fact that Robert Frost had received the $25,000 prize from the National Poetry Foundation: "I was one of the jurors (I voted for Aiken) but evidently a large majority were for the Old Man. The letter informing me of this did not say *Who* got how many votes. I suspect it was rigged."[109] Gardner had been glad to be back in London, seeing plays and sights and their friends, and had enjoyed their visit with Kitty in Paris and the French highlights Chartres and Versailles, but the climax was their long stay in Italy:

A big room overlooking gardens (magnolias—flowering fruit trees) and another room for Allen to work in. We were on half-pension and had breakfast in our room at 7:30 each morning. Then Allen would work. I would roam Florence. At noon we would meet in the piazza Signorina opposite the Palazzo Vecchio. . . . We would always have a vermouth there and read our letters and the papers. Then back to the pensione for lunch—a siesta—then sight-seeing to-gether. Then dinner at a little trattoria where, for a couple of dollars we had delicious food and wine . . . and often with friends—both Italian and American. We had the same feelings about what we *saw*. We both loved the Romanesque churches. We loved Lucca della Robbia—Giotto—Donatello—Masaccio—Mantegna—We went to San Marco to see Fra Angelico. We didn't much like Michelangelo though we admired him immensely and loved the unfinished Pieta in the Duome. We played chess in and out of cafes. We walked and walked and walked. We were immensely happy.

There were side trips. We gave joint readings in Bologna (red, *red* under a deep blue sky) and Urbino with its trompe l'oeil and bells, bells, bells. We went to Assisi which we adored and where Billy Congdon lives in a hundreds of years old house with ducks and a goat and fig trees and olive trees and his *beautiful* post conversion paintings—we went to Siena with its fantastic square where the buildings bend in and out. To Perugia, Orvieto, Gubbio where we saw the town boys practice cross-bow against a target nailed to the Cathedral. San Gimignano . . . and Rome twice—once for a lecture of Allen's. . . . Before sailing we went to Herculaneum and Pompeii. [They were] the most miraculously perfect months of both our lives.[110]

There had been only minor worries. Gardner hated "the sexy jacket" the University of Chicago Press had designed for *The Looking Glass:* "I do not want a jet haired vampire on the cover of a (however 'thin') volume of serious poems."[111] She was so angry that she threatened to withdraw her book, essentially blackmailing Chicago to get her friend the photographer Aaron Siskind to do the cover for the paperback edition. Back in Wellfleet, in July, the Tates' idyll continued. They had Daniel, now seventeen, with them. He was taking drawing lessons, writing poetry, and was a delight to discuss Macbeth, Salinger, or Virginia Woolf with: "He and Allen get along extremely well, though Allen sometimes thinks there should be more emphasis on his punctuation and grammar and less indulgence in discussion."[112] They had a lovely, austere, oriental house near a swimmable pond, its only drawbacks being that there was no hot water and that the neighbors, with whom they shared a generator for electricity, turned it off after 11:00 p.m. Tate testified at the obscenity trial of Hubert Selby's *Last Exit to Brooklyn* and swore solemnly "that the story, which was about a brutal gang rape, was highly moral. Stanley Kunitz said that, too, but the magistrates . . . disagreed. At one point there was such an outburst of hilarity that the Court was cleared," the British critic Frank Kermode recollected, adding: "The truth is, they were, that summer, in a dotingly silly mood."[113]

But Rose was to cause trouble again. She had accompanied Dino to Australia but had suddenly left him behind, gone on to Mexico, and met a Mexican bullfighter and painter, Jorge Luis Lopez, divorced and with a son, whom she was set to marry at once. Touched by a letter that Lopez had written to her and wanting to give her daughter a wonderful wedding to launch her new, bright future, Gardner suggested they marry at Wellfleet. Gossipy Tate wrote his Minneapolis crony Charles Foster of the impending marriage—that his wife was "going all out," that the preparations at such short notice were taking up far too much of her time, that all the Gardners were coming, and that they thought "the marriage a good thing. A bull-fighter at least has courage."[114] Jorge Lopez was very handsome to boot, but the Gardner family, with their close involvement with United Fruit, had connections in high and secret places and were warned just before the wedding that Lopez was notorious for marrying rich American women for their money and then quickly abandoning them. The wedding was called off at the last moment, but Rose flew to the Cape and was oppressively present at Wellfleet: "The poor wretched child doesn't feel anything—not even embarrassment. The most feeling she has shown is to vehemently deny The Embassy's statement that he has not fought a bull for 10 years. It is all in the realm of role and phantasy for her and she even in a way *enjoys* the telegrams and presents and notoriety. I am afraid she has learned nothing from the experience. She is of course at present in this house a rather lovable poltergeist making me ill, and Allen angry and Dan confused. . . . I am tired to my very marrow, but she is blithe and bonny and like an innocent child of 14—God help her."[115]

Exhausted, the Tates gave up their plan to visit the Lytles at Monteagle, Tennessee, as they needed to write. For during their long stay in Europe, Tate had not made much progress on the terza rima poem, though he was keeping up appearances, and Natasha Spender (without hinting once at their earlier affair) wrote him that she was happy that he had been "so prolific."[116] Gardner told Logan that "Allen got more verse written (on his long Terza Rima poem) in Florence than he has done in 7 years," but that was only relative, and Dahlberg heard that "Allen's poem is far from finished."[117]

Chapter Seven

"Book and Bed and Booze and Blunders of the Heart," 1962–1965

There should be a Forest Preserve for poets
each with his or her mate but I remind myself
that the poet is rumoured to be less constant
than the swan. No the bard must do his best with book
and bed and booze and blunders of the heart and
bearing witness burying friends banning bombs
and using onomatopeia with restraint.
("This Room Is Full of Clocks")

In September 1961 the Tates were back in Minneapolis, and praise for *The Looking Glass* growing loud. Katherine Biddle congratulated Gardner on her "enchanting and revivifying book of poems. . . . Your skill, your beautiful craftsmanship, your control, the vistas of you as a warm, feeling human being that comes through all the skill, all the lovely music."[1] Charles Foster, an admirer of Tate, but not of his wife, was surprised into praise: "I confidently predict that there are poems in it destined for permanence in American literature. . . . [The poems] seem to me remarkable in unmistakable individuality of tone and for being true in sight, sound, phrase and sense. I have read no recent poetry of such depth . . . and I dare to add, human warmth. In fact, your humanity, your tenderness (not a drop of sentimentality, a different matter) seem to me the ground of your whole accomplishment."[2] Edward Dahlberg doubted "that Emily Dickinson ever wrote lines with so great a skill."[3] Carolyn Kizer was fulsome: "I'm a little late in acknowledging your book, which I am *so* happy to have! It is beautiful in all ways, inside and outside, like its author. . . . I particularly enjoyed seeing the poems which were new to me: *Nightmare* (the equal of [Louise] Bogan's, no small praise in my canon), *Summer Remembered* (you damn well *do* HEAR every syllable), *Part of Darkness* (a poem several people I know have tried to write, failing miserably), *Writing Poetry* (MARVELLOUS POEM!!!) and *Summers Ago*, which made me weep."[4]

Elizabeth Bishop remarked on Gardner's "poetry of great skill and sophistication. But the best thing about her is that in poems like SEARCHLIGHT, LITTLE ROCK, and A PART OF THE DARK, while using her skill and sophistication, she also uses them up, dissolving them in real feeling, deep, and 'feminine' in the good senses of that word."[5] As one of Tate's ex-lovers, Elizabeth Hardwick's inimical feelings for Gardner showed in her dubiously complimentary response ("the poems *feel like you,* so sharply and rightly, a genuine achievement of your own voice"), while her husband Cal Lowell liked best Gardner's "freedom to dart into all sorts of subjects and passions that would scare me. Some of the poems I like are the Snail ["The Widow's Yard"] Mea Culpa, the long one about acting, the Looking Glass, Little Rock. Few give so much of themselves in so small a space. The language is rich, and nervous and has a lyrical jump to it. What next? You have many useful styles started and I suppose can only wait what the various chances and pressures draw from you."[6]

Tate was on the Bollingen Committee and speculated in a letter to Katherine Biddle on who ought to get that prize: "The 1961 books are rather dreary, except for Jack Wheelock's. Isabella has published too little, is too young; and has other disqualifying circumstances."[7] Her husband's being on the Bollingen Committee would have precluded Gardner from getting the prize anyway, but when she read this, Gardner was embarrassed, and Tate hastened to inform Biddle that "she thinks you may get the impression that she believes she is in some way eligible, etc. Of course she doesn't think she is, nor do I. I am sure I know why I mentioned it. I had just received from Yale a list of the 1961 books of verse, and I suppose I was annoyed that her book wasn't even listed, although some thirty very small poets were."[8] That year's prize was shared between John Hall Wheelock, then seventy-six, and Richard Eberhart, at almost sixty. Tate disliked Eberhart both as poet (too prolific and safe) and person (for his literary politicking).

Like *Birthdays, The Looking Glass* was a leading contender for the National Book Award. The reviews, though fewer than for her first book, were almost unreservedly laudatory. But self-educated Virginian critic Carleton Drewry—later Poet Laureate of Virginia—took exception in the *Roanoke Times,* devoting almost as much space to attacking the book's blurbs as Gardner's poetry, which he chided for its "verbal antics" and attitude of "deliberate disdain, not only for poetry itself, but for its readers."[9] And Hal Smith, comparing *The Looking Glass* to Thom Gunn's *My Sad Captains and Other Poems,* praised Gardner's poetry for being "full of verve and flash; insatiate of forms she never rests," but ended with a platitude: he could not "find, in all the abundant virtuosity of her technique, the rock bottom of her poetic being."[10] Referring to this review, Logan wondered "whether we are not again in the presence of a frustrated poet (whose jealousies are roused more by the awareness of the achievement of an American woman than by those of an English gentleman)."[11] Gardner was far less thin-skinned than she had been when *Birthdays* came out; but the review that hurt was by Harvey Curtis Webster in her own *Poetry*. Instead of commending Gardner for suiting her forms to her feelings and themes, Webster contended in his omnibus article that she was "too involved still with the struggle to find appropriate forms," but appreciated her "Writing Poetry" as well as her translations of Yvan Goll, because they "dare in a promising, less rhyme-ridden direction."[12]

Earlier, Carroll, a perceptive critic who never rolled with the fashions of the times, had written Gardner: "I think your new book is your best (and if that analphabet, Ragoo, doesn't see to it that you receive a review of your own, I will take it upon myself, here in Chicago, to lock him, naked, in a room with Ellen Borden Stevenson, and pitch the key to the gulls)."[13] To what measures Carroll resorted is unknown, but Rago asked him for a review to balance Webster's and printed his ecstatic "A Note on Isabella Gardner" in the same issue.

> Miss Gardner celebrates nothing but the bald essentials . . . death, sexual desire, children, and the mystery, ugliness and pain of human relationships. . . . Few poets I know can delineate the odd, sometimes beautiful twists in a relationship between people as well as Miss Gardner without padding some Big Message into the poem. . . . No woman poet (and I know that Miss Gardner, Miss Denise Levertov, and Miss Carolyn Kizer will read this phrase with contempt) describes sexual desire with the vividness of *Letter from Slough Pond,* and the earlier *Gimboling, Cock A'Hoop* and *Lines to a Seagreen Lover.* Such poems make Elizabeth Barrett Browning and Edna St. Vincent Millay (Dylan Thomas's lady poet pursuing him with a fistful of sonnets) sound as if sex occurs only among the Hottentots and then only prior to beatific illumination by Presbyterian missionaries. . . . *Writing Poetry* is surely one of the most biting, honest, and witty poems written on the subject. Unlike Miss Moore's famous *Poetry,* this poem delineates, with a scalpel keen as my father's Irish tongue, the kind of men and women who write verse.[14]

In 1968 Carroll published his eclectic but seminal *The Poem In Its Skin* and in the final essay, "The Generation of '62," he included Gardner as the only woman among ten very different poets—the others being John Ashbery, Robert Creeley, James Dickey, Allen Ginsberg, John Logan, W. S. Merwin, Frank O'Hara, W. D. Snodgrass, and James Wright—who were "barbarians . . . inside the gate," the ones who were "the alien or the enemy of prevailing contemporary standards of correctness or purity of taste" and radically innovated poetry even before *Howl* by the young Beat poet Allen Ginsberg in 1956.[15]

Van Allen Bradley in Chicago mentioned Gardner's discriminating hand in the affairs of *Poetry* and celebrated her as "the finest woman poet to emerge in Chicago since Gwendolyn Brooks won the Pulitzer Prize more than a dozen years ago"; Rose Mary DeLancey remarked on her "excellent poems which hold up to the looking glass the author, people she has known, and situations on which she wishes to comment"; Fred Holley lauded them for being "intensely personal and intensely contemporary"; Robert Holzhauer (though starting off with "Miss Gardner, whose husband is the distinguished poet and critic Allen Tate") noted that "she peels off the obvious level of reflection, going beyond glittering mirages into another dimension which envelops body and spirit. Heart to heart, yet with an awareness of the conflicts of the world, Miss Gardner writes with golden ease, a passionate perturbation"; and Burton Robie noted her versatility and the "startling and charming liberties with words and forms that only a real poet would dare to do."[16]

Reviews by fellow poets were not only more incisive, but also even more complimentary. Ralph Mills Jr. acclaimed Gardner a "poet of talents *essentially poetic:* that is, an innate sense of language and its possibilities and the ability to think concretely with the words she uses."[17] James Wright, reviewing Gardner's volume together with *The Jacob's Ladder,* by Denise Levertov, called them "two noble women, who are also two of the best living poets in America," and perceived Gardner's "dreadfully strong gift which I will call the power of incantation. It is the rhythmic and musical form of the authentic poetic madness, the madness of the ancient poets and rhapsodists."[18] Gardner was most moved by Logan's "The Poetry of Isabella Gardner" in the *Sewanee Review:* "You have quite a terrifying insight when you say 'It is almost as if our being in love committed us to being abandoned and hence as if commitment to love meant commitment to death.' John, John, that shook me! because it *is* 'almost as if.'"[19]

The best review from a promotional point-of-view was by Karl Shapiro, who had initially been hesitant to write about her: "I am mixed up in too many lunatic fringe affairs to be of any real usefulness to you."[20] In his review for the *New York Times,* he recollected the encomia *Birthdays* had gathered on both sides of the ocean because Gardner's poetry was "paint raw from the tube— without being amateurish or offensive. It had the quality this reviewer admires most, of being primitive, the direct opposite of the modern, extremely fashionable baroque. . . . The present volume, though small, is even better than the first." The poems in *The Looking Glass* were "beautifully complete, rich with the human vibration, without being a strutting Work of Art. Many of her poems are colloquies with persons, somewhat formal and yet highly emotional, at least by present standards. . . . It is an outstanding book. If I had anything to do with it I would nominate it for the Pulitzer Prize."[21] *The Looking Glass* was indeed nominated for the Pulitzer, and Gardner "allowed herself a little fantasy of winning and turning down the Pulitzer Prize," but it went to Alan Dugan's first book, *Poems,* which also won the National Book Award.[22]

Like *Birthdays, The Looking Glass* sold thousands of copies (no thanks to the University of Chicago Press, which barely exploited Gardner's nominations for the two top awards), but while gathering garlands, Gardner hardly mentioned her successes in her letters. The poems in *The Looking Glass* had all been written before she had met Tate; and as her beloved was "feeling more and more isolated from the 'literature'" of his time and battling his long creative drought without success, she considered it treasonous to try to upstage him.[23] Paradoxically, now that she was finally a poet amongst poets, she opted to be a handmaiden to her husband's vocation. They continued to throw parties for the many poets reading in Minneapolis, with most of them staying as overnight guests. Tate wrote to Katherine Biddle about the Lowells' visit, with Lowell "in excellent form," but his wife's lecture "a little short of that." He worried, though, about Lowell's "megalomania—grading the poets, rating their poems, first, second, third, etc.," which was so "all-inclusive that there are no distinctions or standards, literary or personal, and it all comes down to The Career."[24] And about their invitation to the Kennedys' White House: "The Lowells . . . are going. Isabella had decided agin it, but I think she couldn't bear having the Lowells go and our not going; so she sent off an acceptance, saying . . . that we could telegraph regrets at the last minute. Then Peabo was on the telephone from Boston, and he averred that we couldn't treat the White House in such a cavalier fashion. My guess is that we shall go."[25]

Assisting friends continued to take up much of their time: they worked extensively on Reuel Denney's poems, convinced the University of Chicago to publish them, then got him to write the University of Minnesota Pamphlet on Conrad Aiken. Tate also helped Reed Whittemore organize the conference of the Association of Literary Magazines of America in Minneapolis. They did not succeed in all their endeavors, for Maurice English, now heading the University of Chicago Press, refused to publish John Logan's manuscript. If all these friends, including Logan, greatly valued the Tates' exertions in their behalf, Edward Dahlberg, typically, proved an embittered malcontent. The Tates had written numerous letters in his behalf to get him noticed, published, and reviewed; they got him grants, and Gardner often sent him some of her own money. But why, Dahlberg whined to Gardner, had her husband not written to the University of Detroit Press: "You must know, my very dear friend, that it is most awkward for me to ask the same kindness of Allen repeatedly; it was hard enough to ask it once." It had been his "fervent hope also that Allen might be able to suggest some appointment for me at a university, where I could talk to students, and be of some use to people. How many fools are at our academies of nonsense, and despite my so-called reputation for which I would not give a cumin seed, I am helpless." He continued: "Why with all the conferences that are held each year, and what with so many people teaching writing who cannot write themselves, am I always the pariah?"[26] Tate wrote a blurb for *Because I Was Flesh*, which catapulted Dahlberg into renewed recognition, but was, as always, too shrewd to get into a literary fracas with him. He did get embroiled in Minneapolis literary politics in alcoholic, cranky, cruel but often brilliant John Berryman's behalf, whom he wanted to get promoted. His chairman John Clark refused, and Tate got on his high horse: "I owe it to you as well as to myself to say that I will not be intimidated. You have perfectly sound reasons for opposing Berryman. But that you should interpret a different point of view as an act of personal hostility I find incomprehensible."[27] Tate got his way.

His daughter, Nancy, had grown into a warmhearted, responsible woman despite the haphazard treatment she had received from her writer parents; their turbulent lives had centered around themselves, never around Nancy, whom they had left with others for months at a time if it so suited them. Gardner's children, however, were affected by absent fathers and a mother who, though constantly worrying about them, had relegated them to second place. Rose had gone back to Dino ("a mulatto boy who allowed her to support him by posing in the nude") and wanted to marry him.[28] Daniel graduated from Brooks after all, and Rose attended "heavily made up and orange haired with a gigantic pink pouffe of a hat."[29] Daniel was slowly being poisoned against his mother by his big sister—who was living an unfettered druggie, hippie life—and by his father—who had never forgiven Gardner for betraying him and taking his son away and had vilely told Daniel that his mother had behaved like a tramp during their marriage. Gardner's protestations that she had been unfaithful with Sarkissian only—she even got an affidavit to prove this—did not convince Dan. (Myra Cholden was curious to know which other names Seymour had mentioned apart from Sarkissian: "What in heaven's name possessed him to name [Sydney] Harris—it was the only thing that made me laugh."[30]) Dan was feeling more and more adolescently antagonistic toward Gardner and, particularly, Tate, who, unlike McCormick, did not care for him but played the autocratic father when he decided the occasion demanded it. Gardner, much more deferential to Tate than she had ever been to McCormick, mostly allowed this without protest, and Daniel felt cast aside. In an unguarded, alcoholic moment Gardner had conveyed her anxiety about Dan to Elizabeth Hardwick, falling into her "life-long trap of confiding in a woman I know to have a tongue plus *some* hostility to me. Like Mary [Manning]. And so I terribly regret having told Elizabeth something (not all) about Seymour's monstrous telling of untruths to Dan, and discussed Rosy too much. . . . I don't know *why* I am so unnecessarily open with women I know I shouldn't trust—partly masochism and partly fear and some superstitious notion that by being candid I disarm them? I make the grotesque mistake of thinking they will behave as I do in similar circumstances."[31] As even Fanita English spontaneously affirmed, Gardner did not betray trust and was too loyal to gossip, which did not go down well with either the caustic Lowells or the vitriolic Minnesota English department, which got its kicks from the (extra-) marital and other strife amongst its often eccentric and always imbibing members. (Tate's physician Boyd Thomes said of his colleague Franz Montgomery that his blood was "*almost* pure alcohol," while his lawyer John Goetz reported that he had lunched with the young American Studies specialist Leo Marx, who "remarked that this must be the hardest-drinking English department in the United States. He seemed awed."[32])

In April 1962 Gardner had written Dahlberg that Tate's "terza rima poem will be finished by autumn," but that summer found them feverishly visiting all their friends in Europe again instead of working.[33] In June, Isabella wrote to Charles and Doris Foster that they had scarcely had time to draw breath:

> We arrived in London about midnight last Thursday and found many messages including a summons to Edith Sitwell for Friday at 5:30. Poor Edith was in bed with a slipped disk but was gallantly arranged in a pink bed-jacket and served us drinks and malicious wit in equally delightful doses. . . . We had a noon drink that day with Louis MacNeice and lunch with Julian Mitchell . . . and dinner with Jack and Phyllis Wheelock after Edith's soiree. Saturday we went to Red Hill to lunch with Jack and Chatz [?]. Both blooming as was their lovely garden. We had drinks with the [Marcus] Cunliffes at 5:30 and went to *School for Scandal* directed by Gielgud with Ralph Richardson as Peter Teazle and Margaret Rutherford as a delightful but rather implausible Mrs. Candour. Sunday we had lunch with old friends of mine in the country and dinner with the Wheelocks. Monday night we went to dinner at the Eliots (Valerie's gotten very *fat!*) and the Yvor Richards were there and I enjoyed them. Tues. we saw the Richards again at lunch . . . and Tuesday night was a dinner party at the Spenders. Wed. night we had dinner at Allen's publisher's apt. Thursday (yesterday) we went to Hampton Court with Louis MacNeice and in the evening went to a party with Stephen Spender.

There were also meetings with Auden, Graham Greene, and David Rolt and more plays as well as museums. The Tates were looking forward to a "quiet fruitful month in Florence."[34]

Gardner's sister-in-law Lee was treated to less-exhaustive but more salient details about their stay in England: "I finally met Natasha Spender (once Allen's love) who is far younger (41?) than I expected but far *less* interesting both to look at and be with. But extremely nice." Gardner had gone to a retrospective of Francis Bacon's paintings, which she thought were "marvelous and horrifying," but when she met the man at a party she was surprised that he seemed "very friendly and likable and totally (on the surface) unlike his Peter Lorre-ish portraits." Mary McCarthy was also present: "an extremely attractive woman in addition to her other gifts. I suppose all she lacks is a heart."[35] Reveling in being so feted, Tate loved London and "we now think of coming here in 2 or 3 years to live when Allen retires," Gardner told Dahlberg, apologizing for the fact that they still had not found an academic job for him.[36] After these "rigorous gayeties" in London, it was France with the Joseph Frank, then to Florence, where the Tates stayed at their Pensione Annalena again, Tate working in his separate study in the mornings, while Gardner, as before, walked the city.[37] But Florence proved too hot, and soon they were once more too restlessly wandering to work.

Back in the United States at summer's end, they had to get Dan out of a scrape with the law, but Gardner took this, Tate wrote to Foster, "with more philosophic calm than she could have felt a year ago. This is the result of her belief, which I share, that he is a good boy and will pull through."[38] In October the Poets Festival would take place in Washington, D. C., and Tate was looking forward to carousing with the Biddles, Ransom, and Read there, but not to the festival itself: "This is going to be a very rough three days, after which we go to Princeton and New York. I am too old for all this."[39] He refused to go and listen to keynote speaker Randall Jarrell (second choice after Mark Van Doren, who had replied that he would not give the main lecture if his life depended on it), who had at long last won the National Book Award for his *The Woman at the Washington Zoo* (1960). Herbert Read hoped Gardner would accompany Tate: "She should come and heckle Jarrell."[40] The festival was draining, "not at all in the too many cocktails and late hours sense but just too many poets (egos) too much of the time! . . . We all shook our heads about Steinbeck winning the Nobel Prize, and poor Delmore Schwartz wrecking the hotel room at The Continental and being thrown into jail and the fight the last evening after Herbert's [Read] lecture between Kunitz and Oscar Williams. Oscar for no reason picked the fight shouting to Stanley (and he was cold sober) 'You are a climber'—Stanley rose to his feet and said 'You are a worm and I hate you.' I rose to my feet and said to Oscar that I was outraged by his attack etc. etc.—on such a note the poets parted! . . . I think Oscar made the scene to attract attention to himself."[41] Although Gardner thought Léonie Adams, James Cunningham, Stanley Kunitz, Howard Nemerov, Karl Shapiro, and, of course, Tate splendid—and Berryman heroic in getting Schwartz out of jail—she decided to pass on poets reading their poems for some time to come. When Tate, fatigued and frustrated, heard that Jarrell had called him a neglected poet in his lecture "Fifty Years of American Poetry," he exploded: "Neglected? Me? I had not thought so. But to say so in public is a sly way of getting one neglected. I would write Mr. J. this except that it would give him too much pleasure. I thought his public reading was disgusting."[42]

Meanwhile, Gardner was "in a perfect swivet of Christmas shopping for the myriad family connection. Every niece and nephew, and there are thousands. Beside she is directing a play for children at an under-privileged school. I am feeling under-privileged myself. I want to be at Captiva or in Sicily," Tate complained.[43] Now sixty-four, Tate was dissatisfied anyway and wrote Robert Penn Warren: "I'm so bored with giving the same thing every year that I would be tempted to resign if I could afford it. I seem not to have the energy to work up new material. I'm still giving your Interpretation of Poetry, and I'm so sick of interpreting poetry that I sometimes hope I'll never see another poem."[44] He had undergone a minor operation ("All those pipes and electronic devices in the nether regions begin to burn out a little"), suffered as a bronchial asthmatic chain-smoker from the foul Minnesota climate, and was generally feeling under the weather.[45] He took heart when he received from Florence the Medaglia d'Oro della Societa di Dante Alighieri for 1962, which pleased him more than any other honor he had ever had. And he had great fun as one of the three hundred select guests at Gardner's parents' glorious golden nuptials in January 1963, but he was deeply disturbed again upon hearing that his old friend Conrad Aiken, drinking fifteen or so martinis daily, had had a heart attack at seventy-three.

Gardner influenced her husband's political views. When she had been a picketing fellow-traveler, Tate had been a southern racist as well as an agrarian—be it an unlikely one as he could not tell "a tulip from a radish"; Pat Knowlton Stange "could not imagine Allen even knowing what a plough was, let alone getting behind one."[46] Now both had voted for Kennedy against Nixon, for Tate had given up his cherished prejudices about Irish Catholics and Bostonians: "Isabella, of course, is to be credited with the increasing flaccidity of my prejudices: they are daily getting to be like tired rubber: they stretch but they don't snap back."[47] The Confederate flag was still prominently displayed in their mixed Minnesota household and Tate wore his Confederate vest to their most formal parties, but he lectured his old comrade Donald Davidson, still an unconverted bigot, on his views: "I object to having States Rights invoked and the Confederate flag waved only when the race problem becomes acute. This gives the case away to the North, and retroactively confirms the view of the Northern historian that the War was fought only to preserve slavery."[48] He would not feel at home in an integrated South, he continued, but segregation was a lost cause. Some weeks later he added pragmatically: "If you can't lick 'em, join 'em, might well be the Southern slogan: that is, take over integration and do it gradually the Southern way."[49]

Friends continued to ask favors. Theodore Roethke asked them to arrange a reading for him in Minneapolis, as he needed the money. "And I guess the real reason (deep in my heart of hearts, where there is nothing but wormy ambition) is that I would so much like both of you to take a gander at *Dance On, Dance On, Dance On* the manuscript of the new book; and if you don't think it's one hell of a book, I'll turn in my suit. I say this, I suppose, because I always have the terror that I won't write another, etc. Ach Gott, you know. Enough of slobbering egomania and four I's in one sentence."[50] Paul Carroll treated them to a story of similar poetic egos:

> Over the weekend Jim Dickey who was between readings came for a visit and on Saturday I gave a cocktail party for him, which I wish you could have been at: it was a Ragooooean fiasco of limited but intense mirth. Henry arrived, huffing and puffing with artificial dignity—of late he has done a fair imitation of the Pope receiving Bishops from the lower Sudetenland—beet-red because Jim Dickey was "my friend" and hadn't done homage to Poetry magazine by crawling on his hands and knees to visit the Shrine. By chance, John Logan arrived down stairs at the same moment that the Ragos did, and so shared an elevator with them. "Why does God hate me tonight?" John whispered, nervously, in my ear: "Of all moments to arrive at the elevator!" Later, John was seen mumbling to Jim Dickey: "Watch out: Ragoo is The Enemy." In another corner John Frederick Nims was hissing dark thoughts about Henry. Boiling with venom, Rago was inviting Jim to dinner the next night, as he crawled into his overcoat, and I stuck my face right in Henry's mouth, filled with Shelley and cashew nuts, and bellowed: "Can I come, too?" with as much rudeness and poverty of good manners as I could summon. Henry met us the next night with a false, Christmas grin tattooed on his face. . . . [and] stuffed with, as Jim said later, "as much shit as a Christmas goose down home in Georgia." . . . Then, later, at a dreary Chin[e]se joint to which Henry had shepherded us, after, first, a "little visit," as he put it, to Poetry's offices, where he was visibly miffed because neither Jim nor myself genuflected when we entered his office—later, at dinner, Jim, with genuine, Southern charm, blurted, "Why do you literary folks up here in Chicago have so much hate and spite for one another? Why, everybody was hating everybody last night at Paul's." Henry, who as you know is incapable of a plain or straight answer, began a series of labyrinthine lies, all attempting to give Jim the illusion that everybody in Chicago loved everybody else, including and especially, the poets, who were all involved in a love affair because Poetry is so beautiful, etc. When he began slamming John Logan, in a lousy, back-of-the-hand way, claiming that John's verse was "unmeritorious" and trivial, Jim bellowed, "I think Logan is one of the best poets in the country." . . . It was cold, there, in that chop suey joint, cold. "Well," Jim Dickey reflected, over a beer, after we had said good night to Henry and his wife, "I guess I just blew the National Book Award."[51]

Dahlberg kept on beleaguering them for jobs, blurbs, books, and, most of all, attention. Gardner answered Dahlberg's avalanche of letters, and to him as with all bothersome correspondents, Tate had her answer on his behalf. While he used his second wife as his secretary, he lobbied industriously in behalf of his first, trying to get her into the Institute of Arts and Letters; but this was one of the few times he failed to make his influence felt. Gordon, anyway, was hardly interested in temporal affairs; she agonized about Tate's soul and asked him if he wanted an annulment of their marriage as this would reinstate him in the Catholic Church. Tate refused, arguing that as they had been truly married he did not want a legalistic annulment: "To put the matter in extreme terms, I would rather risk damnation, but with the hope of God's grace in the end, than accept the rigmarole of the *merely* legalistic process of establishing a 'diriment impediment.'"[52] He ended by asking Gordon to pray for him, assuring her that he mentioned her in his daily prayers. (In fact, references to his still being a practicing Catholic are to be found only in letters to Gordon and converted friends like the Cheneys.) A few months later, in another caring letter, he comforted Gordon, who had flagellated herself about their upbringing of Nancy, by stating categorically that they had been fine parents and that Percy Wood, Nancy's psychiatrist husband, should be held responsible for any problems Nancy had had or would have: "If after all these years you don't know that Percy is an ambulatory paranoiac kept under relative self control by his profession you have not observed him very closely."[53]

Although rhapsodizing to Logan that she was "marvellously happy with Allen," Gardner was, in fact, despondent, in part because of the never-ending stream of visitors (Paul Carroll, Reed Whittemore, James Wright, and Galway Kinnell came for dinner and Stephen Spender for a few days at the end of February alone), but mainly because of her children, who were "always in some sort of crisis so that for four or five years there's been scarcely a month without some acute worry."[54] Tate became more and more irritated by these crises and took it upon himself to subjugate Daniel:

> If I had the responsibility for you—that is, could tell you what to do and control your allowance—I would feel that under the circumstances I have the following courses that I might pursue:
>
> 1. If you refused to enter a school, academic or art, by September 20th, I would cut off your allowance entirely, and let you shift for yourself.... I would take the risk of your going to the dogs and / or destroying yourself.... Being on your own is a dishonest fiction: you know she [Gardner] will always bail you out. I would *not*, if you were my son.
>
> 2. This course is less tough, and is a compromise. I would still pay you your allowance so long as your father is willing to keep you on and to pay you a rea-

sonable salary, say $40.00 a week. . . . Your mother may settle for this, but I think it would be folly, and in your worst interests. . . . You would be camping in your father's studio waiting to get your money when you are twenty-one. . . . . I don't like the *smell* of this possibility.

3. The third alternative would be to give you your allowance indefinitely under any circumstance until you are twenty-one. This I am convinced would destroy you as completely as cutting you off entirely, or even more so. . . .

You know how fond I am of you, and how greatly I want you to make something of yourself. Won't you please do me the favor of thinking carefully about what I have said?[55]

In March 1963, seventeen-year-old Daniel ran away. Gardner tracked him down to Chicago, where he had ended up with Helen Donohue Butler's son, but she was "sick to death of talking about it." She described her children's troubles and other family news in a letter to her mother. Dan had tried to get to "'Frisco," in the 1960s the haven for the antiestablishment flower children. "As Kitty pointed out for an imaginative restless gifted boy of to-day the running off to Bohemian jungles is the equivalent of running off to sea or to the Yukon in an earlier day. The sad and important difference being that in the old days there were physical hard-ships (elemental ones) to be contended with and thus in itself constituted a kind of discipline. I still have great faith in Dan and I believe he is honestly searching if misguidedly. He'll come through in his own way and in time. Meanwhile I wake up each morning ill with anxiety because despite all his charm and conversational expertise and natural kindness and gentleness and generosity he is still terribly immature and not ready to look after himself." As to Rose: she was "so lonely that she thinks continually of seeing Dino again though she knows she should not. . . . She doesn't seem to understand that a belly-dancer in Puerto Rico is not apt to meet let alone attract a serious and decent person."[56]

"I feel absolutely helpless with these children," Tate wrote Katherine Biddle a few weeks later. "Isabella blames herself—which is the same as blaming the environments she made for them through her divorces. I can't accept this. Both these children have bad heredity—*bad blood* on the paternal sides." At the time Dan was in Baltimore in the hospital, seriously ill with what doctors initially feared might be leukemia, Hodgkin's, or tuberculosis, and Gardner had flown to be with him. Meanwhile, Rose had unexpectedly turned up in Minneapolis and camped with Tate: "She had gone back to that Negro rascal [Dino Campbell] who got $5000 out of her last year; now I suspect she is running away from him. I do not know what to do until her mother returns."[57] For good measure, Tate had Dino Campbell privately investigated at thirty-five dollars per day, with Gardner's knowledge.

In April, after Dan was released from the hospital with a clean bill of health, Gardner tried to be stern and sent him a typed missive with stylistic and moralistic Tate-ian overtones:

> I am afraid I am an appeaser by nature (except politically) and this quality in me based on an [optimistic?] faith in the essential goodness of human beings has not been good for anyone close to me, especially you and Rose. It has led you both to take advantage of me (I'm not necessarily speaking of money here) and to continually "test" me though I should think I have proven my love over the years. In any case this appeasement has resulted in pain all around and has contributed to moral deterioration for you and for Rosy. I had the apparently mistaken and sentimental, wishful-thinking notion that my love and understanding would give you all necessary moral support. . . . I have done you an injustice by not being tougher with you. My abhorrence of scenes and fights is to a large extent a weakness, in so far as it often confuses and even hurts those one lives to protect. . . . I know that you currently reject morality but I think nevertheless that it is deeply ingrained in you. . . . As far as legal obligation to you on your father's part is concerned, at the time of our divorce I felt that although I needed no money for your support, it was better for his own self-respect, and better for your feeling for him when you grew up, if he gave me a token sum of $50 a month. Very shortly afterwards I realized he was in difficulties with the studio, etc., and I informally released him from this obligation. . . . If you choose to return here, I will send you your fare. I will pay your tuition, and an allowance to go with it, at any reputable school of your choice. You are welcome in Wellfleet, and welcome to come abroad with us if we go, provided you employ your time constructively. It has been reported to me that you have said you want to do nothing except wait out the three years for your inheritance. This is a thoroughly demoralized point of view. I am taking the firm position that I refuse to contribute to the possible moral (not legal) delinquency of my beloved son.
>
> This stand is being taken a little late. I hope not too late.
>
> You know how much I love you.
>
> Mom[58]

In the midst of her family troubles, Gardner continued to care for her friends. She sent Dahlberg one hundred fifty dollars to help him with doctor's bills after he had had a stomach hemorrhage; and when Kizer told Gardner that Logan was in financial difficulties, she sent him a check of one hundred dollars immediately, asked him if he perhaps needed another hundred, and impressed on him that she did not believe in loans: "This is a token of friendship and faith and someday somehow you'll pass it along to some-one else."[59] At least as important was her moral support. Karl and Evalyn Shapiro's marriage had reached a new low. Evalyn, deeply depressed, saw a psychiatrist several times a week and worried about Karl's alcoholism, as she, a bootlegger's daughter, perceived it. Karl had a girlfriend whom he saw several times a week and, in his view, was drinking only moderately. Both bared their souls to Gardner in long letters, Evalyn's painfully open, Karl's layered with irony. Drink "only begs the family issues that are never, never resolved," Evalyn grieved. "Maybe *dis*solved in the dregs, but never helping anyone else beside Karl hi[m]self. . . . Which family should I worry most about? Yours or mine? Between us we might categorize most of the sins and virtues of the entire world?! I send you very much love always. Don't doubt it."[60] When Karl got his lover into trouble, Gardner stood by them. Much in love and sure of Gardner's loyalty, Karl then suggested she meet his mistress.[61] But his beloved left him, Random House intended to publish a bowdlerized version of his *The Bourgeois Poet* (1964), and he became job- and penniless after he gave up his job as editor of the *Prairie Schooner* because the University of Nebraska's administration banned a story he had accepted. Shapiro wailed: "It's been the worst year of my life, much worse than 4 in the army. . . . You've been wonderful to me always and especially this year."[62]

Gardner consoled him by return mail, which, Karl acknowledged, he had needed badly. He was glad to hear Tate's poem was coming along and praised him unstintingly: "Some day people will recognize his mastery everywhere."[63] But Tate continued to suffer from writer's block. So did Gardner, although publications such as *Encounter,* the *New York Times, Midway,* and *Poetry* solicited her work. For *Poetry,* Rago accepted what he thought were new poems, "Feminine Ending" and "Nor Good Red Herring," but Gardner informed him that they had been written six years earlier, and she had only submitted them because he had requested work for *Poetry*'s fiftieth anniversary issue. When they did not appear in print for months, Gardner wrote Rago several times, impatiently inquiring about their publication date. After they were finally in proof, Gardner changed her mind and withdrew them as she "would be embarrassed by publication"; she paid for the typesetting.[64]

While planning his fall sabbatical, Tate remained actively involved in departmental politics. An irate mother had written anonymously to the university's president, complaining about James Wright's drinking with underage students. Like Berryman, Wright was indeed often drunk and depressed and hardly the perfect role model for young students, but now Tate withheld his support, partly because Wright had become friends with Robert Bly, whom Tate detested. Tate was initially in favor of terminating Wright's appointment, then wavered, but finally voted against him, not so much because of his drinking, as he explained to Wright, but because he had not met his classes or had taught them badly: "If you were not a poet and a fine one, I should probably have been less hard on you in the voting. I leaned over backwards in severity because I think the poet in the university must lean over backwards in being severe with himself, or else he is doing harm to the university-poet relation."[65] Leaving aside that Tate himself was notorious for not meeting his classes—and a heavy drinker—his letter is a masterpiece of equivocation, and Wright felt betrayed by what he called Tate's Judas kiss. Tate felt he had acted honorably, yet blew up at Wright for showing his letter to Robert Bly and badgered Wright into eating humble pie. (Bly wrote his poet friends that that "spineless shit-eating Tate didn't have the guts to stand up for [Wright]."[66]) Wright, who had revered Tate, would always feel hurt by Tate's perfidy and his second wife, Anne, could "never forgive [Tate] for firing James. . . . But Belle took care of him, because, after his divorce (when he was so lonely and did not know how to take care of himself) she would make soup for him . . . so he would have something to eat. . . . She might have been embarrassed that Allen had been in the position of someone who had fired James."[67]

John Berryman, whose drunken behavior was far worse than Wright's, was a poet much closer to Tate's heart and remained in his good graces, although Tate thought Berryman "ought to be shot" for his treatment of his first wife, Eileen Simpson.[68] Gardner told his biographer, John Haffenden, in 1974 that Berryman disliked women, women poets in particular, and her especially, and that he was "brutally rude." He would "quite often telephone me (really Allen, but Allen would refuse to talk to him) and recite to me on the telephone poems that he had just finished, or half finished, or was beginning to make."[69] Berryman dedicated "Dream Song 70015" to them, and Tate wished Berryman would "write 100,000 Dream Songs, but damn it I hope you will also some day start writing something else."[70] Berryman was "more sick of being (as you put it) the Dream Song Man" than even Tate could imagine, but, he apologized, the songs took him by the throat, trapping him into writing them.[71]

Tate had also told Berryman that "Isabella's daughter Rosie married about two weeks ago her colored boy and plans to go to Europe with him. He's a scoundrel but both he and Rosie want to believe that I will not receive him because he is colored. I will not be blackmailed."[72] In reply Berryman suggested that Tate search his conscience: "*is* he a scoundrel Allen? I never knew no coloured people good—Ellison somewhat. They is people, though. I [am] not of course accusing you of prejudice: we all have it and they have it."[73] Tate wrote bigoted Dahlberg that Gardner had flown to Chicago to meet her son-in-law against his wishes and that although "Rosie has told [Dino], and convinced herself, that I was opposed because I am a Southerner," he was, in fact, "opposed because I learned things that make him out clearly to be a scoundrel, white, black, yellow, or green."[74] Tate was fed up with both children: "[Dan] is with his father, and his mother gives him an allowance while he pretends to work in his father's studio. He refuses to go to any school whatever. . . . He has every advantage; and to say that his generation all over the country is behaving this way explains nothing, and justifies nothing. . . . Isabella will sooner or later, perhaps sooner, have to take the responsibility for any children, for Rosie is completely irresponsible, and will desert not only her husband within two years, but the inevitable child. . . . .The tension of anxiety kept me so nervous that I could write nothing, not even letters. But all is better now—not objectively perhaps, but simply as the result of time; that Isabella is now serene again makes all the difference."[75]

Gardner was, however, "somnambulistic" and "in a sort of trance," rather than serene and apologized to Nancy for having been a bad hostess during the Woods' recent visit to their summer house in Wellfleet. She was trying to put together a manuscript of selections from her two books for a possible British edition of her work, but she still had not screwed up her courage to write. "Maybe if a woman truly loves a man as I do Allen and makes her life with him she can't write poetry? Maybe a woman with children shouldn't write poetry or a woman with 'a touch of the poet' shouldn't have children? Anyway, I am feeling inadequate on all fronts except for Allen and me."[76]

On August 1, 1963, they sailed for Great Britain, where Tate required the constant company of his old friends: "Spenders, MacNeices etc,. are around, and we see Uncle Tom [Eliot] tomorrow. We expect to go to Dublin a week from today. . . . . . We are very sad about Ted Roethke's death."[77] Tate's poem progressed "in millimetres: I do move a little," he was happy to tell Dahlberg.[78] After a fine time in Dublin with the Denneys, but without Louis MacNeice, who had the flu, they came home to London to find that Daniel had apparently "rolled a queer" and intended to travel around the world with his friend Stewart Reichlin, of "great charm and absolutely no scruples, or cash."[79] Writing to her brother Robert on September 4, the day after MacNeice's unexpected death of pneumonia at age fifty-six, Gardner admitted to having been close to a breakdown because of "profound emotional and spiritual exhaustion and a black feeling of failure toward the children." But she was sure she had weathered it: "Thank God that *never* in those two weeks of fatigue caused by depression did I withdraw from Allen, I became only more than usually dependent."[80]

Their new friend Muriel Spark had found a cheap apartment for Gardner to work in and there she wrote her first poem in years, "This Room Is Full of Clocks," about poets Roethke, MacNeice, Thomas, and Cummings, all of whom had died so early, while even "coddled alligators / (safe from such random killers as love or neglect) / are able to thrash and lash and grin at sixty-eight" (87). The poem was gladly taken by Stephen Spender for his magazine *Encounter*. But Gardner remained despondent and was doubly saddened when Rose heckled her in an incoherent letter: "I do not regrettably have much influence . . . over Danny—He knows a little too well my problems and unhappinesses—You had better dismiss me as any kind of cause for his rebellion and search your own conscience."[81] Gardner was by now so blue that she, out of character, complained about Tate, for though mornings were restful, at Tate's insistence they always saw so many people later in the day "that I cannot keep them straight." She would prefer to be alone, "[b]ut no. 'Twill be the dear Biddles in Florence etc. etc. etc."[82]

While they were in Florence in October, the blabby Minneapolis crowd caused more anxiety. One of Tate's colleagues had written a nasty letter about long-haired Daniel, who upon his return from Europe, was staying at Pat Stange's house, thus adding to her income, but, according to her divorced husband, Bob, as well as the academic community, being a bad influence on her children. The Tates would be receiving the cold shoulder, it was rumored, because they had foisted their wayward son upon innocent Minneapolis, while they themselves gallivanted in affluence in Italy. Upset, Tate had again an excuse for being unable to write, although added distractions were Francis Fergusson and Nancy Hale as fellow guests at the Pensione Annalena and freely flowing alcohol.

The Tates visited Congdon, who had become a member of a Catholic lay community near Milan. Congdon's conversion had turned him into a preachy moralist, and he blamed Gardner for the predicament of her children and all but called her a whore. Her worst sin, however, was marrying Tate, for this had resulted in his excommunication; Gardner could not atone for this if she spent the rest of her life on her knees. Tate defended her:

> I agree with you that a firmer policy with her children might have prevented some of their excesses, but I can't agree that she has destroyed them or is destroying me. In spite of being out of communion, I have had greater serenity and felt more at peace with God in the past five years than ever before in my adult life. . . . What creative powers I once had were in abeyance; they have been coming back, slowly, but coming. . . . I could not live with my former wife; I was going under; and I would have destroyed her as well as myself.
>
> I have never said this to anyone before.
>
> I think you have come to the perfect solution for you. With most of us, that is not possible. I am thinking here of Isabella. Grant that she made some bad mistakes: she has never repudiated them—she has had to live with them through her children. I don't think that either you or I am in a position to judge her.[83]

Believing that Congdon's conversion had saved his life and reason by salvaging him from alcoholic and homosexual dissipation, Gardner saw it had also destroyed his once acute compassion and insight into the essences of things, creatures, and people. However, never rancorous, she continued to love him like a brother.

Back in London, the shock of the murder of President John F. Kennedy, on November 22, brought both Tates to tears and made them feel isolated expatriates. Soon after the assassination, plans were laid for an anthology of Kennedy poems with an introduction by Arthur Schlesinger Jr. The Tates thought it a commercial swindle and wanted nothing to do with it, even though it was supported by their beloved Katherine Biddle. Tate was haughty: "I had the impression that I was 'invited to submit a poem.' Well, I am too old to 'submit:' I have to be invited period. . . . I could not write an occasional poem if my life depended on it. And as a partly alienated character I cannot identify myself with public personages, however greatly I admire them, as I admired Kennedy."[84] Gardner pointed out to Katherine that her own "Dylan elegy in part mocked the leaping into verse of every verse-maker on the occasion of Dylan's death. But in the case of the Dylan anthology of elegiac verses a good deal of time elapsed and the selection was made not too eclectically."[85]

She still had not shed the partly menopausal depression that had settled on her but was feeling somewhat better and spent much of her energy helping Paul Carroll, Edward Dahlberg, John Logan, and the women Logan (separated from his wife) was involved with. With both his best book, the autobiographical *Because I Was Flesh,* and his idiosyncratic collection of essays, *Alms for Oblivion,* about to be published, Dahlberg claimed most of her, and some of Tate's, time. On January 2, 1964, she wrote him: "Allen agrees that I am incompetent to review *Because I Was Flesh. He* cannot because of [writing] the blurb. What we can do is try to rally people whose taste and judgment we trust to do it properly." She suggested reviewers and wrote to editors she knew, even Rago: "It is not that I am on *bad* terms with Rago—just that I don't like or respect him very much though he is decent."[86] Asking Rago to have *Because I Was Flesh* reviewed in *Poetry,* Gardner attested: "Dahlberg is a difficult man. A lonely man. An ill and impoverished man. But he has written a truly great book."[87] She again sent Dahlberg money, and Tate convinced the Institute of Arts and Letters to grant him eight hundred dollars. Dahlberg continued to whine nevertheless: could not Tate get him some Bollingen money, too? And would he please write the introduction to his forthcoming book of poems, *Cipango's Hinder Door?*

After years of neglect, Dahlberg was coming into a brief, intense period of fame. Part of the Tates' correspondence with him at this time concerned the making of *The Dahlberg Reader,* edited by Paul Carroll, which was to include a number of his letters to them. Gardner told Dahlberg that they trusted Carroll completely and that he could use what he wanted. She thought Carroll himself had been treated shamefully, as his manuscript of poems had been turned down time and again. Carroll admitted he was "in despair," as his poetry did not fit into the accepted niches of academic and New York School poetry, or even Beat. He went on to describe a reading for a Beat audience at which he turned up wearing a Brooks Brothers shirt and told them to read Horace: "I almost got lynched."[88] Gardner got Maurice English at the University of Chicago Press to consider his manuscript, but Carroll feared his chances were slim because of the university's continued hard feelings over his involvement with the *Chicago Review* and *Big Table* turmoils. He mourned the lives of the poets:

> James Laughlin ... told me Corso had flipped and had been put into a hospital. ... Then you told me of poor Jim Wright's current breakdown. It is a melancholy thing to see one's contemporaries cracking into pieces. I remember Karl Shapiro telling me some years ago that he felt that his generation of poets—Lowell, Berryman, Roethke, and Delmore Schwartz in particular—was a blighted, doomed group of men, so many of them victims of crippling emotional lives and alcoholism, but all the time I felt that my generation seemed spared and, in a way, blessed, so few having exhibited, at the time, the usual occupational hazards of being a poet. Over the years, however, ... I came to see, sadly, that my generation was no different from any other generation of poets. ... Both of you, I know, are aware of the tragic fact that most poets must suffer through violent, driven lives.[89]

Unhappy, insecure, and in and out of analysis, Carroll found a temporary anchor in his Lutheran Latvian wife, Inara Birnbaum, whom he married in October 1964. The Shapiros attended, and John Logan was best man in white tie but later that day had to be bailed out of jail by Evalyn. Almost completely cut loose from the church, Logan was miserable at Catholic St. Mary's, where he was teaching and drinking to excess. He was looking, with the Tates' help, for a summer job, as he needed to make at least twelve thousand dollars annually because by now he had to support nine children. Tate exerted himself, but, Gardner wrote Logan, the English department at the University of Minnesota was not interested: "They *like* [Allen]—he is their pet parlor ... poet but he has no PHD and *they* (Clark who is head of the English Dept. and Montgomery who is his Assistant and runs the summer school) don't *like* or maybe don't trust writers. They love scholars who write erudite books. Preferably single-minded specialists. I've watched (and helped) Allen battle this for the five years I've been here. ... If something doesn't break right for you let me know and I'll help out—*No loan*."[90] In the end, thanks to Tate, Logan substituted for Glauco Cambon at the Indiana School of Letters: "One of the funny things is that Rago and I will be facing each other in elevators and walkways again. Perhaps he will drink and be human then. Would like to see his face when he hears I will be there."[91]

Rago had never fitted in with the hard-drinking crowd of Chicago poets and had behaved boorishly when Gardner left *Poetry*, but their relationship had improved over the years, perhaps because he no longer considered her a threat. He gladly accepted the second poem she had written since her long drought, the witty "A Word from the Piazza del Limbo," on Congdon's detached moralistic coldness after his conversion: "Infrequently but massively I hear / from one who until recently seemed crammed / with *caritas.* Now, since the saving of his / soul his letters speak only of himself and / of Him and their correspondence. / Indeed he declines to address himself to my / distress. Although I have written him of / various despairs he does not even / upbraid me for Sloth, the sin with which / I wake and eat, that monkey on my back" (88). Gardner began "to feel I'm able to write again, but even when I was I'm a snail's pace type!"[92] She longed for more peace and quiet and wished Tate would resign, and put, as usual, his work first: "I would give an arm and a leg if he could finish the long poem."[93] Although they could afford early retirement, she knew Tate did not really want this. He complained about teaching and pressures but relished "the Departmental feuds, the councils of war, the telephoning back and forth. It is painful for him to be still, he needs to be caught up, to be needed, to be engaged, to be active with people. Unlike me he has little joy in nature and to be active, to be sociable, keeps the cold wind from his back."[94]

In March 1964 Gardner wrote to Katherine Biddle: "I thought Minneapolis was a long way from everywhere but everyone seems to find his or her way here."[95] W. H. Auden, Frank Kermode, John Logan, Robert Speaight, Stephen Spender, Robert Penn Warren, and several relatives had all planned visits, so Gardner did not even have time to think about a poem, let alone write one. Even Tate admitted that they "had more house guests this spring than ever before, and Isabella particularly is rather numb as a result. I spare you the list— lest it sound like Homer's catalogue of ships. Auden, for one, was lots of fun, but he *would* get up at seven and raid the ice-box." Still, they had managed to do a little work, both translating poems by Ungaretti "at the last minute," though Tate had been "a little put out by the high-pressure exerted by the Italian Institute and Mrs. Bullock's Academy to dragoon American poets."[96] After a joint reading in the spring at the Poetry Center in New York City, where Gardner had read "very beautifully," Tate reported, while he had performed "like a zombie," Tate flew to Kenyon College for a Ransom symposium and dedication of Ransom Hall there, but had to give up on planned trips to Louisville and Philadelphia because of the flu.[97] In May he went to Sewanee to stay with Andrew Lytle, who had undergone a successful operation for cancer; "having a ball with his Nashville chums," as Gardner, alone in Minneapolis, phrased it.[98]

Gardner would have gladly stayed near her beloved icy ocean at Wellfleet for the entire summer, but Tate insisted on first going to Europe again, as he could not take the Cape for more than a month. Their trip centered once more on friends, rather than work. As always, they stayed in the Pensione Annalena and, once again, Florence proved brutally hot. Gardner was at work, with much trepidation, on a manuscript of collected poems with her few new ones added, which Houghton Mifflin was pleased to publish. Tate mentioned his long poem in most of his letters but was drinking so much that thirty years later the Italian chambermaids still remembered him as intoxicated most of the time.[99] Tate admitted to his fellow New Critic—kind, courteous Cleanth Brooks, who was the cultural attaché in London and whom they had planned to visit—that the "work hasn't gone as fast as I like, and too much travel is certainly not good for it."[100] So, instead of going to Great Britain, the Tates sailed back at the end of July, straightaway to Wellfleet, the ostensible reason being Tate's desire to work with fewer distractions. But incorrigibly hospitable, Tate made sure that on Cape Cod, too, there would not be much time for writing. As if the Wellfleet colony of artists, writers, and diplomats were not sociable enough, he invited the Fosters, while Gardner invited her old Foxcroft school principal, Charlotte Noland. But Tate did not stay put. "Daddo's teeth were bothering him so he flew to Mnpls yesterday to see his dentist and will be back [F]riday," she wrote his daughter and son-in-law on August 19, telling them that Tate's grandson, Allen, and his friend were very welcome and that, of course, the Tates would also love to have them stay in their paradisiacal, artsy-craftsy house. The only blemish on their summer, Gardner sorrowed, was that she had lost her wedding ring in the surf.[101]

The loss of her ring proved to be highly symbolic. For Tate's motive for going to Minneapolis was not to see his dentist, but his lover, Helen Heinz, a nun and nurse, with whom he had been involved for quite some time, and who was to become his third wife. But at the time that was not a foregone conclusion, for Tate wrote to Foster, his main confidant, that "on the way to the airport it was agreed that we would not see each other again, *ever*."[102] Gardner was to live in a fool's paradise for one more year, declaring repeatedly: "I love him so *much*, and I am so cherished—and not deserving but grateful for my blessings."[103]

She had need to count them, for her children were acting up again. Rose was divorcing Dino Campbell after the briefest of marriages and living in Spain with gypsies; she had decided that flamenco dancing was her future. Daniel seemed to have shaped up, and in March Tate had proudly written to Francis Biddle: "Our boy Dan has made the Dean's list this quarter. Isabella has bought him a sports car as a reward. The sudden change from beatnik to student gives me huge satisfaction."[104] But in September, Gardner wrote from Wellfleet that Daniel was causing "great grief. . . . He cannot stay out of trouble, quitting college, marijuana, auto accidents etc. It is terribly hard on Allen who feels, quite rightly, I suppose, that I am not stern enough. The fact is I've faith in Dan and I guess I feel guilty about separating him from Bob McCormick who was good to him and firm with him. His own father is no use at all. Allen of course cannot play the role of a firm stepfather . . . at this point in his life. But it is difficult for a woman to be both mother and father and I seem to have been a failure." Tate had gone to Kentucky "in the hope that re-visiting the scenes of his early childhood might help him to finish the long poem," but he had cut his trip short and flown home to Minneapolis. Gardner "thought he wanted to be alone" and stayed "quietly on 'Aunt Mary's Pond.'"[105] "Alone" in Minneapolis, Tate trysted with his lover.

Tate, Gardner wrote the Fosters (who were at Bowdoin for the year) in all innocence, had "felt very frustrated in Wellfleet though we loved the pond-side house and its isolation." She "wished to God I could make it possible for him to finish the poem. . . . I've told him I'll go to Monteagle next summer if he wants to."[106] Since their return from Europe, Gardner had written nothing. "*Time* is not necessarily my problem but the parcelling out of emotional and spiritual energy certainly is as it must be for any woman 'artist' who does not lead the life of Emily Dickinson or Marianne Moore!" Back in Minneapolis she had cared for "[p]oor Jim Wright who spent 3 nights here on the point of breakdown and went from here to the hospital for four days. His psychiatrist was in Europe and he was suffering terribly because of the rejection by his girl. [Tate's student and Wright's friend] Roland Flint was very helpful. Jim spent another night here two days ago but could not sleep all night. We *care* about him but we are glad for our sake as well as his that his psychiatrist will be back soon. It is heartbreaking to see a man suffer so." They had partied with the "Berry Man mit Beard" and his "Saint Kate," Pat Stange, John and Bobby Clark, and other members of the English department. They had also had James Dickey to their house: "I like a little of his poetry and some of his criticism but he is, to say the least, a rude, vicious, prejudiced and unpredictable *man.*"[107]

Then Gardner was planning birthday parties for Tate's sixty-fifth birthday in November and she had been busy reading four of six manuscripts "penned by friends or friends of friends."[108] John Goetz reported that Tate's official birthday party "was a great success" with Gardner as a "self-effacing and adroit hostess," Hunt Brown wearing black tie and "a top hat, cape and gold headed cane," John Clark reading "a beautifully composed Latin epigram," and Sam Monk delivering "a schmaltzy, but elegant eulogy of Allen's attractive daughter Nancy, who was present. It was amusing to observe her swell and billow next to her slender splinter of a father."[109] Another reason for celebration was that thanks to the Minotaur, as they called Conrad Aiken, Tate was to be "*assumed* into the American Academy of Arts and Letters" in December. He was paid to go "to N.Y. for the laying on of hands next Friday the 11th. We are both going; . . . I can't resist it: my character is weak." He was dismayed, though, "that Katherine Anne [Porter] is *not* a member of the Academy, and continues to languish among the Common People of the mere Institute."[110] He let Porter know that it "was outrageous that I was *elevated* to the Academy before you. Next year it will be done—or I'll resign" and begged her to "stay settled," adding "I'm settled but still *bum around* too much": his affair with Heinz was ongoing.[111]

Gardner was troubled by Daniel, who had been hospitalized for an emergency appendectomy, after having been "in the workhouse for 30 days for driving after his license had been revoked." She was distressed, too, by Edith Sitwell's death in December 1964: "She was a witch, I suppose, cruel to some and to others (me for example) marvellously generous. We were *friends*. And both born on Sept. 7th."[112] The new year also brought Tate "unusual" sadness, because Eliot died, which, "though long expected, was not easily accepted. . . . I feel that an older brother had died."[113] Maurice English empathized: "As soon as I read of Eliot's death, I thought of what it would mean to Allen. Though I do not believe Conrad Aiken's statement that this will be remembered as The Age of Eliot, the very fact that he could propose it, suggests the degree to which Eliot really *reversed* the course poetry in English had taken for a century before he published."[114] English then went on about the few mentions *Midnight,* his first book of poems, had received and asked Gardner to review it. Although the Tates had helped him to get it published, Gardner hardly ever turned a request down, and she gave in hesitatingly knowing academic criticism was not her forte. She warned Charles Newman at the new *TriQuarterly,* who had professed an interest, that her appraisal would be short and affirmative, without intellectualizing. That suited him just fine.

Meanwhile, English had turned down the book submitted by Paul Carroll, who was "hurt, angry, and disappointed."[115] By return mail, Gardner wrote Carroll such a "spirited and caring letter" that his faith in his work, though rejected by ten publishers, was restored. He decided to submit his manuscript to Horizon Press: "I refuse to send the mss to any of the Beat presses, although I consider Ferlinghetti a fairly good friend, and feel that City Lights has published a few good titles. My poems have nothing to do with the Beat or that kind of hip New York experimental poetry written by such bad poets as Leroi Jones and Frank O'Hara."[116] At Gardner's request, Tate offered to write Horizon in Carroll's behalf, and Carroll was duly appreciative. Reading "a mountain of letters" for *The Dahlberg Reader,* Carroll had noticed that whenever "Edward mentions you or Isabella, it is always with warmth and considerable admiration, which is not the case, I discover, with many of the men of letters he mentions."[117] The Tates were, as always, laboring in Dahlberg's behalf. He tried to farm out the editing of his very rough manuscript to the Tates; Gardner, characteristically, spent days on his poems. She drew the line, though, when Dahlberg suggested they edit his poems at will and send the unapproved draft directly on to the University of Texas Press. To soften the blow, she offered to pay the cost of typing the manuscript.

This was in mid-March, a few weeks after the disastrous and disrespectful reception Dahlberg deemed he had received in their Minneapolis house. Gardner had organized a party, at which Dahlberg signed books, which she had bought for their guests; had made soup for him and a cooked breakfast and had taken him out to dinner. But Dahlberg was gravely offended. In numerous letters he went on about the fact that he had been invited to stay for a few days only and that Gardner had not cooked a proper dinner for him. Besides, they had argued bitterly about the Civil Rights Movement and Selma, where after Bloody Sunday on March 7 (when peaceful protesters for Civil Rights were brutally attacked by the police) thousands were ready to march again. Gardner had spoken of joining them, while Dahlberg had argued violently against them. The day after the third march, Gardner, again home alone, tried to enlighten Dahlberg once more:

> I'm not ashamed of having a social conscience, but I have no inclination to re-turn to the marching, picketing, working in strike headquarters etc. of my youth. I do find it odd, in view of both history and humanity, that you feel my having a private income (I am *not* and never will be a "millionairess"!) disqualifies me from caring about the human condition. My attitude in the past when I was as active as possible when caring for two small children, cooking etc. was never that of "the social worker"—I was quite simply deeply concerned and as engaged as was possible under the circumstances. I wish that Rose and Dan might feel now as I did then. In any case I minded your attack on me far less than I minded your intemperate way of talking about "niggers" etc. etc. Your reason is that you tried to help Negro individuals and were in various ways betrayed. . . .
>
> I have never been able to feel that one should lose faith in a person or in one's own convictions of the heart even if one is let down or betrayed or vilified or 'tromped' or whatever. Even if that should happen 99 times out of a hundred, there is still the hundredth chance![118]

At the time, Tate was lecturing in Texas and spending time with old friends in Tennessee, particularly Lytle, now editor of the *Sewanee Review,* who had asked him to be guest editor for a memorial Eliot issue. Gardner herself was doing her duty by dead poets by organizing a memorial Oscar Williams read-ing and by editing the memoir written by his son, Strephon. There was little time left for her to work on her forthcoming book, to be titled *West of Child-hood.* She therefore turned to Logan, who had become her sounding board. Sending him a short version of her poem "Roundelay" about her last Christmas with McCormick, she commented, "Allen preferred the longer one but my own judgment about my poems is apt to be intuitively sound." The deadline for her book was extended to April 15, "*but* Father Lynch, Dan's birthday and Dahlberg this week[,] so there's *no* time. Cooking, party-giving—house, turtle, plant and people-care!! Reminding Allen to write letters, trying to write my own. Files in a muddle. . . . I am the most fortunate of women as regards husband, whom I adore, physical health and enuf worldly goods but sometimes I long for a padded cell or even maybe a room at the YWCA!!" Logan had told Gardner that he felt guilty toward Dr. Kraus, as his analysis seemed to have failed, in spite of inordinate amounts of money and time spent. Gardner empathized: "I've done exactly what you say you have. That is tried to make him think he helped more than he did." Still, thanks to Kraus she might have become slightly less clumsy "when I have to face something that provokes anxiety. [And] I don't have the guilt about being financially secure as much as I did. But I still *suffer* the anxieties and guilts while being less self-punitive." In all, though, she had found "dear Kraus" too indulgent to be of much use. "Both Seymour and Bob McC. thought I drank too much. But Kraus insisted I didn't and said I'd make him worry about his own drinking if I kept on about it." She insisted that now she hardly ever got smashed anymore, although she still drank to control anxiety. "Allen who is *not* neurotic, really, gets very drunk on occasion quite often, but always just for fun—because he *likes* it. It is ironic that I often at parties ask him not to have another drink but he never drinks because he needs to and I feel like a whited sepulchre when I *appear* to be so sober!"[119]

As for *West of Childhood,* she wrote Logan, "I really want to chicken out," but she made her deadline, then flew to Washington, D.C., with her husband for a bone-crushing conference on little magazines, where "the fur flew and feelings were hurt."[120] That spring, Tate lectured at different universities, and during the Tates' customary European summer he was "to read again" at the Edinburgh Festival. As he put it: "One conference breeds another; or conferences spread like V.D. before the discovery of penicillin."[121] Gardner, meanwhile, had sent Carroll all but a few of Dahlberg's letters to Tate for his *Dahlberg Reader;* those withheld were too unkind to the critic Stanley Burnshaw. She had also kept back about forty of his letters to her, because they were too personal about Bob McCormick and her children. "I think I have protected everyone," she informed Dahlberg, waxing teary-eyed about how his letters had sustained her during the grueling time of her affair with Tate. She ended with a sentiment that often enters her letters during her marriage to Tate: "I've *no* intellect. A *little* intelligence but as Allen says I live by my sensibilities."[122] Tate's manic personal life proves that he was led by his emotions at least as much as was Gardner, but while he hid behind his mask of brilliant, often mendacious intellectuality, Gardner sought to be vulnerable and could, therefore, be mistaken for sentimental. Intellectual poet-academics John Logan and Paul Carroll knew better and treasured Gardner's critical intelligence, and she had long since made up for her lack of a formal education by her wide and sensitive reading from philosophy to mythology and poetry to fiction.

Dahlberg had had word from Carroll "that the best letters I had written were to you [Gardner] and Josephine Herbst. He said they were 'masterpieces.'"[123] Gardner replied that she had sent his poems with her tentative corrections and suggestions to Texas University Press and for once spoke up for herself: "Allen is, as we both know, a marvellous man and artist but any 'labor' involved with your poems is entirely mine." She went on to say that she loved "Allen too much to be able to work! Because for work I need (for myself) nature (close-ness to it—and solitude from time to time)—Allen is cerebral as well as passionate—I have only sensibility—my antennae and in order to preserve an edge, a focus, I must not *see people* constantly. I can only tolerate them for about two hours a day—even my closest dearest friends. . . . I would love to be with Allen *alone* close to nature, but he dislikes nature and teases me, very lovingly, about my Thoreau cum Wordsworth feelings and needs."[124] Pouncing on Gardner's sad remark about a surfeit of friends, Dahlberg once more bitterly upbraided her for her presumed inhospitality and political viewpoints: "unlike yourself, I do not insult my friends, and tell them they are intolerable after a pair of days. . . . I have never had any confidence in the abstract Marxist, and that is all that you are, only about 40 years too late at this boring and murderous [c]reed."[125]

For once contrite, Dahlberg sent off apologetic letters within a week, asking Tate's and Gardner's forgiveness for his offensiveness. But Tate had read Dahlberg's first splenetic missive and, insulted on his wife's behalf, had sent off a fuming reply (which crossed Dahlberg's apologies), threatening to withdraw all Gardner letters for Carroll's reader if Dahlberg did not include this last nasty one revealing his true colors. In turn, Dahlberg was infuriated and sent off pages and pages justifying himself, positioning himself as Gardner's mentor and insinuating that Tate and he shared the same reactionary political viewpoints: "Have you forgotten, my dear Allen, that when we had private words about the Negro problem that you were in *absolute* agreement with me?"[126] Tate refused to answer, and Gardner took it upon herself to make peace, emphasizing once more that she had not meant to wound Dahlberg and that Allen felt "his letter to you was a very mild rebuke for your unkind and bitter letter to me."[127] Dahlberg came down a peg or two when he received a Rockefeller grant, thanks to Tate's exertions, and saw Gardner's "exceptional suggestions" about *Cipango's Hinder Door* (1965): "As for the acrimonious and doubtless ill-worded letter I sent, it is bootless to relate that I did so because I was utterly crestfallen, for all excuses are fusty."[128]

Tate had defended his wife against Dahlberg's allegations, as a southern gentleman would, but he had long been living a loutish double life.[129] What had started out as just another affair, with Tate attracted by Helen Heinz's youth (she was half his age) and innocence (when she was his student she was a nun, and her husband was always "very partial to nuns" Gardner had noted in 1961) had become paramount in his life.[130] Heinz had left her order, and she did not doubt his commitment to her.[131] Gardner had no inkling of what was going on and regarded Tate as the loving and loved mainstay of her life. But in June 1965, on the eve of their departure to Italy, Tate wrote to Charles and Doris Foster that he might be back earlier than planned:

> The situation is more serious than I led you to believe. What I can do I do not yet know. My life, since we returned from England in December 1963 has become almost intolerable. How shall I put it? Well, let's say that the circumambient *past*, including all the former husbands, the former step-children, to say nothing of my step-children and the emotional and financial dependents, has become so difficult that I almost literally do not know where I am. Then I met the girl. I was ready to meet her. . . . She has *no past,* neither her own, nor her family's. Had the "dispensation" not been granted nothing further could have happened; for what I wrote you last summer would have remained true. For me, it really comes down to a powerful desire to simplify my life of which I haven't too many years left; and there's something selfish about it: I must have composure and serenity if I am to complete the modest task that I asked God to assign to me forty years ago.—This trip to Europe is mere escape—the old fallacy of change of place; for the "circumambient past" will be with her there, poor darling.—I *may* come back alone and soon; so don't please, be surprised. I have the utmost confidence in you both; if there are rumors please lie for me and say they are not true.[132]

History was repeating itself. During his marriages to Caroline Gordon, Tate had considered it her fault that he had started his affair with her cousin Marion Henry, for Gordon had been too involved, he asserted, with her Meriwether family. He also held Gordon responsible for his many other affairs, for did she not keep on harping on his past liaisons and had she not stopped trusting him? Tate found it equally easy to blame Gardner this time, dragging God and poetry into it for good measure.

The bomb fell in Spoleto at the end of June, at the very beginning of their stay in Europe. Too spineless to tell his wife that he was involved with another woman, Tate left love letters by Heinz in the wastepaper basket for Gardner to find—and fled to London. The next day he wrote her that "we, together, were living in a true paradise. I let the serpent into it"; that he would "not see [Heinz] again"; but also that he was not equal to the "task of restoring your confidence in me" as it "would be *Sisyphean.*" He ended his letter: "I love you as I have never loved any other woman. Ending this letter is like ending my life. You have *all my love.*"[133] He gave Margaret Goetz a very different glimpse of that "true paradise." "He was dying to tell somebody and he was like a child. He said he had not been able to consummate the act of intercourse with Isabella, that she turned him off. But when he got Helen down to the bed for the first time, he was not able to perform either. And he felt terrible, but he said that she was so knowing and understanding, she helped me and we made it!"[134]

If extramarital affairs are never fair to the deceived, Tate's behavior was beyond brutal. At the beginning of October Gardner summarized her suffering for Katherine Biddle:

Allen has been having a love affair since last March [sic]. I found out about it in Spoleto about July 1st. He went to London from Spoleto. I went to Florence to meet my parents and was to join him in London. He wrote me from London to say he feared I could not forgive him and would reproach him all our life and so was flying home. I went at once to London but he had already gone. I telephoned him to say he *was* forgiven and that I *would* not reproach him. He told me he loved me but wanted to be *alone* in Tennessee to work and would join me in September in Florence.

He wrote me nearly every day saying that he loved me but also mentioning two great resentments that he had not spoken of during our marriage. One is what he calls my "hostages." My concern for my former step-children and for Dan's father's family that is, his sisters and his niece. The other resentment is that I *should* have "intuited" that he wanted to go to Tennessee the last two summers and not to Europe or to Wellfleet which he *hates* except for you and Francis. You know very well that I would have gone happily to Tennessee had he made his wishes known to me.

I have said nothing to anyone because until the other day I've *hoped.* I've fought desperately hard but it looks as though I've lost. He recently wrote me (day before yesterday) that he "should like very much" to marry her. The letter ended "I love you." . . .

He wrote me a few weeks ago "I have never loved a woman as I love you." He used the present tense. We were happy to-gether in New York (and *were* reconciled) on my return from Europe. I flew back when he wrote me that he was not coming to Florence. But the reconciliation failed because he went straight to her from me and spent a week in Minneapolis seeing her before going back to Tennessee while I was in the hospital in Boston. (I'm physically well. It was just emotional exhaustion.) . . .

We suffered and struggled so hard to *be* married, and hurt others especially my son to whom this will be another blow. I wish Allen would not let us go down the drain without fighting *for* us.

It is ironical that in one letter he said that it was not him I wanted but our "public life." *That* is the one aspect of our marriage that I minded. I wanted peace and wanted him more to myself. The world was too much with us, I felt.[135]

Since his defection at the end of June, Gardner had only seen Tate once, during their "reconciliation," celebrated with a new necklace and ring (which Gardner, true to type, also lost) in New York City in September. In early October she found a temporary refuge at the artists' colony Yaddo. Before agreeing to a separation or divorce, she wanted to meet him again, and Tate agreed to come to New York City on October 15. Gardner came in from Yaddo, but Tate cabled that he would see her the next day, specifying the exact time; then did not turn up, phone, or cable. Back at Yaddo, she found that he had started divorce proceedings and began to realize that, though he continued to protest that he wanted to break up with "The Girl" as he called Heinz, and that he loved Gardner, Tate did not, in reality, need or want her: "I lack guile and do not suspect it in others. This has put me in the last few months completely at Allen's mercy. It has been hard on him because it must have been frustrating and exasperating to have me consistently turn the other cheek, apologize, affirm, love, reassure etc. when what the poor darling may have hoped was that I would be driven (out of outrage and despair) to rejecting *him* thus saving him from the necessity to do the rejecting."[136]

For once angry, Gardner had hit the nail on the head, but she clung to every thread of hope, and whenever Tate spoke of resuming their old life, which he did often, Gardner wanted to forget that he had blown hot and cold since the summer and hoped against her better reason. Caught between dream and despair, she was wholly dependent on Tate's letters to her, and as these were full of rage-provoking recriminations, evasions, and lies, yet larded with love, she did not know what to believe; it was hard for her to differentiate between Tate's assertions that he had no plans to marry The Girl, but on the other hand would like to marry her, or to understand why, as he claimed, a divorce meant the Tates could start with a clean slate. Gardner tried to defend herself against Tate's now deep-seated resentments, which when they were still together he had expressed in his drunken rages only, always apologizing as soon as he was sober: "I know the crises of my children have been tough on him because they have made me suffer and so that has taken from him. But we both knew what we might be in for. . . . I would go to Alaska or Timbuctoo if he had told me his need. The fact is that he made *all* plans for Europe and I went at times when I thought I should be here in America."[137] For Tate the epitome of Gardner's failure as his wife happened at a small, informal dinner party for his 65th birthday, during which Daniel, at twenty, had monopolized the conversation, whereupon Tate had commanded him to leave the table, which Gardner had prevented. It was impossible for him to forgive her this grave insult to his manly pride.

Dahlberg quite agreed with him: "Above all, if you and Allen are reunited, please remember that your obligation is to him first, second and third. Nor can you irk a man, your husband, whom you are honoring. . . . What do you expect a husband to feel when you are willing to humiliate him in order to defend a son who is speaking when Allen should talk. What has your son to say that Allen could not utter with far great[er] clarity and wisdom?"[138] And writing from idyllic, but small-town Monteagle, Tennessee, Lytle was sure Gardner had been sorely remiss in not sensing that Tate needed to be in the South:

> You cannot abstractly isolate a husband from his background, his environment and his sense of family, which always finds location in some geographical spot. To be concrete I think when he wants you to come to this part of the country, you ought to come with him. This may have had something to do with the failure of the bed. He is in that time for slowing up, but men can last awhile, if not with the vehemence of youth. The mind gets in the way. If there is a basic misunderstanding, it can bring down the tower of London. . . .
>
> In this country, and you've got to see Southerners of our generation as belonging to a distinct society, location, geographical and family traditions mean a lot. And finally in your human and familial communion the man must head the house.[139]

Paradoxically, Gardner was being blamed both for hanging on to her own pasts and for failing to understand the importance of her husband's pasts to him. Moreover, Tate had remained much closer, in love and hate, to his ex-wife Caroline Gordon than Gardner to her three ex-husbands. He corresponded with Gordon regularly and lovingly, tried to propagate her work, and even, once, tanked, in a taxicab with Gardner's parents, had called out: "Caroline is my only wife."[140] But none of that counted. Gardner simply could not win, as Tate (and his cronies) were bound to find examples of Gardner's not having been the perfect, submissive wife. One would almost forget that it was Tate who had been cheating and lying. His betrayal and subsequent wily, dastardly behavior devastated Gardner, but loving him deeply, she was nevertheless eager to take him back without reproach, flagellating herself for the smallest past failures and improprieties, although she knew that the much-touted dinner-table incident should not and could not be the cause of the disintegration of their marriage. After months alone, in desperation but in all seriousness, Gardner suggested her husband divide his time between his wife and his mistress: she would not make scenes or complain. In a letter to Dahlberg, who, while married to Rlene, had his mistress and next wife, Julia, living with them, just a trace of bitterness comes through: "You have in your life Rlene *and* Julia. I am glad that you do. Allen has his young trained nurse; and me, his wife, for the asking."[141]

To Carolyn Kizer it "seemed preposterous that Al[len] would leave Belle, when we all thought it would be the other way around. We referred to them as

'Beauty and the Beast.' I always thought Tate a remarkably *un*attractive man; however ... stories were also rife about his having students on the desk or floor of his office etc.; while Belle was a beauty—the most glorious peaches and cream complexion and divine Titian hair."[142] Although Tate had at first juggled all options, the balance soon swung in favor of Heinz, whom he saw often during the summer and fall. His avowals of love to Gardner followed by broken promises came to seem like a calculated campaign to alienate and break her. Planning his future, Tate now intended to stay in Minneapolis with his young bride-to-be until his retirement. He insisted Gardner leave the city where her son and friends lived—that she give up her comfortable house, for her presence might prove awkward for the new Tates. Gardner had come to feel at home in her adopted city, but the Minneapolis academic community chose sides and rallied around its exciting, powerful philandering professor, rather than his somewhat outlandish Bostonian wife, who, in spite of her wholehearted attempts, had never fit the mold of the self-effacing faculty wife. The Fosters, Gardner realized, had been sniggering behind her back for over a year, but Tate's other colleagues closed ranks, too, with most of their wives following suit. Even Tate's physician, Boyd Thomes, who had used Gardner as "a sort of rescue operation" as "Allen used to drink a bit and at times his behavior would be very aggressive, childish, and embarrassing to lots of people, but when Isabella was associated with him he was just outstandingly good," and who had regarded her as "a worthy celebrant to Tate's greatness," dropped Gardner now that Tate no longer needed her.[143] The exceptions were the Clarks, outsider Bob Stange, for once in accord with his ex-wife, Pat, and Hunt Brown's outspoken wife, Biddy. Biddy Brown had known the Gardner family since childhood, as her father had been one of Kitty's pediatricians. A former Bostonian herself, she had never, unlike others, been daunted or put off by Gardner's aristocratic accent and bearing, and now was infuriated by Tate's preening at having seduced a nun:

> He came to tell me he had found the woman he was going to marry and so he sat down beaming all over. "I am going to get married again," he said. "She was a nun, but I am sure now that she has left the order, and I shall marry her." And I said: "You mean you proposed to her, when she was still in nun costume?" And he said: "Oh, yes indeed," which was a great triumph. He was thrilled to death to think he had got her out of the convent and won such a wonderful battle and I was really fed up and I walked right over to the front door and I said: "Allen, I do not want to see you anymore, goodbye." [144]

As with many anecdotes concerning Tate's conquests—and this situation was made to measure for myriad Minneapolis jokes about Tate's getting her out of the habit, his laying a lay nun and so on—Brown's reportage may be hyperbolic, but there is no doubt that Tate was proud that his charms had won over a good-looking young nun half his age; he had, once more, proven his manhood to himself and others. He knew, too, that with Gardner his life would never be without complications, while he foresaw a peaceful yet sexually exciting future with Heinz, the Galatea to his Pygmalion or his tabula rasa as Gardner called her. Now that he was going on seventy, it crossed Tate's Machiavellian mind that Heinz's qualifications as a registered nurse came in handy, too.[145] Also, he hoped against hope (much of his best poetry having been written before the end of World War II) that this new love would revive his creative energy.

More than in her previous marriages, Gardner had bent over backward to fulfill her husband's wishes, subjugating her considerable personality to Tate's, making him the focal point of their marriage and "letting him shine."[146] She had minded not being able to write, but far less so than when she had hit a dry patch with McCormick, for during the first years of her marriage to Tate the importance of her poetry had paled beside the magnitude of her Poet. Yet, in January 1966, Tate put salt in raw wounds by accusing her of being rivalrous and of disliking to stand around at readings watching him being admired. "Such a notion never crossed my *mind*," Gardner wrote Katherine Biddle, "let alone my lips. . . . I am enormously proud of him and needless to say have never thought of myself as *remotely* in the same league. Even with those I do feel that I am on some sort of par with I am almost neurotically uncompetitive. It frightens me, the mere thought."[147]

Tate may have felt threatened by his wife, who, when they became involved, had recently published her first book of poems to extraordinary acclaim, and expectations for her second book could not have been higher. By contrast, Tate's impersonal, modernist, dense, hypercerebral poetry had become dated after the breakthroughs of Lowell's *Life Studies* and W. D. Snodgrass's *Heart's Needle* in 1959 in the wake of Ginsberg's *Howl* (1955). An authority, still, in the American literary world, revered for his unwavering dedication to his vocation, and an adored mentor to many, Tate was feted for his stature and past achievements, but his diminished influence as a poet as well as his inability to write frustrated him no end. Carroll remembered a party where Tate, "a burnt-out poet, his long terza rima poem like bad Dante," shouted drunkenly: "I am not a poet, you are a real poet, Isabella is a real poet, Robert Lowell is a poet, but I am not."[148] Late in life, according to the publisher Al Poulin, Gardner came to feel that Tate "had attempted to squelch her reputation and tried to make sure that she would never be more famous than he was." Poulin spoke of "the silence that Tate imposed on her."[149] On the other hand, Helen Heinz confirmed that he respected Gardner as a poet: "He never made a negative remark about her writing. . . . He used to say a lot of negative things about Robert Penn Warren's poetry, but never about Isabella's."[150]

After the first frisson of his affair with Gardner and a few halcyon years of blissful harmony as a married couple at the bacchanalian center of the literary life in Minneapolis, Tate had reverted to being, in the words of his would-be biographer Ned O'Gorman a "sexually carnivorous character" and "one of the most tormented, repressed, unhappy, unfulfilled men who ever lived on earth."[151] Gardner's clearheaded aunt Catherine Mayes (though matriarch of the American theosophical center in Ojai, California) did not mince words: "Of the 4 problem children you have married Allen would appear to be the most 'lost,' therefore to appeal to your magnificent, but maybe sometimes misguided, desire to help at all costs. . . . [A]s I see it, he has, all through his life, misused and exploited the devotion of others and for his own sake this can't be allowed to go on."[152] Gardner, however, was sure the failure of this marriage was her fault, too, and she berated herself for having made a mess of her life since she had wed Van Kirk. But Mayes knew: "The only real failure is to fail in love, compassion, understanding. Failures of judgment are . . . inevitable. . . . You have had a most chaotic and difficult life so far, yet you have always seemed to me to be of a different, and larger, caliber than the rest of your very delightful and charming family. Whether you started out that way . . . or whether the way you have always met things . . . there is a depth to you that is certainly not 'run of the mill.'"[153]

Gardner's family had gathered around her. Her parents had met her in Italy in July, just after Tate had deserted her. In September, Kitty came down at once from Paris after Gardner called her in agony when Tate failed to join her in Florence as promised. Kitty wrote their worried, aged parents that she had found her sister looking "better than I would have believed possible, but she eats virtually nothing and smokes incessantly—(she cannot be spoken to about this—). . . . She is drinking very mildly but as always it seems to affect her. . . . God knows I don't disapprove but I realize how cumulative this is when taken in conjunction with calmer-downers." She took immediate command of Gardner's wardrobe, as Gardner had almost no clothes left, her baggage being lost in an Italian strike: "she bought two very reasonable and pretty things to wear in N.Y. and Boston."[154] Kitty's being there for her, caring, listening, supported Gardner more than "a little" as she had been alone in Europe since her parents had left. She had besieged an elusive Tate with calls, cables, and letters, but she had in effect had nobody—least of all Tate—to talk to for months. "In every single point of view Belle and I are so apart in our thinking," Kitty wrote her parents, "and yet I know I have the greatest admiration for her qualities—some of which I think are *saintlike*—although I confess there are moments when I want to shake her!" For, though aggrieved and bewildered, Gardner (unlike

Gordon with her violent temper) never got angry with Tate; Kitty was "thankful an ocean divides Allen and me at the present" for his behavior had been downright "sadistic."[155]

Tate's cruelty to Gardner knew no bounds and continued up to the very end of their marriage, as it had with Gordon. They had a dramatic exchange in January 1966, when Gardner threatened to show his recent letters to her to Heinz or publish them, and Tate warned her that if she did, or opposed the divorce, he would never communicate with her again. He was scared, for Heinz would have been horrified to find that her elderly beloved was vacillating. A month later he wrote his "darling Isabella" that he felt lonely without her, and four weeks before the divorce was to go through, he wrote her a long letter filled with plans to be together again. He proposed that Gardner change the divorce action into a legal separation; this would put an obstacle in the way of his marrying Heinz and could, after a temporary separation, be annulled by mutual agreement without them going to court. "I do not try to justify morally this devious strategy, or stratagem it had better be called," he wrote his wife. "[I]t looks like the end trying to justify the means. If so, I take the responsibility on my own conscience. I suppose I make this plea to you on the ground that you love me and I love you." Feeling "in the depths of my being that a divorce was all wrong for us," Tate promised Gardner that he would never ask for one again, only to do so just three weeks later.[156] The Tates were divorced on March 28, 1966.

One would have expected Tate to lay off now, but a few weeks after their divorce he had found another stick to beat Gardner with: her participating in an anti-Vietnam read-in organized by Robert Bly, to Tate the exponent of everything that was wrong with the (poetry) world. "I was a little surprised that you could let Robert Bly insult you and insult me by saying that now that you were no longer married to A.T., you would want to participate in that disgraceful read-in. I am not trying to stop you; it is entirely your affair. . . . Matters of this sort are an obstacle to our meeting at present. I will have to be firm about this; and please understand that I am doing it for both our sakes."[157] Gardner did not go. As his plans for marrying Heinz took firmer shape, Tate pined for Gardner: "I miss you, as you would very well expect me to. I am trying to deal with my Problem [Heinz]. . . . Love, darling—and write to me."[158] On July 11 he hastened to assure Gardner that he was not married to Heinz; a week later that he would probably marry her at the end of that month; then that they would not exchange vows at Smyrna—which is where they got married on July 31, 1966.

Although he knew that Gardner was still irrevocably bound to him, Tate refused to communicate with her as this would put a severe strain on his relationship with Heinz, but she remained abreast of the developments in his life via Nancy, who, though ever-loyal to her mother, had come to love Gardner and continued to correspond with her all through her life. Tate contacted Gardner only very sporadically. In November 1974 he told her that her love letters to him remained his property; if she paid him $2,000, he would consider them sold to Gardner, who had deposited them at Washington University, St. Louis. He ended his letter: "I was astounded to learn that you had given Nancy's children $3,600 or $900 apiece. . . . You gave them money that I should have received!"[159] In the end, Gardner gave him $1,000.

Chapter Eight

"The Unaired Flat," 1966–1973

I will take Sloth's
arm and go to a cryable movie
come back to the unaired flat
pick up the glass left on the mantle
rinse it fill it with wine
white iced and Tuscan go to my files
find under A: A.T.
I.G. letters: I need the earliest, the
in-the-beginning ones—
Spring Tide: Tug of the sun Pull of the moon.
("One Sunday in 1966")

Finding Heinz's love letters left by Tate in a wastepaper basket rang in the most excruciatingly painful year of Gardner's life. At almost fifty, she was, for the first time, deserted—by the man she had loved and admired most. Gardner came to feel that Tate's leaving her was deserved retribution for her leaving of Bob McCormick: "He was wonderful to Dan who loved him and respected him. Dan was doing so well in every way. I was able to write. Then I fell profoundly and irrevocably in love with Allen and ruthlessly, willfully left Bob and nearly destroyed Daniel. I carried guilt to Daniel into our marriage and was too soft with him and at the same time Daniel knew I put Allen first, as did Rosy."[1]

In the fall she took refuge at Yaddo to bridge the time until she could return to Minneapolis. Pauline Hanson, self-effacing, proper secretary to Yaddo's renowned director Elizabeth Ames was sure that Tate had helped get Gardner into Yaddo at such short notice. This way he could be reasonably sure that Gardner was taken care of and out of his and Heinz's way. For over eighty years Yaddo,

242 Not at All What One Is Used To

with its huge trees, sprawling gardens, and turreted faux-baroque castlelike mansion, has provided bed and board for aspiring and arrived artists, rich and poor, black and white, gregarious and shy, giving them a few weeks or months off, away from telephones, spouses, and children. All were filled with hope that their stay at Yaddo would give their novel, painting, or sonata that much-needed push; an astounding number of them received Pulitzer Prizes and National Book Awards, and one, Saul Bellow, the Nobel Prize. While some guests at Yaddo were determined to see as few people as possible, joining the group only for dinner, most were more gregarious: John Cheever bragged that he had had sex on every flat surface of the mansion.

In the mornings Gardner could often be found outside doing calisthenics with a few like-minded residents. After breakfast she would retire to her studio to work. She ate her lunch, which was left in a box at the door, tried to work some more, and in the late afternoon invited people for cocktails. Dinner was communal, and Gardner blossomed in the gorgeous baronial splendor of the mansion. "Bella needed friends, needed company. She could talk the night away: she wanted to be part of a loving group," New York painter Rosemarie Beck recollected.[2] The writer Jane Mayhall frequented Gardner's "salon" but saw that "some people were jealous and criticized her," partly because Gardner was drinking excessively, even by Yaddo's lax standards.[3] One of her detractors was Hanson, who not only disapproved of Gardner's boozing, but also found her "sick and selfish." She never forgot or forgave Gardner for remarking that she had "a miserable income," whereas to Hanson, Gardner was enormously wealthy; Hanson ached to be a poet but had to work full time serving artists like Gardner to make ends meet.[4] Worried about Tate's unpredictable behavior, Gardner frittered and drank much of her time away, but Yaddo did make her feel that even if her husband had cast her off she still belonged to the world of writers.

While Gardner's poetry had always been a powerful, distanced transformation of her experiences, the three poems Gardner wrote at Yaddo were more directly autobiographical and almost too close for comfort, though technically accomplished: "I have written two Sapphics and another poem while here—all three about our situation and therefore probably not good."[5] One Sapphic asked, "Are you mine my love? Have I lost you to her? / Tell me. I am cold and afraid and I must / Know for I grow old and am lonely. Please SPEAK. / Hold me in your arms as you tell me and be brave." And in "The Duet" "It is said that a marriage / between two poets cannot last / past the first lyrical stanzas / after the year of Epithalamion. / What then of two composers / chimed in the dissonant / assonance of wedlock? / Yesterday evening I heard / and watched two such / play the piano. It was not / Schubert or Mozart / made me weep but the marriage of four hands."[6]

In November, amidst all this emotional turbulence, Gardner's third book, *West of Childhood,* was published by Houghton Mifflin. The Boston press wanted to hitch its wagon to the commercial and critical success of Gardner's *Looking Glass. West of Childhood* was dedicated "To Allen," and on its flyleaf was a quotation from Rilke, whom Gardner revered: "Love consists in this: that two solitudes protect and touch, and greet each other." The collection included the poems from *Birthdays* and *Looking Glass* and three new ones: "Roundelay," written during Gardner's last Christmas with Bob McCormick, "This Room Is Full of Clocks," and "A Word from the Piazza del Limbo" constituted the meager poetic harvest of Gardner's years with Tate. Gardner's steadfast admirer Karl Shapiro, whose long-suffering Evalyn was divorcing him, "thought you are a true poet, more so than say Lowell (who in my novel [*Edsel*] is named Wigglesworth, or Wigg.) . . . I wish your book would win the Pulitzer, for your sake, for the fun of it. I think it deserves it highly. . . . About you and Allen I have nothing to say. My mind is a blank about marriage. People keep telling me how much E[valyn] loved (s) me and it doesn't register. I remember once Spender said to me (long ago) marriage is murder."[7]

To Gardner's "sorrow and fury" *West of Childhood* was sold out eight days after publication. Houghton Mifflin was pleasantly surprised, but could not guarantee the book's second printing before December 10, 1965, rather late for the Christmas sales. And Gardner fretted about the lack of media attention; the reviews were slow in coming, although her publisher had sent out a generous 150 copies. One of the first was Peter Stitt's "In Praise of Isabella Gardner" in her old hometown *Minnesota Review.* Stitt declared Gardner's "versatility astounding—her imagery . . . brilliant, her music superb," noted that her "lighter poems also give us a glimpse of the dark side of the coin" and concluded: "If 'fools admire, but men of sense approve,' I must plead folly at this time. Miss Gardner is an excellent poet, one of our best. Reviewing *West of Childhood* is not a burden; it is a privilege."[8] In a surprising twist, in *Chicago Review,* Peter Michelson contrasted Elizabeth Bishop's sentiment to Gardner's artifice, demonstrating how Gardner uses form to facilitate understanding: "Giving life a definable and isolated form would seem to provide a perspective on it. Perspective permits a kind of control, the absence of which may be chaos. . . . Miss Gardner's grand style indicates a growing development [in American poetry] that emphasizes artifice and rhetoric as devices for making the ambiguity of modern sentiment meaningful for a sceptical contemporary imagination."[9] In *Poetry,* Robert Huff concentrated on Gardner's confronting death in many guises, "often at once fearsome and humorous," and singled out for scrutiny the previously uncollected "This Room Is Full of Clocks" to underscore his admiration.[10] Months later, in the *New York Times Book Review* of March 1967, Gene Baro analyzed three inimitable women poets: Elizabeth Bishop, Carolyn

Kizer, and Gardner. He applauded the "vigorous play of mind" characterizing Gardner's poetry, her "enviable breadth of stylistic attack," and aptly spoke of her poems as having "the excitement of a dramatic encounter."[11] Bishop "was very pleased" with *West of Childhood* and used the book in her classes. "Some of your poems have marvellous meters and song-like [rhythms]."[12]

That Gardner's slender book, a virtual reprint, was so positively reviewed in the *New York Times Book Review* showed that she was still regarded as very much on the map, in spite of her minimal output during her years with Tate. However, her reputation in Tate's South took a hit in sour articles in *Shenandoah* ("Though her intentions and her humanity . . . are worthy and vital, the poems are just plain bad") and *Virginia Quarterly Review* ("Miss Gardner is willing to sacrifice idiom and normal syntax, to employ archaisms, and to magnify words . . . which some people imagine to be quintessentially English or truly [unpoetically] poetic.")[13] Tate had asked Andrew Lytle, editor of the *Sewanee Review,* to pay attention to *West of Childhood:* "It is a fine book and under the circumstances such a review would do her a lot of good."[14] Although somewhat put off by the fact that "Miss Gardner is a New Englander and at first sight her poems seem to be forthright, direct and blunt," *Sewanee*'s critic was fair, balancing Gardner's "respect for words and their rhythms" with her sometimes "narcissistic" pride and "fretful" nostalgia.[15]

Meanwhile, Gardner was looking back on her marriage but at first blamed neither her husband nor Heinz, whom she thought of as a love-struck young nun, "a good and innocent fool helplessly in love with him," until she found out that Heinz was "a high powered administrator. Very calculating and certainly without conscience. I had sentimentally thought she was a naïve innocent. Technically she doubtless was."[16] Slowly and reluctantly, Gardner came "to the conclusion that Allen's cruelties since July have been a calculated campaign to break my will and provoke me to anger, so that I will divorce him and move out of Minneapolis" and was therefore inclined to agree to a divorce even if Francis Biddle (a longtime admirer of Tate and his Don Juanism, who knew Peabo and had always treated Gardner like a spoiled little rich girl) now counseled her not to let her marriage go so casually.[17]

In November 1965 Gardner had started to look at a future without Tate. "If Allen, by March, is still hell-bent—and it *is* hell-bent—I suppose I will fly to Mexico and do the bloody deed. . . . In April I'll have to go back to Mnpls and do a lot of packing and arranging. May 1st—end of June at Yaddo. Then Wellfleet—maybe. I don't intend to sell the house. The mortgage is paid. I can always rent it. If I have to make my life alone I think now I'd want to spend a few months of the year there. It's *home* for me, and Rosy and Dan. . . . It would be *impossible* to go to Chicago. Difficult to go to Boston. I might live in an apt. hotel in N.Y. part of the year."[18] She sent Rago her burning, bitter Yaddo poem about "The Accomplices":

Must now accomplish the division of remains.
Assassins they will now be scrupulous
take pains to be exact in the division of each part
(Let not the question of the genitals impede
the disposition of their singular dead.)
Each must be left with half a
head and half a heart a hand
for him a hand for her a lung apiece
and a iambic foot for each and then surcease. (95)

"Just in the event that you might think Allen would be offended by its being printed I will tell you that he thinks it is the 'best' poem I've written in years and is all for submitting it," Gardner clarified.[19] Rago accepted by return mail, and Gardner was "glad you want the poem; but I wish I had not had to write it."[20]

After getting the divorce in Mexico in March 1966, Gardner went on a reading tour in California, visiting the Manulises and Myra Cholden and then returned to Minneapolis, where Tate now and then deigned to visit her. He vastly preferred spending time with Heinz, and as she lived just around the corner, to spellbound Minneapolis bystanders their situation became ever more dramatic, even comic, with Tate scuttling back and forth between his ex-wife and his lover. For Gardner the position was untenable, and she was relieved to be asked back to her sanctuary Yaddo. In May 1966 she wrote Richard Eberhart that she was "so grateful to be here":

> I'm eating and sleeping for a change, the Spring here is, as you know, beautiful, and the company is quiet and congenial—added to all the above I've actually written two poems! . . .
>
> I've been given a room facing the sun-rise. At about 5:30 anyone who wants to brings his or her tipple to my room where we relax and talk. It's been nearly a year since I've laughed without the shadow of irony implicit in the laughter. . . .
>
> I fear for Allen who had a bad bout of flu and was laid up alone in his hotel for a week. Theirs is an odd situation. She does not live with him, never has. She of course works till late in the day at General Hospital, he does not (he says) intend to marry her. His last letter said "I am trying to solve my Problem." His caps. I wish he could. I even wish he would marry her as I hate to think of him being alone.[21]

Gardner was surrounded by new friends and even lovers at the artists' colony. Jane Mayhall was admiring: "She was adventurous. She picked up men, which I have always believed in. She put herself at risk quite often. At Yaddo she was all over the place and she would fall in love with somebody for a day."[22] In June, two months after the divorce, Gardner confessed to Katherine Biddle that for "a while I didn't want to live. Now I do. Allen speaks of 'reconciliation.' I *don't* think I could re-marry Allen though I'll always love him. . . . My life as a woman is *finished*. I may flirt. I hope for tender and congenial companionship but anything else is out of the question. . . . I want to live an orderly, tidy, but unconventional life, which is to say I am not up to any conjugal or social, or structured life."[23] During their marriage, Gardner had been faithful to Tate, but attractive at fifty and passionate as ever, Gardner now seduced men (younger as well as older) with zest. She often took the initiative and enjoyed one-night stands. Such sexual behavior by a middle-aged woman was frowned upon, but Gardner did not mind much, as her young admirers gave her a new lease on life. Robert Phelps, editor, translator, and expert on Colette and Cocteau, and Arnold Weinstein, playwright and librettist, became her true friends.[24] They picked bunches of lilacs and wild violets for her, typed her poems, played ping-pong and croquet, drank, and flirted, and for a while Gardner indeed fancied herself in love with Weinstein in an escapist fantasy.

Feeling alive and loved again, Gardner mustered the energy to help old friends and new acquaintances. After his manuscript had been rejected by the alternative Grove Press, the umpteenth publisher to which he had submitted it, Paul Carroll had sunk into a depressed gloom. In a fit of rebellion against the publishing world that did not recognize his masterpiece, he founded his own avant-garde Big Table Press, so that he could enter his manuscript for the Lamont Prize for first books of poetry. He counted on winning, but Gardner feared he was far too optimistic. Again, Carroll's hopes were dashed and through raising money—providing most of it herself—Gardner was instrumental in both getting his first manuscript, *Odes* (1969), into print, and, indirectly, in launching Big Table Press. Carroll was greatly "*moved*": "I'll never forget it. I'm going to go ahead and publish [my] book under Big Table Books imprint. . . . I want to publish Bill Knott's . . . first book; and a lot (the best) of the young poets out at Iowa and elsewhere! . . . Ferlinghetti and Ginsberg keep urging me to start Big Table magazine again; but I don't know." He ended, "I *love* your poems. I think I'll write [an] essay on 'Widow's Yard' for [a] book I'm writing on all of us."[25]

Gardner sent numerous comforting letters to the beautiful young Indian poet Shreela Ray, who, while at Yaddo, had fallen hopelessly in love with the handsome, husky-voiced Galway Kinnell, who had no intention of committing himself to any of the many women who could not resist him. Gardner was more touched by Ray's heartache than by her poetry, but, as with all of her protégés, read and criticized her work, wrote references, and introduced her to editors and publishers. Earlier, she had done the same for Barbara Harr Overmeijer, who "when very unhappy and miserably confused over trying to be a wife and a poet and a real live separate person all at the same time" had contacted Gardner on Kinnell's advice, then had had a painful affair with John Logan, and ever since had been pestering Gardner with interminable self-centered letters.[26] Overmeijer invited herself to Minneapolis and Wellfleet, threatening to appear on Gardner's doorstep, hippie guitar in hand, and sent her her book-length manuscript of poems, which Gardner, out of friendship for Logan, critiqued with care. Gardner also spent days on word changes and on revisions of whole lines in Weinstein's poems and helped him organize them into a book suitable for submission by suggesting separate sections, sequences, and headings. When Weinstein then invited numerous other friends to look at his work, Gardner, miffed, wrote Phelps's down-to-earth wife, the painter Rosemarie Beck, that while he was a charming, cultured, talented playwright, he also was "selfish, spoiled." She was sure he would not "get another friend who understands his stuff as well as I do *and* understands editing and will work as hard. . . . I lack confidence in most areas but as to my work I would never allow *anyone* to go at it the way he wanted me to go at him."[27]

As to *West of Childhood,* by mid-1966 Gardner knew that compared to her first two books it had "fallen with a very dull thud though it's in a second printing (*that* was January) and has sold 1250 copies. When married to Allen—when he and I were happy I cared nothing for all this. I must begin now, I suppose."[28] The critic Joseph Frank, a friend to both, consoled her in an insightful critique of both her life and work: "The comparison that occurred most to my mind was that of Blake—I suppose because of your empathy with animals, the kind of Adamic innocence of vision that you manage to get in your best work, and the sense of evil and death which yet somehow never quenches or obscures the purity of innocence. What I like best, I think, is the kind of wild, childlike cunning that is constantly fighting to maintain itself underneath the experience of life with its inevitable maimings (as in the poem on the looking-glass, or less defiantly in your 'Piazza del Limbo'). The person who wrote those poems, I know, will weather whatever life may bring; after reading them, I began to feel less uneasy about your state of mind in view of what's happened."[29]

Congdon tried to help, too, sent her a painting, and referred to their shared talents: "come what may, I, *as have you,* have an extraordinary source of redemptive creativity. Allen may have temporarily suffocated yours which may, perhaps now, burst forth."[30] A few weeks later, in an honest but blunt attempt to help, Congdon gave Gardner a blueprint of how her life should be lived from now on: "[T]he first condition . . . is that each of you disappear from the other's (physical) horizon. . . . The second condition, I see as your entrusting yourself to some authority—probably psychiatric or 'religious.' . . . A third condition, I see, as not to discuss Allen or those aspects (causes etc.) of your problem which are now passed with anyone. . . . Emotionally charged rehashings can only increase confusion and keep you, as the Bible crudely puts it, 'stewing in your vomit.'"[31] Stung by his insensitivity, Gardner let Congdon stew for months, and it was only after he sent a contrite note in March 1967 that she started corresponding with him again.

In the summer of 1966 Gardner left Yaddo for Wellfleet but soon saw that it had not been sensible of her to return to the place where she had fallen in love with and married Tate. Her old friend Maurice Donohue joined her there, uninvited, only weeks after the death of his wife, Milly Cohen Levin. (After having smarted under her long-distance adulterous affair with Donohue for years, she had finally divorced Henry Levin, but her married happiness with Donohue was short-lived, as she soon fell gravely ill.) Gardner felt for him but wanted him gone to salvage herself and to work, for although Donohue was on the wagon, he was manic as well as ill from smoking four packs of cigarettes a day while suffering from emphysema.

> It's been helpful having him here in that we've known each other for 30 years and it has made the-seeing-for-the-first-time-without Allen of friends and places [easier]. He rented a car and he is a cheerful and considerate companion which is extraordinary in view of what he's been through in the last three years of his wife's illness and then her, I think, merciful death.
>
> But it's been trying too in the sense that he is a compulsive TALKER (he talks *well,* but one has to listen and respond) about history, politics, economics, welfare work, mythology, etymology, philosophy, our youth etc. etc.—. . . .
>
> The other trying thing is that he came here assuming we'd be lovers. Eros has never entered into our 30 years of close friendship and what Arnoldo [Weinstein] calls my "cancerous charity" does not extend to the bed.[32]

Rumors of Tate's impending wedding reached Gardner and did not make for peace and quiet. She wrote James Wright: "This week is a tough one as I think Allen is marrying his 'registered Nun' on July 30th in Tennessee. I still love him you know. I think he still loves me. At least he's told other people so, and me too. . . . I have written four poems which aren't bad since October. Once Allen *is* married I'll be able to work again."[33] She told Rosemarie Beck: "I'm not jealous. Of course I'd like him to have the courtesy of the heart to write me but I doubt if he will. Like all my husbands he's a spoiled-by-women problem CHILD fighting ghosts. He needs his cold efficient German registered nurse-nun now."[34] Beck was not fooled and urged Gardner to "want to see him miserable with that wretched nun. . . . If you've got any rage or black bile, let's have it. Be shameless for once."[35] Gardner obliged, sending her what she came to call her hate poem, "Spousall Verse," a savage prothalamion for Tate full of rage and spleen, supposedly written by "Daphne and Chloe," the names by which he had addressed her breasts while making love: "Hail to the Groom! How lightly / Lie his nearly sixty-seven years, / As lightly as he's lain on her. / As lightly as he'll lie to her. / His ladies all have lain with lies. . . . Hail to the almost Bride of Christ / (Anti-Christ will do, if he be old and famous) / Hail to the Nurse who'll count each cough / And take her groom's pulse and his temperature."[36]

Her anger armored her, and being uncharacteristically bitchy helped her survive gossipy Wellfleet: "It amuses me that old friends here expected to find me a broken reed and are either pleased or disappointed (according to their natures) to find me apparently in a state of wit and well-being."[37] She resisted the temptation to send Tate a telegram on his wedding day with best wishes from Daphne and Chloe, and instead of wallowing in self-pity concentrated on those she had met and felt kinship with at Yaddo, the writers Phelps and Weinstein and painters Beck and Boston-based Richard Yarde. Slightly infatuated, Gardner was an early admirer of the latter's work and brought it to the attention of influential Bostonian trustees, but when she tried to interfere in his daily life, Yarde's wife, Susan, called a halt—and Gardner apologized: "A great trouble with being a woman alone is that I act on impulse. I've no-one to guide me. . . . My own son would have been angered by my sticking my onion nose into the running of his life."[38]

With Tate's desertion now certified by his marriage, Gardner picked up the pieces of her life and tried to rebuild. As Tate had not yet retired and so was living in Minneapolis with his new bride, and as in the past year it had become crystal clear to Gardner that apart from the Browns, the Clarks, and the Flints the Minneapolis ranks had closed against her, she chose to live near her new friends in New York City, both close to and far enough away from her family in Boston. She rented an apartment at the Chelsea Hotel, familiar to her because Rose had stayed there before one of her world tours in search of love and the meaning of life. Rose, too, had fallen for Weinstein, who, for Gardner, was one of New York City's chief attractions. This was the first time both mother and daughter were interested in the same man; thereafter, when Rose came to New York over the years, she would often set her sights on the men involved with her mother. Gardner's feelings for Weinstein were skin-deep, but they presaged the pattern of her love life for the years to come. She had never lived without a man and was not going to; however, she was no longer going to give her heart away so easily and passionately as she had done with Childers, Van Kirk, Seymour, and, most wholly and painfully, Tate. Whereas in the past she had changed roles, lifestyles, and cities for her men, she now resolved to consider men mere appendages, for she knew she could not survive another ordeal like the one Tate had brought upon her. Gardner resolved to seize the day; men might be cherished companions and pleasant bedfellows, safeguards against terrible loneliness, but she would no longer commit herself heart and soul to one man, no longer alter herself to please him.

The famous redbrick Chelsea Hotel at 222 West Twenty-third Street with its characteristic wrought-iron balconies, high ceilings, and winding iron staircase offered the perfect ambience for her new life. After eighty-some years, the Chelsea had long since slid from a fashionable cooperative building for Broadway stars to a slightly sleazy Bohemian apartment hotel, where (would-be) actors, musicians, composers, writers, and painters were welcomed by its eccentric proprietor, Stanley Bard, who permitted some residents to pay for their rooms in kind instead of in cash. When too many of them were behind on their rent, and the hotel could not make ends meet, Bard would allow in prostitutes to make a quick profit. Next to (paid) sex, drugs were in evidence everywhere, and Barbara Van Rensselaer Spalding was horrified: "If you went up in the elevator it reeked of marihuana, so you were high if you got up to Belle's floor."[39] Herbert Krohn, M.D., singer and aspiring poet living at the Chelsea, thought the hotel

> VERY Isabella Gardner, because it was a real cross section of society. Isabella really liked to travel from the top to the bottom of society. And she did not have any racism, unless it was reverse racism, and did not have any classism, unless it was to actively seek out classes that were different from the one in which she grew up. She always had friends who were street people, drug people, low life, underworld, into shady dealings, and her two children were just true to type, followed what their mother did, rather than whatever she might have told them. In the Chelsea, there were welfare families there, there were ambulatory schizophrenics living in rooms that were scarcely more than a closet, there were whores and their pimps set up in extended apartments there, and then there were several grand people like Isabella herself and Virgil Thompson, who had these white spacious, luxurious apartments, all in the same building. Then there were clusters of apartments in which rock bands and their managers would all camp. There is no place like the Chelsea, there is no other place quite like it.[40]

Gardner's forbearing parents and concerned brother George were worried: respectable Gardners lived in splendor on Park Avenue (as Kitty would a few years later) and not in a dangerous dump like the Chelsea. But Gardner's real identity was now not in Brahmin Brookline or Boston's Back Bay, where she had always felt a misfit and an embarrassment to her parents, nor among the wealthy on New York's Park or Fifth Avenues, but among the wilder creatures at the Hotel Chelsea, where creativity, real or imagined, and a little madness were assumed, even required. The Chelsea's maids cleaned her apartment and made her bed; its bellmen arranged for tickets and taxis, kept her in liquor, and brought her purchases up. Gardner tipped royally and was relieved of the responsibility (or guilt feelings) of having her own servants. The writer Florence

Turner, spirited participant and historian of the Chelsea Hotel, reminisced in 1987:

> And who comes there? Walking with grace, a flower in her hand. It is the Lady of Shallot, vertical, red hair theatrical against cream skin. But that is not a flower she carries. It is a vodka martini and it is Isabella Gardner Tate who approaches. A beautiful poet, author of 'West of Childhood,' Isabella not only wrote, but lived poetry as well. She was in fact a poem, a rime royal, perhaps. She wore splendid capes and wide-brimmed hats; and made no secret of the fact that she was immensely rich. She had been married to, among others, Allen Tate, the poet.[41]

At the Chelsea, Gardner wanted to be known as Mrs. Tate, or Isabella Gardner Tate. Portraits of Tate and posters for his readings were very much in evidence in the different apartments in which she resided at the Chelsea from September 1966 onward. Like Tennyson's tragic Lady of Shalott pining for bold Sir Lancelot, Gardner continued to yearn for her knight; like the Lady of Shalott she faced her eternal dilemma: seclude herself from society for her art or live what was left of her life to the fullest.

Tate had left her, but at the Chelsea she never needed to be alone. When she went down to its Spanish restaurant El Quichote, where she ordered very rare steak or shrimp with green sauce, other Chelsea people were always there, many of them all too happy to join her, as Gardner, not "immensely rich" but wealthier than most, usually picked up the tab. The most dramatic aspects of her persona were given free rein at the Chelsea, and even among its flamboyant characters Gardner stood out with her regal bearing, majestic voice, and dazzling wardrobe. Her fellow poet Josephine Jacobsen dubbed her "the queen of the Chelsea scene."[42] Gardner's Boston background, her years as an actress, her Chicago connections from the mob to the McCormicks, her long association with *Poetry,* her reputation as a poet, and her marriage to Tate meant that even in New York, where it is easy to get lonesome and lost, she had a diverse group of friends and acquaintances to fall back on.

She invited old and new friends to her literary gatherings, and such invitations soon became prized; any poet passing through New York, new book, or rebellious broadside merited a party. She ordered hors d'oeuvres from El Quichote and lots of liquor, had a bellman serve, and had writers read their work. Two of her most loyal friends (in their different ways), Edward Dahlberg and James Wright, also were living in the metropolis. Wright had recently become engaged to Anne Runk, and Gardner was his first friend to be told, a sure indication of their intimacy. Wright's bride-to-be was "very entranced" by Gardner's get-togethers, meeting points for Robert Bly, Stanley and Elise Kunitz, the poet and *New Yorker* editor Howard Moss, the poet William J. Smith and his French second wife, Sonia, Galen Williams, the director of New York's famous YM-YWHA Poetry Center and her husband, the witty anthologist Bill Cole, Ford Madox Ford's biographer and the founder and director of Columbia University's Writing Center, Frank MacShane, the delicate novelist Hannah Green and her eccentric Pop painter husband, John Wesley, and Gardner's Yaddo friends Robert Phelps and his wife, Rosemarie Beck, and, of course, Arnold Weinstein.[43]

Of the friends Gardner made at the Chelsea, none was more welcome than Mildred Weiss Baker, director of the Newark Museum. They seemed an incongruous pair; Baker was Gardner's antipode: she was resolute and determined, rather than undecided and vague, and sense rather than sensibility guided her actions. Baker had an erect, neat appearance, wore her hair in processed violet-and-white waves, and dressed in an inconspicuously prim but distinguished style like Queen Elizabeth the Second on a rainy day, while Gardner's sweeping, colorful dress sense favored the first Elizabeth's, even if her long, dangly earrings, clunky necklaces, and enormous rings were often secondhand junk. Known as the Chelsea's "First Lady," but called "Jellyroll Baker" behind her back because nothing could be more inappropriate than referring to her as a sexual virtuoso, Baker looked down her dignified nose somewhat at the antics of Chelsea's oddballs, yet they also fascinated her. She moved to the Chelsea in the 1940s when she married Jacob Baker, a business executive, and she stayed until her death of a stroke in 1998 at age ninety-three.

Gardner and Baker became fast friends when Baker was widowed soon after Gardner settled at the Chelsea in 1966. They were opposites in many ways, but most of the female residents were much younger and submerged in pop culture rather than the high culture, visual arts, and literature that Gardner and Baker appreciated. They enjoyed each other's company, going to the Met, seeing a play on Broadway, or attending poetry readings. A man's woman, Gardner preferred male escorts who would provide the many gallantries she expected, but men were not always at hand, and Baker was a worthy substitute. Clearheaded, intelligent, and formidable, with an impressive career in the arts, a member of the best clubs, Baker was not intimidated by Gardner's background or imperious manner, and she spoke her mind, taking no nonsense. Simultaneously, she felt protective of Gardner, loving her for her acute sensitivity, her extreme loyalty toward friends, and her excessive generosity. Gardner found in steadfast and slightly malicious Baker a high-powered friend she could trust and talk and drink with.

Baker had become close to Virgil Thomson, another longtime resident, and Thompson and his entourage were also included in Gardner's literary gatherings. One of Andy Warhol's associates, handsome, aspiring photographer and poet Gerald Malanga, remembered that Gardner "held court like Edith Sitwell" with acolytes sitting at her feet.[44] She often had her guests read poetry or Greek tragedies in harmony; but for a few poetic egos bickering to get the best parts, "people felt lucky to be invited," Frank MacShane remembered—"and then it got all spoiled."[45] For over the years the atmosphere of the Chelsea changed from aberrant Bohemian to shabby criminal, and so did Gardner's get-togethers. Instead of reading major Greek tragedies, minor poets now made scenes about which of them was greatest, and hangers-on crashed the parties for the free food and booze or the easy pickings among the guests, as Reed Whittemore's wife found when she put her purse down for a moment in Gardner's apartment.

The North Dakota poet Thomas McGrath, also known as Tom Fool or Tommie the Commie, was at a party in honor of self-styled bourgeois poet Karl Shapiro and attacked him verbally and physically. But Anne Wright thought Gregory Corso "the lowest," and Chelsea's passionate sculptor Stella Waitzkin agreed, calling him "demonic, a bully."[46] Corso was no longer the youthful, adoring admirer of Gardner's poetry, no longer the handsome, gifted young Beat poet of "Bomb" and "Marriage" of the late 1950s, but a blocked writer, a junkie constantly on the lookout for drink and drugs, which were to be found in abundance at the Chelsea. While his impossible behavior worsened, loyal friends like Allen Ginsberg or Patti Smith stood by him. A sometimes-charming consummate liar, Corso tried to convince himself as well as his publishers that he was writing as he sank deeper into silence. His most outrageous stunt was trying to convince the literary world that Gardner had stolen his manuscripts because she was envious of his success. Corso told the story to interviewer Gavin Selerie, explaining why he had published so little since the mid-1960s:

> GC: See, there are two books missing in all this. They were lost. One was stolen and that book was called *Who am I—Who I am.* . . . . It was in two suitcases and I was living in this fucking Chelsea Hotel in New York City. A supposed friend, a woman, who's a very rich lady and all this shit, a poet named Isabella Gardner, got hold of it; once it was in her hands, it was lost.
>
> GS: What did she do with it?
>
> GC: Well, she was very jealous of me, you see. . . . I was writing the goodies and she knew that that was my book. So there was a big gap—1970–1974, four years' work, gone. I got so fucking pissed at that shit, man, I said, "*Forget* it" for two years. That led up to 1976 and I said, "Hey wait a minute, the poet's not gone. They can fuck my poetry around but they didn't fuck the poet around." And that's from *Heirlooms,* which is the work I'm reading lately to people—the new poems.
>
> GS: Do you know what happened to those other poems?
>
> GC: Destroyed or stolen or hidden.

GS: Do you think someone's sitting on them?

GC: Sure. She doesn't need the money so she ain't selling.[47]

Anne Wright knew that Corso had "claimed that valuable manuscripts—which were worthless, you would have to pay someone to cart them away—had been stolen. And he charged Belle for it. She remained kind and he was rude to her, he was rude to everybody, he was really a horrid person."[48] Roland Flint told a similar story of Corso storing some beat-up old suitcases in a little room that Gardner used for her own files, two floors below her apartment, and that, when they were gone—"A tragedy for America letters," Flint added sarcastically—Corso blackmailed Gardner. In his "Verse Testament for Isabella Gardner," Logan remembered how "Gregory Corso, that hood, conned her. / He'd left two bags in her workroom / and they were stolen. He solemnly claimed their value / at two thousand bucks and threatened / to smash to bits her apartment / if she did not produce the cash. / She paid, this great-hearted woman, who had subsidized / many needy writers and painters, never loaning / money but always giving it."[49] Gardner's and Corso's lives had become closely intertwined, for Corso had moved in with Rose, who, when in New York City, also stayed at the Chelsea. It was easy for "that frightful monster, that alleged poet," as Carolyn Kizer called him, to dominate Rosy, who was enthralled by him, but Corso also "would deliberately, verbally torture her [mother]. . . . He is one of the nastiest pieces of work I have ever met."[50]

In September 1966 when she moved into the Chelsea, it still showed Gardner its softer side: there were the young long-haired hippies, writing, singing, making love for a better world, drifting on marijuana clouds; there were the international artists of any age for whom the cheap Chelsea in the middle of Manhattan was the gateway to New World fame; and there were the old-timers like Mildred Baker, who cherished its tolerant diversity and the creative energy that swept through its badly cleaned corridors. Anything went at the Chelsea: one of its best-loved inhabitants was George Kleinsinger, composer of "Tubby the Tuba," who had rented a penthouse studio to escape the hell of suburbia, creating there his own exotic tropical paradise complete with doves, monkeys, skunks, a dancing turtle, parrots, and the obligatory snake that fed on trembling live mice, until Kleinsinger "had forgot to close the Python's door / which led into the aviary. The Composer / was unable to save his favorite toucan. / Right in the region of the Python's mouth / lay one last token feather. (One cannot / scold a snake, nor retrieve, / he sighed, the irretrievable.)"[51]

Gardner's apartment was more traditional. While to the biographer Jean Gould "there wasn't anything about her apartment that would make you feel that this was a woman who came from a well-known and wealthy family," Anne Wright's impression was very different: "She had a lovely apartment with all her treasures and wonderful pictures on the wall. It was like being in a little museum."[52] There were paintings by Congdon and, soon, by her new friends Beck and Yarde; treasures from her travels with Tate; and bowls with agate, amber, and amethyst eggs everywhere, many of which ended up at her friends' houses, as Gardner gave them away as easily as she gathered them. Gardner knew she tended "to be untidy *unless* I've a man to please" and was happy that the Chelsea provided maid service. "I suppose my untidiness is mostly laziness but maybe partly a reaction against the sterile immaculate suffocating tidiness of my parents' house. We weren't allowed to sit on our beds because of the bed-spreads or to have anything to eat or drink in the privacy of our bed-rooms with our friends in our childhood and even the disorder of the Sunday papers irritated my mother."[53]

A few weeks before her big move, Gardner had told Rosemarie Beck that she felt "euphoric, perhaps overly so, about the apt. and OPERATION NEW LIFE."[54] And soon she wrote Charles and Doris Foster: "I've a wonderful set-up at The Chelsea Hotel. *Big* living room with high ceilings *and* a fire-place, big bed-room, small hall, nice kitchen and bathroom, plenty of closets, maid service, switchboard, heat, air-conditioner, all utilities and linens for $325.00 a month. . . . I'm told I'm very fortunate and indeed I'm positively elated. I've many friends, both old and very new in New York; and [it's] been about 25 years since I've gone to plays, museums and galleries there."[55] Gardner laid it on thick, as she knew the Fosters would blab to Tate; but to Rosemarie Beck, who had become her bosom friend, she had confessed that "[p]acking and unpack-ing, arrivals and departures have always been very traumatic for me. I've had to dismantle so many lives. . . . Minneapolis was hellish. I telephoned a friend there before I left Boston and he told me that Allen and wife would be there the exact same time (the 8th, 9th, and 10th [September]) and that on the 10th a large party was being given by our mutual friends 'To meet Mr. and Mrs. Al-len Tate.' I told Allen in *July* that I would be in Mnpls. the 8th 9th and 10th. . . . There are only about 5 people in Mnpls. who give a damn about me now that Allen and I are divorced. I loved it there but hate it now. . . . As we used to say in my theatre days 'Duse is dead, Bernhardt is dead and I don't feel too good myself.'"[56]

Gardner had pretended to be glad about Tate's marriage to Heinz, but the reality of her irrevocable loss was sinking in. She began entertaining at a fran-tic pace and saw Nancy and Percy Wood, the Lowells, also based in New York City ("Cal seems *fine*"), the Franks, the French poet-essayist Francis Ponge and his wife, and a new friend, the lyric novelist Glenway Westcott, and his lover Monroe Wheeler, curator at the Museum of Modern Art: "I *loved* Glenway! I'd *always* liked his books and oddly enough had never met him. I thought him ab-solutely charming and he cooked the most heavenly dinner." She kept in touch with a Yaddo companion, the "wonderful" wood engraver Claire Leighton, had lunch and cocktails with Marcel Breuer's wife Constance, and saw a lot of the widowed poet and Chelsea resident Léonie Adams. She attended a reading by Adams and Langston Hughes at the Guggenheim. They were introduced by poetry's fairy godmother, Marianne Moore, almost eighty and dashing in her signature tricorn hat and black cape. Gardner thought Adams "marvellous," Hughes "long-winded," and Moore "frail but superb." The reading's organizer, Elizabeth Kray, had hoped Gardner would give the after-party, but Gardner no longer wished to be an official "saloniste"; that part of her life belonged to Minneapolis when she had a large house and a husband by her side.[57] Another reading was by "*two* Prima Donnas," Marianne Moore, "a bit tottering . . . but radiant and ineffably charming" and W. H. Auden.[58]

With her new work coming out in *Atlantic Monthly, Nation,* and *Poetry,* Gardner intended to concentrate on writing. Protesting a bit too much to William Smith, she explained, "[I] cared *nothing* about my own work during Allen's and my wonderful years till late 1963. Now I have to *try* to care."[59] Gardner had written a sensitive letter to Alexander Laing upon the death of his wife, Dilys, and Laing now asked her to write a "free upwelling" appreciation as introduction to Dilys's *Collected Poems* (1967). She initially accepted but soon copped out, as was her wont on assignments of—even celebratory— criticism. Gardner was still in demand and gave a reading with James Wright at the YMHA in November and another a month later in Washington, D.C., at the request of the gay poet Elliott Coleman, one of Josephine Jacobsen's closest friends. She was also asked to teach a poetry workshop at the New School in early 1967, which she dreaded. But *West of Childhood,* after its first surprise sell-out, was no longer doing so well: it did not even earn back its advance. And the Oxford University Press frustrated Gardner's hopes for a British edition, for although the press did not doubt that the collection "deserve[d] to be published on this side of the Atlantic," to them it seemed "(rightly or wrongly) slightly lacking in intensity and force"; an unorthodox view to say the least.[60]

Gardner spent part of December 1966 in Minneapolis in order to clean up the last debris of her marriage, shipping books and mementos to her own apartment or Tate's. Having to gut her home rent her heart as is apparent from her unfinished "Letter from an Empty House":

> A matter of months after the "young woman" (it
> was thus you referred to her) married you I saw fit
> to return to our house for a few belongings and prized
> letters. I found my letters to you (I was not surprised)
> in a trunk in the cellar. I foolishly read them line by line

last night as I sat in our tomato-colored kitchen lapping wine
in the company of tattered cook-books and the crockery
of other marriages. How sustaining is self-mockery!
    When I entered this dismantled house, myself dismembered,
I went straight into your study and remembered
that I once wondered why you never lit a fire in your grate
you then remarked that it was warm enough without.
It used to please me that you never closed your door
while you were writing typing keeping score
or reading at your desk. You were kept safe by all
your Lares and Penates on the shelves and wall.
There is nothing in this room that can remind
me of you, I am relieved to find,
except the wedding picture we both left behind.
    Upstairs in the bedroom your closet and bureau, of course
are empty but by trick of eye and force
of habit, not of will, I imagine that I see
what is not there, or so it seems to me.
Each dapper suit and jaunty jacket bobs, and those
sky-blue, green-blue-indigo, red and black ties
hang on the racks you'd fastened to the closet door.
I go to your bureau and pull out the top drawer.
How it bulges with its muddle of keep-sakes
handkerchiefs medals crucifixes keys and socks.
The second drawer is tidier, blue and white shirts . . . Good
God this is not a laundry list—although that could
be one way (like scanning old grocery lists) of rifle—ing through a marriage or a life.
            Old heart's eye lacks the heart to fill
            the bed where we made love until
            you turned the corner down the hill.[61]

Back in New York City, Christmas and the New Year 1967 loomed without
Tate, but fortunately her dear friend John Logan was in town. Drunk, lonely,
and longing for others, they made love out of a mutual need for momentary
physical comfort. Confused by having had sex with Gardner, his role model and mentor, Logan fled the scene. Writing on New Year's Eve, waiting for
Robert Phelps to drink with her and for James Wright to take her to Anthony
Hecht's poets' party, Gardner let him down easy:

Now, John darling, the *last* thing for either of us to brood about is our Thee
and Me.—We "came to-gether" out of loneliness and a profound affection. I was

happy for the closeness. It is of course no answer for either of us but in future we can do so or *not* do so as our inclination goes.

Certainly I am not either dependent on you or demanding—nor are you in regard to me. I still love Allen and am therefore however much I wish it otherwise a dry "virgin" to another man. You are the *only* man since Allen. I'm glad it *was you* but that does not mean you are obligated to continue. I *always* want to see you. But we need not make love. You were splendid and dear. I am glad we came to-gether, in intimacy. Perhaps we will, perhaps we won't. It doesn't *matter*.[62]

At the beginning of 1967, Gardner stopped writing. She hardly ate, and she was drinking again. She existed in limbo, caught in a haze of ruined dreams. Depressed, troubled by an eye infection, awkward as ever, and probably tipsy, she broke a bone in her foot. Confined to her apartment, she had to hobble around in a knee-high cast, leaning on a chic golden aluminum cane, for weeks. Her poetry workshop at the New School for Social Research, which was to start at the end of January, had to be cancelled, but her fame had not yet faded. The University of Pittsburgh Press asked her to be a reader, and she was invited to join PEN, and, in May, to consider being poet-in-residence at the University of Washington in Seattle, where the bearlike, baby-faced Theodore Roethke had left his indelible imprint. Her old flame Maurice English paid tribute to her in *TriQuarterly,* but Gardner felt he had done her a disservice, as English had not written analytically about her poetry but had used her "slender" output, "born out of passion and the gains and losses it brings," as a touchstone for a diatribe against the lack of personality and passion in much of contemporary poetry, "a compilation of the quasi-stenographic notations of anonymous sensibilities."[63]

In February 1967, Shapiro and his lover (soon to be his second wife) Teri had been "knocked out" by hearing Gardner on the radio. "You should have seen us last night. We were in bed reading and had the FM on when we heard you announced. I ran and got two copies of WEST OF CHILDHOOD which were in the next room, and then ran and got another little FM radio, as the first one wasn't working too good. So we heard you in style." Shapiro had "lots of wild and [H]erzogian news" about his divorce from Evalyn but preferred telling it in person, but he took the opportunity to thank Gardner for yet another check to tide him over.[64] Gardner had always been generous to a fault, but now that she was alone, she gave to almost everyone who came to her with hard-luck stories—and the Chelsea was crammed with artists-manqués who needed a little money to get their masterworks published, sponges who wanted handouts to keep Stanley Bard from chucking them out, or freeloaders who sucked up to her for drinks and dinner. Gardner usually knew that she was being used; nevertheless, she did not mind sharing her wealth, particularly with young writers, especially as much of her money stemmed from United Fruit's ill-gotten gains.

She was happy to send a check to the Wrights, who had given a dinner party to celebrate their engagement, saying that "anybody who is about to get married should not have to worry about paying for dinner."[65] And what if she had to pay for Erica Jong's dinner before Jong became famous with her sexy *Fear of Flying* (1973), if it led to her being immortalized in "Chinese Food": "Belle ordered spareribs / sweet and sour. / "I have given my life to men," / she said. / Like Eve in the garden she chewed the rib / & regretted nothing."[66] Gardner's old friends and dependents were not forgotten either, and she sent Anneke Van Kirk a considerable monthly allowance, about a quarter of what her Greek husband was earning.

Edward Dahlberg, long a beneficiary, chastised Gardner for her liberality but accepted large amounts of money himself. Gardner gave him $750 in April 1967 and, a few months later, another large check "to help with moving" as Dahlberg and his Julia, whom he married in July, were leaving New York City for Dublin.[67] In July 1968, in a wounding letter full of old grievances about Tate, Dahlberg asked her to give him an annual salary. But Julia had told her she was convinced that Dahlberg had a small fortune of $40,000 salted away and Gardner refused. She realized Dahlberg would "resent [her] negative reply and interpret it wrongly," adding: "Please know, however, that if either you or Julia is ill at any time you have only to tell me and I will help."[68] By that time, Dahlberg had physically abused his young wife and had left her, battered, alone, without money in Dublin, while he himself took off for Rome and Tel Aviv. When Julia begged for help, Gardner immediately cabled her five hundred dollars for the hospital, food, and the rent. Dahlberg directed his fury at Gardner:

> I have your very cruel letter: you have humiliated me for the last time. You told Julia from whom I have parted, and definitely, that if I were in need you would aid me. Now you propose to be my sick and burial society. . . . You run about for causes, but not for a friend who dearly loved you. I am the most eminent figure in American Literature and were I dying you would be so benevolent as to send me money? Friendship, eh! . . . You would never have met Allen were it not for me. I wrote you countless letters, knowing only that you were an unhappy woman, and had you gone to an humbug psychiatrist it would have cost you thousands of dollars and not for the wise counsel I gave you. . . . Just find another friend like Edward Dahlberg. He doesn't exist. When you are dust my fame will just begin to emerge.[69]

With friends like this who needs enemies? Yet, till death parted them, for better or worse, Gardner remained loyal to Dahlberg. Her true talent for friendship forged ties stronger than the vows of love and marriage. Gardner's friends knew they could count on her coming to their rescue time and again, on her forgiving them anything—as she did when Shag Donohue wrote her a pathetic begging letter: "Was I not supposed to pay you back the two-hundred-and-fifty real ones six months ago, by November 11th? And was I not supposed to deliver the short-story novel to my publisher four years ago? And did not Sylvia and my three children expect some sort of financial support which they have not been getting for the last three years? Did I not promise my mother to be good? ... None of the things I said I would do have I done. . . . But I do not want my stupidities to make me lose touch with you. I have no phone anymore, and unless I get 250 more bucks by Monday I may be evicted from this address."[70] Donohue was not thrown out of his Village apartment.

Gardner spent the summer of 1967 at America's oldest artists' colony, Mac-Dowell, in Peterborough, New Hampshire. Like Yaddo, though without a baronial castle and in general a little less elegant, MacDowell offered artists an inspiring interdisciplinary work environment, the colony offering room and board in isolated studios scattered over almost five hundred wooded acres. Here, where Thornton Wilder had written *Our Town,* in which both Gardner and her daughter had acted, Gardner felt at home, enjoyed the fresh air and, as she wrote Nancy Tate Wood, was "getting some work done"; she ranked her fellow guests as "nice but not ve[r]y inte[r]esting."[71] She was more open with Dahlberg, although characteristically putting herself down: "[T]hough I have made some friends (acquaintances) I've no companion, my work is no good at all, and my back hurts hellishly all the time. The chiropractor does not seem to help it. Why? because it is just *angst.* Allen—frustration in work, lack of love—race riots *et cetera.* Yes this *is* a sick and terrible society."[72]

Gardner was asked to act as hostess for that year's awarding of the Edward MacDowell Medal to Marianne Moore. Moore was grateful ("What can I say of the gifts and ministerings as though it were fitting you should wait on me! I never can forget—your lovely appearance and sometimes pensive air"), but Beck remembered that Gardner, though charming, was as disorganized as ever and depended on her to arrange the ceremony. Gardner was "embarrassed by a forthcoming article in The N.Y. Times Book Review about this Colony. . . . I am (to my distress) referred to as being better 'known' than the others here. . . . I shall have to write a letter. I have a horror of ending my days as Edith Sitwell did writing outraged letters to various organs of the press."[73] Gardner did send off a letter to protest her mention, suggesting that its author, Lawrence Bensky, should have written "the kind of piece that would demonstrate the immense value of the MacDowell Colony to writers—as also to painters, sculptors and composers. . . . The Colony is no place for dilettantes."[74] Bensky answered tersely that "I singled you out for mention because you were the only name I thought might be recognizable to the public, for whom the article was written."[75]

Gardner also wrote to the *New York Review of Books,* where Robert Adams had reviewed Paul Carroll's *Edward Dahlberg Reader* side by side with Edwin

Seaver's *Epitaphs of Our Times: The Letters of Edward Dahlberg,* both of which contained letters to her, Seaver's including Dahlberg's epistolary quarrel with Tate over which letters to Gardner should be included. "Did Mr. Tate indeed kick Mr. Dahlberg out of the house over this issue?" Adams wondered.[76] Angry that Dahlberg had been dissected by Adams's "tidy stiletto," Gardner defended Dahlberg's stature as a great American writer but explained that "Allen Tate did not kick Edward Dahlberg out of the house. The quarrel came after the visit when Mr. Dahlberg wrote me a cantankerous letter berating me for a lack of courtesy and inadequate hospitality and for my opinions about the equal rights movement."[77]

At MacDowell, Gardner drank, procrastinated, went skinny-dipping, and made some new friends, foremost among them the painter Louis Tytell. She also swam in the nude at Roque Island, which she visited for the first time in a decade to celebrate George's fiftieth birthday (and her own fifty-second) en famille. But among her successful siblings Gardner felt alone, depressed, a failure. Tate's young new wife had given birth to twins prematurely (they "just missed being born on the living room floor," Tate informed Robert Penn Warren); Houghton Mifflin was remaindering *West of Childhood;* and Gardner's new poems were "just plain NOT any good."[78] When Marcia Lee Masters, daughter of Edgar Lee Masters, asked Gardner, as one of America's leading poets, to contribute to the *Chicago Tribune,* Gardner replied that she was played out. Masters was shocked: "Dearest Belle; not so, not so. You must not stop being a poet. I remember what Edith Sitwell said about you—that you would be the next great woman poet. You have wonderful subject matter all about you—that Chelsea Hotel (where my father lived) and all the people who have come and gone, and left that silent cold floor, and the memorable spittoons. Forget the world news for a while, and turn your imagination loose. Stevens would have done it; so would Yeats. I intend to hear from you soon—with a dazzling poem."[79]

Gardner's despair was not only directed inward. She feared for America as the Black Power movement grew increasingly critical of the nonviolent approach to inequality as proclaimed by Martin Luther King: "I think that there are bloody years ahead . . . unless the slums are razed and the people who live in the ghettos whether white, Negro or Puerto Rican educated. They cannot be educated unless they have a full belly and a pair of shoes and a warm coat. They cannot be singled out and patronised and given these essentials as a handout—who wants 'benevolent paternalism'?" Gardner had no answers and was "going South to Negro colleges with 4 other poets under no do-gooding illusions. I suppose I think that if *one* poem by *one* of the 5 of us speaks directly to *one* human being in each of the several colleges it means something more than nothing. Personally I think more and more of leaving this country and living in Ireland, but not yet."[80] Reporting to the National Foundation on the Arts and Humanities, which underwrote her trip south, Gardner suggested that she would like to teach together with a black writer or activist at black colleges for short stints even at her own expense; in fact Margaret Danner had just asked Gardner to join her at Virginia Union University at Richmond. However, when Danner (no longer "the stuffy, middle class minded Margaret you once knew") warned Gardner that the climate at her university was not ripe for a visit by a white poet after all, she believed that Danner held off because of the color of her skin.[81] Danner denied this with vehemence: "Don't ever, not even in jest, think in honkie nigger terms where we are concerned. I was sure that you knew by now that I absolutely am not like that. . . . I DO NOT THINK OF YOU AS WHITE OR BLACK. I THINK OF YOU AS A POET. I THINK OF THE WAR-LOCK POEM CONTINUALLY AND THE MILKMAN AND OF OUR DAYS AT POETRY AND KARL SHAPIRO AND THE MILITANT MESS AND THE BLACK POWER OR WHITE FASCIST UGLINESS NEVER INTRUDES IT-SELF."[82]

Reed Whittemore, another of the sponsored poets, traveled part of the way with Gardner. Not surprisingly, given their mission, they "were political allies," but Whittemore soon found that Gardner preferred discussing Tate—"how sad that was for her. . . . That's all she wanted to talk about, at one point—" rather than the combustible political situation.[83] Yet, Gardner was trying to wean herself from Tate and had gotten involved with Louis Tytell. The Wrights were happy about Gardner's new relationship: "He was a lovely man. Both James and I were very, very fond of him and had hopes, because he seemed to be a stable influence on Belle. When she tried to order him to come to her parties, he would just be calm about it and say: 'No, Belle. I have told you I am busy, I cannot come.' He was much more serious, he was a very good man, very sweet."[84] Indeed, by all accounts, Louis Tytell, "stereotypically a late mid-dle-aged American Jew with a bald head, carefully groomed . . . with a sweet, beautiful, beatific smile," as Roland Flint described him, though running "to fat a little," was a good man, who had fallen deeply in love with Gardner, in many ways his opposite. Tytell was short, while Gardner was tall, portly while she was gangly, supportive while she tended to be domineering, sober while she loved her drink, and rooted in the earth while she often had her head in the clouds. Soon, introvert Tytell became Gardner's main escort. Dressed in conservative, tweedy Brooks Brothers suits, he accompanied Gardner to open-ings, the opera, museums, readings, and parties, taking solicitous and chival-rous care of her. Rosemarie Beck was sure that Gardner slipped Tytell money for his services, but he came to care for her deeply by all accounts.

Gardner was fighting hard "to make some sort of life for myself" with Tytell and to "keep [Tate] out of my thoughts," but Dahlberg made that impossible.[85] In letter after letter he enlarged on what he perceived as Tate's misdeeds to-ward him: abandoning him as a friend and plagiarizing his work. Writing from

MacDowell, Gardner rushed to Tate's defense: "Edward, darling, *please* do not attack Allen in print. . . . Far from being your opponent he has praised and affirmed you because he unquestionably respects and admires you as a unique and powerful man of letters." She added "one last word about Allen and me. It was more of a grand passion than a marriage. Therefore there was no way to mend us when he lost his feeling for me and turned elsewhere."[86] Tytell advised Gardner that unless she "cut things completely," she would "continue to be hurt by [Dahlberg]. I don't think anything you say to him will stop him from hating," but Gardner paid no heed to his sensible suggestion.[87]

Her mind soon turned back to Tate, whose baby Michael had choked on a toy and died. Her own children were abroad. Rose was living with gypsies in caves in southern Spain, and dancing the flamenco as Rosa La Americana; Daniel was, Gardner guessed, in Amsterdam making a film. Rose kept in touch, and planned to be home for Christmas, but Daniel hardly wrote. When he finally gave a sign of life, her worries were not assuaged, as he was hardly coherent: "my fellow americans, I wont go to jail for grass, I wont, I wont. . . . I like amsterdam very much. it is a more human and more intelligent place than the states . . . more free love. . more free thought[.] I have met here a film-maker friend of uncle bob's, Louis van Gasteren. [He has] been of some help to me here, more than uncle bob ever was, for instance! I don't like . . . the guy . . . he is a bad man, pathetically corny, sort of a pompous . . . buffoon . . . I don't like the way he talked about uncle bob."[88]

At MacDowell, Gardner no longer even tried to write poetry; she spent most of her time turning Congdon's turbulent scribblings on his beliefs, life, and art into publishable prose. Back at the Chelsea there were enough diversions related to poetry to make her feel (sometimes) that she was not a total has-been. In the fall of 1968 alone, the Academy of American Poets proposed that she guest-edit an issue of their magazine *Poetry Pilot;* Samuel Hazo asked her to read with Logan; William Packard invited her as a speaker for his course on New York Poets; the composer Paul Earls set some of her poems to music; and she was asked to be a juror for the Brandeis University Creative Arts Awards. She wrote letters of recommendation for her difficult Chelsea friend, writer Carol Bergé, to get her into MacDowell, and for her Korean MacDowell writer friend, Kim Young Ik, to get him a Guggenheim, but although Gardner, out of friendship, wrote glowing letters for them, she was not truly impressed by their work. Young William Knott's poems, on the other hand, bowled her over: "They touch me in all my quicks (or whatever still is quick) they draw blood and I thought I was drained. . . . I am amazed to find that you make *me* want to again attempt the terrible struggle which I have, in cowardice and sloth, evaded."[89] Knott gushed, "If only I were as handsome as Mark Strand or someone, I could come kiss your eyelashes and fingertips and toes. But I have kissed your letter, which is worth more than my poems because it is life-generous, and the poems are selfish. Not any of the poems begins to equal the beauty of your face, body, soul and mind. . . . I do worship beauty and you seem to contain more of it than any other woman I've seen."[90] In Knott's subsequent letters, Gardner reached the goddess stage.

Tytell's letters had become more intimate over the months but never reached Knott's epistolary peaks. In February 1969 Gardner went to Saint Martin with Clare Leighton, and the two enjoyed themselves so much with booze and men that Gardner rarely responded to Tytell's almost daily devoted letters in which he spoke of his longing for her, his feeling lonely and lonesome: "I so much want to know how you are feeling, how you are enjoying your stay, if you're writing as planned, if you've decided on a definite date for your coming back—and I don't know nothing."[91] Gardner, however, felt unfettered without Tytell around and wrote Nancy Tate Wood of her "marvelous five weeks" on the island.[92] Her generosity had drawn hangers-on, and on her return she received begging letters from islanders: "Your like a mother to me. I want you to send me some money to help pay my passage to come up to new york."[93] Gardner sent money.

Gardner thought transatlantic travel without Tate "a little traumatic," so Tytell accompanied her to Europe in the summer of 1969.[94] They first visited Ireland, where Gardner joined Mary Manning (who had returned to Dublin after her husband's death in 1967) and gave a reading at the Lantern Theatre with James Tate. They then went to Florence, where they stayed in (of all places) Pensione Annalena. Tytell flew home from Milan as he had to go back to teaching at City College in New York. Gardner spent two more weeks in Great Britain, meeting up with old friends.

The high point of the year was a performance of musical adaptations of Gardner's poems at Mrs. Jack's Fenway Court on October 2. Next to the erotic "Letter from Slough Pond," written for McCormick, Paul Earls had set three of Gardner's divorce poems ("Salt," "The Accomplices," and "Who Spilled the Salt?") to music for piano and tenor; he had also included her in a piece for solo violin entitled "Five Notables" (among the others were Glenway Westcott and Rosemarie Beck); then there was a solo piano performance "derived from Kennedy, King, Kennedy assassinations" played by Gilbert Kalish, and in conclusion an untitled work for the young violinist Paul Zukofsky.[95] Gardner's siblings rallied: George and Tania and Bob and Lee vied to give the after-concert party for about eighty people, and Kitty and her second husband, Jimmy, postponed their return to Paris to attend.

A few weeks later, Gardner taught her first workshop in the venerable YW-YMHA program at 92nd Street. Never having taught, she felt insecure and asked Herbert Krohn to sit in as her backup. Krohn was glad to oblige. He had felt isolated as a poet and found Gardner "very helpful. . . . She made connections for me, she introduced me to people, she recommended me to MacDowell colony where I went three times, and she really helped get me into the world of poetry." However, with respect to both his own poetry and the work of the aspiring writers in her workshop (which soon gathered in her apartment instead of at the Y), he noticed that Gardner "did not feel comfortable critiquing":

> She found herself unable to separate the human relationship from the poetical relationship. She would wince up her face in a pained look, as if she were afraid of one's delicacy, or that it would spoil the friendship. She always seemed to feel that giving criticism other than praise and encouragement might be hurtful to a person. And she was not really trained enough in a setting of people working on their craft dispassionately, anything like her husband Tate certainly was, in the explication de texte criticism: tinker with this here, change your verbs, see which way it goes, rearrange order, let's play with this verb and see how it works, and which way it works better. . . . With herself she got a kind of a favorable salutary severity, though with others she seemed to be unable to do that.[96]

Gardner, always an excellent reader of poetry, had criticized even during her years at *Poetry* by praising the good parts of poems instead of pointing out less successful elements, and she had done so by letter, hardly ever in person. Now, at the end of the 1960s, in a workshop atmosphere with aspiring poets, Gardner stimulated emotion and intuition, rather than craft, meeting, overall, the expectations of her freewheeling students; some of them became Gardner's devoted friends and correspondents.

The next year she gave a similar workshop, and members of both groups told her of their attempts at publication, offered up new work, requested recommendations and letters of support, and updated her on their lives and loves. They included Alice MacIntyre, a total technician who could write in almost any form; and Betty Kronsky, a psychotherapist who dabbled in poetry. The youngest, most dedicated, and closest to Gardner were Daniel Papish, a rich stockbroker-turned-poet who joined a Vermont commune; Michael West, a widely read but (self-confessed) prideful, drifting graduate student with alcohol and drug problems; and Vera Gold, who had fled extreme poverty and abuse in the Appalachians in order to become an actress and writer in New York City:

> It was Michael, Dan, and I who formed this great attachment. Maybe it was the decadence of our own lives at the time, or drinking in the Chelsea together, but it was our approach, and our love, and our passion for poetry. She met with each of us before we met as a group and she took what was not even formed in

us and nurtured it so that we did far more than I would have ever expected. . . . We were almost soul mates and we loved her work also, even though she never talked about it. . . . We did get so much from her, but I remember Alice thinking we should have an assignment and it would not have occurred to Belle to give an assignment. She would encourage you to be yourself in any style. And I remember Betty Kronsky saying: "I really don't think that we're on a very high level" and we were ready to wage war! . . . She never criticized anything severely: she would find the line or two that worked in the poem. She would often praise the skill, but what really spoke to her was something that had a lot of feeling, very like her own poems that had so much feeling, but also the technical skills. . . .

She was parental, more than that, she was like a goddess.[97]

Gardner had hoped that teaching might help her write again: "I have so *much* I burn to write but I am afraid of the pain of the confrontation and the *work*."[98] She hid in alcohol, and it debauched her: "Isabella took us to dinner . . . and disgraced herself, and us. We took her (she paid) to Charlie's. She immediately hated the decor (who wouldn't?) and proceeded to insult the waiter, a poor kid who spoke weak English (now who could do a thing like that but a savage)? . . . She got drunker and drunker, until she was eating some sort of goddamned fr[ui]t and whipped cream confection with her fingers. By the end of the evening she had humiliated the waiter, dropped food all over the table, and insulted us almost anytime we said something remotely conversational. Then she had the [Gordon] O'Briens over while she sobered up on Chablis."[99]

Calm, trusty Tytell, loving Gardner, tried—and failed—to keep her from drinking to excess. History seemed to repeat itself: Gardner had begun a relationship with him after having been deserted by the wolfish Tate, as she had married sensible, nice McCormick when on the rebound from the roguish Seymour. Once again Gardner left a generous, good—if too restrained and uptight— man for a more ardent relationship with an unreliable lover. Daily life with Tytell (even at the Chelsea) failed to satisfy her senses and to appeal to her longing for the different; where marrying a Jewish immigrant in the 1940s had been a provocative act, having a Jewish academic painter for a lover at the end of the 1960s was mainstream. In the summer of 1970 Gardner traveled to Europe, this time without Tytell. She felt "lonely in Ireland and London. I am lonely everywhere," she wrote to Dahlberg: "Life just seems barely desirable."[100] She did not answer Tytell's letters, and back in New York she broke off with him, suggesting they remain friends. Tytell was disconsolate: "We can't meet 'as friends'—my feelings for you are too strong."[101]

Gardner, though despondent and drinking heavily, had no intention of resuming her liaison with Tytell. A few months later she wrote William Smith that she felt "*alive* for the first time in 5 years but it *hurts*."[102] Gardner's resurrection was inspired by the new man in her life, the Chelsea's handsome black bell captain, Ernest Gill, who was, like Tytell, close to her own age. She described him to Riva Blevitsky, with whom she had remained in close contact, as a "brown-skinned reddish gray haired, freckle faced 'Black.'. . . Gill's done about everything a colored man (he *always* says colored) his *age* could have done. I mean in that generation and getting most of his education on the street. Long shore man, merchant marine, alto sax musician, cleaning shop, catering, etc. etc."[103] Often called "Red," Gill was tall, lanky, and handsome, "very dashing" and "really gracious."[104] Tate's biographer, Ned O'Gorman, came to know Gardner and Gill well. He thought Gill "kind of a primitive, but very intelligent," with Gardner "trying to civilize, like Pygmalion, this irreducible, wonderful, intelligent sensibility." Gardner, with her ritzy Boston accent, was always correcting Gill's black grammar and pronunciation, but he would have none of that: "They used to fight a lot; it was incredible. I used to sit here like some kind of a bored in-law, listening to these silly quarrels."[105]

Gardner was "a little ashamed of Gill and could not carry him around to Boston." Mildred Baker, the Wrights, and the Phelpses all looked down on Gill.[106] Only a few of Gardner's friends welcomed him into her life. Gill's background was shady, and if he was not a drug runner, he certainly snorted coke, and if he was not a bookie, he bet and was heavily in debt. He was street-smart, a hustler, though a charming one, and Gardner fell in love once more. Krohn remembered that when "she met Gill, she was trying to get dark to be more like him and she gave herself a serious burn as she fell asleep under a sunlamp, I guess under the influence of white wine. I had to treat her for extensive second degree sunburn all over her back, and her legs, and everything."[107] But Anne Wright was indignant that Gardner "would go to his apartment and cook for Gill. She cooked for darling Louis Tytell who deserved every bit of home-cooked food he could have. But she cooked for that ruthless Gill. She was smitten by him, just obsessed."[108] Gill's dangerous edge aroused Gardner's senses. In a society where interracial marriage had been illegal in the southern states, Gardner had taken a black, "gangster type" lover.[109] If her parents had hoped that after a long string of disastrous relationships, Gardner, at fifty-five, could no longer shock them, they were disappointed. Rose Grosvenor Gardner's reaction is not known, but Peabo, who had undergone open-heart surgery, wondered publicly why he had to live to his seventies to see his daughter "shack up with a negro."[110]

Gardner felt at ease with Ned O'Gorman: he, too, straddled two worlds; he came from an immensely wealthy family but worked in Harlem and had a black adopted son. "We used to have Sunday lunches and my son, Rickie, adored Belle and called her Aunt Belle. They were great friends and they used to go to the theater together and she gave Rickie a portrait of Malcolm X; it is still in his bedroom."[111] Because O'Gorman did not need her money, he would not be bossed around as easily as most of her new friends. For research on his Tate biography, he and Gardner traveled to Minneapolis:

> I met her at the airport and there she was standing in this great black cape, at the ticket counter, looking like Mata Hari and Captain Gray and the shepherdess out of a Rubenesque landscape. She was waiting for her wheelchair: she had told everybody at the airport that she was ill because then you board before everybody. . . .
>
> One of the poignant things about that trip to Minneapolis was our visit to the house that they had. . . . Belle walked in and proceeded to give me a tour of the house. . . . Belle said: "I will show you our bedroom," the bedroom where she said Allen and she would lay on the bed and have orgasms and look up through the Venetian blinds! The naked bodies. She talked about it all the time. I mean, nothing could stop Belle about this. . . . Then we walked into the study, Allen's study. And the roof was broken and you could see the outside of the study. And Belle just fell apart. Because this was where Allen did his writing. . . .
>
> Our plane from Minneapolis was leaving very shortly and Belle wanted me to take all these goddamn pieces of luggage with me. I said: "I am not going to do it! Get yourself a porter!" Oh, I remember what she said! She said: "I want men to carry, I want men to treat me like a lady." "Sure as hell not me, Belle," I said. And we are standing there: "Flight so-and-so to New York, last call." I said: "Belle, we are not going to go. You get a porter to help you and you pick up one of your bags; we will share these bags." She absolutely froze, because she wanted me to do her bidding: "Pick up my bags, do this, do that," and I would never, ever, do it. She was really pissed at me. We got on the airplane and of course proceeded to drink seventy-five gin-tonics on a two-hour flight to New York.[112]

Gardner could be pushy, but her innate self-contempt, dormant during her marriage to Tate, had burgeoned in the dissipated, slothful years at the Chelsea. Through much of her life, poetry had been her saving grace, but now she could not summon the courage to write. As was her nature, Gardner remained loyal and generous to old friends like Logan or Carroll and continued to turn the other cheek to Dahlberg, but booze made her more difficult. Krohn, her doctor-poet friend, was sure that Gardner's drinking kept her from writing: "I had the impression that she was somewhat intoxicated a good deal of the time. That is why she sprained her ankles always, was accident-prone. She went through the entire day with a certain level of alcohol in her blood and that kept her from being as sharp or well focused as she could have been at the time. It did not help her writing at all." He noted that the alcohol made Gardner touchy: "She was sensitive of anything that might be a criticism of her. One was always watching carefully not to offend Isabella and to say things that she expected if she asked you something. You did not want to overturn her expectations, or say anything the least bit challenging."[113]

Gardner knew all too well that Gill was taking her for a ride, but she was convinced that she was not worthy of a man of higher caliber. Through the reverse classism and racism paradoxically bred into her by her blue-blooded, lily-white family, Gardner had always been drawn to both the underbelly of society and to other races, and Gill fulfilled her erotic propensity for the exotic. Gill was not a choice of love, but of loneliness, low self-esteem, and sexuality, and he appealed to her latent sadomasochistic tendencies. In February 1971 she took him on a honeymoon trip to Kingston, Jamaica, where a mature, biracial, unmarried couple did not make too many waves. Animated and energized by her new beau, Gardner tried her hand at writing again, and for a few days she kept a notebook meant to be the fond for future poems. Entitled "Gill and I," the text did not rise above the level of a typical travel diary, even though the start of their trip was more exciting than most: "G. picked me up in a cab in front of the Chelsea at 7:30 a.m. We boarded the plane for Kingston just before nine. The immense plane was full to capacity. Our take-off was delayed for 3 hours. The pilot told us that a hijacker had been removed from the plane and that the luggage was being sorted out in order to locate and remove his suitcase containing explosives." The remaining pages dealt with rooms, food—and lots of drink: "After a couple of stiff vodkas with apple juice"; "[a]fter dinner we shared our wine"; "[w]e had a couple of drinks and watched several young women do the sort of bumps and grinds (*fantastic* cans) that I used to see *years* ago in after hours 'clubs' in Chicago"; "[a]fter 2 hours G and I wanted to stop at a mountain road-side shack bar."[114]

On Valentine's Day, Gardner, schoolgirl-like, noted in her calendar, "Love from Gill." Gardner feared Margaret Danner's reaction to her sleeping with a black man, but Danner was far less militant than she had been in her *Poetry* days ("the woman who hated Paul Robeson has gone with the wind") and approved. "I liked your guy. He WAS FOR REAL as the kids say."[115] Compared to Danner's lover ("He embarrasses people by being a know it all and has many lady friends") Gill may have seemed a catch, but Gardner's euphoria was muted by his living in Harlem, where he was involved in illegal activities while still working as bell captain at the Chelsea.[116] Besides, Gill started treating Gardner with swaggering machismo as if he were her pimp, rather than her gigolo. The ups and downs of her relationship with Gill and, even more, the general emptiness and uselessness of her life dragged Gardner down, and James and Anne Wright, deeply concerned, put her in touch with "the love of our lives," James's therapist, the Jewish intellectual Dr. Irving Silver: "He saved our marriage; he saved James's life, in many ways."[117] Silver specialized in creative people with dependency problems and had helped Wright, also an unstable alcoholic, stop drinking. Gardner initially saw Silver almost every day, and he remained her father-confessor till the end of her life. He was softhearted but strict with Gardner: "She was suicidal. Of course it was greatly related to the drinking and what happens to one's mind when one is drinking. The enormity of depression and helplessness, futility of existence, all of this. I made it clear to her that at any time she came to a session where I could see that she evidently was drunk, I would not see her, but I would charge her for it." Gardner learned to control her drinking (and smoking) somewhat but still spent most of the day with a glass of white wine in hand, though perhaps the wine was watered down a little in the mornings. Silver wanted to get Gardner "to start writing: this is the only way to get away from suicide, to be active," but she tried her hand at poetry even more halfheartedly than she attempted to stop drinking. Gardner knew poetry was the only place where she could not hide and "had to be open enough to see herself as she was."[118]

Gardner had outfoxed Dr. Kraus and other therapists, but Silver realized that she "thought of herself as some kind of pseudo personality who had everybody fooled. All these brilliant PhDs and all these incredibly intelligent doctors were so stupid that they would fall for her lying." He was not taken in nor did he succumb to her charms as a woman both seductive (though now on the decline) and smart. Trying to "see the world as she perceived it," Silver thought it "really scary how she blended in with and hid herself in her environment." Through years of therapy, Silver obtained a good sense of the extreme paradoxes and contrasts of Gardner's character, calling her "a woman of unusual intelligence, not from education, but intuitive," while realizing that she was "very quick and analytical about the whole world, except for herself." He saw her self-centeredness, selfishness, and imperiousness, but also, paradoxically, the "poor little rich girl" who was panic-stricken when she had to go to Boston to confront her disapproving family, though George remained, still, "the only secure place in the world." Above all, though, he plumbed Gardner's "sense of shame: she felt so unequal, so undeserving: the wagging finger of Isabella was much worse than anything her parents or George or whoever had said to her."[119]

Her children's lives were even more messed up than her own. Daniel was rich and handsome and a talented photographer and filmmaker. He worked with Robert Frank, photographer of the seminal *The Americans* (1958) and filmmaker of the experimental *Home Is Where the Heart Is,* a drama about a day in the life of a heroin addict, in which Daniel's closest friend, Paco Grande, and his young wife, Jessica Lange, acted. With Frank, Daniel made the notorious documentary *Cocksucker Blues,* commissioned by the Rolling Stones about their North America tour in 1972. (In the end, the Stones did not want the film released, because it showed them debauched and doing drugs.[120]) He also knew John Lennon and Yoko Ono, who filmed *Fly* in Daniel's loft, while he filmed them for his movie *Ono* (1970).[121] According to Krohn, for *Fly*, a movie supposedly celebrating women, a prostitute was picked up from the street and drugged; then half-frozen flies were let loose on her naked body to crawl around in a stupefied daze. It was all shot in extreme close-up; the prostitute became known as the actress Virginia Lust.

Daniel was friends with most of the great musicians of the 1960s, and, "obsessed with the idea of pop musicians as the truly creative artists of our culture," he took "every opportunity to photograph, film, record, or just watch them work"; among them bluesman Mark Naftalin and guitarists Michael Bloomfield and Jimi Hendrix. They were all portrayed in his soulful photo autobiography *A Loud Song* (1971), the first book to be published by the influential underground press Lustrum, founded by Ralph Gibson and funded in part by Daniel. Named after the poem his mother had written for him, *A Loud Song* was, Daniel explained, "an attempt to use the photographic image as a language, and with that, to make literature. . . . It is an attempt to survive—to preserve my identity." Dedicated to Seymour, "the best photographer in the world," *A Loud Song* is an impassioned documentary consisting of photographs enhanced and personalized by Daniel's handwritten running commentary: "My mother and father come from very different backgrounds. It is often difficult for people to imagine the two of them together. My mother is from a very rich Boston society family—generations of money and privilege. My father has struggled all his life, passing through periods of relative success and failure." Describing McCormick as "quite down to earth," Daniel included a loving letter he had written as a child to "Dear Pop": "I love you very much. You do so much for me." But "my mother fell in love with Allen Tate. . . . I was quite fond of Allen, but more influenced by his intelligence—the quality of his mind, than by his affection for me, which was dubious." He included a relentlessly honest picture of his dissolute mother, but wrote: "I had a great deal of respect for her work, and have been powerfully influenced by her hyper-sensibility. . . . She has pursued life with a passion and devotion to emotion, to the heart, to love, to intensity, and to the highest reaches of the intuitive; she has not yet stopped trying to live the most beautiful life possible."[122]

One of the first stream-of-consciousness photographic diaries and a poignant visual account of both the author and his times, *A Loud Song* has reached cult status over the years; it is a testimonial to Daniel's talent. But in his contribution to the book, Robert Frank was chillingly prescient and honest: "I liked Danny right away. Danny is 26 and I am 47. We live in the same building—look out on the same street, the Bowery in New York City. Danny has a lot of dope and a lot of d[e]s]pair. He also has friends who share it with him. But Danny is an artist and if he'll survive—we all will be richer to see what he has done."[123] But Daniel was already addicted to heroin, a victim of his own character and circumstances, of his mother's laissez-faire attitude and taking him from the fathers he loved and putting him in an anti-Semitic school, of money enough to dawdle and to keep himself and his hangers-on supplied with drugs in the psychedelic explosion of the counterculture. Like his mother, he crested high on the waves of emotions, prone to addiction and undisciplined. A large part of *A Loud Song* was reserved for Rose: "she has always been 5 years older than me. This has had a strong effect on me. She has influenced the direction of my life—the way in which to begin. She is a rare and special spirit which remains at once naïve and cynical." Pictures of Rose as a child alternate with photos of her as a stripper and belly-dancer, but most are from her life in Andalusia with the gypsies, including her then-lover, Ansonini, who lived with her on a farm she had bought in 1967, and the pioneering master of flamenco guitar, Diego Amaya Flores, better known as Diego del Gastor, star of Daniel's film *Flamencologia* (1971) and godfather to Rose's son, Raoul, born in the fall of 1970.

In the spring of 1970 Rose had written from Spain that she was pregnant; Gardner, already depressed, sank even deeper with the added worry about the unborn child. Gardner was all too familiar with Rose's irresponsible way of life. When in New York, usually staying at the Chelsea, Rose mirrored her mother's behavior with men and drink, even going so far as to provoke her mother by having sex in the halls and elevators of the hotel. Promiscuity, drinking and smoking, and traveling whenever the whim struck, Gardner wrote her, were unfair to the baby, who needed a caring mother and a home. Upset because Gardner, while in Europe, did not intend to visit her, Rose burst out: "The whole gist of your letter is Don't depend on me—It was your decision and I won't take *ANY* responsibility."[124] Rose went on to say that Manolo, a waiter at the El Quichote, should not be too sure he was the father, for there were enough other candidates: both Chelsea one-night stands and her gypsy lovers—Ansonini, Curro [Velez?], or perhaps even Diego.

Gardner's grandchild was born in September 1970, looking "like his mother."[125] Gardner's parents disapproved, and Rose Grosvenor Gardner wrote the new mother: "This child of yours did not ask to come into this extremely difficult world we are living in, and very soon he . . . is going to find out that he . . . is without a father—So I hope that you realize the seriousness of this situation and that you will do everything in your power to make up for this great lack in the child's life."[126] In December, Rose was back in Spain with baby Raoul, having left Gardner instructions: "If Bard asks about my rent, just say I'll be back soon. . . . You can tell him I checked out Sun.—*Make sure Charles cares for the cat and parrot.*" But the main subject of Rose's letter was Chelsea's Harry Smith, under whose dangerous spell she had fallen: "I know you are extremely ambivalent in regards to Harry especially in relation to me but I will *never* forgive you if you don't keep me posted as to how he is—*often.* . . . And try to impress on him that he means as much to me as *anyone* in the world."[127] Smith, a smallish man about fifty years of age with long grayish hair that he wore in a ponytail tied back with a ribbon, was an ethnomusicologist and radical filmmaker, using "a kind of a cartoon juxtaposition of symbols . . . working out some kind of a symbolistic film poem."[128] Many artists (among them Corso, Ginsberg, Patti Smith, and Janos Mekas) thought him a genius; others, like Krohn, thought him a "weasel weighing about ninety-five pounds of distilled ironical VENOM":

> He collected Seminole with his birds flying around everywhere in this room, shitting. He would open his closet, and instead of his own clothes—I do not think he ever changed his clothes—he had a collection of seventy Seminole costumes that he had written a study on, an anthropological study. . . .
>
> He was always trying to get people to kill themselves, suggesting suicide as a serious thing. He was a very destructive person. He had many acquaintances, friends if you will, in all walks of life. There was a guy there named Stanley Amos, very close to Isabella's room. He was a magician, he did the tarot, he did astrology, many people believed in him. He had bags THIS big of LSD tablets at his parties. . . .
>
> Harry used to keep company with Rosy a lot, and Danny worked with Harry, that is another connection to that family. Harry was making this movie, the Brecht and Weil Mahogany. Arnold Weinstein was living in the hotel then with his new bride, and he put the play on. And Larry Rivers did the sets.[129]

Smith easily dominated Rose, the more so as he was an occultist, and the occult, voodoo in particular, had always wielded a bizarre power over her. So Gardner was happy that Rose was traveling for a while, and away from Smith, but she was also sure that Rose was neglecting Raoul, treating him like a doll rather than a child. Back in New York, Rose took Raoul everywhere in his little basket, from restaurants to bars to discos, but just as easily dropped him off at one of her friends' homes and then forgot where she had left him or failed to collect him, sometimes disappearing for days, as Betty Kronsky—unmarried and clueless about children—found to her distress when she accompanied Rose to Haiti on what should have been a relaxing vacation. Impulsive and addicted to alcohol, cigarettes, and sex, Rose was even less fit to be a mother than Gardner had been.

She fought constantly with Gardner when both were at the Chelsea, Krohn remembered. "They would argue and they would compete with each other and they would flirt with each other's beaux." Rose was taking revenge on her mother for she "did not care at all. . . . If Rosy were taking risks of destroying herself, Isabella would get upset, but she never got upset by anything that Isabella did. So she had the upper hand."[130] Traveling all over the world, with a farm in Spain and a lease at the Chelsea, Rose was squandering her money so quickly that she exhausted Peabo's patience. He wrote, "when I told you that you were in very, very serious trouble and would have to take drastic steps immediately to reduce your expenses and suggested that you pack up Raoul with you to your place in Spain, you packed up and took a trip to Haiti, called for $5,000 and, of all things, bought some pictures. Unbelievable! You simply have to take quick action. Why should not Raoul's father (if you know who he is) help support his son and for that matter you also? . . . Needless to say I am deeply concerned about you but I see no ready solution to your problems. It is up to you to work them out."[131] Rose remained unrepentant, defending her buying of art ("Art is safe. Even if God forbid the stock market should crash there are always a few people w/ money who want art"), Raoul's father ("he is a 'poor' gipsy"), and her lifestyle ("I will not give up my lease or stop making trips"); she was also unrealistic, telling him that she was "beginning a book which will make money."[132]

Concerned as she was about her daughter's being in thrall to Smith while neglecting her son, Gardner was no happier about her relationship with Gill, which seemed to be getting nowhere. To make matters worse, from February to mid-May 1972, she was immobilized by a fractured hip; depressed, she discouraged visits and hardly wrote or phoned anyone. Still, the literary world had not forgotten her. Kirkland College in New York asked her to teach part-time, but Gardner begged off hastily when she found out she could not freewheel as she had done at the Y. This job necessitated her residence on campus most of the week. Small Centre College of Kentucky, in Danville, offered her their writer in residence post on far more generous conditions, which Gardner also declined, for she had other plans. She had traveled with Gill to Hawaii and met her old friends the Denneys there, as well as the Wrights, and she had taken Gill to Ojai, California, where her beloved aunt Catherine Mayes lived, the only relative, Gardner felt, who had never judged her and who seemed to understand her—the mother she had never had. Small-town, New Age Ojai in Ventura County was everything New York City was not: peaceful, quiet, and laid-back, without the enticements and dangers of the metropolis in which Gill was so mired that Gardner had been forced to pay off the mob to ensure his continued health.[133] Weary of her life in New York, disturbed by Rose, Gardner wrote Congdon that she "must move out of the cesspool of the Chelsea" as she had "wasted my time and my talent." She planned to live in Ojai with Gill, near Aunt Catherine, hoping that their new life together would give her so much strength that she would "dare to write again."[134]

Chapter Nine

"The Dead Center of All Alone," 1974–1981

I will be lonely at half past dead
Weep none one or many beside my bed.
At the dead center of all alone
I must unwillingly work at dying
I will be crying crying crying
Not I not I this flesh these bones.
("Knowing")

Nestled in the mountains not far from Los Angeles, with a balmy climate, Ojai was a haven for artists, musicians, and the spiritually inclined. Gardner's Aunt Catherine had found peace there after having been mistreated and deserted by her first husband. Her second, one-legged William Mayes, was the leader of Ojai's burgeoning Theosophist religious colony. Another prominent member of the Theosophist community was the potter Beatrice Wood, known as the "Mama of Dada" because of her early connections with Marcel Duchamp. Wood was friends with Reginald Pole and the Indian Brahmin sage and teacher-philosopher Krishnamurti, a former Theosophist who lived in Ojai and remained on good terms with many members of the colony. Ojai was also home to psychics, palm readers, and flower children, and Meditation Mount and marijuana gardens added to its general mystical atmosphere. Excellent hiking and riding trails wound through magnificent scenery; the perfume of citrus fruits and Mediterranean flora scented the air; Bart's exceptional outdoor bookshop (which operated after hours on the honor system), a few galleries, and a small museum offered entertainment and diversion, all of which made Ojai into a veritable paradise, which Frank Capra chose as his Shangri-la for *The Lost Horizon* (1939).

After the violent confusion of the Chelsea, Ojai offered Gardner the promise of rural tranquility, and she hoped to find, together with Gill, a restful, poetry-inspiring equilibrium. "The years till we moved to Ojai were rough," Gardner wrote Riva Blevitsky in December 1973:

> [Gill] lived *way* uptown and I at the Chelsea where I met him—he was a bell-man there and tended bar for people's parties. He quit when he broke his hand. Then he got to be part owner of a bar and got swindled. He was away a lot of the time. Anyway we made several trips to Ojai. My aunt who lives there adored him. Finally on the last trip we bought a house. About 3/4 of an acre surrounded by a huge chain fence because of Gill's Doberman. The house isn't much but it already *had* a swimming pool and avocadoes. We've planted loads of corn, to-matoes etc.—We're eating corn right now. Gill's made friends with *everyone* and the people we [see] most of are the Fearings—She's Bob McCormick's cousin and a very big wheel in The Santa Barbara Museum. Fishing is Gill's passion and he fishes all day. Bob's cousin Connie Fearing also loves it and they go to-gether often.[1]

From the first, however, it was clear that trendy small-town California was not Gardner's cup of tea, and soon after their arrival Gardner already realized that "Gill adjusts faster than I do."[2] After years of virtually no cooking at the Chelsea, it was "hard to be a house-wife again but Gill hates to go out. He loves T.V. and I never did but when I broke my hip I got hooked on it in the hospital." Ojai did not, as Gardner had hoped, bring her relationship with Gill in calmer waters: "We laugh a lot, we fight a lot, we seem to need to be to-gether. He's not an easy man to live with and my untidyness, and absent-mindedness are rough on a neat, organised, fast moving, efficient man. He's very protective, I guess he thinks I'd lose my head if he wasn't around to keep it screwed on. He has a work-shop for welding sculpture. I've a study and he *longs* for me to try to write again, but I doubt it."[3]

Daniel was much on Gardner's mind, as she hardly ever heard from her heroin-addicted, globe-trotting son. Rose reassured her: she had seen her half brother on his new boat, the *Imamou*, in Haiti, where she herself, to her immense grati-fication, had been anointed a voodoo priestess. Rose intended to visit Ojai in the late spring to meet with the Theosophists for further spiritual develop-ment. Gardner, who had fled the Chelsea scene in part to escape Rose's cease-less emotional demands, told her off; there could be "*no possibility* of a meeting of minds or spirits, as voodoo represents, *forcibly,* an aspect of the forces of evil to those, who like Catherine, are actively, constantly and profoundly engaged in a struggle against the power of evil."[4] Having been put down as wicked and immoral by her own mother, Rose retaliated by characterizing Gardner as Jesuitical and ignorant and told her to read Maya Deren's and Alfred Metraux's standard anthropological works on voodoo. As for Daniel, Rose informed her coolly, he was on a two-thousand-mile trip from Haiti to Columbia on the *Imamou* and could not be reached.

With a longer stay in Ojai out of the question, Rose returned to her home base, the Chelsea, with Raoul, now two, in tow, but even three thousand miles away, it was easy for Rose to upset her mother. Weak-willed as she was, she now became a virtual slave to draconian Harry Smith who, Gardner wrote Maurice English more than once, was "the most sick man" she had ever met.[5] Besides, Rose broadcasted that she had embarked on an affair with Gill's artist son, Jimmy, while denying that she had tried to seduce Gill himself, too: "In the days I didn't know you were together I may have flirted w/ him as women do and he *is* attractive. But he never appealed to me sexually. I wanted *NO* sexual dealings with Negroes after Dino—absolutely turned off. He'd come up and we'd have a drink, coke, talk, but that was it." Thanking her mother for the two thousand dollars she gave every February, she wondered how much Raoul would inherit and "if 1—I will get anything [, and] 2—wild guess how much (when Grandpa dies)??"[6]

Rose's irresponsible, competitive behavior, graphically depicted in her many letters, did not contribute to the peace of mind Gardner sought in her "very badly designed little house" in Ojai, but Daniel's continued silence troubled her even more. She had last seen him at the Chelsea, in March, around his birthday, when his parting words had been: "Goodbye Mom, I'll love you forever," but six months later, "quite lame" from arthritis, Gardner was "in grave distress" as nobody had heard from Daniel since the spring.[7] As Daniel had always looked up to and loved his half sister, Gardner flew to New York to discuss him with Rose. The visit was an unmitigated disaster as Rose made constant scenes, blaming Gardner for Daniel's addiction and disappearance. On Gardner's return to Ojai, shaken, having "thought over *everything,* not only my recent 9 days at the Chelsea, but the way you have treated me for many years," she forbade her daughter "to visit me for at least a couple of years—until such time as you can get yourself together. You are 34 years old; not 14."[8] Gardner did not know if her golden boy was alive or dead; he might be cruising the seas on his yacht, or wasting away in a South American prison for drug smuggling; he might have overdosed, or even, though Gardner refused to believe this, have committed suicide.

Not until much later was Gardner able to piece together the events leading up to Daniel's disappearance. At his twenty-seventh birthday party some of his old Minneapolis friends and the elite of the New York underground had admired his pictures of the 1968 Paris revolution; they had listened in to Keith Richards singing "Happy Birthday" to his friend on the phone from London;

and they had heard Danny complain about having too much money.[9] About a month later, he had paid a staggering $70,000 for his boat, intending to sail the seas with "the light of [his] life," his lover Kathy Moore, a dancer from California, and her two-year-old son, Jason, as well as some friends, Susan and Robert Duran.[10] Daniel had told Kathy that kicking his heroin habit was his main objective for their trip, but in truth he was using more than before, and they quarreled so constantly that the Durans abandoned ship and returned to the United States. This left just Daniel and Kathy to manage the yacht, and during a harrowing storm which lasted for days, Jason almost drowned. Trying to keep the boat from capsizing, Daniel and Kathy had to strap tiny Jason, terrified and screaming, to his berth. Finally back in safe harbor, in Cartagena, Colombia, Kathy had had enough of boats and flew back to Miami with her son. At the time, Cartagena was awash in raw cocaine waiting to be shipped to America by anyone wishing to get rich quickly, and Daniel may have been tempted. At any rate, he needed extra deckhands and soon found another American hippie, John Kent Breckenridge, who, in turn, knew two experienced French sailors, Jean-Pierre Guy and Denis Nelkene. This crew of four sailed for Colon, Panama, on May 19, 1973.

Daniel Seymour and John Breckenridge were never seen again. A few weeks after Daniel's departure from Cartagena, the *Imamou* was spotted at Port Royal, Jamaica, with only the two Frenchmen aboard. Kathy had been anxious since late May 1973, as Daniel had promised to call her from Colon. When she did not hear from him, she contacted Gardner, who, in turn, called Boston. United Fruit, "the Octopus," had leverage everywhere, and as its former chairman, George Gardner called in a few favors. In the early 1970s, numerous private American vessels had disappeared in the Caribbean Sea, hijacked by pirates who used the boats for smuggling drugs—and left no witnesses. American government agencies had not considered it their problem and had not undertaken expensive inquiries. Now, listening to George Gardner, FBI, CIA, DEA, navy and coast guard all worked together in an unprecedented search for his nephew and the missing boat.

George Gardner and Daniel's father, Seymour, kept in close touch about the findings of the state agencies, but left Gardner, Rose, and Kathy out of the loop. Desperate, Rose called Bob McCormick, who, in spite of the pain Gardner had caused him, "went to a great deal [of] trouble to find the right person" and came up with a private eye in Chicago who spoke a number of languages and "had knowledge of drug smuggling etc. in the area."[11] This notorious detective went by the pseudonym "Mr. Brown," but his real name was Richard Cain, and his connections reached as far and as deep as George Gardner's and Seymour's put together. Cain may have known both personally, as he had joined the Chicago police force in the 1950s, was on good terms with most of the city's main mobsters, and "was caught bugging the office of Mayor Richard Daley's organized crime task force"; later, he was involved in one of the many bungled plots to kill Fidel Castro (which United Fruit likely had a hand in, too).[12]

This shady detective told Kathy that "he owed George a favor, and that is why he was trying to find Danny," while letting Rose know that "George seemed uptight about spending a lot of money."[13] Gardner distrusted Cain, but he delivered the goods. He traced the two Frenchmen and told the authorities, who arrested Guy and Nelkene on the French island of Guadeloupe; they were suspected of involvement in other murders. In this instance, they protested their innocence, testifying that Daniel and Kent had been too doped up to stay on board, had gone ashore on one of the San Blas Islands, and turned over the boat to them. They swore that they had arranged to rendezvous with Dan in Miami in March 1974 and that they had subsequently received three letters from him with money enclosed, the last one originating from Colombia and dated December 1973. Even when three bullet holes were detected in the *Imamou*, the French gangsters stuck to their unverifiable, unlikely tale. As no bodies were ever found, nothing could be proven, and after about a year they had to be let go from prison. Sure they had gotten off scot-free, Guy and Nelkene sailed from Guadeloupe, but then they, in turn, disappeared forever, and it was rumored that the long tentacles of the Octopus had dragged them down into the watery depths of the Atlantic in revenge for the death of one of its sons. Always living on the edge, Cain himself had already come to a bad end: he had been shot in a sandwich shop in Chicago in December 1973, but whether this was a mob hit or a liquidation by the intelligence community has never been ascertained.

"After learning of 'Mr. Brown's' death," Kathy Moore had felt "such d[e]spair. I really thought he was our only hope and I felt completely confident in that man." Moore seemed, however, as interested in the boat as in her lover's whereabouts: "There are things on there Danny and I hid together and only we know where they are," she wrote Gardner about a year after she had left him.[14] Wondering why "Seymour and my brother want to keep both you and me out of all this," Gardner implored Moore to "[s]ay nothing to the F.B.I. or anyone."[15] As late as January 1974, Gardner was willing herself to believe that Daniel had "*chosen* to disappear and gone in quest of his innermost identity," but as the horrible facts surfaced after months fraught with uncertainty, deep down she knew better.[16] Perhaps Daniel had been doomed from birth. Then Gardner's Aunt Catherine had made an astrological chart and predicted that he would "be caught between the mesh of the emotional . . . and the rotting timbers of the Mayflower."[17]

With her talented, addicted son lost, heartbroken and overwhelmed by feelings of guilt, Gardner turned to saving her surviving child, her drifting daughter,

Rose. She sent money for living expenses and Raoul's playschool and invited them to Ojai after all, but on condition, as Rose saw it, that afterward they would settle in Hawaii with Kathy and Jason. In a confused eighteen-page answer, Rose emphasized that she loved her mother "as much as I love *anyone*, naturally," but insisted that she was now sure that not Hawaii, but Salvador, Brazil, was Nirvana; that she had found her true medium (filming instead of writing); that although she was moving out of her apartment at the Chelsea, she did intend to rent a room there by the week. Harry Smith had been helping her "with the Kabbala—tree of life—etc. He *finally* started teaching me seriously—any where from one to 12 hours a day, very few breaks." Rose admitted that she "drank too much, had blackouts, . . . been bitchy and angry—*furious*," but went on to challenge Gardner's insight that she was "a parody of you." She denied being a bad mother, even defending the drug-ridden Chelsea as a good place for raising a young child. Besides, she argued, many people were happy to take care of Raoul, among them Seymour and his motherly wife, Helena, who, with their children, lived close by and had taken the neglected little boy, though no blood relation of theirs, to their hearts. On the other hand, Rose did not want to depend too much on her stepfather, even if she acknowledged that he had "been extremely anxious, helpful etc. about Dan. I think he's done *everything* in his power to help find him and is still."[18]

Not reassured at all by her daughter's contradictory letter, and in a feeble attempt to shock her into maturity, Gardner sent Rose numerous pages describing the crises she had caused. Rose was unmoved: "I don't thank Aunt Kitty for putting a detective on [multi-marrying] Jorgé. We had a good life. . . . . He *was* a creep before. . . . but during the year I spent w / Jorgé he became very passionate about working and he loved me."[19] Gardner then sent her a thousand dollars to extricate herself from the perilous temptations of the Chelsea, and Rose came to Ojai to spend with her mother their first Christmas without Dan. There she started drinking hard liquor as soon as she got up and fell into her old, adolescent pattern of hurting the mother she depended upon too much; making scene after scene, she even went so far as to blame Gill for Daniel's death. In early 1974, Rose's behavior went from bad to worse; simultaneously, she began to comprehend that there was something seriously wrong with her. From her farm in Spain, she wrote of her plans to return to New York City in June. "I am decidedly not well. I haven't been for the last few years, but it's steadily gotten worse. I am 2 people at this point. One personality is *totally* disorganized and irresponsible—I have memory blanks (that may last hours) where I say and do disastrous things. The other is my old and true *self* except that I am continuously under an *overwhelming* depression and so unable to do anything. If it weren't for Raoul I would just 'carry on somehow' but . . . I love him more than anything in the world so I *must* get well—Mom I know you're having an operation in July. I don't want to put you out in *any* way. But only—if you have any ideas as to who to see. I need professional help."[20] Despair about Dan, her messed-up life, and a dawning realization of responsibility toward her son had finally led to her turning a corner; Rose was taking herself in hand instead of counting on her mother to rescue her. Gardner was only too happy to call Silver from Ojai and impress on him that "Rosy must not be allowed to be outside, because she could provoke any kind of hostility towards herself"—that she was too gullible for the dangerous characters who roamed the Chelsea and needed a quiet, isolated place to rest.[21] Silver obliged, and with Rose, who trusted him, visited an excellent private mental health center, the Institute of Living, located on beautifully landscaped grounds in Hartford, Connecticut, where, at great expense, patients were treated by the best doctors for their behavioral, psychiatric, and addiction disorders. Rose was ready to commit herself voluntarily, and the institute accepted her as an inpatient at the end of July 1974.

Gardner herself also "looked forward to the womb of hospital care." Her osteoarthritis had intensified; she could barely move about and was suffering from such severe pain that she was scheduled for hip replacement surgery in Los Angeles in July. Gill was not supportive but instead "ever increasingly abusive and irrationally unkind. Perhaps he is fearful for me—perhaps I just aggravate him. . . . In any case, it is no soothing preparation for a radical operation. . . . I am vague, confused, anxious, depressed and not at all sure I've anything to live for," Gardner wrote Logan, asking him not to "reply to my whines but send me a FUNNY *Get Well Card*."[22] A revitalized and exuberant Logan—"I'm a grandpa"—came through for his beloved friend, visited her in the hospital and reported "some good luck with [*West of Childhood*]. I wrote to Robert Bly and sent him your inscribed copy. He is going to send another copy to Jonathan Cape in England, and he expressed in his letter how much he had always admired your poetry and your personal warmth as well. He did say that the publishing scene is bad in England—money is so tight there—but I am sure his recommendation will mean a lot."[23] The hip operation had gone well, and although Gardner had to spend weeks in the hospital to recuperate, she was cheered by the many letters she received from family (Kitty: "Seymour called— I was *so* surprised. . . . I told him everyone grateful for their care of Raoul—and that I always had Jimmy's picture he took beside my bed.") and old friends such as Edith Kennedy's son Robert ("So if youall git to writin, honey, don't youall go tossin it out, heah!") and Josephine Jacobsen ("Someday you are going to send me the golden news that you are again writing your splendid poetry.")[24]

Then the unthinkable happened. While Gardner was recuperating in Los Angeles, Rose was waiting to be admitted to the institute. During her last free weekend, she decided to party, was overdosed and beaten, and ended up in St. Vincent's Hospital. Horror stories abound about what exactly happened to her; most incriminate Harry Smith as an evil genius who lured her into a drug-infested, sadistic, black magic ceremony; others, less likely, blame the Hell's Angels. Helpless, laid up in her sickbed thousands of miles away, Gardner received alarming communiqués and angry letters from Rosy's friends: "Rose changed so drastically after she met Harry Smith, she didn't seem to be the same person at all. . . . Those sons of bitches at the Chelsea, may they get double what they deserve."[25] One of the hotel's few altruistic inhabitants, Herbert Krohn, had immediately gone to St. Vincent's to find out about Rose's state of health; though a medical doctor, he was turned away from its intensive care unit. In early August, Gardner's former student psychoanalyst Betty Kronsky was allowed to visit Rose but found her "very weak and awfully confused and disoriented. She had trouble hearing and her speech was very strange—almost a poetic babble that was only intelligible at times."[26] Gardner was optimistic about Rose's eventual recovery and wrote Kathy Moore about her daughter's "real dream to keep house with you and Jason" and her own plans to fly East to visit Rose as soon as she was allowed to travel.[27] Gardner's relatives were as positive about the outcome of Rose's "dangerous brush with her maker," Robert hoping that it would "bring her into closer harmony with reality," and her mother that she would "be taken care of . . . in a reliable retreat where she will not . . . lay herself open to temptation."[28] And Jimmy Gill, who had joined the ranks of Gardner's dependents, wrote his "Dear Mom" that he hoped "Rose deals with life on a positive basis from now on. She got everything a young woman needs and I mainly mean strength. She needs a man who will stand behind her and with her, and I hope she does find this. It's all been tough on you within the last couple of years. You've been stronger than most women."[29]

Gardner needed courage because when, clutching a cane, she went to see her child at the Institute of Living at the end of August, Rose was deaf and delusional, and her doctors feared she had sustained irreparable brain damage. She was put "in a maximum security ward, all her clothes[,] trinkets, etc. in a hamper on wheels, watched day and night. . . . They are considering shock treatment."[30] Rose became so aggressive and irrational when her mother was around, hitting out at her and screaming that Gardner had murdered Daniel, that Rose's doctors soon forbade Gardner to visit. Rose was not left all alone, though. Faithful visitors were Seymour and Helena, who had taken Raoul into their family. And Rose's half sister, Anneke, whom she had always respected, now lived close by and visited her often even though she had her own burdens to bear. Her daughter with Woody Guthrie, Lorina, whom Mrs. Koeth had raised, was now living in Los Angeles, with a man twice divorced, and was sure, Anneke wrote, that this time the "affair will be 'forever.' Just to think that she came to NY 3 times, to Pennsylvania once (separate trips) and never came to see me. I think she is a person with a hole in her, just like Rosie."[31] Soon after, tragedy struck, when Lorina, at nineteen, died in a car accident.

Broken in body and spirit, with her son gone and her daughter brain-damaged, Gardner returned to Ojai. "You know it has occurred to me how felicitous for our parents it is that all the shame and unhappiness resulting from erratic behaviour etc. has been generated by me, my daughter, and my son," Gardner wrote her brother Robert.[32] At almost sixty, she was an alcoholic, living with a black illiterate hustler, spending her days watching television and desultorily growing corn and avocados. Whereas during her most productive years as a poet and associate editor of *Poetry,* Gardner had written numerous scrawly letters in longhand to her friends, now, with nothing to do, nowhere to go, living in unaccustomed isolation, even scribbling a postcard often seemed too much effort, because the story of her life was too painful to recount. It was easier to send gifts and money, and Gardner just added hangers-on of Dan's and Rose's to the many friends and cadgers who had come to count on her openhandedness over the years.

Sporadically, for her old and true friends, Gardner managed to transcend her grief and emerge from the alcoholic fog in which she now chose to live. When Katherine Biddle was seriously ill, she sent her "bright yellow and white chrysanthemums—big and gay and cheerful—. . . kind, kind notes and such lovely cards" and the Biddles were "just overwhelmed . . . with admiration that you could think of anyone else outside yourself at such a time of your own mental and physical anguish."[33] And when David Cavitch wrote a devastating personal attack on John Logan's *Anonymous Lover* (1973) in the *New York Times,* Gardner stepped into the breach in an emotional letter to the editors: "He is a reacher who *reaches.* There are no 'cosmetics' in any of his poems. Any poet who is truly a poet is 'torn by beauty and frightened by death.' But Logan has courage and virtu. He is a *poet's poet.* Perhaps that is why your reviewer, Mr. Cavitch has failed so sadly in his review of the 5th book of one of our *best* poets."[34] For all his drinking, philandering, and picking up of lover boys, for all his problems of confused sexuality and loneliness, Logan, in contrast to Gardner, always returned to writing as the one constant in his life. His way of helping Gardner through her tragedies, therefore, was trying to get her to write again by convincing his friends that they should help her publish a new volume. But publishers were not lined up for a poet whose last book (a compilation of earlier books) had flopped, and who had written virtually nothing new in the ten years since Tate had left her.

Still, at a time when no respectable university could do without a poet in residence, Gardner was invited by several, one as far away as Michigan, to grace their campuses. Frank MacShane had recommended her to Irvine, but Northridge clinched the deal, and during the spring of 1975, Gardner was to be "a full fledged member of our staff in place of [Donald?] Salper, who has a sabbatical for cogitation. He may do more cohabiting than cogitating, but why not?"[35] Meanwhile, in May 1974 Gardner had given a reading at another California campus, at Riverside, at the invitation of Steven Gould Axelrod, who had interviewed her for his *Robert Lowell: Life and Art* and remembered her as "kind, charismatic, vulnerable, lovely—sort of like a faded movie star":

> She spoke a lot about Tate, with whom she still seemed to be half in love. She spoke about choosing the poems he would read at poetry readings, about arranging the order and so on, about "The Mediterraneans," which as I recall she considered his best poem. She spoke tearfully about her son, who at that time was missing. . . .
>
> Her boyfriend was up in the mountains fishing. He was uninterested in poetry and intellectual talk and just drove her out and picked her up. She was wonderful, kind, talkative, unpretentious; I did not realize how kind until years later when I had had more experience with poets. She was happy to chat with my students, happy to be nice to them.
>
> One felt the terrible sadness in her—over her estrangement from her children, her break-up with Tate, her loss of friends and respect, her aging, her exile in the hills of Ojai, her sense that her whole life hadn't quite worked out, as in the line from "On Looking in the Looking Glass": "I see that maker that you want and aren't." In retrospect I visualize a talented woman marking time, effortlessly charming an assistant professor and his graduate student wife, and his students and colleagues: a woman who knew on some level that her life was already over."[36]

Too terrified to teach, Gardner in the end reneged on her Northridge acceptance. As a self-titled "aging has-been," she then applied to MacDowell, yet its director, Conrad Sponholz, welcomed her for the winter of 1975 as a "[m]ature artist . . . as long as they continue productive."[37] "I wish we could have done together (Sitwell fashion?) the things we once talked of and wanted to do," Gardner wrote her brother Robert, who had released two new documentary films in 1973, *Mark Tobey Abroad* and *Rivers of Sand*. She knew that her brother shared her impulse to preserve human experience through form, that he attempted to engage and touch others through his visual medium, just like she did through her poetry.[38] Strong-willed, of similar sensitivity and sensibility, both were uncompromising in their art. Unfortunately, the two had always lived too different lives too far apart to bring about a Sitwellian performance, since Gardner had left the parental home for Ireland and Great Britain in the fall of 1937, when Robert was only eleven. Gardner no longer looked forward to a possible collaboration with her productive, successful brother; she had, she felt, wasted her talent and wrecked her children's lives as well as her own, and there remained nothing for her to do but grieve or perhaps give up altogether. She knew better than anyone what wonderful possibilities she had been given as a gifted Gardner, and she blamed herself most bitterly for having thrown them away. She envied her cousin Lowell, she had told Axelrod, for being "intensely ambitious, making himself a poet and then a noted poet almost by act of pure will."[39] Indeed, it is as if the main male poets of the 1950s and 1960s, such as Lowell, Berryman, Jarrell, and Shapiro, had to prove their manhood through an intensely macho competitiveness, while Gardner established her femininity by putting the men in her life before her work and her children; sensuality and sensitivity but also, as she well knew, sloth were her guiding principles. An early, autobiographical poem describes "the scarce and lonely sloth, obedient prisoner in space, / astonished by perpetual pain," who travels "having no heels / to take to on your unsoled feet, no hole to hide in, and no / way to fight. / Doomed to the trees, 'good food for many,' your one safety is in flight" (10).

Looking backward, Gardner could not even find protection in the past. Erskine Childers had become the fourth president of Ireland in 1973 but had transmogrified from a dashing rebel into a man whose pomposity was, according to Mary Manning, "beyond belief. He is making a perfect fool of himself turning up with entourage at whist drives tea parties and openings. His wife never stops talking."[40] Childers died after only fifteen months in office, "enjoying the job immensely and doing well," Manning had to admit, but "[n]ot the same Erskine you knew, or I once knew. Do you remember 'The night is young.' [W]ords forever on his lips." Childers's death made Manning think back to her own affair with Samuel Beckett, whose biography was being written by Deirdre Bair, who had "uncovered some letter from Sam . . . in 1937 saying 'Mary Manning has just given birth to a daughter. . . . I must consult my chemist about more efficient condrums.' [O]r words to that effect. I had trouble putting that rumour down. . . . Ah well who cares now. It['s] all over."[41]

Gardner's old nurse Molly Laughlin still cared, for although plagued with arthritis in her arm and hand she just "had to write" her after she had heard about "sweet girl" Rosy's drama.[42] And Gardner still cared about Tate when she heard from his daughter, Nancy, who was embroiled in a feud with Helen Heinz, that he was ill with emphysema in Nashville and had become so isolated from most of his old southern friends through his wife that he was thinking of moving back to Minneapolis: "When I think of the tale you told I feel desolate for Daddo; but also fury. Fury that Ms. Heinz could not have made it possible for Allen to live out his remaining years in peace with himself, his friends, his colleagues; and with occasional gayety, *loving* his friends, and once upon a while laughing his unique waterfall-cadenced laugh, a laughter that always was fresh and spontaneous when you were near him, Nancy. I used to like to fantasy that he was rocking on a porch at Andrew's, sipping maybe a bourbon or two."[43]

Gardner's own present was as depressing as Tate's. From the first day onward in Ojai, she had missed the museums, galleries, and lively literary atmosphere of New York City. She felt she had outlived her life: she "was not seeing very many people" and "was lonely."[44] But Ojai, she wrote George, was "perfect for Gill. His dog, his outboard motor fishing boat, his rods and reels, the outdoors." "As for me," she continued:

> Liver is neither enlarged nor *tending* to shrink and dry up to cirrhosis. . . . My body is more supple and flexible than women 30 years younger than I am. I have fantastic recuperative powers, and an iron will *when* I use it. Too seldom.
> *Debits*
> I have drunk too much since the age of 19 when I found that my "shyness"— my *fear* of people, the strangle in my voice could be eased by booze. . . .
> When we talked on the telephone you asked me why (how) I could say I had a ferocious will to live, but also a strong desire to "cease upon the midnight with no pain." I think our father understood me, to a degree. . . . [H]e said, (and I paraphrase) you are a composite of *extreme* opposites. . . .
> Dear brother of my heart I am so terribly tired, and I grow old . . . but often a sunset, a sunrise, a tender new green leaf, a soft south west wind—my being can be anywhere from 9 years old to 99 years old.[45]

Gill did not even "fit the stereotype of the great black stud," Gardner had told Roland Flint, and indeed felt that "orgasm shortened life," but attracted to his otherness and paying his way, she counted on his being a steadfast, stable, loving companion who would take care of her, share her meals, hold doors, and zip up her dress.[46] As Gardner and Gill were thrown back upon each other for company in rural, remote Ojai, the conflicting barriers of class, race, and personality led to inevitable clashes and proved, in the end, insurmountable. Supercilious, Gardner often treated Gill like a particularly unsatisfactory and uncouth servant, while he took a sadistic pleasure in taunting her as a "stupid bitch"—not something a Boston Brahmin, however deeply she had sunk, could ever get used to. Their quarrels soon surpassed the verbal stage, and they were "hitting each other over the head, or throwing coffee pots at each other almost daily."[47] Josephine Jacobsen, who felt that Gardner had been so battered by life that she needed and deserved some shelter and warmth, had had high hopes for this biracial relationship but was shocked into sense. "When I heard that she had eloped with this black man from the Chelsea Hotel I thought—now maybe this is a racist remark—but some of my black friends do seem to be having a peculiar cherishing quality that is very special." Gill, however, "was aggressive and just the exact reverse of everything that I had fantasized for her: tough, tough, tough. . . . He was so spectacularly lacking in the kind of characteristics that are exceptionally appealing in black people, that kind of a richness, a luxuriance of emotions and affections. He was so sharp and vulgar, while Belle really was a very patrician person and very, very bright. And you just felt that nothing except absolute desolation could have pitched her into this."[48]

Guilt-ridden about her children and her wasted life, and in almost constant pain from arthritis, Gardner clung to her daily comfort dose of wine and vodka, becoming ever more confused, vague, and irritable. Gill reacted by becoming ever more abusive and started beating her up. Far from her family and friends, with hardly anybody to talk to, Gardner suffered in silence for the most part, convinced that she was so worthless as to deserve such gruesome treatment. Only her closest friends, like John Logan, knew of her predicament, and he told her there "must be an end to such assault and battering."[49] Yet it was not until Gill broke her arm that Gardner started thinking of leaving him and returning to New York City: "I'm a little afraid of being physically assaulted again by Gill but he does not *mean* to hurt me. . . . Perhaps I must summon the courage to leave Gill and move back to New England."[50] When months later Gardner finally did, she blamed herself as much as Gill and continued to feel responsible for him, making sure that he and his were well taken care of for as long as she lived. She could never sever ties, and Myra Cholden thought Gardner was going overboard when she gave him the Ojai house, continued to pay for Jimmy Gill's tuition for art school, and in later years even came to support Gill's new young wife, Sarah, and their baby son: "Why, God knows, because he had more than sufficient payment for his services. . . . It is all guilt money."[51]

True to form, Gardner did not leave Gill until after she had found other loves. One was Raul Caraballosa, a Cuban with a "colossal belly" with "beautiful blue and bloodshot eyes," whom she had met during one of her trips East and who, though "[t]oo far gone in booze to truly care," had nursed her for days when she had been ill with bronchitis at the Chelsea ("Bronchitis at the Chelsea—Or Salud Raul," 119). Much more important, though, was the young singer, writer, sculptor, painter Jay Bolotin, whom she met at MacDowell at the end of 1975. Hailing from Tate's Kentucky, with a dark, seductive southern drawl, the age of her son, Bolotin personified "Pan cum Orpheus" for Gardner.[52] When she arrived at MacDowell in November 1975, she was "not too stable, but holding my own, or so I think," Gardner had written Logan.[53] Only two weeks later Gardner, at sixty, confessed to Bolotin, who was in his twenties: "All my long mixed up life I've longed for intuitive tenderness. You've given me that. When I came here I was at the point of seriously thinking about suicide. Now I *want* to *live*, and now I feel that perhaps, *not* perhaps, but certainly as long as I survive, I now have the inside courage and will to *try*."[54] Gardner was physically attracted to Jay as she was to any good-looking man, but insisted that her letters were not "'love letters' but letters of love. I have lived long, I've loved greatly, but never with this inward peace, this stillness and clarity and joy, without any fear of hurt or hurting, without any obsessive desire to intrude, invade, possess, or disturb."[55]

Gardner was more than half in love with Bolotin, a sensitive, kind young man, who looked deeper than the alcoholic, lecherous, irritable dame, who, in the words of Ned O'Gorman, "gobbled men like weenies and I do not think Belle had one single conscience problem about it, at all."[56] Bolotin was Gardner's new muse, personifying the possibility of hope, the future (and was, clearly, though with erotic overtones, a stand-in for Daniel). The older poet Marguerite Harris noted that "Bolotin has really turned you on. We are sisters under the skin with respect that we can get as excited about someone else's talent as our own."[57] For the first time in years, Gardner went all out to promote the work of a young artist, offering to introduce him to Betty Parsons, to get him invited to Harris's Dr. Generosity poetry readings or the Manhattan Theatre Club, or to have him meet Allen Ginsberg. Ginsberg is, she warned Bolotin, "very much aware of my horror of his friend Harry Smith and my own and my daughter's difficulties with Gregory Corso who when I first met him seemed gifted (to some degree) and although we were never friends in any real sense, there was something rather disarming, not charming, in his infantilism. That was 20 years ago and now he is corrupt, and therefore, I suppose, pathetic because of self-destruction and wanton destructiveness to others, but I cannot like him. Allen, no matter what is felt by anyone, pro or con, in regard to his own poetry, is a *good* human being, generous and compassionate to the Harry Smiths and the Corsos of this world."[58] When soon after Gardner's departure from MacDowell, Bolotin fell in love with a young resident painter, Lorna Ritz, Gardner did not mind overmuch and kept up a barrage of unselfish letters in which her main concern was encouragement of his work. Bolotin valued his elderly mentor and wrote her that their communal friend Hannah Green "thinks it is of high importance that you continue to write. . . . We speak of you with much love in our voices."[59]

Gardner had indeed started writing again and would, during these last wine-drenched years of her life, manage to wring out a number of sharply moving poems that came up to her own high standards. At MacDowell she had, at first, just dawdled, drinking and bemoaning the terrible tragedies that had befallen her children, reminiscing about their halcyon days at Union Pier, until one night a fellow resident told her she should stop talking and start writing as she had the makings of a poem right there. Years of pain culminated in "That Was Then," a very melodious, prosy poem evoking an idyllic past and horrific present without the slightest touch of melodramatic sentiment. "That Was Then" was emblematic of Gardner's best new poems, which were far more explicitly autobiographical than her earlier ones, and they may have inspired her remarks in an interview quoted in the *Boston Globe:* "I realize that it is impossible for me to make any statement about my work without making continual reference to lived experience and that, correspondingly, I can't talk about my life without wanting to turn it into writing. Most of the poetry I have written has been just this: a track or series of footprints indicating where I have been."[60] With her own life rather than myth and folklore as their framework, these new poems were loosely lyrical and a pleasure to the ear through her magisterial use of rhythm and the interplay of assonance and consonance. Particular and precise, poignant, "That Was Then" shows Gardner to be still a past master at communicating raw emotions through structured form:

> Instead of a play-pen, my husband, Seymour,
> called Simcha which means joy, made a paddock
> for him. Dan did not like to be cooped up
> (Nor did Rose, my daughter Rosy; nor did she)
> not then, not later, never. Dan was last
> seen in Columbia, South America.
> ("That Was Then," 120)

Gardner recognized the poem for the breakthrough it was and sent it to her parents for their sixty-third anniversary in 1976, defensive (at sixty!) and wanting to prove that even if she was their black sheep, she was also a poet, capable of creating beauty, though she doubted they could appreciate what she had wrought. "It may not *seem* a poem to you but it meant a great deal to old and young artists, visual and writers, poets etc.—I enclose notes that were left in my mailbox at MacDowell. This *seldom* happens, if ever. . . . They are only to bear witness to the fact that I did not waste either my time or my substance while at MacDowell. . . . You may not like or understand the poem. But people wept, openly. . . . I don't use end rhyme. But the structure of the poem is very strict and I use poetic devices within the line. The poem is essentially elegiac—as to Rosy and Daniel."[61] Karl Shapiro "was truly moved by it—the last line brought tears to my eyes. I read the poem as an 'insider' because I could recognize almost everything in it and almost all of it I had long since forgotten came flooding back. It was rather amazing to be shot back twenty years. . . . I think it is one of your richest poems."[62]

For the spring of 1976 Gardner was accepted at the writer's colony at Ossabaw Island, but she wrenched her back and could not go. Gill was of no help when pain rendered her immobile for weeks, and his unfeeling behavior strengthened her resolve to move back East without him. She settled on New York and, in spite of what had happened to her daughter, on the Hotel Chelsea, where Harry Smith still resided; Corso often appeared; drunks, junkies, and whores had proliferated; and Bard had installed a TV monitoring system in the lobby in a feeble attempt to prevent more holdups. Gardner listed its pros and cons for Bolotin:

[Stanley Bard] is hated by the entire staff, and deplored by the more stable inmates of the cess-pool cum lunatic asylum to which he has reduced the once rather noble Chelsea. When I was twenty three I remember going on a pilgrimage there to pay a call on Edgar Lee Masters, with my daughter Rosy's father.

When Allen Tate and I were divorced I went there at the suggestion of a painter friend, Bill Bomar. I had an apartment and stayed several years. The hotel has deteriorated terribly as far as the inhabitants are concerned. It is full of lonely hearts and the hotel is a comfort to them (all of us). . . . The owners of the restaurant [El Quichote] and the waiters are friends of mine and are protective of me. Especially protective as far as the tragic gifted monster Harry Smith is concerned. I am hated by some denizens of the hotel, and bad-mouthed by many.

You will meet my friend Mildred Baker, formerly associate director of the Newark Museum, Virgil Thomson, the composer. George Klei[ns]inger, *kindly and frivolous*—composer of Tubby the Tuba, Archie and Mehitabel etc.—he has cobras, other snakes and tropical birds and fish in his penthouse place. I *like* George but he is febrile and brittle, but good-hearted. . . .

Except for Stella Waitzkin and Mildred Baker the people I cared for left (Bill Bomar included) because of the prevalence of drug pushers, pimps, call girls and whores.

Robberies are rife. Beatings, rapes, even homicides. The police appear to be paid off, by both the hotel and the restaurant. . . .

Why do I return?

Because of the friendships of Mildred Baker and Stella—because of the warmth and kindness of the waiters and owners (especially Manuel a man of great dignity often behind the bar) and Jose, the chef, a man of dignity, soul and beauty—the third owner Gilbert is Maître D', glossy, pleasant, and fairly recently in jail for possession and selling. . . .

Again—why do I come? I know the neighborhood, the laundry, dry cleaner, shoe repair, 5 and ten, optometrist, movie house, liquor store, food store, bank etc. The bell captain, *Al Lewis*, is a friend of mine, and Gill's. The telephone operator (*not* in the morning) is a friend, *Josephine Brickman.* Two or 3 of the bellmen are nice.[63]

It is clear that Gardner struggled over her decision to set up house in the Chelsea again. Her brother George was appalled at her plans, so Gardner enlisted Kitty, who wrote him that while aristocratic Green Hill suited him and fashionable Park Avenue her, the Chelsea was their sister's true habitat. Sadly, because of her minimal self-esteem, this disreputable hotel was indeed the one place where Gardner did not feel out of place, and the Chelsea was to be her last home. She moved there in the summer of 1976, leaving Gill not only her house, but also her station wagon and boat, so that he would remain in Ojai, "safe from all that he was into in N.Y.C. I know that he *hurts,* and that he loves me as well as he can but I *cannot* live without *affection* and that is difficult for him. If I were younger I might try to 'hang in' but my daughter, my grand-son, my parents, 3 brothers, 2 sisters and my friends are all back East and the West Coast is not my heartland. I want to write new poems. I cannot here and I have no time to waste."[64]

At the Chelsea, Gardner was all alone, for her new lover Raul Caraballosa had walked in front of a truck while drunk on the very day she returned to New York City. In "Bronchitis at the Chelsea—Or Salud Raul," Gardner memorized in word and sound the violence of his death: his "skull cracked" and he died "not knowing the racking / sobbing of the man" whose truck his "undirected body attacked / At the funeral parlor your mother rocked / Aiee Aiee she cried but never cracked / Nor loosed the easier tear. Raul you can't come back" (119). Unable to live without a man, Gardner at once fell for a distinguished-looking, white-haired, well-made Australian named Ed Berryman, "very slender and very fit" with a "kind of masculine assurance, a hard edge."[65] She felt that she owed Roland Flint, who had come out to California to help her pack up and break away from Gill, an explanation:

Before World War 2 he came to America. At the onset of the war he was navi-gating officer on a freighter (2 were sunk under him) in the North Atlantic con-voy route. The British connived with the Americans when we entered the war to remove him from freighter duty and train him as a commando in Scotland. He spent much time in the Burmese jungle with knife on leg, knife on back and, of course, a gun. He did a *lot* of killing of Japanese, contracted malaria from which he still suffers. . . .

After the war he captained freighters, did store and harbour duty etc.—Ten years ago the booze caught up with him—his marriage broke up he had shock treatments and for 10 years has been in and out of de-tox units. He is not stable, but appears impeccable. I met him at the Chelsea. I was with Mildred who likes him much. . . . He is meticulously almost compulsively tidy. He can sew, paint, spackle, carpenter and do anything and everything. . . .

He is delightful company drunk or sober, kind, tender affectionate, and what he does by just looking at me or touching me softly, delicately, I thought I'd never feel again and / but he wants to make love day and night. *But* I am not so emo-tionally dependent that I cannot endure being without him. On the other hand, he *is* terribly dependent on me. . . . He is a gentle man, and a gentleman, but as a commando killing *was* his profession, perforce during the war. . . .

Like Gill, if I touch him or approach him when he is asleep and I've been up his reflexes go instantly into action. The street man and the commando man react the same way in that sense. . . . Meanwhile trust me because I *am* putting work first.[66]

Gardner was not fooling Flint, or even herself. However courageous Berry-man's actions might have been during the war, he was now in Stella Waitzkin's words "a very destructive, very violent, very crazy alcoholic."[67] And far from liking him, Baker had told Myra Cholden to stay clear of him because he was "dangerous." When she did meet him, Myra was "terrified. He was crazy, just sheer, absolute crazy. If he were drinking, Belle would not let him into her room. . . . Then he would go and get dried out and he would come back vow-ing everything. And then he would go again."[68] Around this time the poet-critic Robert Phillips came to know Gardner and to love her as a poet and a person. Because Berryman did not have "a literary bone in his body," Phillips would accompany her to readings.[69] He noted Berryman "was drinking even more than she was. The battles between them got to be rather large scale."[70] As he was an aggressive, vicious drunk, no detox institution would take him a second time, so every few months, Gardner would have to find a new place for him to dry out—at her expense—as well as make sure that he could not enter her own apartment, because otherwise he would trash it and beat her up: "Everything is BAD—EVERY place turned him down," Gardner explained to Flint, who was staying at the Chelsea to help her with filing her correspondence when Berryman got into one of his alcoholic rages. "He's finally at some place called Kimbro—where he pissed on the floor and they'll take him for one night only. I want to go to [the restaurant] Simply Good—but it's the first place he'll look for me."[71] This "really slimy character" was the man Gardner decided she deserved for the remaining years of her life.[72] She was too ashamed of him, though, to introduce him to the Wrights, the more so as James was no longer drinking, but John Logan, who was still a drinker, got to meet him.

Although the poet Robert Peters "thought they were boozing as fast as pos-sible to see who would die first," Gardner was, in fact, taking her writing more seriously than she had done in years. The deaths of her lover Caraballosa and, in January 1976, her old friend Paul Robeson, and, saddest of all, her beloved father at eighty-eight in September 1976, spurred her into elegiac poetry, much as the loss of her friends Lemuel Ayers, Louis Cholden, and Barbara Ransom Jopson had done twenty years before. Peabo Gardner's obituary in the *New York Times* described him as "a financier, philanthropist and member of one of Boston's oldest and most noted families," listed his trusteeships of the Isabella Stewart Gardner Museum as well as Boston's Fine Art Museum, his numerous directorships from the General Electric Company, the First National Bank of Boston, the Chase Fund of Boston, the Amoskeag Manufacturing Company to the Eastern Steamship Company, his prowess as an athlete and his membership of the top Boston clubs.[73]

He had also been a former director of the American Telephone and Tele-graph Company, and Gardner wrote a series of haikus for him beginning: "The telephone rang / in my dream Long Distance from / my dead father" ("The Telephone," 106). She was experimenting, and her elegy to Robeson was diametrically opposite in technique, a prosaic epic rather than a taut lyric: "Once (a gambit of yours?), / you spoke of knowing I'd been a professional actress my playing / Desdemona to your Othelllo. Seymour feared you and I were / lovers. I wish it *had* been so. One evening you and I / were together at 'the mission,' an apartment several blocks from where Seymour and I lived. Three or four stouthearted / young women / shared there. Pat Haskell, Ruth Frank, others. I sat beside you on the sofa. My hand was in your hand when Seymour walked / in. Seeing his ire I muttered to you 'The old man of the / tribe.'[74] Gardner also tried her hand at poetics once more and paying homage to Marianne Moore (who had died in 1972) in "Are Poets Ball Players?" used a sustained but rather repetitive baseball metaphor for the art of poetry ending: "There are no free Walks for Poets to first / base on balls. The umpire counts and chooses / So we Warm the Bench, jounce back to Left Field / or, maybe, we touch all three bases and / slide in peril to Home Plate / That Home Run at last" (110).

When Logan did not take the Robeson poem, and haiku priest-poet Raymond Roseliep rejected the rambling baseball one, Gardner lost some of the confidence she had gained with "That Was Then," but as she knew these two were not her best, refusal for once did not deter her from persisting and from being unusually productive. She wrote a loving nature poem for Jay Bolotin on her communion with "a palpable moth quivering on the path" ("The Moth Happened," 102), as well as a repulsively realistic one on her massacre of cockchafers: "I wake to 19 ½ corpses. Some squished flat. Those / still twitching mine the floor. I put on solid shoes / and stamp on you cocky twitchers CRUNCH / Crunch-crunch, and sweep you up, / and out" ("Cockchafer," 101). "Your Fearful Symmetries" was an incisive pictorial commissioned tribute to the painter Alice Neel ("Whether you, Alice Neel, assess / define or collect souls / it is the internal structure / that matters" [105]), while "Card Island or Cod Island?" evoked the warm fairyland she created as a child as a refuge from feeling a misfit, from loneliness and her distant disapproving imperious mother: "At bedtime my father played God / The King the Queen the Ace the Jack / I was the joker in the pack" (114).

In the end, Gardner placed all these poems, but *Poetry*'s John Frederick Nims took only "The Telephone." It was a sop to her feelings when Julia Bartholomay, president of *Poetry*'s Modern Poetry Association and a former student of Paul Carroll's, invited her for two readings in Chicago, mentioning that "[y]ou and John [Logan] are probably the two people for whom Paul has felt more love and loyalty, over the years, than anyone else. If he has ever idolized a woman it is you: he used to tell our workshop that he and John 'worshipped at your feet'—a jocular remark but, in many ways, a true one."[75] "Only you could have warmed up all us Chicagoans when the temperature was—19," Nims's wife, Bonnie, wrote Gardner after her visit. "I have been reading *West of Childhood*. What a splendid collection. There was a review that John had written; tucked inside the covers it was. He said that 'That Craning of the Neck' was a poem 'in which insight, passion, phrasing and rhythm, all brilliantly fuse.' And John is right. And your new poems go right on."[76] Nims, however, continued to turn down her new work with what Gardner regarded as "incredibly patronising notes."[77]

In the summer of 1979 she had more cause to be upset with *Poetry*, as Daryl Hine and Joseph Parisi had not included her work in *The Poetry Anthology 1912–1977* (1978). Supposedly comprehensive, the anthology did not include Jacobsen, Wright, or Gardner, while Rago was there "in plenitude," Gardner fumed.[78] Jacobsen wrote to Gardner that she had appeared in *Poetry* "under H. Monroe and published under *every* editor, including the unlamented D. Hine. I doubt if *any* poet had as many poems in P. I do feel that my exclusion was shocking, but not as shocking as yours. I feel sure D. H. was the poo-bah. Well, my dear, what really can it matter?"[79] Angered on Gardner's behalf, Shapiro had written to Parisi and received a lukewarm apology in return: "I am beginning to realize what dubious enterprises anthologies are, since so many people are bound to be displeased."[80] Nims wrote Gardner that he "was very surprised you weren't there.... But please do not think that the anthology represents the opinion of your work that we now at Poetry have of it. (It's true I sent some poems back lately, but only because they weren't the *best* you.) . . . Do you see James Wright? Judy [Bartholomay] said he was aggrieved? upset? mad? or whatever at being omitted. Please tell him I like his work very much, and look forward to publishing it. Yours too."[81] In contrast to Hine and Parisi, Nims was indeed a true admirer of Gardner's work, but although she exonerated him from responsibility for the anthology, she had had it with him, she wrote, because of his "exacerbating habit of including homil[ie]s and comments. . . . I cannot think why you feel it incumbent on you to instruct poets you reject about the quality of their work. All of us submit what we are *not* ashamed of! I don't honestly think that many poets of those you reject saying 'it's not the best *you*' are inclined to try again. I, for one, will not."[82] Sending out new poems after all these years, Gardner was touchy about their reception, and poor Nims, who was just trying to be as encouraging as Gardner had been when she was associate editor, had to bear the brunt of her hypersensitivity.

Gardner had never been subservient or compliant, but now she became more arrogant and easily offended than she had ever been. She snubbed and hurt friends who did not dance to her tune (paradoxically cherishing some who dared disagree or object), insulted acquaintances, and, inebriated, shouted at waiters, maids, and other personnel. Those who did not get to know her well only saw her haughty manner, the befuddled flamboyance, "an operatic heroine in her last changes," or, less compassionate, the "epitome of the crazy, eccentric poet."[83] They reacted to the theatrical, aristocratic quality of her "strange kind of fallen state," her height and hair, now dyed a fiery red, the strong hurt that she radiated.[84] Although Gardner hobnobbed with Thomson, Kleinsinger, and other luminaries at the Chelsea, and was a constant on New York's extensive and lively poetry circuit, from Galen Williams's YM-YWHA Poetry Center to Harris's Dr. Generosity series, only a few people in New York City were her true friends. James Wright cared deeply, but was too much in awe of Gardner to tell her home truths when she needed them; Rosemarie Beck Phelps was loving and sympathetic but refused to be at Gardner's command, which irritated Gardner no end; and Mildred Baker was a dependable companion but loved her liquor as much as Gardner did and did not instill much-needed moderation. Dahlberg, a constant if often troublesome presence in Gardner's life, had died in California by Julia's "side in his sleep" in February 1977. Julia had "buried him as an Orthodox Jew" and, "a very broken woman," wondered if she could ever thank Gardner "enough for all that you have done for Edward and for me."[85] Gardner's longtime, steadfast friends Shapiro and Logan also were in California, with Shapiro now a happily married bourgeois poet and Logan trying to stay out of sexual trouble, while Carroll, the fourth friend from her propitious Chicago days, could be counted upon to be in distress himself. Her supportive younger male friends were far away, too: Roland Flint lived in Georgetown and Jay Bolotin in Kentucky. Both wrote frequent affectionate letters and came to New York City every so often, but neither was there to sustain her in her troubled day-to-day. Berryman was, of course, no help at all, and Gardner wished in vain "someone would wrap me in a mantle of love and take care of me."[86]

Now that her father had died, Gardner dreaded going to Green Hill even more than before, but she did her duty as a daughter, even though she was sure her mother hated the visits as much as she did. She often took along an escort: "You have to come and defend me from my family, and help me out, Oh God, Stephen," Gardner implored the poet Sandy. He remembered that his formal night with Gardner at the grand household in Brookline with its Sargents and servants galore ended with a visit at a louche bar in the Combat Zone, Boston's skid row, and Gardner, even more drunk than he was, coming on to him: "It was very theatrically worked out. . . . she played the comedy."[87]

When in Boston, she always attempted to visit Rose at the nearby Institute of Living, but Gardner was hardly ever allowed to see her, as she set off Rose's most violent episodes. Rose bombarded Gardner with disturbed letters, her handwriting affected by shock treatments, saying, "I love you with all my heart" and in the next sentence asking, "*Why* did you kill Daniel my brother?"; accusing her of being "a cannibal," then asking "Why the fuck don't you come to see me?"[88] Catherine Mayes, who had been doing her "very best to help Rosie, with letters, books and . . . helpful thoughts and prayers," felt compelled to warn Gardner that Rose had become "violently insane and should be kept under surveillance. Principally her accusations against you have been so appalling that no sane mind could think up such things. I feel that if she ever got loose you would be in very great danger. . . . I shall continue to keep in touch with her, as she must be kept from suicide."[89]

As a young poet Gardner had vowed that "in a sewer of waste / a thicket of pain a mountain of fear or the sea- / wrack of sorrow" she "would beg, steal and betray to be" ("Of Flesh and Bone," 31), but now she no longer believed in the sanctity, desirability or purpose of life however tenuous and had "rather my own dear Dolphin, Porpoise daughter had died . . . than exist brain damaged, stone deaf and full of hate."[90] When Rose's doctor, Raymond Veeder, suggested that Raoul at eight meet his mother, Gardner resisted vehemently: "I have decided that at all costs I must put what I feel to be Raoul's well-being first. Therefore, under no circumstances do I want Raoul to go to the Institute, either to see you or his mother, at Christmas or anytime thereafter until he is 12 or 13."[91] Veeder urged her to reconsider, but Gardner was adamant, delineating details of Rose's mental history and abuse of Raoul over the years:

> I'm not certain that you are aware of Rose's life-long obsession with arson. When she was about 11 she told me of the fires she had set on the South Side, in Chicago . . . When Rose moved to the Chelsea she gleefully boasted of setting off fire alarms all around the neighbourhood. . . .
>
> There is the history of drug-taking, abuse of alcohol, extreme and exhibitionistic promiscuity. . . .
>
> The Society for the Prevention [of Cruelty to Children] twice called me with complaints of her neglect and exploitation of Raoul. . . .
>
> I think it possible that there were two factors involved. 1) *Genetic.* Her father had a character disorder: amoral, manipulative, and no 'affect' except whatever he assumed when he deemed it suitable. 2) Birth trauma. She was a 'shoulder version' and very nearly lost her infant life. I had, at her birth, no anaesthetic except a whiff of ether at the end. Throughout her pregnancy I was allergic to alcohol. I've never taken drugs of any kind.
>
> *Needless* to say I do not overlook my depriving her of two fathers. However after Seymour's and my divorce he rejected her most cruelly. . . .
>
> When Raoul was a baby I was told that Rose took him to discos at 3 A.M. and literally threw him back and forth to people like a football. I don't now want him to be used as an emotional foot-ball—or a *pawn.*[92]

Gardner had hoped her beloved brother George would understand and support her as always, but he let her down. For now that Peabo had died, the weight of the Gardner name and responsibilities lay on his shoulders alone, and because Raoul was illegitimate, fatherless, and of, presumably, low birth, George, in patrician fashion, pretended he did not exist except as a financial burden. Supervising Gardner's finances, George knew that after she had paid the institute's huge annual bills for Rose, there was not much left for what he deemed her extravagances, even though she had inherited money upon Peabo's death. He upbraided her for blowing her money on tuition for Anneke Van Kirk and Gill's sons and others; for buying paintings of artist friends and acquaintances such as Rosemarie Beck, Larry Bigelow, Bill Bomar, Larry Calcagno, Blanche Dombeck, Ethel Edwards, Margo Hoff, and Richard Yarde; for subsidizing magazines like *Choice, Poetry, New York Quarterly,* or *Unmuzzled Ox.* He let pass that she kept an unsavory lover, but why did she have to put up and pay for every one of her friends who came to New York City? Why, for that matter, did she so often foot the dinner bill of freeloaders? Did not she know that she was using up her capital? "Do bear in mind Belle," he admonished her, "that you may be a vulnerable target to others—some of whom may really not mean that much to you and most of whom you probably have no obligation to whatsoever. Use me, if you will, as the nasty person whose approval you have to get first. This will honestly afford you some protection."[93]

But Gardner reckoned that there would be enough money for herself always anyway and took pleasure in it mainly because she could give it to worthy causes like the education of the young and be a patron of the arts like her great-great-aunt had been. She had dreams of building and endowing a film studio at MacDowell in Daniel's name and was saddened by her brother's disapproving meddling: "I found that I am not only incapable of doing anything for Mac-Dowell *or* anything else, but was sternly but kindly told by George that I was (as regards capital) in arrears and must *NOT* indulge myself in my favourite vice which is to give non tax deductible money to loved but indigent friends and causes. In fact unless I outlive (*unlikely*) Mother and Aunt Catherine all I will inherit will go to poor Rosy! . . . Rosy *still* has funds but for some reason they— George and the lawyer . . . don't want to exhaust her money. So I must, it appears, 'pull in my horns.'"[94] The last straw for George was when Gardner, in a fit of naïve independence, handed over the Georgian family silver to a dealer, who disappeared without a trace: "What seems to have happened is that you have a modest amount from him as a theoretical 'down payment' and he has the silver. Unless I malign him it would seem he has the far better of the bargain."[95] Notwithstanding her brother's admonishments, Gardner preferred to err on the side of trust even more than she had done in her earlier years. She proved sensible and steadfast, however, where she was most vulnerable, with Raoul, and, still, Tate. She fought like a tiger for Raoul's position in her family and (even if she sometimes wearied of Seymour's claims) made sure that Seymour and Helena were well compensated for their loving care of her grandson.

Then after years of silence, in July 1978, came a demand on Gardner's lar-gesse from Nashville, Tennessee, where Tate was spending his last years in in-creasing isolation. It came via his friend David McDowell, who had known him in Nashville when he was sixteen (and had followed John Crowe Ransom to Kenyon College in Ohio together with Lowell):

> I did want you to know that Allen's marriage to Helen is wrecked. He is semi-invalid, partly in bed or using a walker. As you know he has emphysema and has great difficult[y] breathing after any physical effort.
>
> Helen has withdrawn from him and plans to put him in a nursing home—which I don't think he needs and which I feel would kill him. At least she has the honesty to say over and over that she hates him. This situation has alienated his two little boys, John and Benjamin, whom he loves very much, and they avoid seeing him as much as possible.
>
> Helen says he must get out, and that will take about half of his income, which, he tells me, is about $34 to $36 thousand a year. Helen will, of course, take cus-tody of the children.
>
> Allen can't live with his daughter as her husband will have nothing to do with him. Allen feels this is because he paid for Percy [Wood's] psychiatric training.
>
> Allen says that he should never have left you, and that the primary reason he did was that he could not cope with your two children and their father who seemed to be almost always present in your house.
>
> In the past year Allen has thought of you constantly, and he wishes you would come to Tennessee to help rescue him from his disastrous situation.
>
> It is so sad. I don't know what you will think about this matter, but when you answer, please enclose the letter in an envelope addressed to me, and I will pass it on to Allen.[96]

Tate had in fact dictated this letter to McDowell and in a draft version had added: "Helen has no interest in or understanding of his works."[97]

Robert Phillips remembered Gardner's agonizing "for days. Should she just swallow her pride and go down there to be with him, or should she leave well enough alone? And if she did go, what would be her relationship with the other wife and so on? . . . And Caroline Gordon was still alive and I wondered if he had called for Gordon, too. They could have all just surrounded the bed. Ring around the rosy."[98] Gardner's answer was the epitome of sensitive sense.

> Thank you for writing, though your letter distressed me.
>
> Yes, I knew of Allen's emph[yse]ma. And when I talked to Nancy Wood in June, or maybe in May, I think she told me that Allen and Helen were having problems. She told me that she *and* Percy hoped Allen would come to stay. I've never heard

Percy Wood express anything other than affection and admiration for his father-in-law. . . .

The last direct word I had from Allen forbad my writing him ever again. I used to send, after that, snapshots etc. he might like to have, in care of Andrew Lytle.

My circumstances prohibit any assistance of any kind to Allen.

Financially

The money I inherited at my father's death makes it just possible for me to maintain my daughter, Rose Van Kirk, for life, in a private mental institution. At a time when I was living in California and having my arthritic right hip removed and replaced, my daughter was brutally beaten and over-dosed. She had cardiac arrest at St. Vincent's hospital. She suffered *irreversible brain damage* and is totally and permanently deaf.

My son Daniel was last seen in Col[o]mbia, S.A. and has not been seen since. He is presumed dead. Murdered. The Col[o]mbia Connection.

My daughter's son, my grandson, is being raised by my son Daniel's father and his wife. I of course underwrite that financially.

I have also undertaken the tuition of my daughter's half-sister, Anneke Sakellariou's son.

There is no foreseeable financial assistance available from me.

Emotionally, or shall we say in terms of what is left of my life, I have nothing to offer Allen.

I've no recriminations. The most joyous time of my life was spent with Allen while he loved me. The demands of the ever-recurring crises of my children were too much for us both. Then a clinical depression I experienced with the change of life. We were in London. Allen said it was "the megrims." In any case he was *open* to Helen, and turned from me. I cannot blame him.

Somehow or other I patched my life together. I don't choose to be nearly destroyed again.

I feel sorry that his marriage failed, that his wife, Helen, failed him.

I shall always love him, and care *about* him. I cannot care *for* him in any tangible way. . . .

P.S. You are welcome to pass this letter on to Allen, though he always thought I wrote at too much length!

For the record:

Allen *never* even met either my daughter's father *or* my son's father. So of course neither husband was *ever* present in my house.

Neither of my children spent much time in our house either. Christmas, Easter, Summer—at most a few weeks a year. I'm having your letter to me, and this letter, zeroxed. I very much fear that Helen unduly influenced Allen in regard to all those who loved, *and love,* him most—Nancy, Percy, his grandchildren, Pete,

Allen, Caroline, Amy, Andrew Lytle, Peter Taylor, many others, and, of course and *understandably,* myself.[99]

A few months later, on February 9, 1979, Allen Tate died a lonely death. Mc-Dowell knew they would "miss Allen, but at least he is at rest. It seems as if Helen had been withholding a good deal of mail from friends. . . . Allen's death so soon after Cal [in September 1977] makes it almost unbearable for their friends. And all the others gone these past years: Ransom, Davidson, Jarrell, Berryman, William Carlos Williams, Auden, Moore, Roethke, Stevens, Delmore, and a few years earlier, Agee. Do you know Hardy's poem, An Ancient to Ancients in which he addressed the young? It ends: 'Yea, rush not. Time serves. We are going, Gentlemen.'"[100] Andrew Lytle, who had washed his hands of Gardner after Tate's marriage to Heinz because he thought her a meddlesome pain in the neck, now sent a compassionate note: "The last years, as you no doubt know, the situation was such that I saw Allen very little. Nor was he himself, but that is over and done with. I heard, and pass on, as I know you will like to hear it, his last hours or so. It is called hallucinations, but he saw hundreds of people in his presence, he was talking with Henry James and they were playing charades. Helen entered the room, and you know how he could bow; he asked his companions if she could play, too."[101] Gardner helped organize a memorial reading for Tate in New York City, and cried throughout, feeling very much the widow. The poetry consultant to the Library of Congress, William Meredith, described the evening as "one of those moving moments at a funeral, where the recognition of loss is complete and yet, because so many share it, acceptable. This continued to happen at that lovely gathering you gave us at your house (you have made the apartment into your house). What a good difference Allen Tate's life made, in sum. I look out the window of this office and try to realize that I am one of his successors, if only in this job. I suppose what I see is in part because of what I learned from him to see. How much more you must feel that."[102]

When Nims asked Gardner to write a poem on her ex-husband for *Poetry,* she obliged a few months later with the overly prosy "The Four of Us and the Monkey" about a snapshot with a borrowed primate taken on an ecstatic day spent in 1962 with the poet Louis MacNeice and his lover Mary Wimbush:

> We were four hilarious
> middle-aged lovers out boating from London to Hampton
>   Court. What a
> *jubilant joy-ride* those four lovers had!
>
> At a hotel in Dublin the following summer A.T. and I
>   waited as planned
> for Louis to join us. Mary called us from London, Louis in
>   hospital

mortally ill. We flew back to London. Louis had died.
    Mary came to
our flat the next afternoon and in an extremity of pain
    spoke of Louis,
his spent lungs and that he'd foolishly gone down into a
    mine, a heedless
needless enterprise and then the hospital, the oxygen. She
    told us Louis
smiled when he said Tell me about the monkey.
Rest in peace Allen Tate, Louis MacNeice, while Mary
    and I, not yet late,
contrive to stay alive.

In a postscript Gardner added that somebody "had visited Allen in the nursing home some weeks or months before he died. I was told that this particular visitor (Spender?) was puzzled when Allen said 'tell me about Louis MacNeice when he was dying.' Maybe, just for the flash of an instant, Allen, too, remembered the June day at Hampton Court. The four of us and the monkey."[103]

While Maurice English loved "The Four of Us and the Monkey" because it "manages to recapture a real sense of that vanished fulfillment" and Shapiro enjoyed its "poignancy" because Gardner had "savor[ed] the past so well," Nims returned the poem, explaining she had sent it in too late for the Tate issue.[104] Although Nims's reaction came down to a dismissal of a solicited elegy by the poet who had both spent years of her life as an associate editor of *Poetry* and had been married to the subject of its commemorative issue, Gardner's reaction was rather mild; she may have just given up on her magazine. Then, too, she was working on a new and, she thought, last book, and this took up all of her emotions and energy. Three years earlier, a few months after the breakthrough of "That Was Then," Gardner had asked Princeton University Press about the possible publication of a book of her new and collected poems, and Princeton had professed interest even though very few Gardner poems had appeared in the past ten years. Princeton's positive response had given Gardner the courage to continue writing, and in the fall of 1978 she decided she had enough new poems for a book but was "frightened about submitting it," fearing "both rejection *and* exposure. . . . I have been out of the rat race for so long."[105] In the end she submitted her manuscript to Farrar, Straus, and Giroux on the advocacy of Robert Phillips, who had become an unselfish, powerful, and passionate promoter of Gardner's work: "It had been 15 years since she had a book and I think she felt passed over. She was not invited to give many readings, she was not invited to judge things. And one night after many delays, we had dinner at that little place across the street, called Simply Good. And we went back to her apartment and as I was getting ready to leave I said: 'Belle, where is that manuscript?' And she says: 'Why do you want to know?' And I said: 'Well, why don't you let me send it out?' And she said: 'Would you do that?' And I said: 'Yes,' and this tear rolled down her cheek."[106] Phillips took care of most of the handiwork for her manuscript, from copying reviews to typing acknowledgments, dedication, foreword, and contents, as well as her covering letter to Robert Giroux. Adding some minor editorial suggestions about her proposed preface, he then thanked Gardner "for trusting me with your work."[107]

Giroux read the manuscript "with pleasure and admiration" and thought it "worthy . . . of publication," but he rejected it "for hard reasons of economics" and suggested she try Atheneum.[108] Harry Ford at Atheneum begged off, too, letting Gardner know that he published only six books of poetry by their own poets per year and had finished manuscripts through 1980. Gardner then tried Doubleday and became impatient and irritable when they (requiring three outside readers) did not respond within weeks. Having dared submit her final manuscript to the scrutiny of the publishing world, knowing that she was all but forgotten as a poet, Gardner was even more irascible than usual about the reception of her work and thus, Phillips found, hard to deal with. A firm believer in her work (as he was in Karl Shapiro's), he then approached Al Poulin, poet, translator, and editor, who had started his own alternative poetry publishing house, BOA Editions, a few years before. Poulin told Phillips over the phone that he "would love the chance to do that" and stepped into the breach when Doubleday declined.[109] Poulin strained every nerve to turn Gardner's book into a success, getting photographer Aaron Siskind to do the art for its cover.[110] And upon Poulin's request, the engaging leftist feminist poet Muriel Rukeyser was "glad to write something about [Gardner's] work, which is valuable," but Gardner preferred blurbs by the less politically engaged Elizabeth Bishop or, even, Robert Penn Warren.[111] Phillips and Poulin had their work cut out for them by their demanding author, as Gardner showered them with requests and then forgot what she had wanted and was so insecure that she kept on asking for suggestions, only to bridle at what she regarded as editorial intrusions.

The only one who managed to stay on Gardner's good side through most of the process of putting the book to bed was Roland Flint, although she brushed aside most of his suggestions as well; as before, Gardner was sure she was the best judge of her own work. As Flint was still living in Georgetown and visited her in New York City only a few times a year, the best part of their relationship remained epistolary, and Gardner was therefore less likely to be offended by real or imagined slights, discourtesies, or criticisms of her work. Once, though, in a long letter discussing the new book, to be titled *That Was Then*, Flint spoke of having enjoyed dinner with her in their "usual lovely, rather filial scene;" Gardner, who desired a sexual thrill in the relationships with all her men, whatever their age, saw red: "Filial?? Explain yourself, sonny!"[112] Flint had to eat his words and tried, with little success, to convince her that "[a]ll I meant by 'filial' was 'familial' (which I thought it meant), 'fraternal,' 'just us chickens,' etc. . . . I sure as hell don't think of you as my mother or as myself as your father. *Christ!*"[113] Gardner had been hurt, too, by Flint's dislike of "Letter to Paul Robeson" and his suggestion she omit those poems "in which the love of sounds and pure song runs away with the poem, leaving the meaning behind."[114] Gardner retorted:

No matter what you or anyone else said I wd. have included *many* of the poems you originally appeared to exclude—and I *shall exclude* certain poems you wd. like included. For example—

The Panic Vine

3 Rings or 5 Rings

At the Zoo

I agree about the Lem Ayers poem which however does *not* "leave the meaning behind" viz. grief and loss—it *is* an elegy. *Certainly At a Summer Hotel* (mother-daughter-age-youth etc. etc.) does not leave meaning behind, nor, God *knows* does Cock A' Hoop (am changing title) nor *Mathematics of Encounter.* Logan quoted from it in his long article in The Critic and it is thematically important and central to any collection, selected or not, of my work. I think the intention of Reveille is clear, if slighter.

My voice is mine, Roland, and cannot, and would not if I could resemble yours or Jim's or John's or any one else[']s. . . .

As far as inclusion or exclusion is concerned I don't trust *any one's* opinion (Logan, an exception) but my own.

Sequence and arrangement are something else. . . .

As to the Robeson, it doesn't have as many problems as the Marianne Moore Baseball poem which to me has *never* come off properly. . . . I *may* make changes in the Robeson but there is a syllabic count control plus a forward thrust that I do not want to interfere with. I fully realize it is a *flawed* poem—but sometimes like the fault in a stone or the flaw in a person one fumbles with these flaws and faults—or cherishes them.

As to the dedication I shan't change my mind. The dedication is not to you as a poet (though you know I care greatly for your poetry) but it is to you as friend who helped me to survive the end of my marriage to Allen, the loss of both my children and the break-up with Gill not to mention the times in between.[115]

On November 14, 1979, she wrote James Wright: "I talked to Al Poulin today. He told me you had written words for me. Scared, happy, I said, 'please read them to me'—And dear Jim; I cried. The tears came out of joy. I began to feel that maybe the slight output of mine *does* add up to something to be proud of—anyway not to be embarrassed by."[116] Just a few weeks before he was diagnosed with the cancer of the tongue he was to die of the following spring, Wright had written: "Isabella Gardner's NEW AND SELECTED POEMS is a rare moral and artistic achievement. It contains work of unmistakable serenity and wholeness, in which the trendy and meretricious have no place. I am grateful for this triumphant book." [117]

Poulin was busy with all kinds of promotional activities, including a publication party on January 24, 1980, at the elegant intellectual bookstore Books & Co on Madison Avenue. But first Gardner had another party to attend, one hosted by President and Mrs. Jimmy Carter on January 3, "to honor Poetry and poets . . . at the White House." The *Washington Post* called it "one of the most enjoyable White House parties in recent memory" and *Poetry* "the most powerful concentration of American poetic talent ever assembled under one roof."[118] The literary world was also invited to the launch of *That Was Then*, from novelists Louis Auchincloss, John Gardner, Jean Stafford, and Kurt Vonnegut, to the critic Harold Bloom, to poets Anthony Hecht, James Meredith, and May Swenson, to new New York acquaintances Gerald Malanga and Erica Jong, and steadfast literary friends such as Eberhart, Herschberger, Kizer, Kunitz, Whittemore, and Robert Penn Warren, as well as, of course, Flint, Logan, Phillips, and Anne Wright. The celebration had to go on without its protagonist, however, as she had been rushed to hospital with cardiomyopathy that very same day. Mildred Baker reported blow-by-blow "on the day's happenings beginning with your sad departure on a stretcher bound for the hospital." She enumerated the participants, among them some of the above, Gardner's friends Pat Haskell and Frances Pole Sacco, Nancy Tate's daughter Amy Wood, the writers John Ashbery, William Cole, (belly-dancer) Daniela Gioseffi, Hannah Green, and Ned O'Gorman ("a great admirer of yours") as well as the artists Lillie Brody and Alan Davis. The appearance of famous singer and actress Kitty Carlisle Hart, the chair of the New York State Council of the Arts, was "amusing . . . with the young assistants of the bookshop, etc. suddenly crowding in to be photographed with her so that suddenly I was facing a row of backs." Gardner's sister Kitty called the next day and "was very perturbed that she had not come to the bookshop because she thought all parties had been cancelled," but Baker explained "that that would have been impossible because many had been invited and that you wanted a good showing for Al Poul[i]n and that there was indeed a good showing. . . . It was an impressive tribute to you and one not to be forgotten."[119]

That was not all, for there was a second party, four days later, at another cultural landmark, the Gotham Book Mart, about which Baker duly reported at length. Shortly thereafter she wrote to keep Gardner abreast of calls by concerned friends. Gardner had been at death's door, and after weeks in intensive coronary care went, at Silver's suggestion, to the chic Gramercy Park Hotel to recuperate with room service and rest rather than returning to the shabby Chelsea where troublesome Ed Berryman was at large. Her old friends supported Gardner by praising in their often reminiscent, nostalgic letters what mattered most: her new book of poetry. Frances Pole Sacco called *That Was Then* "an experience of joy and laughter weighted with an anchor of grief and anger. . . . Usually I avoid the word God. But I am so grateful for your gift to this world that I am urged to acknowledge the maker of life in some small way."[120] Helen Donohue Butler knew "what a fighter you are but you have been asked to survive too much for any person, so I fear for you. You are in my thoughts constantly—the happy days we spent (now, at last I have *time* to sit and remember) the parties—the riding around Bucks County."[121] The indefatigable mischievous Mary Manning—who was getting married again at 73 to "a Boston lawyer one Faneuil Adams. . . . He's 82 . . . so it isn't a boy and girl relationship"—wrote a second letter as she felt her first "was not nearly warm enough or admiring of your poems":

> I cried over That Was Then last night. All the memories that the words brought up. . . . My memories of you in Ireland, both you and Betty Stockton, the cocktail party in the Shelburne with Sam Beckett glowering, glass in hand. Then the Erskine Childers episode. J. J. O'Leary. Michael Mac Liammoir. All dead Belle, all dead. You coming to see us in Cambridge with Seymour. Rosie in Wellfleet talking to [my daughter] Fanny about her boy friend in who[se] arms she had been locked in the car: 'I[t's] all completely Platonic Fanny.' . . . You've known a great deal of tragedy Belle and I have too but nothing compared to you[rs], but you have also had intervals of wonderful happiness the few that are allowed us in this life. And you've been privileged in your friendships with poets and writers. You've had recognition. I think you are one of the most gifted American poets and I am not alone in this.[122]

Richard Eberhart wrote her that *That Was Then* "enthralled me, thrilled me and I lived totally in their extreme goodness for a day and night. What a grand book!"[123] Josephine Jacobsen "spent enrapt and envious hours going over and over it," admiring the "[m]usic, wit and pith" of this "stunning" book.[124] Novelist Hannah Green, an obsessive perfectionist, was stirred by "the passion and elegance" of Gardner's poetry, "the pure vibrant electric *life* of it" but had held off writing about *That Was Then* because she had been having "a bad time," tearing down her own book, *Little Saint,* instead of building it up: "I should have taught this semester but thought I'd finish book this spring. (Ha!)"[125] Karl Shapiro, a veritable bundle of contradictions who kept changing his passionately polemical mind about poets, poetry, and poetics, remained bracingly constant in his admiration for Gardner: *That Was Then* is "certainly what they call in the review world a Solid Achievement. You know my opinion of your poetry. This collection proves my opinion. I put it with E. Bishop and all the hooplah diving-in-the-wreck poets as one of the best, if not *the* best book of poems by any member of your or our generation. . . . It has a freshness that is very rare and hard to find in most modern work. . . . You have had such patience over the years about your work. I think it's your turn for a standing ovation."[126]

Tributes from her friends salved her soul, but Gardner wanted *That Was Then* reviewed and suggested bookshops and magazines for Poulin to approach, implying he had not done enough and that she would have done more but could not for she was "made to REST two hours of the day" as she still tired very easily. Nevertheless, she remained hopeful, even speaking of a future "small book of *ALL* new poems and as starters I've got the 3 that were too late for That Was Then."[127] Phillips commiserated with Poulin, who had pulled out all the stops to plug *That Was Then:* "As you know, one can start intending to do Belle Gardner [a] favor, and end up incurring her wrath."[128]

Phillips had written an early, commissioned essay for *Parnassus,* a nationally respected critical review; another was Jerome Mazzaro's inclusion of *That Was Then* in a survey of almost twenty poets in *Hudson Review,* in which he traced the, to him, overwhelming presence of influences and echoes, while describing her real achievement as "inventive and infectious ceremony."[129] There were the incidental reviews in local newspapers, such as Leon Driskell's in the *Louisville Courier* in which he praised Gardner's "fine poetic voice," feeling he was "being offered up a lifetime of experience—whole but maturing," but in all the book's reception was disappointing; Gardner's poetry seemed no longer seminal or central.[130] Gardner's luck changed in one stroke, however, with Vernon Young's admiring review in the *New York Times Book Review,* ending: "Substantial poetry, this. Nothing here of the characteristic feminine sensibility—which has its own taut appeal—in so many contemporary poems, a solipsistic or embattled voice. Isabella Gardner writes from the whole of her self; her subject is always *out there,* at the haunted center of our disappointed lives. To steal a line from Chorus, in Henry V, and shift its meaning: She pieces out our imperfections with her thoughts."[131]

William Smith then nominated *That Was Then* for *Poetry*'s Lenore Marshall Poetry Award, because "the poems give off those 'dark sounds' that Lorca said were the recognizable sign of any true work of art," because of their "strong appeal to the senses" and "extraordinary directness," but although the book was one of the finalists, the award went to *The Poems of Stanley Kunitz, 1928–1978.*[132] Much more gratifying was being recognized once more as a major presence in the American poetry world at large when *That Was Then* was nominated for the American Book Award. Of the more than forty thousand books published in 1980 in the United States, one thousand were submitted for consideration in different categories, ranging from autobiography to children's books, fiction and poetry, and out of these eighty were nominated for the final round. Gardner's competitors were Philip Booth, Lisel Mueller, Mark Strand, and Robert Penn Warren. She told Bonnie Nims she was "*happy* to have been nominated for the A.B.A. For so long so much could only silence me."[133] When the award went to Mueller she was sure Bonnie's husband, who was on the jury, had "wanted Lisel Mueller—anyway not me. To be expected—this way people can be sorry I didn't win, not sorry I *did!*" Nevertheless, the nomination had boosted her confidence: "Wish the P[ulitzer] prize had been in the cards. Twice I came close there."[134]

Gardner wrote this from Italy, where she had gone to be present at the opening of the first major show in years by Congdon who, like his cousin, had come to be regarded as a midcentury relic. Gardner's trip to Europe was in the spirit of reconciliation, for Congdon had wounded her severely when upon the loss of her father he had told her not to "grieve but to live the gift of your father's death," in essence saying that she should be glad because Peabo's passing had freed her.[135] Then, too, in his missives he had never even mentioned the murder of Daniel or the brutal sadomasochistic assault on Rose but had harped on in his insufferable, arrogant way about his celibate life in God, accusing Gardner of being a Jezebel and suggesting she should give up her wanton ways and live, like him, in chastity, as only then would her God-given talent return to her. Disenchanted, Gardner had virtually stopped writing him, but when Congdon asked her in 1979 to return his letters for his book *America Addio: Lettera a Belle* (1980) she obliged and forgave him: "Unlike you I am sustained by no faith; except the faith in those I've loved and will always love. You see, Billy, I love whom I love as *much* for their flaws as for their 'virtues.' I cannot *not* love you."[136] In as far as that was possible, Congdon was remorseful: "Your letter is such a radical recall to my conscience that the only real answer would be in my appearing at the Hotel Chelsea. You have forgiven me even before I 'confess.' . . . [Y]ou who profess no faith are this Misericordia to my 'heart of stone' . . . my crass indifference, fear to be entangled in the trials of others, hypocritical [ph]arisaic judge of others. It is the insensibility of the spirit: death, even before physical death occurs."[137]

Gardner begged her cousin, brother "semblable," not to castigate himself and referring to Unamuno's *Tragic Sense of Life* forgave him his narcissism. While she could understand his "reluctance to be involved in the pain and peril of others," such entanglement enabled her "to continue to feel engaged in being alive."[138] Most of his subsequent letters were as egocentric as ever, but Congdon did try harder, managing to keep his distance from Gardner's convoluted, chaotic, sensual life, while touching her spirit through apt quotations such as the following from Jacques Maritain, the central 1950s philosopher for converted American Catholics: "Poets are obliged to be at the same time at two different levels of the soul, out of their senses and rational, passively moved by inspiration and actively conscious, intent on an unknown, more powerful than they are which a sagacious operative knowledge must serve and manifest in fear and trembling. No wonder that they live in inner solitude and insecurity."[139]

Their renewed relationship stimulated Gardner to visit him in Italy for what she realized would be her last trip abroad, for though her doctors said she had made an "extraordinary recovery, much to their surprise. . . . they warn me it is a long time, if ever, before I am able to live as I did."[140] Gardner's doctors—and her mother—advised against air travel, but she was determined to go to Europe in the spring of 1981 to see Congdon and his show in Milan. Although he had not seen her in years, Congdon was self-centeredly afraid Gardner would trespass on his time, so she hastened to assure him that she intended to stay at the Pensione Annalena in Florence for old times' sake as well as visit friends and haunts in London; besides, she thought her translator Alfredo Rizzardi might arrange some poetry readings for her. (Rizzardi did not and later stood her up in Florence because he was ill.)

In the end, Gardner did not stay at Pensione Annalena, as she needed comfortable care because of her infirmity, and Annalena had no elevator and did not serve dinner. Instead she lived in monastic moderation on the fourth floor of a small pension, with only a narrow bed and a washbasin—not even a toilet or shower of her own. But she did not mind, she told her concerned mother, for "beautiful Billy, white haired, otherwise exactly as always, met me in Milan. It was a most loving reunion. . . . After 3 days he came to Florence and it was as though there'd been *no* years of not seeing each other."[141] Ed Berryman received a less censored version of her adventures: in typical Gardner fashion she had injured her back when stumbling out of the aircraft's lavatory and had hurt her (artificial) hip when she slipped on the marble floor of a bank in Florence. Besides, she was tired all the time because the elevator in her hotel was not working. Yet, in the quiet tranquility of her Florentine cell, she was so contented that Berryman, who missed her when he was sober, promised "[n]o more bickering from now on . . . or snide remarks to get a rise and a reaction from you. I shall be Mr. Agreeable himself. The original Yes Man. It will probably kill me but I'll try."[142]

The reconciliation with her blood cousin and soul mate after so many years brought Gardner some much-needed peace and a renewed sense of belonging to her family, even if it was only from the bonding of its two artistic reprobates. For Gardner had been hurt to the quick by her beloved banker brother George, her former beacon and mainstay. When George's son and namesake was about to be married, Gardner intended to take Raoul along to Roque, so that he could get to know his great-grandmother and other Gardner kin. George then explicitly refused to acknowledge Raoul as a member of the Gardner clan, stating peremptorily that Raoul was not welcome and besides, would not feel at home with the upscale Gardners anyway. Never had Gardner been so disappointed and furious with her brother:

Daddy would turn in his grave could he have heard you attempt to deny Raoul a visit to Roque while some of his cousins are there. I am deeply thankful that [other relatives] do not share your peculiar aversion to accepting Raoul as the member of the family that he *is*. He is a radiant, *bright,* loving and loveable child. . . .

Of *course* Helena and Seymour are in loco parentis and his immediate family. Helena and I consult about everything. She is a fine person, I like her, Raoul loves her and Seymour and their family. But he is aware of his other family, and so he should be. He loves me *very* much. It is hypocrisy of the worst kind to say it is "better" for Raoul not to be friendly with his cousins, aunts and uncles. . . .

To be illegitimate these days is neither shocking, disgraceful or *contagious.* My love for the brother of my heart, the soul of my childhood, I shall always love him with all my heart *and* soul. I do not love the brother who revealed himself at dinner and whose letter continues to reveal a brother I do not recognise. . . .

You know I am *not* speaking of money, or old school ties, or A.D. clubs or Christmas dinners. I speak of humanity.[143]

In one of the last poems she was to write, "Fly in Amber," she mixed her sorrow and anger about George's cold behavior with a forgiving farewell, but because she did not want to bare her wounds too openly, or wound her brother too deeply, she sought distance and refuge in myth as she had done at the beginning of her poetic career: "Myth tells us amber is the concretion / of tears wept by Meleager's sisters / before and after Artemis changed them / into long winged birds with horned beaks while they / mourned at Meleager's funeral pyre; / . . . Should a tear drop upon a leaf or an insect, on a fly, for instance / then that tear drop would lumpen into clear / amber and the fly would remain visibly / intact until Armageddon because / a dropped tear congealed an ambience to amber" (156). Flint thought it "The steepest / Song belle Bella ever made / . . . / Sheer at its edges and amber-hard," and Gardner submitted it together with the evocative "Eros in May at MacDowell" ("Shafts of lilac / arousing opening thrusting / heedlessly. / Never was I taken so / rashly and remembering / I nearly die! Again" [157].) to *Poetry.*[144] Nims failed her again, and Gardner burst out in fury: "If you read carefully the poems I've sent you, you would I think see that my voice never changes, but I *structure* each poem (cf. my Afterword to *That Was Then*) in accord with that which I wish to *say*. It astounds me that you rejected *Fly in Amber* which by any standard is equal to the best I've seen in your pages. No matter, I have now released us both. *I* am released from the unreasonable impulse to give *Poetry* first refusal. *You* are released from pondering ways in which to phrase your consistent rejections."[145]

In these last few months of her life, Gardner had finally come to believe that she was leaving a valuable, if small literary legacy and was looking forward to publishing a book of all new poems. She wrote more, because her ill health forced her to drink less, and appeared almost ethereal, as beautiful as before the alcohol had ravaged her face and figure. Yet, she realized that she was a very sick woman and updated her will (including generous gifts to Gill and his son Jimmie), decided who was going to inherit which of her artworks, and made Roland Flint her official literary executor. In her letters, she looked backward, wondering why she had not married her "delightful, brilliant Childers," mourning James Wright who had died in March 1980 ("I miss Jim terribly. He was very much a part of Allen's and my life in Minneapolis.") and remembering Van Kirk who had died half a year later.[146]

Gardner returned wholly worn out from her visit to Europe in May and told fellow resident Carol Bergé that she could not see her: "Right now I get exhausted if I talk on the *phone* for 2 minutes!"[147] In early June, Gardner was "just *hoping* I won't have to go to the hospital" and therefore did not "want to take house calls or incoming calls for a couple of weeks anyway."[148] Flint sent a concerned, gossipy note to Gardner: "I really don't have anything important to say; I just wanted to be in touch, to let you know I'm thinking about you and hope things are well, that you're feeling better already." "We had a nice visit with Annie; she seems to be adjusting well, and is full of plans for editions of Jim's work. . . . She likes to drink and I think feels unrestrained—released from temperance, maybe—without Jim's problem to worry about. Even so, I can't imagine her ever getting drunk."[149] Gardner received this letter in the hospital where she had been taken after all, shortly before being discharged against her will. She then again chose to convalesce at the Gramercy Park Hotel, away from that cesspool Chelsea and free of Berryman's drunken antics, watching the soap operas to which she had become addicted, but too bone-weary to see anyone. On July 7, 1981, Gardner died all alone in an impersonal hotel room, after years "of hurly-burly / . . . intolerably early," having lived, like her "Masked Shrew," a "*fastpaced gluttonous life.*"(9)

In his poem for Gardner, "Queen Anne's Lace," Robert Phillips commemorated: "Belle, hours before your death / you called and we spoke. Later / / I cried. You'd thanked me for what / I'd not remembered doing. Your purpose, / valedictory. You knew. That night / at the hotel, death gave room service."[150]

The next morning Baker called, and when Gardner did not pick up the phone, she alerted the authorities. Gardner was found in bed, reading glasses on her nose, apparently having died peacefully.[151] In Colombia for the making of his film *Ika Hands* (1988), Robert Gardner noted in his journal: "It has been more than a week since I put down any thoughts at all in a time of substantial change in my emotional status. One whole continent of love and care has sunk beneath the horizon with my sister Isabella's death. I learned of it on the night of July 12th from Adele when I called after flying to Cartagena from the Corazzi airstrip near Valledupar. Fulton and I had just come down the mountain. I was told she had died while reading. She always read, Belle did, to sleep and to death."[152]

Epilogue

Whereas Gardner's death seemed almost too serene to be in character, its aftermath was more appropriately muddled, chaotic, and scandalous. When Robert returned to the United States, he was called by his friend Viva, the Andy Warhol superstar, who told him that Gardner's apartment was being looted by other Chelsea residents and that he should come down to rescue the remaining artwork. He succeeded in salvaging David Rolt's London portrait of his sister, but much had disappeared. Most put it down to the routine pilfering by the junkies and prostitutes at the Chelsea Hotel, but some fingers pointed at Berryman, who needed money now that Gardner was no longer there to take care of him. Far away in California, Myra Cholden blamed the Gardners for not minding enough: "They had to come and get things, because otherwise Berryman would have sold everything. He had a key, he was untrustworthy and may have gotten away with a lot of things. The family, when they got the paintings, put them all in a garage, as if they had no value."[1] Gardner's third husband, Bob McCormick, was treated as indifferently, for the Gardners did not notify him of his ex-wife's death, and he only found out because one of his sisters happened to see the obituary notice in the *New York Times*. It quoted Gardner: "If there is a theme with which I am particularly concerned, it is the contemporary failure of love—the love which is the specific and particular recognition of one human being by another."[2]

The *Boston Globe* quoted Richard Eberhart: "She wrote of love and death with fervor and conviction in poems that have a quality of justice and truth" and referred to Gardner's belief in "the democracy of universal vulnerability."[3] The *Globe* announced that services for Gardner would be held in St. Mark's Episcopal Church in Southboro. On Monday, July 13, Gardner's friends gathered there for the last farewell. Roland Flint was determined to accompany Ed Berryman so he would not make a spectacle of himself but in the end had to leave him behind at the Chelsea, as he was far too drunk to attend. Even so, the Gardners and Gardner's friends remained worlds apart, in death as in life.

George had written a moving graveside prayer, in which he avowed that "if we did not seem to understand her sometimes, it was because her hopes and aims were so much higher than ours."[4] But in true Gardner fashion the family did not shed a tear and showed little feeling in public, which some of Gardner's friends took for indifferent coldness. Eric Stange, son of Bob and Pat Stange from Minneapolis, related that "Maurice Seymour and his wife were the only people who really showed emotion, especially his wife. . . . She just could not stop crying very loudly during the service and I thought: 'Thank God.'"[5] Afterward there was a lunch at Green Hill. Flint went but felt "they had tolerated me as a prole, one of Isabella's working class friends."[6] Riva Blevitsky, too, felt cold-shouldered and was shocked by what she perceived to be an unfeeling, indifferent ceremony, but Daniel Jones's memory was different: as a member of the upper class himself, he knew better how to assess its expressions, and in his perception everybody was in tears, if not visibly.

In February 1981, the New York State Council on the Arts had established the biennial New York State Walt Whitman Citation of Merit Award, in effect New York State's poet laureateship, with a prize of $10,000 and two readings. A jury consisting of Robert Bertholf, Thulani Davis, Virginia Elson, Jonathan Galassi, and May Swenson chose Gardner as its first recipient. With the publication of *That Was Then,* including almost twenty new poems, its being nominated for the American Book Award, and her election to the poet laureateship of New York all during her last days, the epitaph Gardner had written for herself in the 1960s had become a little less appropriate: "Gone not to God but to her Rest / Is one who never did her best."[7] Told in advance that she would be named the Whitman winner, Gardner had decided to give the $10,000 to Yaddo, New York's writers' colony. When she died, the jury decided to award the prize to Gardner posthumously, and May Swenson volunteered to give the two public readings. The *Rochester Democrat and Chronicle* was snide: "Gov. Hugh Carey has accepted the nomination of Isabella Stewart Gardner as New York state's first poet laureate, even though she is dead and out of print and from Boston, it has been learned."[8] The award was celebrated in March 1982, with Kitty Carlisle Hart giving a gracious speech and John Logan, inebriated, disgracing himself by badly slurring the poems he read.

There were two other readings in honor and memory of Gardner. One was put together by Anne Wright and Daniela Gioseffi at the Writers' Voice, at the West Side YMHA, and among the speakers were George Gardner, Hannah Green, John Logan, and Ned O'Gorman. Anne Wright spoke of Gardner's "courage and lack of self-pity when faced with tragedies in the lives of her son and daughter," of her being "a lady, white gloves and all, a woman of great dignity, sometimes curiously aloof, a loving person who stopped what she was doing to reach out when friends were troubled."[9] One of these friends, Robert

Phillips, was troubled, for he was asked only at the very last minute and therefore so miffed that he did not participate. He was present at the second, less formal memorial held at the library at Great Neck, New York, on Sunday April 4, 1982, organized by the poet Harriet Zinnes, where Roland Flint and Daniela Gioseffi also read and feelings ran high as the participants started gossiping and complaining about Gardner's imperiousness and then complained about each other's complaining.

It no longer touched Gardner, finally at rest in the small, very select graveyard reserved for Burnetts and Gardners behind St. Mark's Church. Years later George Gardner wrote Roland Flint:

> *Many* times during the year the spirit and image of Belle comes on strong. Just last week I was trying to cull through . . . my and her letters and photographs. Bitter sweet it was. And two weeks ago I revisited (as I often do) the small graveyard in Southboro, Mass where Belle and my mother and father are buried. A flat stone tablet spreads itself under an absolutely *giant* oak tree. It simply says

> In loving memory of
> Isabella Gardner
> POET[10]

Notes

Prologue

1. Marian Janssen, *The Kenyon Review (1939–1970): A Critical History.*
2. Wallace Stevens to Houghton Mifflin, March 13, 1955, copy in Isabella Gardner (IG) Papers (hereafter, unless otherwise indicated, correspondence may be found in the Isabella Gardner Papers); William Carlos Williams to Houghton Mifflin, January 13, 1955; Delmore Schwartz to Houghton Mifflin, n.d.
3. Sylvia Plath, *The Journals of Sylvia Plath,* ed. Ted Hughes and Frances McCullough, 211.
4. Isabella Gardner, "The Fellowship with Essence: Afterword," *The Collected Poems,* 161, 162.
5. The phrase was coined by her friend John Logan. See *A Ballet for the Ear: Interviews, Essays and Reviews,* edited by John Logan and A. Poulin Jr.
6. James Wright, "Gravity and Incantation," 424, 426.

Chapter One "The Walled Garden," 1915–1933

Unless otherwise indicated, Gardner's poems are from *The Collected Poems.* Page numbers and, where applicable, titles are cited parenthetically in the text.

1. IG to Julia Bartholomay, February 9, 1974.
2. Catherine Gardner Mayes to IG, January 14 [1972?].
3. George Peabody Gardner (father) to Isabella Stewart Gardner, September 7, 1915, Isabella Stewart Gardner Papers.
4. Interview with William Congdon, April 26, 1990.
5. IG to Percy Wood, July 7, 1975, Gordon Papers.
6. "George Peabody Gardner," speech by a fellow Taverner, May 2, 1977.
7. The Gardner genealogy is traced in Frank Augustine Gardner, *Gardner Memorial: A Biographical and Genealogical Record of the Descendants of Thomas Gardner, Planter.*
8. Ibid., 255.
9. Joseph J. Thorndike, "Mrs. Jack and Her Back Bay Palazzo," gives many amusing anecdotes.
10. Dixon Wecter, *The Saga of American Society: A Record of Social Aspiration 1607–1937,* 427; newspaper quotation, 349.
11. Louise Hall Tharp, *Mrs. Jack: A Biography of Isabella Stewart Gardner,* 290.
12. Ibid.
13. Cleveland Amory, *Who Killed Society?* 85.
14. Nelson W. Aldrich, *Old Money: The Mythology of America's Upper Class,* 52.
15. Francis Biddle, *A Casual Past,* 215.
16. Aldrich in *Old Money,* 38–39, opines that "Old Money Americans simply want to make themselves new in the most radical way a New World can imagine, by making themselves old. This requires long and intensive training. From dancing class to the varied 'lessons' of the country

club, the yacht club, and the Grand Tour, from Fay School to St. Paul's School to Harvard, from the Porcellian Club to the Somerset Club and the Knickerbocker Club, from the summer place at Northeast Harbor, Maine, to the winter place in the firm, at the bank, and, most important, 'on the board'—all these stations of Old Money life appear not only as constitutive of the class but instructive of it: as so many courses that have to be taken, so many credentials tested, so many qualifications proclaimed. Before it is a status, *while* it is a status, Old Money is composed of a curriculum."

17. George Peabody Gardner Jr., *Chiefly the Orient: An Undigested Journal,* 4.

18. Ibid., 124.

19. Ibid., 251.

20. Ibid., 371–72.

21. Ibid., 374.

22. Gilbert Hovey Grosvenor to George Peabody Gardner (father), June 8, 1951, Grosvenor Papers.

23. "'Roslyn,' A Newport Villa: The Summer Home of Mr. William Grosvenor, on Beacon Hill," 10.

24. "News of Newport: Tableaux Vivants at Casino Theater a Financial and Artistic Success"; "Newport Amateurs in a Wilde Play."

25. "Simplicity a Feature of the Wedding of Miss Harriot Daly and Count Anton Sigray Von Febre."

26. "Sidelights on the Smart Set."

27. "Grosvenor-Gardner Nuptials Expected."

28. "Sidelights on the Smart Set."

29. "Fashion's Fads and Fancies"; "Society at Home and Abroad."

30. Wecter, *Saga of American Society,* 268.

31. Catherine Gardner Mayes to IG, April 16 [1981].

32. Tharp, *Mrs. Jack,* 301.

33. George Peabody Gardner (brother) to IG, May 7 [1931]; George Peabody Gardner (brother) to IG, n.d. .

34. Tharp, *Mrs. Jack,* 309.

35. Ibid., 31.

36. George Peabody Gardner (father) to Isabella Stewart Gardner, March 13, 1920, Isabella Stewart Gardner Papers.

37. Interview with Robert Gardner, November 29, 1989.

38. Interview with Robert Gardner, June 22, 1990.

39. George Peabody Gardner (brother) to IG, May 7 [1931].

40. George Peabody Gardner (father) to Isabella Stewart Gardner, July 13, 1921, Isabella Stewart Gardner Papers.

41. As quoted by IG to Percy Wood, July 7, 1975, Gordon Papers.

42. Interview with Robert Gardner, June 22, 1990.

43. Interview with Anabel Holland, July 10, 1990.

44. Interview with George Peabody Gardner, November 19, 1989. This is Gardner's brother; her father died in 1976.

45. Interview with Robert Gardner, November 29, 1989.

46. Interview with Robert Gardner, September 27, 1989.

47. IG to Julia Bartholomay, February 9, 1974.

48. Tharp, *Mrs. Jack,* 88.

49. Eleanor Palffy, *Largely Fiction,* 305. Eleanor Palffy was born Eleanor Greene Roelker and was one of the many wives of the Hungarian Count Paul Palffy.

50. Interview with George Peabody Gardner, November 19, 1989.

51. John Peabody Monks, *Roque Island, Maine: A History,* ed. Diana Whitehill Laing, 4.

52. Interview with William Congdon, June 29, 1990.

53. Interview with Nina Herrick Kearns, January 14, 1990.

54. IG to Robert Gardner, August 3, 1974, Robert Gardner Private Collection.

55. IG to Robert Gardner and Lee Gardner, August 8, 1954, Robert Gardner Private Collection.

56. Interview with Rose Gardner Cutler, October 4, 1989.

57. Ibid.

58. Interview with Robert Gardner, December 6, 1990.

59. Interview with George Peabody Gardner, November 19, 1989.

60. "Welcome Home to Mum and Dad," manuscript, n.d. .

61. Interview with Nina Herrick Kearns, January 14, 1990.

62. Interview with Robert Gardner, June 22, 1990.

63. IG to George Peabody Gardner (brother), July 7, 1975; Vivian Cochrane Pickman, born Vivian Wessel, the daughter of a New York voice coach, was a minor actress. She married Alexander Lyndon Cochrane in August 1917. Cochrane died in 1928, and two years later she wedded another rich Boston bachelor, Dudley L. Pickman Jr. The time frame of her affair with Peabo Gardner is hard to determine.

64. IG to Robert Gardner, September 10 [1950s], Robert Gardner Private Collection.

65. Esmee Brooks to the author, March 25, 1991. Rose Grosvenor Gardner was Esmee Brooks's indifferent and scary godmother.

66. Katherine Gardner Herrick Coleman to IG, n.d. .

67. IG to Edward Dahlberg, June 27, 1958, Dahlberg Papers.

68. IG to George Peabody Gardner (brother), July 7, 1975.

69. Interview with Robert Gardner, June 22, 1990.

70. Interview with Mary Manning, September 20, 1989. Mary Manning explicitly referred to her first husband, Mark De Wolfe Howe, Harvard law professor and civil rights champion, and her daughters, the writers Fanny Howe and Susan Howe.

71. IG to George Peabody Gardner (brother), July 7, 1975.

72. Interview with Nina Herrick Kearns, January 14, 1990. George "Peabo" Gardner (Gardner's father) told her this story about his daughters; Kitty (Nina Kearns's mother) became a social hostess like Rose Gardner, Belle a poet, and Rose a nurse.

73. Interview with George Peabody Gardner, November 19, 1989.

74. Ibid.

75. Suzie Micklay to IG, April 5, 1955.

76. "Christmas Carol Christmas Card," manuscript [Christmas 1926], IG Papers.

77. "Epitaph to a Mouse," manuscript, n.d., IG Papers.

78. "Report of Isabella S. Gardner," Beaver County Day School, February 1930, IG Papers.

79. Interview with Rose Gardner Cutler, June 8, 1990.

80. In *Who Killed Society?* Amory calls Foxcroft "*the* of America's private girls' schools" (14).

81. Interview with Robert Gardner, November 29, 1989.

82. *Foxcroft Yearbook 1932,* 49.

83. Aldrich, *Old Money,* 92.

84. Joan Ryerson Brewster to the author, April 23, 1990.

85. Interview with Nina Herrick Kearns, January 14, 1990. Kearns attended Foxcroft in the late 1950s.

86. Wecter, *Saga of American Society,* 241.

87. Joan Ryerson Brewster to the author, April 23, 1990.

88. IG to Rose Grosvenor Gardner, January 31, 1931, George Peabody Gardner Private Collection.

89. IG to Richard Eberhart, April 26, 1956, Eberhart Papers.

90. IG to George Peabody Gardner (father), March 29, 1957, George Peabody Gardner Private Collection.

91. IG to George Peabody Gardner (father) and Rose Grosvenor Gardner, February 19, 1931.

92. Interview with Robert Gardner, November 29, 1989.

93. "I Am Alone upon a Bleak High Hill" won "First Prize—Older Girls' Poetry" and was published in the *Foxcroft Yearbook 1932,* 55.

94. "Portrait" won "Honorable Mention—Older Girls' Prose" and was published in the *Foxcroft Yearbook 1933*, 75.

95. Wecter, *Saga of American Society*, 188–91; Lawrence H. Officer and Samuel H. Williamson, "Purchasing Power of Money in the United States from 1774 to 2008," MeasuringWorth, 2009, convert the minimum lay out of $5,000 to, roughly, $75,000 in today's money, http://measuring worth.com/powerus/

96. Interview with Rose Gardner Cutler, June 8, 1990; certificate, comprehensive examination in English, College Entrance Examination Board, June 19–24, 1933. Gardner's result was 85. The year before, she had scored 70 in English, 34 in Latin, and 73 in French, George Peabody Gardner Private Collection; interview with Robert Gardner, November 29, 1989.

97. Betty Alden, "Beacon Hill," clipping, George Peabody Gardner Private Collection.

98. Marion Lyndon, "Dinner before Large Dance: Affair for 50 Guests to Precede Ball in Honor of Isabella Stewart Gardner—Mrs. Theodore E. Brown Also Entertaining."

99. [W.H.O.?], "Gossip of the Debs," clipping, George Peabody Gardner Private Collection.

100. Clipping; "Debutante Excels—In Role of Mannequin," clipping, George Peabody Gardner Private Collection.

101. Interview with Rose Gardner Cutler, June 8, 1990. Cutler thought he might later even have followed Gardner to Ireland.

102. Aldrich, *Old Money*, 240.

103. IG to George Peabody Gardner (brother), July 7, 1975.

104. Interview with Robert Gardner, June 22, 1990.

105. Roland Flint, in an interview on December 27, 1989, talked about the aluminized mittens; interview with Rose Gardner Cutler, June 8, 1990.

106. Some say she died.

107. Interview with Robert Gardner, June 22, 1990.

108. Ibid.

Chapter Two "Not at All What One Is Used To . . . ," 1934–1942

1. As Gardner was such an inexhaustible and loyal correspondent, usually pouring her heart out, it is striking that she does not mention this accident anywhere.

2. Interview with Robert Gardner, November 29, 1989.

3. Interview with Barbara Van Rensselaer Spalding, December 27, 1989.

4. May Sarton, *A World of Light: Portraits and Celebrations*, 89, 87, 91, 94, 99.

5. IG to Julia Bartholomay, February 9, 1974.

6. IG, "Book Report" on Booker T. Washington, *Up from Slavery*, January 15, 1935, George Peabody Gardner Private Collection; IG, "Book Report" on Mary Antin, *The Promised Land*, n.d., George Peabody Gardner Private Collection.

7. IG to Myra Cholden, February 21, n.y., Myra Cholden Brown Private Collection.

8. IG to Julia Bartolomay, February 9, 1974; in this light, it is the more surprising that Sarton regarded Kennedy as her poetic muse.

9. John Nichols Young, *Erskine H. Childers, President of Ireland: A Biography*, 32.

10. Andrew Boyle, *The Riddle of Erskine Childers*, 14.

11. Interview with Elizabeth Farley Stockton, October 13, 1989.

12. Elizabeth Farley, "A Lack of Decorum," manuscript, IG Papers.

13. Interview with Martin Manulis, August 27, 1990.

14. Ibid.

15. IG to Edward Dahlberg, January 26, 1958. The Sidhe are the fairy people of Irish folklore, and Oisin, Naoisi, and Cuchulain are magical Irish heroes. The books Gardner mentions all celebrate mythology: Robert Graves's influential *The White Goddess* (1948; the white goddess is celebrated as the patroness of the magic of poetry); Sir James George Frazer, *The Golden Bough* (1922); Jessie L. Weston, *From Ritual to Romance* (1921; influenced T. S. Eliot's 1922 *The Waste*

Land); Joseph Campbell's Jungian *The Hero with a Thousand Faces* (1949); and Daniel Garrison Brinton, *Myths of the New World* (1905; on Native American mythology).

16. Much of the information about Erskine Childers is from Young, *Erskine H. Childers.* The book concentrates on Childers's career, is adulatory and not very personal, yet succeeds in giving a sense of his magnetic personality. Gardner is not mentioned.

17. Ibid., 63.

18. Ibid., 32.

19. Ibid., 77.

20. Ibid., 52.

21. IG to Allen Tate, July 23, 1958; IG to Allen Tate, November 24 [1958]. Gardner seems to feel the need to assure Tate that she was not a fast young woman.

22. Interview with Mary Manning, November 11, 1989.

23. Eleanor Palffy to George Peabody Gardner (father) and Rose Grosvenor Gardner, May 27 [1935].

24. Eleanor Palffy to George Peabody Gardner (father) and Rose Grosvenor Gardner, June 18 [1935].

25. Seamus G. O. Ceallaigh, clipping, George Peabody Gardner Private Collection.

26. Farley, "Lack of Decorum."

27. Interview with George Peabody Gardner, November 19, 1989.

28. Interview with Elizabeth Farley Stockton, October 13, 1989.

29. Interview with Mary Manning, November 20, 1989; Liddy James to IG, April 29, 1969.

30. Telegram, George Peabody Gardner (father) to IG, July 24, 1936, George Peabody Gardner Private Collection.

31. IG to Allen Tate, November 16, 1958.

32. Interview with Martin Manulis, August 27, 1990; the writer H. E. F. Donohue, himself Irish American, was also sure.

33. Maurice Donohue to the author, May 4, 1990.

34. J[oan] Ryerson, "Dramatic Notes," *Foxcroft Yearbook 1932,* 36.

35. Alice Hegan Rice's *Mrs. Wiggs of the Cabbage Patch* was made into a movie starring Pauline Lord and W. C. Fields in 1934.

36. "Junior Leaguer Is Cockney Maid of 'Blithe Spirit,'" clipping [1942], George Peabody Gardner Private Collection.

37. Wecter, *Saga of American Society,* 329.

38. "Dramatic Club Names 'Wind and Rain' Cast." I have not been able to find an "Erskine School of Acting" and suspect Gardner was joking.

39. Isabella Gardner to Julia Bartholomay, February 9, 1974.

40. IG to Robert Gardner and Lee Gardner, n.d., Robert Gardner Private Collection.

41. Leighton Rollins School of Acting is also (indiscriminately) named the Rollins Studio of Acting, the Leighton Rollins Studio, and the Rollins Studio.

42. Much of the information about Leighton Rollins in this paragraph is from Kenneth A. Brown, "Gathering to Celebrate the Art of Leighton Rollins' Life."

43. Ibid.

44. Enez Whipple, "Remembering Mary Woodhouse," 22–23.

45. According to Officer and Williamson, "Purchasing Power," $200 would be around $3,000 now and the $18.50 for room and board would convert to about $280.

46. Sean Axmaker, "Stewart Stern: The Storyteller," http://www.greencine.com/article?action =view&articleID=298

47. Dorothy Quick, "Theater on Huntting Lane—The Leighton Rollins School of Acting," 33, 38. Quick's article originally appeared in *Long Island Forum* in June 1941.

48. *Playhouse 90* won six Emmy Awards in 1956 and was still mentioned in *TV Guide 2002*'s top fifty greatest television shows. Information mainly from Martin Douglas, "Martin Manulis, TV Pioneer, Dies at 92."

49. Interview with Martin Manulis, August 27, 1990.

50. Patrick Troughton was Dr. Who from 1966 to 1969.

51. Interview with Martin Manulis, August 27, 1990.

52. Maurice Donohue to the author, March 28, 1990. Henry Levin also worked with, for instance, Charles Coburn, Connie Francis, Anthony Perkins, Jill St. John, Clifton Webb, and Jane Wyman.

53. Ibid.

54. Interview with Martin Manulis, August 27, 1990; see also Diana Rico, *Kovacsland: A Biography of Ernie Kovacs.*

55. The Finch School for Girls was located on East 78th Street and was one of the most famous finishing schools in the country. In 1937 the school became Finch Junior College, and in 1952 Finch College, a four-year college. It remained all-female. Arlene Francis, Suzanne Pleshette, and Patricia Nixon are among its well-known alumnae. Finch College closed in 1975.

56. IG to Julia Bartholomay, February 9, 1974.

57. Interview with Martin Manulis, August 27, 1990.

58. Ibid.

59. Ibid.

60. IG to Robert Gardner and Lee Gardner [ca. 1954], Robert Gardner Private Collection.

61. "Studio Group Gives Pleasing 'Stunt Night,'" 79; see also Rico, *Kovacsland.*

62. Interview with Frances Pole Sacco, February 22, 1990.

63. Interview with Maurice Donohue, December 30, 1989; interview with Martin Manulis, August 27, 1990; interview with Mary Manning, November 20, 1989.

64. Joan Larkin to the author, April 16, 1990.

65. Anabel Holland to the author, January 17, 1995.

66. Interview with Martin Manulis, August 27, 1990.

67. Interview with Frances Pole Sacco, February 22, 1990.

68. Maurice Donohue to the author, May 4, 1990.

69. IG to Robert Gardner and Lee Gardner, January 17, 1956, Robert Gardner Private Collection.

70. Interview with Martin Manulis, August 27, 1990.

71. IG to George Peabody Gardner (father) and Rose Grosvenor Gardner [ca. October 1937], George Peabody Gardner Private Collection.

72. IG to George Peabody Gardner (father) and Rose Grosvenor Gardner, December 26 [1937], George Peabody Gardner Private Collection.

73. Ibid.

74. IG to Julia Bartolomay, February 9, 1974.

75. Maurice Donohue to the author, May 4, 1990.

76. IG to Carol Bergé, n.d., Bergé Papers. Childers's last—rather impersonal—letter to IG dates from December 20, 1973, the year before he died.

77. Leighton Rollins was to arrange Henry Jesson's wartime letters to him in *And Beacons Burn Again: Letters from an English Soldier.*

78. Interview with Patricia Haskell, March 6, 1990.

79. Interview with Frances Pole Sacco, February 22, 1990.

80. Enez Whipple, *Guild Hall of East Hampton,* 141–42.

81. In my interview with Frances Pole Sacco, February 22, 1990, she explicitly mentioned Ayers and Manulis, but implied that there were a number of others who were bisexual.

82. Quoted in Rico, *Kovacsland,* 20.

83. Interview with Maurice Donohue, December 30, 1989. Donohue refers to Feodor Ivanovich Chaliapin, the famous twentieth-century Russian singer, who established the tradition of naturalistic acting in opera.

84. Interview with Harry Holland, March 22, 1990.

85. Interview with Maurice Donohue, December 30, 1989.

86. Ibid.

87. Ibid.

88. Ibid.

89. Interview with Martin Manulis, August 27, 1990.

90. Interview with Frances Pole Sacco, February 22, 1990.

91. Interview with Harry Holland, March 22, 1990.

92. Interview with Martin Manulis, August 27, 1990.

93. Interview with Maurice Donohue, December 30, 1989; interview with Robert Gardner, September 27, 1989.

94. "Isabella Gardner Weds in November," clipping, George Peabody Gardner Private Collection.

95. Rico in *Kovacsland*: "Van Kirk would surprise everybody when he ran off with one of the East Hampton students, Isabella Stewart Gardner, who came from a wealthy Boston family. The elopement caused a bit of a scandal because of the difference in their ages and because of the clear-cut hierarchy that existed between students and teachers at the time" (26). Rico is the only one to mention an elopement, while the hierarchy between teachers and their older students was not as clear-cut as Rico has it.

96. "Brookline Girl to Wed Mr. Herrick."

97. Interview with Rose Gardner Cutler, December 2, 1989.

98. Officer and Williamson, "Purchasing Power," convert $60 in 1939 to, roughly, $930 in 2008.

99. In legal documents the names of the children are given as Annike and Jan, however, in the general correspondence we find Anneke (sometimes Anni) and Peter.

100. Interview with Maurice Donohue, December 30, 1989.

101. Notebook, 1939–1941, IG Papers.

102. Officer and Williamson, "Purchasing Power," convert $10,000 in 1939 to, roughly, $155,000 in 2008.

103. IG to George Peabody Gardner (father) and Rose Grosvenor Gardner, postmark January 17, 1939; Robert Briffault's book on Great Britain, published in 1938, was a vehement denunciation of that country; his *Europa* was published in 1936.

104. Harold Van Kirk, draft letter to friends, March 24, 1939, and "Thoughts while en route from Beaulieu to Genoa," IG Papers.

105. Ibid.

106. IG to Helen Machat [1939], in the author's possession.

107. Harold Van Kirk, draft letter to friends, March 24, 1939, and "Thoughts while en route from Beaulieu to Genoa," IG Papers.

108. Ibid.

109. Interview with Maurice Donohue, December 30, 1989.

110. G.F.C., "The Festival Theatre: 'See Naples and Die.'"

111. Harold Van Kirk to IG, August 28, 1976.

112. Maurice Donohue to the author, June 7, 1990.

113. "For Peter" and "For Anni" are unpublished poems in the IG Papers.

114. Interview with Frances Pole Sacco, February 22, 1990.

115. Interview with Harry Holland, March 22, 1990.

116. Mary Manning to Orson Welles, June 7, n.y. .

117. Telephone interview with Frances Pole Sacco, February 14, 1990.

118. IG to George Peabody Gardner (father) and Rose Grosvenor Gardner, postmark March 26, 1941.

119. Ibid.

120. Elinor Hughes, "The Theater"; "Comedy Opens at Bass Rocks," clipping, IG Papers.

121. *The Hottentot* is now mainly remembered for its musical film version, *Going Places* (1939), because Ronald Reagan played the role of Jack Withering; "Junior Leaguer Is Cockney Maid of 'Blithe Spirit,'" clipping, IG Papers.

122. "Junior Leaguer Is Cockney Maid of 'Blithe Spirit,'" clipping, IG Papers.

123. Telegram, Harold Van Kirk to IG, February 17, 1942.

124. Charles Gentry, "Coward Comedy Is Tops," clipping, IG Papers.

125. Harold V. Cohen, "Blithe Are Spirits of Mr. Coward," clipping, IG Papers.

126. Fremont Power, "Voice from the Balcony," clipping, IG Papers.

127. Ashton Stevens, "Mr. Coward and Some High Spirits," clipping, IG Papers.

128. "To Join Coward Show," 11, 23.

129. Telegram, Harold Van Kirk to IG, June 29, 1942.

130. The Internet Broadway Database mentions: "The play took a summer rest in July 1942, then resumed." It closed on June 5, 1943. http://www.ibdb.com/production.asp?id=1127

131. Gene Martel to IG, July 27, 1942.

132. Officer and Williamson, "Purchasing Power," convert this to about $500 in 2008.

133. Telegram, Harold Van Kirk to IG, October 6, 1942; telegram, Anneke Van Kirk to IG, October 6, 1942.

134. "Film Stars Seen in One-Act Plays," clipping, IG Papers.

135. "Three Curtains," clipping, IG Papers.

136. Ford's Theatre is the site of the assassination of Abraham Lincoln; Gilbert Kanour, "Gloria Swanson, Francis Lederer at Ford's in 'Three Curtains,'" clipping, IG Papers.

137. Interview with H. E. F. Donohue, February 24, 1990; interview with Barbara Van Rensselaer Spalding, December 27, 1989; interview with Harry Holland, March 22, 1990.

138. There are many different stories about this incident. In an interview on December 27, 1989, Barbara Van Rensselaer Spalding remembered the hole in the molding and Van Kirk's explanation; another story is that Van Kirk shot a towel instead of himself.

139. Interview with Frances Pole Sacco, February 22, 1990.

140. Interview with Martin Manulis, August 27, 1990.

141. Anneke Van Kirk to IG, n.d. .

142. Peter Van Kirk to IG [January 12, 1952]. Peter Van Kirk, who was not very literate, actually wrote "couldn't have stayed together," but it is apparent from the context of this—as well as the following—letter what he means; Peter Van Kirk to IG, n.d. .

143. Peter Van Kirk to IG [May 1965].

144. Peter Van Kirk to IG, n.d. .

145. Lance Morrow, *The Chief: A Memoir of Fathers and Sons,* 43, 44, 7, 133, 108.

146. Interview with H. E. F. Donohue, February 24, 1990.

147. IG to Robert Gardner, January 27, postmark 1956, Robert Gardner Private Collection.

148. IG to Myra Cholden, September 29, 1960, Myra Cholden Brown Private Collection.

149. Interview with Barbara Van Rensselaer Spalding, December 27, 1989.

Chapter Three "Shapiro Shangri La," 1943–1949

1. IG to Helen Machat Donohue, postmark April 12, 1944, in the author's possession. Van Kirk and Vickers broke off in the spring of 1944.

2. Interview with Frances Pole Sacco, February 22, 1990.

3. Harold Van Kirk to IG, May 15, 1964.

4. Harold Van Kirk to IG, n.d. .

5. Harold Van Kirk to IG [August 28, 1976].

6. Julie Van Kirk to IG, January 22, 1974.

7. Interview with Maurice Seymour, May 31, 1990.

8. Interview with Maglet Myrhum, January 11, 1990.

9. Interview with Maurice Seymour, May 31, 1990. Chez Paree was a famous downtown Chicago nightclub, popular with underworld figures.

10. Interviews with Sydney Seymour Fingold, October 6, 1989 and with Maurice Seymour, June 1, 1990. Seymour just briefly touched upon his background in Bessarabia, while Sydney Seymour Fingold, his daughter, gave more detailed information. The two stories do not quite

match, as Seymour mentioned that his mother had left for America with her husband and two daughters, while Fingold is sure she stayed in Khotin.

11. Interview with Maurice Seymour, June 1, 1990.

12. Interview with Sydney Seymour Fingold, October 6, 1989.

13. Interview with Maurice Seymour, May 31, 1990. The four languages Seymour spoke probably were Yiddish, Hebrew, Moldavian, and Russian.

14. Interview with Maurice Seymour, May 31, 1990.

15. According to Officer and Williamson, "Purchasing Power," convert $12 in 1924 to, roughly, $150 in 2008.

16. Interview with Maurice Seymour, May 31, 1990.

17. Jack Mitchell, "Capturing Emotion In Motion: Photographing Ballet Dance," *Dance Magazine,* December 1999, http://findarticles.com/p/articles/mi_m1083/is_12_73/ai_58050370/.

18. Maurice Seymour, "Introduction," *Seymour on Ballet: 101 Photographs,* no page number.

19. Interview with Anabel Holland, July 10, 1990.

20. Interview with Daniel Jones, September 22, 1989; Jean Burden to the author, July 14, 1989. Seymour took pictures of her after she graduated from the University of Chicago.

21. Interview with Maurice Seymour, June 1, 1990.

22. Interview with Maurice Seymour, May 31, 1990.

23. Ibid.; in an interview, April 26, 1990, William Congdon called his own mother, Caroline Grosvenor, and his aunt Rose Grosvenor (Gardner's mother) "ice-cubes."

24. Riva Blevitsky Berkovitz to the author, July 23, 1991.

25. Interview with Riva Blevitsky Berkovitz, October 18, 1992.

26. Interview with Patricia Haskell, March 6, 1990.

27. Interview with Maurice Seymour, May 31, 1989.

28. Ibid.

29. Aldrich, *Old Money,* 277.

30. Peter Chapman, *Bananas: How the United Fruit Company Shaped the World,* 102, 95.

31. Interview with Barbara Van Rensselaer Spalding, December 27, 1989.

32. Interview with Maurice Seymour, June 1, 1990.

33. Interview with John Gardner, September 19, 1989.

34. Interview with Maurice Seymour, May 31, 1990.

35. Ibid.

36. "Becomes Bride Today."

37. Interview with Sydney Seymour Fingold, October 6, 1989.

38. Ibid. The Van Gogh was probably "The Italian Woman with Carnations" (1887) or "Madam Roulin Rocking the Cradle" (1889).

39. Interview with Frances Pole Sacco, February 22, 1990.

40. Ibid.

41. Interview with Riva Blevitsky Berkovitz, October 18, 1992.

42. Interview with Maurice Seymour, June 1, 1990.

43. Ibid.; their friend Victor Weisskopf was not the Manhattan Project physicist.

44. Interview with Riva Blevitsky Berkovitz, October 18, 1992.

45. Ibid.; interview with Sydney Seymour Fingold, October 6, 1989.

46. Interview with Maurice Seymour, May 31, 1990.

47. Ibid. During part of this interview Daniel Jones and Robert Gardner were also present and participated. After his stint with Seymour, Daniel Jones worked with another famous photographer, Nicholas Murray. He went on to cooperate on the successful NBC *Victory at Sea* documentary television series about naval warfare in World War II, which was aired in 1952 and 1953, parts of which can now be seen on YouTube. For much of his working life he was the photography curator at the Peabody Museum of Archaeology and Ethnology at Harvard University.

48. Interview with Daniel Jones, September 22, 1989.

49. Ibid.

50. Daniel Jones was present during the interview with Maurice Seymour on May 31, 1990, and now and then interjected some remarks; interview with Daniel Jones, September 22, 1989.

51. Interview with Daniel Jones, September 22, 1989; Edward Stern worked with Joseph Epstein, also a big Chicago betting commissioner. Their gambling offices were at 10 North Clark Street, close to the St. Clair Hotel. Others in their circle were Jack Terman, Julius Horwick, and James Mondi; the latter used to be a big shot in Al Capone's Chicago gambling empire.

52. Interview with Daniel Jones, September 22, 1989.

53. Ibid.

54. Ibid.

55. Interview with Maurice Seymour, May 31, 1990.

56. Interview with Daniel Jones, September 22, 1989.

57. Ibid.

58. Riva Blevitsky Berkovitz to the author, July 23, 1991.

59. The confusion exists to this day: not many people in the photography world know that "Maurice Seymour" used to be two brothers.

60. Interview with Myra Cholden Brown, August 26, 1990.

61. Ibid.

62. Ibid.

63. Interview with Anabel Holland, July 10, 1990.

64. Interview with Riva Blevitsky Berkovitch, October 18, 1992; interview with Anabel Holland, July 7, 1990.

65. Interview with Myra Cholden Brown, August 26, 1990.

66. Ibid.

67. Ibid.

68. Interview with Maurice Seymour, June 1, 1990.

69. IG to Jay Bolotin, April 4, 1976, Bolotin Private Collection.

70. Telephone interview with Harry Holland, March 22, 1990.

71. Interview with Patricia Haskell, March 6, 1990.

72. Interview with H. E. F. Donohue, February 2, 1990.

73. Interview with Patricia Haskell, March 6, 1990.

74. Riva Blevitsky Berkovitz to the author, April 21, 1991.

75. Interview with Riva Blevitsky Berkovitz, October 18, 1992.

76. IG to Helen Machat Donohue, n.d., in the author's possession.

77. IG to Helen Machat Donohue, August 4, 1944, in the author's possession. The books Gardner mentions are Lillian Smith, *Strange Fruit* (1944); Victor Francis White, *Peter Domanig: Morning in Vienna* (1944); and Arthur Koestler, *Darkness at Noon* (1944); "the Jules Romains" probably is his *The Death of a Nobody* published by Knopf in 1944.

78. Interview with Daniel Jones, September 22, 1989; interview with Patricia Haskell, March 6, 1990.

79. Interview with Daniel Jones, September 22, 1989.

80. Interview with Myra Cholden Brown, August 26, 1990.

81. William V. McDermott, *A Surgeon in Combat: European Theatre—World War II Omaha Beach to Ebensee 1943–1945,* 261–62.

82. Saul Bellow in a letter to Cynthia Ozick written in the late 1980s. Quoted in James Atlas, *Bellow: A Biography,* 247.

83. Interview with Myra Cholden Brown, August 26, 1990.

84. Interview with Daniel Jones, September 22, 1989.

85. Interview with Anabel Holland, July 10, 1990.

86. Interview with Myra Cholden Brown, August 26, 1990; quoted in Michael Wreszin, *A Rebel in Defense of Tradition: The Life and Politics of Dwight Macdonald,* 243.

87. Interview with Anabel Holland, July 10, 1990.

88. IG to Julia Bartholomay, February 9, 1974.

89. Ibid.

90. Strephon Williams to IG, November 24, 1964.

91. Interview with Richard Eberhart, October 25, 1989.

92. Many of his anthologies are still in print, and during his lifetime his books sold over two million copies.

93. The quotations are from an unpublished manuscript, "The Death of Oscar Williams," by Strephon Williams, IG papers. See also www.oscarwilliams.dreamwork2000.com/oscarwilliams/oscarwilliams.html

94. Richard Eberhart to IG, January 17, 1965.

95. Conrad Aiken to IG, February 20, 1965; Aiken wrote on the same day to Edward Burke: "That terrible Isabella Tate is having a Memorial Reading for Oscar next week, and wanted a limerick. What an idea." Joseph Killorin, ed., *Selected Letters of Conrad Aiken,* 320.

96. Karl Shapiro to IG, December 6, 1957.

97. Isabella Gardner, draft of a memorial tribute to Oscar Williams, IG Papers.

98. Oscar Williams to IG, January 29, 1949.

99. Oscar Williams to IG, July 16, 1949.

100. IG to Riva Blevitsky Berkovitz, n.d.; there may be some inaccuracies in this and the following quotes from this letter, as Riva Berkovitz read it aloud to the author during their interview on October 18, 1992, paraphrasing here and there as this was a letter that Gardner had asked her to burn.

101. Interview with Anabel Holland, July 10, 1990.

102. Interview with Maurice Seymour, May 31, 1990; interview with Riva Blevitsky Berkovitz, October 18, 1992.

103. Riva Blevitsky Berkovitz to the author, April 21, 1991.

104. IG to Riva Blevitsky Berkovitz, n.d., interview with Berkovitz, October 18, 1992.

105. Riva Blevitsky Berkovitz to the author, July 23, 1991.

106. Interview with Jean Gould, February 26, 1990. Gould had interviewed Gardner for her *American Women Poets: Pioneers of Modern Poetry.*

107. IG to Riva Blevitsky Berkovitz, n.d., interview with Berkovitz October 18, 1992.

108. Interview with Daniel Jones, September 22, 1989.

109. Interview with Maurice Seymour, May 31, 1990.

110. Edith Tarkov to IG, n.d. .

111. Interview with Anabel Holland, July 10, 1990.

112. Interview with Maurice Seymour, June 1, 1990.

113. IG to Riva Blevitsky Berkovitz, n.d., interview with Berkovitz, October 18, 1992. During that interview Berkovitz added: "But what you do not know and what I am not telling you until Seymour dies is what he said to her, the counter-threats and that is why she went, because of the threat that he would, you know, that is why she did not want the family to know, she told me, but not my mother, not my sisters." I still do not know the exact nature of his threats.

114. Interview with Maurice Seymour, June 1, 1990. The "Agreement between Maurice Seymour and Isabella Gardner Seymour," dated February 16, 1950, was actually signed in Chicago, IG Papers.

115. "Seeks Divorce," 5.

116. "Decree Granted."

117. "Agreement between Maurice Seymour and Isabella Gardner Seymour," February 16, 1950, IG Papers.

118. Riva Blevitsky Berkovitz to the author, April 21, 1991.

119. Interview with Maurice Seymour, May 31, 1990.

120. Riva Blevitsky Berkovitz to the author, July 23, 1991; it should be noted that Maurice Zeldman was better at more demure portrait photography than Seymour.

121. Interview with Sydney Seymour Fingold, October 6, 1989.

122. Ibid. Fingold celebrated her fiftieth wedding anniversary in 2008.

123. Interview with Riva Blevitsky Berkovitz, October 18, 1992.

124. Riva Blevitsky Berkovitz to the author, April 21, 1991.

125. IG to Robert Gardner, September 20, 1956, Robert Gardner Private Collection.

126. Interview with Anabel Holland, July 10, 1990.

Chapter Four "Writing Poetry," 1950–1954

1. IG to Riva Blevitsky Berkovitz, n.d., interview with Berkovitz, October 18, 1992.

2. William Congdon to IG, March 18,1950, Congdon Foundation Papers.

3. IG to William Congdon, June 1, 1955, Congdon Foundation Papers.

4. Interview with William Congdon, April 26, 1990.

5. Robert Gardner to IG, February 14, 1956.

6. IG to Robert Gardner, February 2, 1956, Robert Gardner Private Collection.

7. IG to Robert Gardner, February 29, 1956, Robert Gardner Private Collection.

8. Interview with William Congdon, April 26, 1990.

9. William Congdon to IG, January 5, 1955, Congdon Foundation Papers.

10. William Congdon to IG, August 30, 1955, Congdon Foundation Papers.

11. IG to Robert Gardner, February 17, 1956, Robert Gardner Private Collection.

12. Gardner wrote "in Am. Mercury and first published poem" on the typescript of "Triolet" in the IG Papers, but I have not been able to find the exact reference.

13. Isabella Gardner, "Folkways," *Furioso* 6, no. 1 (winter 1951): 20. Gardner did not include "Folkways" in her books; it finally appeared in the posthumous *Collected Poems;* "Homo Gratia Artis," *Furioso* 6, no. 4 (fall 1951): 47.

14. IG, "Postillion for Pegasus," manuscript enclosed in IG to Karl Shapiro, October 15, 1956, Shapiro Private Collection. As "Postillion for Pegasus" was meant to generate money for *Poetry,* Gardner crossed out "the shrieking slashed throats of pigs, the mooning moos of stunned huge cattle" and replaced it with Upton Sinclair's *The Jungle.*

15. IG to Herman Kogan, October 6 [1963].

16. George Anastoplo, "Maurice F. X. Donohue, 1911–1995," 16.

17. Ibid.

18. Interview with H. E. F. Donohue, February 24, 1990.

19. Maurice Donohue warned me before my visit to interview him in his house in a small town in West Virginia that he was suffering from several illnesses and that he tired easily. In the end, it was I who had to beg for breaks, as his hyperintelligent stream of consciousness was exhausting.

20. Telephone interview with Fanita English, December 26, 1989.

21. Interview with Helen Drutt English, July 8, 1990.

22. Maurice English to IG, October 23, 1979.

23. Telephone interview with Fanita English, December 26, 1989.

24. Ibid.

25. Robert Gardner, unpublished speech for "The Other Isabella: Isabella Gardner, The Poet (1915–1981)," symposium at the Isabella Stewart Gardner Museum, April 12, 2007.

26. Much of the information about Robert Gardner is from his website, http://www.robert gardner.net/

27. Robert Gardner, unpublished speech for "The Other Isabella: Isabella Gardner, The Poet (1915–1981)," symposium at the Isabella Stewart Gardner Museum, April 12, 2007.

28. Robert Gardner did release *Dances of the Kwakiutl* (1951), a short film composed of fragments of "cannibal dancing" made in collaboration with William Heick.

29. IG to Myra Cholden, August 16, 1957, Myra Cholden Brown Private Collection.

30. T. S. Eliot to IG, October 19, 1950.

31. "R. H. McCormick III Sued by Wife for Desertion."

32. Interview with Robert McCormick, October 20 and 21, 1989.

33. Ibid.

34. Judith Cass, "Miss Bersbach Bride of Young R. H. McCormick."

35. Interview with Maurice Donohue, December 30, 1989.

36. Al Chase, "Twin Co-op Apartments Are Planned."

37. Interview with Patricia Haskell, March 6, 1990.

38. Interview with Robert McCormick, October 20 and 21, 1989.

39. Ibid.

40. Interview with Rose Gardner Cutler, October 10, 1989.

41. Judith Cass, "Mrs. Seymour to Wed R. H. McCormick III."

42. Eleanor Page, "Junior League to Hear Tutor of Princess."

43. Interview with Robert McCormick, October 20 and 21, 1989.

44. Interview with Robert Gardner, September 27, 1989.

45. Interview with Anabel Holland, July 10, 1990; interview with Myra Cholden Brown, August 26, 1990.

46. Interview with Maurice Donohue, December 30, 1989; before my interview with Robert McCormick his wife, Mary, whispered: "I hope you can get him to talk."

47. William Congdon to IG, December 3 [1954?], Congdon Foundation Papers.

48. The house was finished in 1953; it was moved from 299 Prospect Street in Elmhurst to the new Elmhurst Art Museum in 1994.

49. Interview with Patricia Haskell, March 6, 1990.

50. IG to Robert Gardner, February 1, 1955, Robert Gardner Private Collection.

51. Interview with Robert McCormick, October 20 and 21, 1989.

52. IG to Theodore Roethke, December 16 [1953], Roethke Papers.

53. Karl Shapiro to IG, quoted in her "Postillion for Pegasus," in IG to Karl Shapiro, October 15, 1956, Shapiro Private Collection; Gardner's poems were "The Panic Vine," "Cadenza," "The Last Trump," and "Cowardice."

54. M. L. Rosenthal, *Poetry* 151, no. 1–2 (1987): 218.

55. IG, "Postillion for Pegasus," in IG to Karl Shapiro, October 15, 1956, Shapiro Private Collection; Karl Shapiro, *Reports of My Death,* 58.

56. IG to Julia Bartholomay, February 9, 1974; IG, "Postillion for Pegasus," in IG to Karl Shapiro, October 15, 1956, Shapiro Private Collection.

57. Shapiro, *Reports of My Death,* 59; IG to Lee Gardner, March 18, 1955, Robert Gardner Private Collection.

58. IG to Robert Gardner, n.d., Robert Gardner Private Collection.

59. Shapiro, *Reports of My Death,* 59.

60. Ibid., 58.

61. Modern Poetry Association, minutes of the meeting of trustees, October 20, 1951, Modern Poetry Association Papers.

62. Modern Poetry Association, minutes, June 14, 1954, Modern Poetry Association Papers. In the end, thanks to its new president, Stanley Pargellis, *Poetry* moved to the rent-free attic of the new Newberry Library, of which he was the head librarian.

63. Shapiro, *Reports of My Death,* 58.

64. Karl Shapiro to Nicholas Joost and Sue Neil, March 5, 1954, *Poetry* Papers.

65. Patricia Hancock, "Dream House of Tomorrow: Is This It?"

66. Julia Bartholomay, "These Island Citadels," unpublished speech, January 25, 1978, Winnetka Fortnightly Papers.

67. Shapiro, *Reports of My Death,* 59.

68. Interview with Robert Phillips, February 28, 1990.

69. Shapiro, *Reports of My Death,* 37.

70. Karl Shapiro, *In Defense of Ignorance,* 128.

71. Interview with Karl Shapiro, August 18, 1990.

72. Shapiro, *Reports of My Death,* 71.

73. Modern Poetry Association, report of the editor to the trustees [1952], Modern Poetry Association Papers.

74. Interview with Karl Shapiro, February 20, 1990.

75. IG to Robert Gardner and Lee Gardner, Christmas 1954, Robert Gardner Private Collection.

76. John Logan to IG, January 26, 1953.

77. John Logan, "Spring Chill," *Poetry* 81, no. 6 (1953): 350–51.

78. IG to Karl Shapiro, May 21, 1956, Shapiro Private Collection.

79. Gardner's "The Fellowship with Essence: An Afterword," was written in the summer of 1979 for *That Was Then* and also appeared as the afterword to *The Collected Poems;* "A Conversation with Anthony Piccioni and A. Poulin, Jr.," 29–30.

80. "A Conversation with Thomas Hilgers and Michael Molloy," 59.

81. John Logan to IG, August 18, 1953; John Logan to IG, May 19, 1954.

82. Paul Carroll to IG, December 20, 1954.

83. Paul Carroll, "Un Voyage à Cythère," *Poetry* 85, no. 6 (1955): 319.

84. Interview with Philip Booth, October 20, 1989; Gregory Corso to IG, November 18, 1954; Richard Eberhart to IG, May 19, 1954; Theodore Roethke to IG, January 24, 1954.

85. Interview with Richard Eberhart, October 25, 1989.

86. Ibid.

87. Richard Eberhart to IG, May 18, 1952; Richard Eberhart to IG, April 4, 1953.

88. IG to Robert Gardner, May 29, 1957, Robert Gardner Private Collection.

89. T. S. Eliot to IG, June 12, 1955; Karl Shapiro to Wallace Fowlie, August 27, 1952, *Poetry* Papers.

90. The editors, "Announcement," *Poetry* 81, no. 1 (1952): A.

91. Brett Millier, *Elizabeth Bishop: Life and the Memory of It,* 220.

92. Karl Shapiro to R. M. MacGregor, January 23, 1953, *Poetry* Papers.

93. Ibid.

94. R. M. MacGregor to Karl Shapiro, February 5, 1953, *Poetry* Papers.

95. Nicholas Joost to Karl Shapiro, November 5, 1953, Shapiro Congress Papers.

96. Karl Shapiro to George Dillon, June 19, 1952, *Poetry* Papers.

97. Karl Shapiro to Wallace Fowlie, August 27, 1952, *Poetry* Papers.

98. Interview with H. E. F. Donohue, February 24, 1990.

99. T. S. Eliot to IG, June 12, 1952.

100. Interview with H. E. F. Donohue, February 24, 1990. Donohue was mistaken, because at the time Moore was no longer *Poetry*'s editor.

101. Interview with Robert McCormick, October 20 and 21, 1989.

102. Ibid.

103. Interview with Carolyn Kizer, August 21, 1990.

104. IG to Edward Dahlberg [late 1956 / early 1957], Dahlberg Papers.

105. IG to Robert Gardner, September 29, 1954, Robert Gardner Private Collection.

106. Wallace Fowlie to IG, April 10, 1953.

107. Paul Brooks [Houghton Mifflin] to IG, July 30, 1953.

108. William Congdon to IG, February 20, 1953, Congdon Foundation Papers.

109. Interview with Robert McCormick, October 20 and 21, 1989.

110. Chapman, *Bananas,* 154.

111. Katherine Gardner Herrick to IG, undated [ca. 1955].

112. IG to Robert Gardner, September 10 [1953], Robert Gardner Private Collection; according to Officer and Williamson, "Purchasing Power," $76 in 1953 is around $610 in 2008; today the ofay etymology that Gardner mentions is considered dubious and it seems more likely that ofay derives from an African source; "Of Flesh and Bone" was published in *Botteghe Oscure* 13 [1953]: 274–76; "Mindful of the Forest" was published as "Children Are Game."

113. IG to Karl Shapiro, September 24 [1953], Shapiro Private Collection.

114. IG to Robert Gardner, April 28 [1954], Robert Gardner Private Collection.

115. "Nursery Rhyme No. 1" and "Nursery Rhyme No 2" were published in *The Collected Poems,* 146–47.

116. Kathryn Loring, "They Were There."

117. IG to Robert Gardner [early 1954], Robert Gardner Private Collection.

118. Interview with Robert McCormick, October 20 and 21, 1989; IG to Robert Gardner [early 1954], Robert Gardner Private Collection.

119. IG to Robert Gardner [ca. February 1954], Robert Gardner Private Collection.

120. John Logan to IG, November 29, 1953.

121. Telephone interview with Paul Carroll, January 9, 1990.

122. IG to Robert Gardner [ca. February 1954], Robert Gardner Private Collection.

123. IG to Oscar Williams, n.d. .

124. IG to Richard Eberhart [January 1954], Eberhart Papers.

125. Theodore Roethke to IG, January 9, 1954.

126. William Congdon to IG, April 22, 1954, Congdon Foundation Papers.

127. John Logan to IG, June 1, 1954.

128. Telegram, Paul Brooks [Houghton Mifflin] to IG, May 28, 1954.

129. Anneke Van Kirk to IG, n.d. .

130. Ibid.

131. Hela Koeth to IG, June 19, 1956. The Koeths rechristened Lorina Renata.

132. William Congdon to IG, February 21, 1954, Congdon Foundation Papers.

133. Interview with William Congdon, April 26, 1990.

134. William Congdon to Robert McCormick, March 1, 1956, Congdon Foundation Papers.

135. Sue [Neil] to Karl Shapiro, February 25, 1954, Shapiro Papers.

136. "New Magazine Is Out; Sales Brisk."

137. IG to Robert Gardner, June 28, 1954, Robert Gardner Private Collection.

138. IG to Oscar Williams [ca. mid-1954].

139. IG to Julia Bartholomay, February 9, 1974.

140. John Logan to IG, June 29, 1954.

141. IG to Robert Gardner, postmark September 15, 1954, Robert Gardner Private Collection.

142. William Congdon to IG, July 8, 1954, Congdon Foundation Papers.

143. IG to Richard Eberhart, [late 1954], Eberhart Papers.

144. Karl Shapiro to Sue Neil, October 4, 1954, *Poetry* Papers.

145. Karl Shapiro to Henry Rago and Charlotte Miller, May 7, 1955, Shapiro Papers.

146. Henry Rago to Karl Shapiro, February 14, 1955, Shapiro Papers.

147. Dylan Thomas's poems were "Out of a War of Wits," "This Is Remembered," "Shiloh's Seed," "Before We Mothernaked Fall," and "The Almanac of Time."

148. Karl Shapiro, "Dylan Thomas," 100, 109.

149. Ibid., 109; Roy Campbell, "Memories of Dylan Thomas at the B.B.C.," 111.

150. IG to Robert and Lee Gardner, n.d., Robert Gardner Private Collection.

151. IG to Karl Shapiro, September 28, 1955, Shapiro Private Collection.

152. IG to Richard Eberhart, October 24, 1955, Eberhart Papers.

153. Ibid.

154. Karl Shapiro to IG, March 22, 1954.

155. Interview with Karl Shapiro, February 20, 1990.

156. IG to Karl Shapiro and Evalyn Shapiro, n.d. .

157. Interview with Karl Shapiro, August 18, 1990.

158. Ibid.

159. Gardner, "Postillion for Pegasus," in IG to Karl Shapiro, October 15, 1956, Shapiro Private Collection.

Chapter Five "On the Wing," 1955–1958

1. Galway Kinnell to IG, September 5, 1955.

2. Philip Booth to IG, August 21, 1955.

3. John Logan to IG, August 7, 1955; Wallace Fowlie to IG, August 21, 1955.

4. Richard Eberhart to IG, October 17, 1955. Harriet is Harriet Monroe, *Poetry*'s founding editor; Richard Eberhart to Henry Rago, October 17, 1955, *Poetry* Papers.

5. Henry Rago, "A Statement by the New Editor," 39.

6. Karl Shapiro to IG, July 14 [1956].

7. Julia Bartholomay to the author, June 3, 2000.

8. Joseph Parisi and Steven Young (compiled and edited), *Dear Editor: A History of Poetry in Letters. The First Fifty Years, 1912–1962,* 15, 14; see also Diederik Oostdijk, "Karl Shapiro and *Poetry: A Magazine of Verse* (1950–1955)."

9. Karl Shapiro to the author, June 24, 1989.

10. IG to RG, October 12, 1954, Robert Gardner Private Collection.

11. IG to Robert Gardner, October 12, 1954, Robert Gardner Private Collection.

12. Fanny Butcher, "The Literary Spotlight."

13. Harvey Breit, "Dame Day," 8.

14. IG to Robert Gardner, February 1, 1955, Robert Gardner Private Collection.

15. IG to Robert Gardner, February 1, 1955, Robert Gardner Private Collection.

16. Karl Shapiro to IG, February 4, 1955.

17. William Carlos Williams to Houghton Mifflin, January 13, 1955, copy in IG Papers.

18. Delmore Schwartz to Houghton Mifflin, n.d., copy in IG Papers.

19. Richard Eberhart to Houghton Mifflin, November 21, 1954, copy in IG Papers; IG to Richard Eberhart, n.d., Eberhart Papers.

20. William Congdon to IG, April 6, 1955, Congdon Foundation Papers; Oscar Williams to Houghton Mifflin, November 19, 1954, copy in IG Papers; Mary Manning to IG, March 16, 1955.

21. T. S. Eliot to George Peabody Gardner (father), n.d., copy in IG Papers.

22. IG to Robert Gardner, postmark April 9, 1955, Robert Gardner Private Collection.

23. Josephine Jacobsen, "Two Poets."

24. Karl Shapiro to IG, May 23, 1955. Jacobsen came to admire Gardner, and her own poetry is now internationally known.

25. Ibid.

26. Selden Rodman, "The Content and the Form."

27. Karl Shapiro to IG, June 7, 1955.

28. Carolyn Kizer to IG, June 12 [1955].

29. Galway Kinnell, "New Volumes from Two Poets," 62; Wallace Fowlie, "Three Poets," 237, 238.

30. Edith Sitwell, "A Tidy, Natural Taste," 14.

31. IG to Galway Kinnell, June 8, 1955, Kinnell Papers.

32. William Congdon to IG, April 26, 1955, Congdon Foundation Papers; William Congdon to IG, April 27, 1955, Congdon Foundation Papers.

33. John Frederick Nims, "Poetry: Ironic to Romantic," 3.

34. IG to Karl Shapiro, October 7, 1955, Shapiro Private Collection.

35. Karl Shapiro to IG, October 14, 1955.

36. Randall Jarrell, "Recent Poetry," 122.

37. IG to Karl Shapiro and Evalyn Shapiro, October 27, 1955, Shapiro Private Collection.

38. IG to Lee Anderson [ca. November 1955], Anderson Papers.

39. Rose Van Kirk to IG, May 26 [1955?].

40. IG to Robert Gardner, August 3, 1955, Robert Gardner Private Collection.

41. Ibid.

42. IG to Robert Gardner, September 2, 1955, Robert Gardner Private Collection.

43. IG to Robert Gardner [ca. September 1955], Robert Gardner Private Collection.

44. Harold Van Kirk to IG, n.d.

45. William Congdon to IG, June 14, 1955, Congdon Foundation Papers.

46. William Lynch to Caroline Gordon, January 16, 1959, Gordon Papers.

47. For an extensive discussion of Ransom's editorship see my *The Kenyon Review 1939–1970:*

A Critical History; John Crowe Ransom, "The Poet as Woman," 78, 98. In "American Poetry Now Shaped by Women," Alice Ostriker described being a college student in the late 1950s and early 1960s, pointing out that, "needless to say," hardly any women poets were on her reading lists. (1)

48. See for an extensive description of the Aiken, Dahlberg, Shapiro brawl Oostdijk, "Karl Shapiro and *Poetry,*" 105–10.

49. Edward Dahlberg to IG, December 10, 1965; Edward Dahlberg to IG, November 22, 1965; Edward Dahlberg to IG, May 2, 1968; Edward Dahlberg to IG, May 12, 1968.

50. IG to Edward Dahlberg [ca. late 1956, early 1957], Dahlberg Papers.

51. IG to Karl Shapiro, October 27, 1955, Shapiro Private Collection.

52. William Congdon to IG, June 14, 1955, Congdon Foundation Papers.

53. Interview with Robert McCormick, October 20 and 21, 1989.

54. IG to Robert Gardner, postmark [December?] 10, 1955, Robert Gardner Private Collection.

55. Elizabeth Bishop to IG, October 21, 1955.

56. Elizabeth Bishop to Austin Olney [Houghton Mifflin], March 18, 1956, copy in University of Chicago Press Papers.

57. Elizabeth Bishop to IG, March 18, 1956.

58. John Logan, "The Celebration of Birthdays," 163; John Logan to IG, February 4, 1956.

59. "100 of the Year's Outstanding Books . . . A Selected Guide to Summer Reading."

60. "A List of 250 Outstanding Books . . . A Christmas Guide."

61. Elizabeth Bishop to IG, May 14, 1956.

62. Elizabeth Bishop to IG, May 1, 1957.

63. IG to William Congdon, June 1, 1955, Congdon Foundation Papers.

64. IG to Robert Gardner, n.d., Robert Gardner Private Collection.

65. IG to Myra Cholden, May 2, 1956, Myra Cholden Brown Private Collection.

66. IG to Robert Gardner, n.d., Robert Gardner Private Collection.

67. IG to Robert Gardner and Lee Gardner, July 18, 1956, Robert Gardner Private Collection.

68. Gardner had a massive correspondence with Smith Oliver, which is unfortunately lost. I have not been able to trace his plays.

69. Evalyn Shapiro to IG, August 20, 1956.

70. Karl Shapiro to IG, August 8, 1956.

71. IG to Karl Shapiro [ca. early August 1956], Shapiro Private Collection.

72. Karl Shapiro to IG, August 20 [1956].

73. IG to Karl Shapiro, August 28, 1956, Shapiro Private Collection.

74. IG to Evalyn Shapiro, August 29, 1956, Shapiro Private Collection.

75. Karl Shapiro to IG, September 9, 1956.

76. IG to Karl Shapiro, July 28, 1956, Shapiro Private Collection.

77. IG to Myra Cholden, March 13, 1957, Myra Cholden Brown Private Collection.

78. Ibid.

79. IG to Anabel Holland, October 11, 1957, Myra Cholden Brown Private Collection.

80. IG, "The Fellowship with Essence: An Afterword," 162.

81. IG to Robert Gardner, March 15, 1957, Robert Gardner Private Collection.

82. Robert Gardner to IG, March 24, 1957.

83. IG to Robert Gardner, postmark May 29, 1957, Robert Gardner Private Collection.

84. Ibid.

85. IG to George Peabody Gardner (brother), July 7, 1975.

86. Evalyn Shapiro to IG, January 15, 1958.

87. Karl Shapiro to IG, January 16, 1958.

88. Evalyn Shapiro to IG, January 16, 1958.

89. Karl Shapiro to IG, January 22, 1958.

90. Karl Shapiro to IG, May 13, 1958. IG gave a few thousand dollars, and in the end the Ford Foundation may have stepped in also.

91. IG to Galway Kinnell, June 7, 1957, Kinnell Papers.

92. Galway Kinnell to IG, July 1, 1957.

93. John Logan to IG, September 16, 1957.

94. John Logan to IG, October 12, 1958; John Logan to IG, June 20, 1956; John Logan to IG, September 22, 1956.

95. John Logan to IG, February 19, 1959.

96. Edward Dahlberg to IG, April 11, 1958.

97. Edward Dahlberg to IG, January 23, 1956.

98. Edward Dahlberg to IG, October 8, 1956.

99. Ibid.

100. Edward Dahlberg to IG, January 22, 1958.

101. Robert Lowell to IG, October 27, 1957.

102. Philip Booth to IG, October 7, 1957; Carolyn Kizer to IG, March 8, 1958.

103. Carolyn Kizer to James Wright, May 2, 1958, Wright Papers.

104. Theodore Roethke to IG, May 30, 1958.

105. IG to Dahlberg, December 9 [1957], Dahlberg Papers.

106. *Foxcroft Yearbook 1933*, 75.

107. IG to Edward Dahlberg, January 2, 1958, Dahlberg Papers.

108. IG to Edward Dahlberg, January 30, 1958, Dahlberg Papers.

109. IG to Edward Dahlberg [ca. mid-1958], Dahlberg Papers.

110. Edward Dahlberg to IG, June 11, 1968.

Chapter Six "Courting Lovers," 1958–1961

1. Thomas Underwood in *Allen Tate: Orphan of the South* narrates Tate's early years with great perception.

2. Shapiro, *Reports of My Death*, 8, 7.

3. Underwood in *Allen Tate* has Ysaÿe say: "Your left hand is good, but it is all very uninteresting" (25).

4. Caroline Gordon had become a Catholic in 1947. During the 1940s and 1950s many writers converted to Catholicism, among them John Logan, Robert Lowell, Walker Percy, and Edith Sitwell.

5. Caroline Gordon to Robert W. Barnett, June 8, 1959, copy in Gordon Papers. Gordon's time frame is off.

6. For Tate's relationship with Caroline Gordon, see Veronica A. Makowsky, *Caroline Gordon: A Biography*, and Ann Waldron, *Close Connections: Caroline Gordon and the Southern Renaissance*.

7. Interview with John and Margaret Goetz, August 4, 1990. John Goetz was not only Allen Tate's lawyer, but lawyer and confidant to most of the members of the English department.

8. Interviews with Elizabeth Brown, August 2, 1990, and John and Margaret Goetz, August 4, 1990.

9. Interview with Leonard and Sherley Unger, August 3, 1990.

10. Allen Tate to IG, October 12, 1957.

11. IG to Robert Gardner, July 21 [1958], Robert Gardner Private Collection.

12. IG to Edward Dahlberg, July 24 [1958], Dahlberg Papers.

13. IG to Edward Dahlberg, November 12, 1959, Dahlberg Papers.

14. Brainard Cheney to Allen Tate, August 5, 1958, copy in Gordon Papers.

15. Interview with Pat Knowlton Stange, December 5, 1989.

16. Allen Tate to IG, October 10, 1958.

17. Interview with Robert McCormick, October 20 and 21, 1989.

18. Ibid.

19. Telephone interview with Paul Carroll, January 9, 1990.

20. IG to Robert Gardner, September 4, 1958, Robert Gardner Private Collection.

21. Robert Gardner to IG, October 4, 1958.

22. Edward Dahlberg to IG, November 20, 1958.

23. IG to Edward Dahlberg [ca. late February 1959], Dahlberg Papers.

24. Robert Lowell to Elizabeth Bishop, October 16, 1958. Quoted in Saskia Hamilton, ed., *The Letters of Robert Lowell*, 271–72.

25. Robert Lowell to Elizabeth Bishop, November 19, 1958. Quoted in Saskia Hamilton, ed. *The Letters of Robert Lowell*, 277.

26. Allen Tate to Robert Lowell, November 23, 1958, Lowell Papers.

27. Interview with Robert McCormick, October 20 and 21, 1989.

28. Maurice Seymour told me that Bob McCormick had an affair with Vickers while he was married to Gardner. While there is no proof, McCormick married Vickers almost immediately after his divorce.

29. Interview with Robert McCormick, October 20 and 21, 1989.

30. Interview with Fanita English, December 26, 1989.

31. Morrow, *The Chief*, 59, 57–58.

32. Allen Tate to Katherine Chapin Biddle, January 25, 1959, Katherine Biddle Papers.

33. IG to Edward Dahlberg, January 22, 1959, Dahlberg Papers.

34. IG to Edward Dahlberg [ca. late January 1959], Dahlberg Papers.

35. Richard Eberhart to IG, February 6, 1959.

36. IG to Katherine Chapin Biddle, March [26?], 1959, Biddle Family Papers.

37. Karl Shapiro to Allen Tate, March 2, 1959, Tate Papers.

38. Allen Tate to Andrew Lytle, March 14, 1959, Lytle Papers; Allen Tate to Andrew Lytle, March 26, 1959, Lytle Papers.

39. Allen Tate to Edward Dahlberg, March 9, 1959, Dahlberg Papers.

40. Allen Tate to George Peabody Gardner (father), March 7, 1959.

41. Allen Tate to Katherine Chapin Biddle, March 23, 1959, Katherine Biddle Papers.

42. T. S. Eliot to Allen Tate, April 20, 1959, Tate Papers.

43. IG to Robert Gardner, May 11, 1955, Robert Gardner Private Collection.

44. Elizabeth Hardwick to Allen Tate, June 1, 1959, Tate Papers.

45. Allen Tate to Katherine Chapin Biddle, May 17, 1959, Katherine Biddle Papers.

46. Allen Tate to Andrew Lytle, May 25, 1959, Lytle Papers.

47. Allen Tate to Caroline Gordon, May 29, 1959, Gordon Papers.

48. Caroline Gordon to Robert W. Barnett, June 28, 1959, copy in Gordon Papers.

49. Caroline Gordon to Robert W. Barnett, May 23, 1959, copy in Gordon Papers.

50. Allen Tate to Katherine Chapin Biddle, June 1, 1959, Katherine Biddle Papers.

51. IG to Robert Gardner, May 20, 1959, Robert Gardner Private Collection.

52. Samuel Monk to Allen Tate, June 2, 1959, Tate Papers.

53. Paul Carroll to James Wright, June 26, 1959, Wright Papers.

54. Paul Carroll to IG, July 8 [1959].

55. Paul Carroll to IG, November 21, 1959.

56. IG to Paul Carroll [late 1959], Carroll Papers.

57. IG to Dahlberg [ca. August 1959], Dahlberg Papers.

58. Carolyn Kizer to IG, August 17, 1959.

59. Ibid. Kizer's debut, *The Ungrateful Garden,* was published by Indiana University Press in 1961, Kizer was sure, "[t]hanks in large parts to your [Gardner's and Tate's] efforts." Carolyn Kizer to IG and Allen Tate, October 25 [1959].

60. Allen Tate to Andrew Lytle, August 10, 1959, Lytle Papers.

61. Allen Tate, "Ode to K. and F. Biddle," August 27, 1959.

62. Robert Daniel, wedding poem for Isabella Gardner and Allen Tate.

63. Allen Tate to Caroline Gordon, September 6, 1959, Gordon Papers.

64. IG to Robert Gardner, January 11, 1960, Robert Gardner Private Collection.

65. Allen Tate to Katherine Chapin Biddle, November 16, 1959, Katherine Biddle Papers. *Un'Altra Infanzia,* translated by Alfredo Rizzardi, was published in 1959 by Libraria Antiquaria Palmaverde in Bologna, Italy.

66. IG to Myra Cholden [ca. December 1959], Myra Cholden Brown Private Collection.

67. Interview with Ann Birstein, March 27, 1990.

68. IG to John Logan [ca. December 1959], Logan Papers.

69. Allen Tate to Paul Carroll, August 17, 1959, Carroll Papers.

70. Edward Dahlberg to IG, September 15, 1959.

71. Reed Whittemore to IG and Allen Tate, October 1 [1959], Tate Papers.

72. Allen Tate to Cleanth Brooks, October 19, 1959, Brooks Papers. The *Sewanee Review* 67, no. 3 (July-September 1959) was devoted to Tate; Gardner's poems appeared on pages 450–51.

73. Allen Tate to Katherine Chapin Biddle, May 20, 1960, Katherine Biddle Papers.

74. Allen Tate to Katherine Chapin Biddle, June 1, 1960, Katherine Biddle Papers. The "Hoover portrait" may be the painting by Mary Aiken, which the Tates thought awful.

75. IG to John Logan [ca. early 1960], Logan Papers.

76. " . . . And Thou No Breath at All?" actually appeared in *Poetry* 99 (November 1961): 100.

77. IG to John Logan, October 4, 1960, Logan Papers.

78. Robert Lowell to T. S. Eliot, October 28, 1960, and Robert Lowell to Elizabeth Bishop, April 14, 1962, quoted in Saskia Hamilton, ed., *The Letters of Robert Lowell*, 371, 406; Robert Lowell to Allen Tate, October 22, 1959, Tate Papers; Robert Lowell to Allen Tate, June 27, 1960, Tate Papers.

79. Lee Gardner to IG, October 4, 1973.

80. Herbert Read to IG and Allen Tate, April 3, 1960.

81. IG to John Logan, July 15, 1959, Logan Papers.

82. Barbara Howes Smith to IG, October 13, 1960; W. D. Snodgrass's first book, *Heart's Needle* (1959), won the Pulitzer Prize in 1960; Donald Justice, *The Summer Anniversaries* (1960).

83. IG to Barbara Howes Smith, October 18, 1960, Howes Papers.

84. Paul Carroll to IG, October 10, 1960.

85. IG to Paul Carroll, October 12, 1960, Carroll Papers.

86. Paul Carroll to IG, October 18, 1960.

87. IG to John Logan, October 20, 1960, Logan Papers.

88. Karl Shapiro to IG, August 24, 1960.

89. Karl Shapiro to IG, December 19, 1960.

90. Ibid.

91. Allen Tate to John Clark, October 10, 1960, copy in Tate Papers.

92. IG to John Logan, November 11, 1960, Logan Papers.

93. IG to Barbara Howes Smith, November 22, 1960, Howes Papers.

94. Roger Hancock, reader's report of "The Looking Glass," December 13, 1960, University of Chicago Press Papers.

95. Elder Olson, reader's report of "The Looking Glass," April 3, 1961, University of Chicago Press Papers.

96. John Crowe Ransom, reader's report of "The Looking Glass," December 30, 1960, University of Chicago Press Papers.

97. IG to University of Chicago Press, February 2, 1960, University of Chicago Press Papers.

98. Cecil Day Lewis to Carroll Bowen [University of Chicago Press], March 10, 1961, University of Chicago Press Papers; T. S. Eliot to Allen Tate, May 26, 1961, Tate Papers.

99. Interview with Robert Stange, November 29, 1989.

100. Gordon O'Brien to IG, December 29, 1980.

101. Interview with Boyd Thomes, July 28, 1990; interview with John and Margaret Goetz, August 4, 1990.

102. IG to Barbara Howes Smith, October 18, 1960, Howes Papers.

103. According to Officer and Williamson, "Purchasing Power," $5,000 in 1960 is about $36,300 in 2008; IG to Myra Cholden, November 21, 1960, Myra Cholden Brown Private Collection.

104. IG to Myra Cholden, December 2, 1960, Myra Cholden Brown Private Collection.

105. Allen Tate to Katherine Chapin Biddle, November 21, 1960, Katherine Biddle Papers.

106. IG to Myra Cholden, November 21, 1960, Myra Cholden Brown Private Collection.

107. Robert Lowell to IG and Allen Tate, May 22, 1961.

108. Herbert Read to Allen Tate, November 27, 1960, Tate Papers.

109. Allen Tate to Katherine Chapin Biddle, May 13, 1961, Katherine Biddle Papers.

110. IG to Myra Cholden, July 15, 1961, Myra Cholden Brown Private Collection.

111. IG to University of Chicago Press, May 29, 1961, University of Chicago Press Papers; IG to University of Chicago Press, June 9, 1961, University of Chicago Press Papers.

112. IG to Myra Cholden, July 15, 1961, Myra Cholden Brown Private Collection.

113. Frank Kermode to the author, June 21, 1989.

114. Allen Tate to Charles Foster, August 4, 1961, Tate-Foster Papers.

115. IG to Myra Cholden, August 23, 1961, Myra Cholden Brown Private Collection.

116. Natasha Spender to Allen Tate, October 4, 1961, Tate Papers.

117. IG to John Logan, October 1, 1961, Logan Papers; IG to Edward Dahlberg, August 4, 1961, Dahlberg Papers.

Chapter Seven "Book and Bed and Booze and Blunders of the Heart," 1962–1965

1. Katherine Chapin Biddle to IG, October 2, 1961.

2. Charles Foster to IG, September 26, 1961.

3. Edward Dahlberg to IG, January 6, 1962.

4. Carolyn Kizer to IG, December 2 [1961].

5. Elizabeth Bishop to John Simmons [University of Chicago Press], August 14, 1961.

6. Elizabeth Hardwick to IG, October 9, 1961; Robert Lowell to IG, October 10, 1961.

7. Allen Tate to Katherine Chapin Biddle, November 23, 1961, Katherine Biddle Papers.

8. Allen Tate to Katherine Chapin Biddle, November 24, 1961, Katherine Biddle Papers.

9. Carleton Drewry, "Three New Volumes of Poetry."

10. Hal Smith, review of *Best Poems of 1959*, Isabella Gardner, *The Looking Glass,* and Thom Gunn, *My Sad Captains and Other Poems,* 187, 188.

11. John Logan to IG, Thanksgiving 1961.

12. Harvey Curtis Webster, "Five Poets," 210.

13. Paul Carroll to IG, n.d. .

14. Paul Carroll, "A Note on Isabella Gardner," 215, 216, 217.

15. Paul Carroll, "Fair, Foul and Full of Variations: The Generation of 1962," 206.

16. Van Allen Bradley, "Isabella Gardner: Poet in Search of an Audience"; Rose Mary DeLancey, "Poets' Views of Their Worlds Differ Widely"; Fred S. Holley, "5 Poetic Visions Evaluated"; Robert A. Holzhauer, "Two Midwestern Poets"; Burton A. Robie, review of Thom Gunn, *My Sad Captains and Other Poems,* and Isabella Gardner, *The Looking Glass,* 3286.

17. Ralph J. Mills Jr., "Three American Poets," 105.

18. James Wright, "Gravity and Incantation," 424, 426.

19. IG to John Logan, February 26, 1962, Logan Papers; John Logan, "The Poetry of Isabella Gardner," 252.

20. Karl Shapiro to IG, September 8, 1960.

21. Karl Shapiro, "Voices that Speak to the Critic in Very Different Rhythms," 4–5.

22. In "Judges Name Leading Contenders for 13th National Book Awards," flyer, February 11, 1962, IG Papers, the other contenders were named: Robert Bagg, Philip Booth, John Ciardi, H. D., Abbie Huston Evans, Horace Gregory, John Holmes, Denise Levertov, Ned O'Gorman, and John Hall Wheelock; Gardner's fantasy is to be found, crossed out, in her 1961 notebook, IG Papers.

23. Allen Tate to Edward Dahlberg, January 18, 1962, Dahlberg Papers.

24. Allen Tate to Katherine Chapin Biddle, April 18, 1962, Katherine Biddle Papers.

25. Ibid.

26. Edward Dahlberg to IG, May 17, 1962, Tate Papers.

27. Allen Tate to John Clark, April 22, 1962, copy in Tate Papers.

28. IG to Edward Dahlberg, April 18, 1962, Dahlberg Papers.

29. IG to Lee Gardner, July 1, 1962, Robert Gardner Private Collection.

30. Myra Cholden to IG [ca. April 1962], Robert Gardner Private Collection.

31. IG to Lee Gardner, April 19, 1962, Robert Gardner Private Collection.

32. As reported by Bobby Clark to IG, June 24 [1979]; John Goetz to Allen Tate, July 27, 1962, Tate Papers.

33. IG to Edward Dahlberg, April 18, 1962, Dahlberg Papers.

34. IG to Charles Foster and Doris Foster, June 29, 1962, Tate-Foster Papers.

35. IG to Lee Gardner, July 1, 1962, Robert Gardner Private Collection.

36. IG to Edward Dahlberg, July 1, 1962, Dahlberg Papers.

37. IG to Charles Foster and Doris Foster, June 29, 1962, Tate-Foster Papers.

38. Allen Tate to Charles Foster, September 5, 1962, Tate-Foster Papers.

39. Allen Tate to Katherine Chapin Biddle, October 18, 1962, Katherine Biddle Papers.

40. Herbert Read to Allen Tate, October 8, 1962, Tate Papers.

41. IG to Katherine Chapin Biddle, October 29, 1962, Biddle Family Papers.

42. Allen Tate to Katherine Chapin Biddle, December 17, 1962, Katherine Biddle Papers.

43. Ibid.

44. Allen Tate to Robert Penn Warren, November 29, 1962, Warren Papers.

45. Ibid.

46. Interview with Pat Knowlton Stange, December 5, 1989.

47. Allen Tate to Francis Biddle, October 6, 1961, Katherine Biddle Papers.

48. Allen Tate to Donald Davidson, October 19, 1962, copy in Tate Papers.

49. Allen Tate to Donald Davidson, November 23, 1962, Davidson-Tate Papers.

50. Theodore Roethke to IG, February 17, 1963.

51. Paul Carroll to IG and Allen Tate, December 10, 1962.

52. Allen Tate to Caroline Gordon, January 18, 1963, Gordon Papers. "Diriment impediment" is a reason for annulment.

53. This admittedly extreme quotation is from Allen Tate to Caroline Gordon, August 19, 1977, Gordon Papers, but Tate's references to Percy Wood are almost always very negative.

54. IG to John Logan, February 21, 1963, Logan Papers.

55. Allen Tate to Daniel Seymour, n.d., in Daniel Seymour, *A Loud Song.*

56. IG to Rose Grosvenor Gardner, March 10, 1963.

57. Allen Tate to Katherine Chapin Biddle, April 3, 1963, Katherine Biddle Papers.

58. IG to Daniel Seymour, April 17, 1963, copy in IG Papers.

59. According to Officer and Williamson, "Purchasing Power," $150 was worth over $1,000 in 2008; IG to John Logan, August 1, 1963, Logan Papers.

60. Evalyn Shapiro to IG, April 15, 1963.

61. Karl Shapiro to IG, December 17 [1962].

62. Karl Shapiro to IG, May 9, 1963.

63. Karl Shapiro to IG, May 14, 1963.

64. IG to Henry Rago, Easter Sunday, 1963, *Poetry* Lilly Papers.

65. Allen Tate to James Wright, May 19, 1963, copy in Tate Papers.

66. Quoted by Richard Hugo to James Dickey [August 1, 1963], Dickey Papers.

67. Interview with Anne Runk Wright, March 16, 1990. Anne Wright remembered the only time she ever met Tate: "Tate was asked to give a reading at the Morgan library and I cannot remember the exact date, it must have been '69 or '70. And James was very anxious to show him how he had remade his life. It must have been in '70, because by then James had a beard. So we went to this reading and here was this wispy little man that looked like shredded wheat and he did not even recognize James. And I thought: 'You caused my husband so much misery'—although my husband, of course, had caused it himself—'and here you do not even recognize him!' It was very ironic, a very strange situation." At Macalester College, where he went after being fired, Wright got into similar trouble as at the University of Minnesota.

68. Allen Tate to Caroline Gordon, January 18, 1963, Gordon Papers.

69. IG to John Haffenden, January 25, 1974, Berryman Papers.

70. Allen Tate to John Berryman, June 6, 1963, Berryman Papers.

71. John Berryman to IG and Allen Tate, June 8, 1963.

72. Allen Tate to John Berryman, June 6, 1963, Berryman Papers.

73. John Berryman to IG and Allen Tate, June 8, 1963.

74. Allen Tate to Edward Dahlberg, July 4, 1963, Dahlberg Papers.

75. Ibid.

76. IG to Nancy Tate Wood, July 4, 1963, Gordon Papers.

77. Allen Tate to Robert Lowell, August 21, 1963, Lowell Papers.

78. Allen Tate to Edward Dahlberg, August 24, 1963, Dahlberg Papers.

79. IG to Nancy Tate Wood, August 31, 1963, Gordon Papers; IG to Robert Gardner, September 4, 1963, Robert Gardner Private Collection.

80. IG to Robert Gardner and Lee Gardner, September 4 and 5, 1963, Robert Gardner Private Collection.

81. Rose Van Kirk to IG, September 18 [1963].

82. IG to Nancy Tate Wood, September 25, 1963, Gordon Papers.

83. Allen Tate to William Congdon, October 23, 1963, Congdon Foundation Papers.

84. Allen Tate to Katherine Chapin Biddle, July 18, 1964, Katherine Biddle Papers.

85. IG to Katherine Chapin Biddle, July 18, 1964, Biddle Family Papers.

86. IG to Edward Dahlberg, January 2, 1964, Dahlberg Papers; IG to Edward Dahlberg, February 10, 1964, Dahlberg Papers.

87. IG to Henry Rago, February 10, 1964, *Poetry* Lilly Papers.

88. Paul Carroll to IG and Allen Tate, September 10, 1964, Tate Papers.

89. Paul Carroll to IG and Allen Tate, October 1, 1964.

90. IG to John Logan, January 22, 1965, Logan Papers.

91. John Logan to IG, March 3, 1965.

92. IG to Henry Rago, July 18, 1964, *Poetry* Lilly Papers.

93. IG to Edward Dahlberg, October 20, 1964, Dahlberg Papers.

94. IG to Edward Dahlberg, November 6, 1964, Dahlberg Papers.

95. IG to Katherine Chapin Biddle, March 3, 1964, Biddle Family Papers.

96. Allen Tate to Katherine Chapin Biddle, May 5, 1964, Katherine Biddle Papers.

97. Allen Tate to Katherine Chapin Biddle, April 8, 1964, Katherine Biddle Papers.

98. IG to Barbara Howes, May 18, 1964, Howes Papers.

99. Interview with a few maids at the Pensione Annalena, spring 1991.

100. Allen Tate to Cleanth Brooks, July 7, 1964, Brooks Papers.

101. IG to Nancy Tate Wood, August 19, 1964, Gordon Papers.

102. Allen Tate to Charles Foster, August 22, 1964, Tate Papers.

103. IG to Edward Dahlberg, October 20, 1964, Dahlberg Papers.

104. Allen Tate to Francis Biddle, March 11, 1964, Katherine Biddle Papers.

105. IG to Edward Dahlberg, September 16, 1964, Dahlberg Papers.

106. IG to Charles Foster and Doris Foster, October 1, 1964, Tate-Foster Papers.

107. IG to Edward Dahlberg, October 5, 1964, Dahlberg Papers.

108. IG to Charles Foster and Doris Foster, October 1, 1964, Tate-Foster Papers.

109. John Goetz to Charles Foster and Doris Foster, November 24, 1964, Tate-Foster Papers.

110. Allen Tate to Katherine Chapin Biddle, December 4, 1964, Katherine Biddle Papers. The Minotaur is mentioned in Aiken's poem "Preludes for Memnon."

111. Allen Tate to Katherine Anne Porter, January 5, 1965, Porter Papers.

112. IG to Lee Anderson, [December] 1964, Anderson Papers.

113. Allen Tate to Charles Foster, January 8, 1965, Tate-Foster Papers.

114. Maurice English to IG, January 19, 1965.

115. Paul Carroll to IG and Allen Tate, February 4, 1965.

116. Paul Carroll to IG, February 8, 1965; Paul Carroll to Allen Tate, February 26, 1965, Tate Papers.

117. Paul Carroll to Allen Tate, February 26, 1965, Tate Papers.

118. IG to Edward Dahlberg, March 22, 1965, Dahlberg Papers.

119. IG to John Logan, March 10, 1965, Logan Papers.

120. Ibid., IG to John Logan, April 16, 1965, Logan Papers.

121. Allen Tate to Charles Foster, April 10, 1965, Tate-Foster Papers.

122. IG to Edward Dahlberg, April 23, 1965, Dahlberg Papers.

123. Edward Dahlberg to IG, May 18, 1965.

124. IG to Edward Dahlberg, May 20, 1965, Dahlberg Papers.

125. Edward Dahlberg to IG, June 7, 1965.

126. Edward Dahlberg to Allen Tate, June 12, 1965, Tate Papers.

127. IG to Edward Dahlberg, June 29, 1965, Dahlberg Papers.

128. Edward Dahlberg to IG, July 3, 1965.

129. It is difficult to pinpoint the start of their affair, as Tate gave many different dates in letters to his friends. Probably, he became involved with Helen Heinz as early as the winter of 1962. To John Goetz, asking for a divorce on August 17, 1965, he wrote: "I have been in a false position since the winter of 1962" (Goetz Private Collection). He told Charles Foster on October 6, 1965: "I have struggled with this dilemma longer than anybody, even you and Doris, knows." (In Tate-Foster Papers.) In most letters he mentions their return from Great Britain at the end of 1963 as the time when he was "ready" for an affair, being burdened by Gardner's pasts.

130. IG to John Logan, July 26 [1961], Logan Papers.

131. Interview with Helen Heinz Tate, July 17, 1990. Helen Heinz Tate stated repeatedly that she had never had one moment of doubt about Tate's love for her and their future together.

132. Allen Tate to Charles Foster, June 14, 1965, Tate-Foster Papers.

133. Allen Tate to IG, July 1, 1965.

134. Interview with John and Margaret Goetz, August 4, 1990.

135. IG to Katherine Chapin Biddle [October 4, 1965], Biddle Family Papers. Of course, Tate had lied about the start of the affair.

136. IG to Katherine Chapin Biddle, October 18, 1965, Biddle Family Papers.

137. IG to Edward Dahlberg November 17, 1965, Dahlberg Papers.

138. Edward Dahlberg to IG, November 22, 1965.

139. Andrew Lytle to IG, n.d. .

140. Interview with David Hallman, September 30, 1988.

141. IG to Edward Dahlberg, November 23, 1965, Dahlberg Papers.

142. Carolyn Kizer to the author, December 4, 1989.

143. Interview with Boyd Thomes, July 28, 1990.

144. Interview with Elizabeth Brown, August 2, 1990.

145. In the interview with John and Margaret Goetz, August 4, 1990, Margaret informed me that Tate told her that marrying Heinz "was going to be great for him, because he was going to have a nurse to take care of him in his old age."

146. Interview with Roland Flint, May 15, 1990.

147. IG to Katherine Chapin Biddle, January 4, 1966, Biddle Family Papers.

148. Telephone interview with Paul Carroll, January 9, 1990.

149. Interview with Al Poulin, January 26, 1990.

150. Interview with Helen Heinz Tate, July 17, 1990.

151. Interview with Ned O'Gorman, April 3, 1990.

152. Catherine Gardner Mayes to IG, July 4, 1965.

153. Catherine Gardner Mayes to IG, May 6 [1966].

154. Kitty Gardner Herrick Coleman to George Peabody Gardner (father) and Rose Grosvenor Gardner, n.d. .

155. Kitty Gardner Herrick Coleman to George Peabody Gardner (father) and Rose Grosvenor Gardner, n.d. .

156. Allen Tate to IG, March 1, 1966.

157. Allen Tate to IG, April 4, 1966.

158. Allen Tate to IG, May 20, 1966.

159. Allen Tate to IG, November 18, 1974.

Chapter Eight "The Unaired Flat," 1966–1973

1. IG to Katherine Biddle, October 18, 1965, Biddle Family Papers.
2. Interview with Rosemarie Beck Phelps, February 19, 1990.
3. Interview with Jane Mayhall, March 22, 1990.
4. Interview with Pauline Hanson, December 3, 1989.
5. IG to Katherine Biddle, October 18, 1965, Biddle Family Papers.
6. IG, "Sapphic," manuscript, IG Papers; IG, "The Duet," manuscript, IG Papers.
7. Karl Shapiro to IG, November 11, 1965. Shapiro satirizes Lowell savagely in chapter 11: "I had no particular feeling about Wigg, as poets called him, except envy. Not envy for his poetry, which I thought wooden and fake and lacking in 'the poetry of' anything he wrote about, but envy for his genius for publicity. Whenever there was a Cause, Wigg could be seen on the platform, rolling his eyes and dealing out volumes of righteous indignation. . . . He was handy with conversions. When the real news of the German death camps became known after the Second War, Wigg publicly converted to Judaism and wrote Hasidic poems. He even forced his wife, the travel writer and belletrist, to shave her head and wear a *shaytl*" (p. 118). *Edsel* (1971) is a zany, sexy, undervalued autobiographical novel about a poet on the loose in a midwestern university town. It did not bring Shapiro the commercial success he had hoped for.
8. Peter Stitt, "In Praise of Isabella Gardner," 94, 96.
9. Peter Michelson, "Sentiment and Artifice: Elizabeth Bishop and Isabella Gardner," 193, 196.
10. Robert Huff, "The Lamb, the Clocks, the Blue Light," 45.
11. Gene Baro, "Clear Vision."
12. Elizabeth Bishop to IG, September 30, 1966.
13. Dabney Stuart, "Weights and Measures," 100; Irvin Ehrenpreis, "Solitude and Isolation," 335.
14. Allen Tate to Andrew Lytle, February 15, 1966, Lytle Papers.
15. F. H. Griffin Taylor, "A Point in Time, a Place in Space," 316.
16. IG to William Alfred, November 13, 1965, Alfred Papers; IG to John Logan, December 15, 1965, Logan Papers.
17. IG to John Goetz, October 26, 1965, Goetz Private Collection.
18. IG to Myra Cholden, November 11, 1965, Myra Cholden Brown Private Collection.
19. IG to Henry Rago, January 4, 1966, *Poetry* Lilly Papers.
20. IG to Henry Rago, February 2, 1966, Rago Papers.
21. IG to Richard Eberhart, May 26, 1966, Eberhart Papers.
22. Interview with Jane Mayhall, March 22, 1990.
23. IG to Katherine Chapin Biddle, June 4, 1966, Biddle Family Papers.
24. Robert Phelps is best known for his *Earthly Paradise: Colette's Autobiography Drawn from Her Lifetime Writings* (1966) and *Professional Secrets: An Autobiography of Jean Cocteau Drawn from His Lifetime Writings* (1970); Arnold Weinstein collaborated with the composer William Bolcom and is best known for his *The Red Eye of Love* and his adaptation of Ovid's *Metamorphoses*.
25. Paul Carroll to IG, November 7, 1966; Carroll's book was *The Poem in Its Skin*.
26. Barbara Harr Overmeijer to IG, July 1, 1964.
27. IG to Rosemarie Beck, July 7, 1966, in the author's possession.
28. IG to William Smith, June 22, 1966, Smith Papers.
29. Joseph Frank to IG, May 22, 1955.
30. William Congdon to IG, May 24, 1966.
31. William Congdon to IG, June 18, 1966.
32. IG to Rosemarie Beck, July 7, 1966, in the author's possession.
33. IG to James Wright, July 26, 1966, Wright Papers.
34. IG to Rosemarie Beck, July 12, 1966, in the author's possession.
35. Rosemarie Beck to IG, July 15, 1966.
36. IG, "Spousall Verse," manuscript, IG Papers.

37. IG to Rosemarie Beck, July 19, 1966, in the author's possession.

38. IG to Rosemarie Beck, July 31, 1966, in the author's possession.

39. Interview with Barbara Van Rensselaer Spalding, December 27, 1989.

40. Interview with Herbert Krohn, September 20, 1989.

41. Interview with Josephine Jacobsen, December 15, 1989; Florence Turner, *At the Chelsea,* 84. (She writes Shallot instead of Shalott.)

42. Interview with Josephine Jacobsen, December 15, 1989.

43. Interview with Anne Runk Wright, March 16, 1990.

44. Interview with Gerald Malanga, March 3, 1990.

45. Interview with Frank MacShane, February 15, 1990.

46. Interview with Anne Runk Wright, March 16, 1990; interview with Stella Waitzkin, March 1, 1990.

47. Gavin Selerie (editor), *The Riverside Interviews: 3. Gregory Corso,* 32.

48. Interview with Anne Runk Wright, March 16, 1990.

49. John Logan, "Verse Testament for Isabella Gardner," manuscript, July 12, 1981, IG Papers.

50. Interview with Carolyn Kizer, August 21, 1990.

51. IG, "The Trials of the Composer and His Birds," manuscript, IG Papers.

52. Interview with Jean Gould, February 26, 1990; interview with Anne Runk Wright, March 16, 1990.

53. IG to Rosemarie Beck, August 23, 1966, in the author's possession.

54. IG to Rosemarie Beck [ca. August 1966], in the author's possession.

55. IG to Charles and Doris Foster, September 2, 1966, Tate Papers.

56. IG to Rosemarie Beck, September 11, 1966, in the author's possession.

57. IG to Katherine Chapin Biddle, October 21, 1966, Biddle Family Papers.

58. IG to William Smith, November 17, 1966, Smith Papers.

59. IG to William Smith, October 28, 1966, Smith Papers.

60. John Stallworthy [Oxford University Press] to IG, October 18, 1966.

61. IG, "Letter from an Empty House," manuscript.

62. IG to John Logan, December 31, 1966, Logan Papers.

63. Maurice English, "Isabella Gardner: A Rhetoric of Passion," 147.

64. Karl Shapiro to IG, February 4, 1967.

65. Interview with Anne Runk Wright, March 16, 1990.

66. Erica Jong, "Chinese Food," manuscript enclosed in Erica Jong to IG, October 5, 1971.

67. IG to Edward Dahlberg, July 12, 1967, quotes his criticism of her "humanitarian shib-boleths" and emphasizes that she will never quit, Dahlberg Papers; IG to Dahlberg, January 25, 1968, Dahlberg Papers

68. IG to Edward Dahlberg, August 2, 1968, Dahlberg Papers.

69. Edward Dahlberg to IG, August 13, 1968.

70. H. E. F. Donohue to IG, April 11, 1968.

71. IG to Nancy Tate Wood, July 7, 1967, Gordon Papers.

72. IG to Dahlberg, July 22, 1967, Dahlberg Papers.

73. IG to Dahlberg, August 18, 1967, Dahlberg Papers.

74. IG to Francis Brown, editor of the *New York Times Book Review,* August 21, 1967, copy in IG Papers.

75. Lawrence Bensky to IG, August 21, 1967.

76. Robert M. Adams, "Crier in the Wilderness," *New York Review of Books,* August 24, 1967.

77. IG, draft letter to the *New York Times Book Review* [ca. August 25, 1967].

78. Tate to Robert Penn Warren, September 12, 1967, Warren Papers; IG to John Logan, August 14, 1967, Logan Papers.

79. Marcia Lee Masters to IG, n.d. .

80. IG to Edward Dahlberg, August 22, 1967, Dahlberg Papers.

81. Margaret Danner to IG, May 1, 1971.

82. Margaret Danner to IG, August 20, 1968.

83. Interview with Helen and Reed Whittemore, December 23, 1989.

84. Interview with Anne Runk Wright, March 16, 1990.

85. IG to Edward Dahlberg, August 2, 1968, Dahlberg Papers.

86. IG to Edward Dahlberg, July 25 [1968], Dahlberg Papers.

87. Louis Tytell to IG, August 7 [1968].

88. Daniel Seymour to IG, August 28 [1968].

89. IG to William Knott, February 6, 1969, in author's possession.

90. William Knott to IG, February 18, 1969.

91. Louis Tytell to IG, March 6, 1969.

92. IG to Nancy Tate Wood [ca. April 1969], Gordon Papers.

93. Regina Bryan to IG, April 14, 1969.

94. IG to Myra Cholden, July 16, 1969, Myra Cholden Brown Private Collection.

95. "Program for October 2nd (Paul Earls)," manuscript in IG Papers.

96. Interview with Herbert Krohn, September 20, 1989.

97. Interview with Vera Gold, September 18, 1989.

98. IG to Lee Anderson, December 25, 1969, Anderson Papers.

99. Charles Norman to Roland Flint, June 23, 1970, Flint Papers. Charles Norman and his wife, Anni, were living in Gardner's Minneapolis house at the time and had been thinking of buying it, but the deal fell through, and the Normans were angry.

100. IG to Edward Dahlberg, August 18, 1970, Dahlberg Papers.

101. Louis Tytell to IG, September 2, 1970.

102. IG to William Smith, December 11, 1970, Smith Papers.

103. IG to Riva Blevitsky Berkovitz, December 13, 1973, Blevitsky Berkovitz Private Collection.

104. Interview with Jane Mayhall, March 22, 1990; interview with Rosemarie Beck Phelps, February 19,1990.

105. Interview with Ned O'Gorman, April 3, 1990.

106. Ibid.

107. Interview with Herbert Krohn, September 20, 1989.

108. Interview with Anne Runk Wright, March 16, 1990.

109. Ibid.

110. Interview with Daniel Jones, September 22, 1989.

111. Interview with Ned O'Gorman, April 3, 1990.

112. Ibid.

113. Interview with Herbert Krohn, September 20, 1989.

114. IG, "Gill and I," manuscript, IG Papers.

115. Margaret Danner to IG, May 1, 1971.

116. Margaret Danner to IG, May 11, 1971.

117. Interview with Anne Runk Wright, March 16, 1990.

118. Interview with Irving Silver, March 6, 1990.

119. Ibid.

120. *Cocksucker Blues* can be viewed on YouTube.com.

121. Interview with Herbert Krohn, September 20, 1989.

122. All quotes are from Daniel Seymour, *A Loud Song.*

123. Ibid.

124. Rose Van Kirk to IG, June 18 [1970].

125. IG to William Smith, December 11, 1970, Smith Papers.

126. Rose Grosvenor Gardner to Rose Van Kirk, October 10, 1970.

127. Rose Van Kirk to IG, December 12 [1970].

128. Interview with Herbert Krohn, September 20, 1989.

129. Ibid.

130. Ibid.

131. George Peabody Gardner (father) to Rose Van Kirk, May 4, 1972.

132. Rose Van Kirk to George Peabody Gardner (father), May 16 [1972].

133. Anabel Holland was sure that Gill's connections with the mob had to be bought off.

134. William Congdon to IG, July 28 [1972] quotes Gardner in an earlier letter to him and comments.

Chapter Nine "The Dead Center of All Alone," 1974–1981

1. IG to Riva Blevitsky Berkovitz, December 13, 1973, Blevitsky Berkovitz Private Collection.

2. IG to Vera Gold [ca. late 1972].

3. IG to Riva Blevitsky Berkovitz, December 13, 1973, Blevitsky Berkovitz Private Collection.

4. In Rose Van Kirk to IG, April 26 [1973], Rose Van Kirk quotes her mother on voodoo.

5. Quoted by Maurice English to IG, January 20, 1975.

6. Rose Van Kirk to IG, June 6 [1973].

7. IG to Riva Blevitsky Berkovitz, January 21, 1974, Blevitsky Berkovitz Private Collection; IG to Vera Gold, September 13, 1973, Gold Private Collection.

8. IG to Rose Van Kirk, September 28, 1973.

9. Some of the information on Daniel's disappearance is from an interview with Bruce Rubenstein, August 31, 1990, and from "Danny's Boat" in Rubenstein's *Greed, Rage, and Love Gone Wrong: Murder in Minnesota*. Rubenstein is insightful but a bit too romantic, and he does not always get his facts right, particularly with respect to the Gardner family; Rubenstein, for instance, thinks Gardner was living alone in Los Angeles and mixes up her brothers George and Bob. Much information is from letters by and to Gardner and from speculations in interviews.

10. Daniel Seymour, *A Loud Song*.

11. Rose Van Kirk to IG, November 2 [1973]; IG to Riva Blevitsky Berkovitz, January 21, 1974, Blevitsky Berkovitz Private Collection. According to Bruce Rubenstein, it was George Gardner who got "Mr. Brown" involved, but evidence from a number of letters between Rose Van Kirk and her mother belies that.

12. Bruce Rubenstein, "Danny's Boat," 124.

13. Ibid., 121; Rose Van Kirk to IG, November 2 [1973].

14. Kathy Moore to IG [1974], copy in Rubenstein Private Collection.

15. IG to Kathy Moore [1974], copy in Rubenstein Private Collection.

16. IG to Riva Blevitsky Berkovitz, January 21, 1974, Blevitsky Berkovitz Private Collection.

17. Interview with Myra Cholden Brown, August 26, 1990.

18. Rose Van Kirk to IG, October 18 [1973].

19. Rose Van Kirk to IG, November 2 [1973].

20. Rose Van Kirk to IG, June 4 [1974].

21. Interview with Irving Silver, March 5, 1990.

22. IG to John Logan, June 27, 1974, Logan Papers.

23. John Logan to IG, July 12, 1974.

24. Kitty Gardner Herrick Coleman to IG [July 2, 1974]; Robert Woods Kennedy to IG, July 8, 1974; Josephine Jacobsen to IG, July 9, 1974.

25. Mary Hester to IG, August 31, 1974.

26. Betty Kronsky to IG, August 8 [1974].

27. IG to Kathy Moore [early August, 1974], copy in Rubenstein Private Collection.

28. Robert Gardner to IG, July 28, 1974; Rose Grosvenor Gardner to IG, July 28, 1974.

29. James Gill to IG, July 29, 1974.

30. IG to Nancy Tate Wood and Percy Wood [late 1974], Gordon Papers.

31. Anneke Van Kirk to IG, January 11, 1974.

32. IG to Robert Gardner, August 3, 1974, Robert Gardner Private Collection.

33. Fran Biddle to IG, January 24, 1974.

34. Letter by IG to the editors of the *New York Times* [ca. early 1974], copy in Logan Papers.

35. Fred McMahon, chairperson, department of speech communication, the University of California at Northridge to IG, November 13, 1974.

36. Steven Gould Axelrod to the author, July 29, 1989.

37. Conrad S. Spohnholz to IG, April 24, 1975.

38. "The impulse to preserve lies at the bottom of all art" is a quote by the poet Philip Larkin; Robert Gardner titled his film-making memoir *The Impulse to Preserve: Reflections of a Film-maker.*

39. Steven Gould Axelrod to IG, September 21, 1973, quotes from his interview with Gardner the day before.

40. Mary Manning to IG, January 18 [1974].

41. Mary Manning to IG, January 31 [1975]; Deirdre Bair, *Samuel Beckett: A Biography.*

42. Molly Laughlin to IG, n.d. .

43. IG to Nancy Tate Wood and Percy Wood, July 7, 1975, Gordon Papers.

44. Interview with Frank MacShane, February 15, 1990.

45. IG to George Peabody Gardner (brother), July 7, 1975.

46. Interview with Roland Flint, December 27, 1989.

47. Interview with Daniela Gioseffi, April 2, 1990.

48. Interview with Josephine Jacobsen, December 15, 1989.

49. John Logan to IG, June 13 to 18, 1975.

50. IG to Jay Bolotin, December 21, 1975, Bolotin Private Collection.

51. Interview with Myra Cholden Brown, August 26, 1990.

52. IG to Jay Bolotin, December 30, 1975, Bolotin Private Collection.

53. IG to John Logan, November 11, 1975, Logan Papers.

54. IG to Jay Bolotin, December 13, 1975, Bolotin Private Collection.

55. IG to Jay Bolotin, December 30, 1975, Bolotin Private Collection.

56. Interview with Ned O'Gorman, April 3, 1990.

57. Marguerite Harris lived from 1889 or 1899 to 1978 and bridged the gap between the Imagist and Surrealist writers and the Beats. Marguerite Harris to IG, January 1, 1976.

58. IG to Jay Bolotin, January 25, 1976, Bolotin Private Collection.

59. Jay Bolotin to IG, May 16, 1976.

60. Quoted in "Isabella Stewart Gardner, Author of 5 Books of Poetry," *Boston Globe,* July 10, 1981.

61. IG to George Peabody Gardner (father) and Rose Grosvenor Gardner, January 25, 1976, George Peabody Gardner Private Collection.

62. Karl Shapiro to IG, January 24, 1976.

63. IG to Jay Bolotin, April 6, 1976, Bolotin Private Collection.

64. IG to Jay Bolotin, March 25, 1976, Bolotin Private Collection.

65. Interview with Roland Flint, May 15, 1990.

66. IG to Roland Flint, October 29, 1976, Flint Papers.

67. Interview with Stella Waitzkin, March 1, 1990.

68. Interview with Myra Cholden Brown, August 26, 1990.

69. Interview with Robert Phillips, February 28, 1990.

70. Ibid.

71. IG to Roland Flint, n.d., Flint Papers.

72. Interview with Robert Peters, August 25, 1990.

73. "George Gardner Dies, Art Patron in Boston."

74. IG, "Letter to Paul Robeson (Born 1989—Died 1976)," *New Letters* 45, no. 1 (fall 1979): 92.

75. Julia Bartholomay to IG, December 6, 1976.

76. Bonnie Nims to IG, January 28, 1977.

77. IG to John Logan, July 14, 1978, Logan Papers.

78. IG to David Ray, August 18, 1978, Ray Private Collection.

79. Josephine Jacobsen to IG, September 15, 1978.

80. Joseph Parisi to Karl Shapiro, September 8, 1978.

81. John Frederick Nims to IG, September 5, 1979.

82. IG to John Frederick Nims, September 20, 1978, *Poetry* Papers.

83. Interview with Milton Kessler, March 26, 1990; interview with Richard Kostelanetz, April 1, 1990.

84. Interview with Milton Kessler, March 26, 1990.

85. Julia Dahlberg to IG, March 3, 1977.

86. IG to Jay Bolotin, March 22, 1978, Bolotin Private Collection.

87. Interview with Stephen Sandy, October 26, 1989.

88. Rose Van Kirk to IG, November 30, 1977; Rose Van Kirk to IG, November 19, 1977; IG to Jay Bolotin, July 13, 1977, quoting Rose Van Kirk, Bolotin Private Collection.

89. Catherine Mayes to IG, May 27 [1979?].

90. IG to Jay Bolotin, April 17, 1978, Bolotin Private Collection.

91. IG to Raymond Veeder, September 12, 1978, copy in IG Papers.

92. IG to Raymond Veeder, December 27, 1978, copy in IG Papers.

93. George Peabody Gardner (brother) to IG, May 20, 1977.

94. IG to Rose Gardner Cutler, August 13, 1977, Gardner Cutler Private Collection.

95. George Peabody Gardner (brother) to IG, August 3, 1977.

96. David McDowell to IG, July 26, 1978.

97. Letter, dictated by Allen Tate to David McDowell, n.d., McDowell Papers.

98. Interview with Robert Phillips, February 28, 1990.

99. IG to David McDowell, August 2, 1978, copy in IG Papers.

100. David McDowell to IG, February 27, 1979.

101. Andrew Lytle to IG, March 27, 1979.

102. William Meredith to IG, November 28, 1979. Gardner had also been considered for the job of consultant in poetry to the Library of Congress for 1978–1980.

103. IG, "The Four of Us and the Monkey," *Adena* 5, no. 1 (spring 1980): 9.

104. Maurice English to IG, October 23, 1979; Karl Shapiro to IG, November 25, 1979.

105. IG to Jay Bolotin, October 19, 1978, Bolotin Private Collection.

106. Interview with Robert Phillips, February 28, 1990.

107. Robert Phillips to IG, October 22, 1978.

108. Robert Giroux to IG, November 15, 1978.

109. Interview with Robert Phillips, February 28, 1990.

110. Aaron Siskind had also done the cover of *The Looking Glass*.

111. Muriel Rukeyser to Al Poulin, August 16, 1979, BOA Papers.

112. Roland Flint to IG, June 6, 1978; IG to Roland Flint, June 11, 1978, Flint Papers.

113. Roland Flint to IG, June 14, 1978.

114. Roland Flint to IG, June 6, 1978.

115. IG to Roland Flint, June 11, 1978, Flint Papers.

116. IG to James Wright, November 14, 1979, Wright Papers.

117. James Wright, blurb for *That Was Then,* BOA Papers.

118. Both quotations are from "News Notes: Poetry at the White House," 356.

119. Mildred Baker to IG [January 1980]. Kitty Carlisle Hart (1910–2007) was a singer, actress, and patron of the arts; for years she was the chair of the New York State Council on the Arts.

120. Frances Pole Sacco to IG, February 20, 1980; John Clark to IG, February 21, 1980.

121. Helen Machat Donohue Butler to IG, n.d. .

122. Mary Manning to IG, April 16 [1980]; Mary Manning to IG [early 1980].

123. Richard Eberhart to IG, February 20, 1980.

124. Josephine Jacobsen to IG, December 9, 1980.

125. Hannah Green to IG, April 30, 1980; *Little Saint* was published posthumously by Random House in 2000 to great critical acclaim.

126. Shapiro, *Reports of My Death,* 37; Karl Shapiro to IG, March 22, 1980.

127. IG to Al Poulin, April 2, 1980, BOA Papers.

128. Robert Phillips to Al Poulin, July 30, 1980, BOA Papers.

129. I have not been able to find the essay that *Parnassus* commissioned from Robert Phillips. Perhaps Phillips retracted it, for on July 30, 1980, he wrote to Al Poulin: "I am taking the precaution of sharing with you my review, for PARNASSUS, of her book. Please don't tell anyone I did this—it's highly unusual for a publisher to see a review before the magazine that commissioned it does. But I'm showing it to you because of your knowledge of her reactions to the printed word, based on your working relationship. Could you read this, and tell me where she may be offended? I don't want to jeopardize my friendship with her. If need be, I'll deep-six the whole review." BOA Papers; Jerome Mazzaro, "At the Start of the Eighties," 461.

130. Leon Driskell, "A Sensitive Collection from Poet Gardner."

131. Vernon Young, "Hell and Death," 14.

132. William Smith to IG, October 13, 1980.

133. IG to Bonnie Nims, March 31, 1981, Nims Papers.

134. IG to Al Poulin, May 18, 1981, BOA Papers.

135. William Congdon to IG, September 24, 1976.

136. IG to William Congdon, June 16, 1979, Congdon Foundation Papers.

137. William Congdon to IG, July 15, 1979.

138. IG to William Congdon, September 25, 1979, Congdon Foundation Papers.

139. William Congdon to IG, October 8, 1980, Congdon Foundation Papers. Congdon quotes from Jacques Maritain, *Creative Intuition in Art and Poetry* (1953).

140. IG to William Congdon, July 7, 1980, Congdon Foundation Papers.

141. IG to Rose Grosvenor Gardner, May 11, 1981.

142. Ed Berryman to IG, May 22 [1981].

143. IG to George Peabody Gardner (brother) [ca. August 1980].

144. Roland Flint to IG, October 15, 1980.

145. IG to John Frederick Nims, December 22, 1980, Nims Papers.

146. Quoted by Blanche Dombeck to IG, December 28, 1980; IG to Bonnie Nims, January 12, 1981, Nims Papers.

147. Interview with Ned O'Gorman, April 3, 1990; IG to Carol Bergé [May 1981], Bergé Papers.

148. IG to Carol Bergé, June 2, 1981, Bergé Papers.

149. Roland Flint to IG, June 24, 1976.

150. Robert Phillips, "Queen Anne's Lace."

151. The stories about Gardner's death are somewhat contradictory; some say she was found sitting in a chair and that the television was on.

152. Gardner, *Impulse to Preserve,* 269. Adele would become his second wife.

Epilogue

1. Interview with Myra Cholden Brown, August 26, 1990.

2. "Isabella Gardner, 66; Wrote Books of Poetry."

3. "Isabella Stewart Gardner, Author of 5 Books of Poetry."

4. Quoted in Roland Flint, "A Memorial Reading for Isabella Stuart [*sic*]Gardner, Great Neck Public Library, Great Neck, LI; April 4, 1982," manuscript, IG Papers.

5. Interview with Eric Stange, December 1, 1989.

6. Interview with Roland Flint, May 15, 1990.

7. Isabella Gardner in *Epitaphs by Poets on Themselves,* (Brooklyn Heights, NY: Broadsides from America, 1965), n.p.

8. "New York's Poet Laureate."

9. Anne Runk Wright, "A Memorial Reading for Isabella Gardner," manuscript, IG Papers.

10. George Peabody Gardner (brother) to Roland Flint, June 22, 1998, Flint Papers.

Works Cited

Manuscript Sources

Alfred Papers. William Alfred Papers, Brooklyn College Library, Brooklyn College, Brooklyn NY.

Anderson Papers. Lee Anderson Papers, Washington University Libraries, Department of Special Collections, Washington University, St. Louis MO.

Bergé Papers. Carol Bergé Papers, Washington University Libraries, Department of Special Collections, Washington University, St. Louis MO

Berryman Papers. John Berryman Papers, University of Minnesota Libraries, University of Minnesota, Minneapolis.

Biddle Family Papers, Georgetown University Libraries, Georgetown University, Washington DC.

Biddle Papers, Francis. Francis Biddle Papers, Georgetown University Libraries, Georgetown University, Washington DC.

Biddle Papers, Katherine. Katherine Biddle Papers, Georgetown University Libraries, Georgetown University, Washington DC.

Blevitsky Berkovitz, Riva. Private Collection.

BOA Papers, Beinecke Rare Book and Manuscript Library, Yale University, New Haven CT.

Bolotin, Jay. Private Collection.

Brooks Papers. Cleanth Brooks Papers, Beinecke Rare Book and Manuscript Library, Yale University, New Haven CT.

Carroll Papers. Paul Carroll Papers, Special Collections Research Center, University of Chicago Library, The University of Chicago, Chicago IL.

Cholden Brown, Myra. Private Collection.

Congdon Foundation Papers. William G. Congdon Foundation, Milan, Italy.

Dahlberg Papers. Edward Dahlberg Papers, Harry Ransom Humanities Research Center, The University of Texas at Austin.

Davidson-Tate Papers. Donald Davidson Papers, Vanderbilt University Special Collections, Vanderbilt University, Nashville TN.

Eberhart Papers. Richard Eberhart Papers, Dartmouth College Library, Dartmouth College, Hanover NH.

Flint Papers. Roland Flint Papers, University of Maryland Libraries, University of Maryland, College Park.

Gardner, Isabella Stewart Papers. Isabella Stewart Gardner Papers, Isabella Stewart Gardner Museum, Boston MA.

Gardner, George Peabody. Private Collection.

Gardner, Robert. Private Collection.

Gardner Cutler, Rose. Private Collection.

Goetz, John. Private Collection.

Gold, Vera. Private Collection.

Gordon Papers. Caroline Gordon Papers, Manuscripts Division, Department of Rare Books and Special Collections, Princeton University Library, Princeton University, Princeton NJ.

Grosvenor Papers. Grosvenor Family Papers, Manuscript Division, Library of Congress, Washington DC.

Howes Papers. Barbara Howes Smith Papers, Manuscripts Division, Department of Rare Books and Special Collections,Princeton University Library, Princeton University, Princeton NJ.

IG Papers. Isabella Gardner Papers, Washington University Libraries, Department of Special Collections, Washington University, St. Louis MO.

Kinnell Papers. Galway Kinnell Papers, The Lilly Library, Indiana University, Bloomington.

Logan Papers. John Logan Papers, University Libraries, State University of New York, Buffalo.

Lowell Papers. Robert Lowell Papers, Houghton Library, Harvard University, Cambridge MA.

Lytle Papers. Andrew Lytle Papers, Vanderbilt University Special Collections, Vanderbilt University, Nashville TN.

McDowell Papers. David McDowell Papers, Vanderbilt University Special Collections, Vanderbilt University, Nashville TN.

Modern Poetry Association Papers. Modern Poetry Association Papers, *Poetry*, Chicago IL.

Nims Papers. John Frederick Nims Papers, The Lilly Library, Indiana University, Bloomington.

Poetry Lilly Papers. *Poetry* Papers, The Lilly Library, Indiana University, Bloomington.

Poetry Papers, Special Collections Research Center, University of Chicago Library, University of Chicago, Chicago IL.

Porter Papers. Katherine Anne Porter Papers, University of Maryland Libraries, University of Maryland, College Park.

Rago Papers. Henry Rago Papers, The Lilly Library, Indiana University, Bloomington.

Ray, David. Private Collection.

Rubenstein, Bruce. Private Collection.

Shapiro, Karl. Private Collection.

Shapiro Congress Papers. Karl Shapiro Papers, Manuscript Division, Library of Congress, Washington DC.

Shapiro Papers. Karl Shapiro Papers, Harry Ransom Humanities Research Center, The University of Texas at Austin.

Smith Papers. William Jay Smith Papers, Washington University Libraries, Department of Special Collections, Washington University, St. Louis MO.

Tate-Foster Papers. Allen Tate and Charles Foster Papers, Manuscripts Division, Department of Rare Books and Special Collections, Princeton University Library, Princeton University, Princeton NJ.

Tate Papers. Allen Tate Papers, Manuscripts Division, Department of Rare Books and Special Collections, Princeton University Library, Princeton University, Princeton NJ.

University of Chicago Press Papers, Special Collections Research Center, University of Chicago Library, The University of Chicago, Chicago IL.

Warren Papers. Robert Penn Warren Papers, Beinecke Rare Book and Manuscript Library, Yale University, New Haven CT.

Winnetka Fortnightly Papers, The Newberry Library, Chicago IL.

Wright Papers. James Wright Papers, Kenyon College Library, Kenyon College, Gambier OH.

Published Sources

Adams, Robert M. "Crier in the Wilderness." *New York Times Book Review*, August 24, 1967.

Alden, Betty. "Studio Club Starts Rehearsal for Play at Copley." *Boston Evening Transcript*, April 27, 1937.

Aldrich, Nelson W., Jr. *Old Money: The Mythology of America's Upper Class.* New York: Alfred A. Knopf, 1988.

Amory, Cleveland. *Who Killed Society?* New York: Harper, 1960.

Anastoplo, George. "Maurice F. X. Donohue, 1911–1995." *University of Chicago Record* 31, no. 4 (1997): 16.

Anonymous. "A Conversation with Thomas Hilgers and Michael Molloy." In *A Ballet for the Ear: Interviews, Essays and Reviews*, edited by John Logan and A. Poulin Jr., 51–60. Ann Arbor: University of Michigan Press, 1983.

——. "Becomes Bride Today." *Chicago Daily Tribune*, January 4, 1944.

——. "Brookline Girl to Wed Mr. Herrick." *Washington Post*, August 17, 1934.

——. "Decree Granted." *Chicago Daily Tribune,* February 22, 1950.

——. "Dramatic Club Names 'Wind and Rain' Cast." *Harvard Crimson,* April 21, 1936.

——. "Fashion's Fads and Fancies." *Washington Post,* December 4, 1912.

——. "Film Stars Seen in One-Act Plays." Clipping, IG Papers.

——. "George Gardner Dies, Art Patron in Boston." *New York Times,* September 18, 1976.

——. "Gloria Swanson, Francis Lederer at Ford's in 'Three Curtains.'" Clipping, IG Papers.

——. "Grosvenor-Gardner Nuptials Expected." *New York Times,* September 23, 1912.

——. "100 of the Year's Outstanding Books . . . A Selected Guide to Summer Reading." *New York Times Book Review,* June 5, 1955.

——. "Isabella Gardner, 66; Wrote Books of Poetry." *New York Times,* July 10, 1981.

——. "Isabella Stewart Gardner, Author of 5 Books of Poetry." *Boston Globe,* July 10, 1981.

——. "Junior Leaguer Is Cockney Maid of 'Blithe Spirit.'" Clipping [1942], IG Papers.

——. "A List of 250 Outstanding Books . . . A Christmas Guide." *New York Times Book Review,* December 4, 1955.

——. "New Magazine Is Out; Sales Brisk." *Chicago Daily Tribune,* February 27, 1954.

——. "Newport Amateurs in a Wilde Play." *New York Times,* June 26, 1910.

——. "News Notes. Poetry at the White House." *Poetry* 135, no. 6 (March 1980): 356-57.

——. "News of Newport: Tableaux Vivants at Casino Theater a Financial and Artistic Success." *Washington Post,* August 25, 1910.

——. "New York's Poet Laureate." *Rochester Democrat and Chronicle,* February 11, 1982.

——. "R. H. McCormick III Sued by Wife for Desertion." *Chicago Tribune,* June 20, 1950.

——. "'Roslyn,' A Newport Villa: The Summer Home of Mr. William Grosvenor, on Beacon Hill." *Town and Country,* August 26, 1905, 10.

——. "Seeks Divorce." *Chicago Daily Tribune,* February 16, 1950.

——. "Sidelights on the Smart Set." *Washington Post,* October 5, 1912.

——. "Simplicity a Feature of the Wedding of Miss Harriot Daly and Count Anton Sigray Von Febre." *New York Times,* April 3, 1910.

——. "Society at Home and Abroad." *New York Times,* January 12, 1913.

——. "Studio Group Gives Pleasing 'Stunt Night.'" *Guild Hall Scrapbook* 3:79 [August 5, 1937].

——. "Three Curtains." Clipping, IG Papers.

———. "To Join Coward Show." *New York Times*, June 24, 1942.

Atlas, James. *Bellow: A Biography*. New York: Random House, 2000.

Axelrod, Steven Gould. *Robert Lowell: Life and Art*. Princeton NJ: Princeton University Press, 1978.

Axmaker, Sean. "Stewart Stern: The Storyteller." http://www.greencine.com/art icle?action=view&articleID=298

Bair, Deirdre. *Samuel Beckett: A Biography*. New York: Harcourt Brace Jovanovich, 1978.

Baro, Gene. "Clear Vision." *New York Times Book Review*, March 26, 1967.

Biddle, Francis. *A Casual Past*. Garden City NY: Doubleday, 1961.

Boyle, Andrew. *The Riddle of Erskine Childers*. London: Hutchinson, 1977.

Bradley, Van Allen. "Isabella Gardner: Poet in Search of an Audience." *Chicago Illustrated News*, June 30, 1962.

Breit, Harvey. "Dame Day." *New York Times Book Review*, March 20, 1955.

Brown, Kenneth A. "Gathering to Celebrate the Art of Leighton Rollins' Life." *Santa Barbara News-Press*, April 6, 1980.

Butcher, Fanny. "The Literary Spotlight." *Chicago Tribune*, February 6, 1955.

C., G. F. "The Festival Theatre: 'See Naples and Die.'" *Cambridge Review*, June 8, 1939, n.p.

Campbell, Roy. "Memories of Dylan Thomas at the B.B.C." *Poetry* 87, no. 2 (November 1955): 111-14.

Carroll, Paul. "Fair, Foul and Full of Variations: The Generation of 1962." In *The Poem in Its Skin*, 202–59. Chicago: Follett, 1968.

———. "A Note on Isabella Gardner." *Poetry* 101, no. 3 (December 1962): 215–17.

———. *Odes*. Chicago: Big Table, 1969.

———. *The Poem in Its Skin*. Chicago: Follett, 1968.

———. "Un Voyage à Cythère." *Poetry* 85, no. 6 (October 1954-March 1955): 319.

Cass, Judith. "Miss Bersbach Bride of Young R. H. McCormick." *Chicago Daily Tribune*, September 12, 1937.

———. "Mrs. Seymour to Wed R. H. McCormick III." *Chicago Daily Tribune*, March 2, 1951.

Chapman, Peter. *Bananas: How the United Fruit Company Shaped the World*. Edinburgh, New York, Melbourne: Canongate, 2007.

Chase, Al. "Twin Co-op Apartments Are Planned." *Chicago Daily Tribune*, April 9, 1949.

Cohen, Harold V. "Blithe Are Spirits of Mr. Coward." Clipping, IG Papers.

Congdon, William. *America Addio: Lettere A Belle*. Milan: Jaca Books, 1980.

DeLancey, Rose Mary. "Poets' Views of Their Worlds Differ Widely." *Fort Wayne News Sentinel*, February 10, 1962.

Douglas, Martin. "Martin Manulis, TV Pioneer, Dies at 92." *New York Times*, October 2, 2007.

Drewry, Carleton. "Three New Volumes of Poetry." *Roanoke Times,* November 26, 1961.

Driskell, Leon. "A Sensitive Collection from Poet Gardner." *Louisville Courier,* date unknown.

Editors. "Announcement." *Poetry* 81, no. 1 (1952): A.

Ehrenpreis, Irving. "Solitude and Isolation." *Virginia Quarterly Review* 42, no. 2 (Spring 1966): 332–36.

English, Maurice. "Isabella Gardner: A Rhetoric of Passion." *Tri-Quarterly* 7 (Fall 1966): 145–49.

Fowlie, Wallace. "Three Poets." *Accent* 15 (Summer 1955): 237–40.

Foxcroft Yearbook 1932. IG Papers.

Foxcroft Yearbook 1933. IG Papers.

Gardner, Frank Augustine. *Gardner Memorial: A Biographical and Genealogical Record of the Descendants of Thomas Gardner, Planter.* Salem MA: privately printed, 1933.

Gardner, George Peabody Gardner Jr. *Chiefly the Orient: An Undigested Journal.* Norwood MA: Plimpton Press, privately printed, 1912.

Gardner, Isabella. *Birthdays from the Ocean.* Boston MA: Houghton Mifflin, 1955.

——. *The Collected Poems.* Brockport, NY: BOA Editions, 1990.

——. "The Fellowship with Essence: An Afterword." In *The Collected Poems,* 161–62. Brockport, NY: BOA Editions, 1990.

——. *The Looking Glass.* Chicago: University of Chicago Press, 1961.

——. *Un'Altra Infanzia.* Translated by Alfredo Rizzardi. Bologna: Libraria Antiquaria Palmaverde, 1959.

——. *That Was Then: New and Selected Poems.* Brockport, NY: BOA Editions, 1979.

——. *West of Childhood: Poems 1950–1965.* Boston MA: Houghton Mifflin, 1965.

Gardner, Robert. *The Impulse to Preserve: Reflections of a Filmmaker.* New York: Other Press, 2006.

——. "The Other Isabella: Isabella Gardner, The Poet (1915–1981)." Speech, Isabella Stewart Gardner Museum, April 12, 2007.

Gentry, Charles. "Coward Comedy Is Tops." Clipping, IG Papers.

Gould, Jean. *American Women Poets: Pioneers of Modern Poetry.* New York: Dodd, Mead, 1980.

Griffin Taylor, F. H. "A Point in Time, a Place in Space: Six Poets and the Changeling Present." *Sewanee Review* 77, no. 2 (April-June 1969): 300–318.

Hamilton, Ed. *Legends of the Chelsea Hotel: Living with Artists and Outlaws in New York's Rebel Mecca.* New York: Thunder's Mouth Press, 2007.

——. www.hotelchelseablog.com

Hamilton, Saskia, ed. *The Letters of Robert Lowell*. New York: Farrar, Straus and Giroux, 2005.

Hancock, Patricia. "Dream House of Tomorrow: Is This It?" *Chicago Daily News*, May 12, 1954.

Hewitt, S. Tobie, ed. "A Conversation with Anthony Piccioni and A. Poulin, Jr." In *A Ballet for the Ear: Interviews, Essays and Reviews*, edited by John Logan and Al Poulin Jr., 21–37. Ann Arbor: University of Michigan Press, 1983.

Hine, Daryl, and Joseph Parisi, eds. *The Poetry Anthology, 1912–1977: Sixty-five Years of America's Most Distinguished Verse Magazine*. Boston MA: Houghton Mifflin, 1978.

Holley, Fred S. "5 Poetic Visions Evaluated." *Norfolk Virginia-Pilot*, July 29, 1962.

Holzhauer, Robert A. "Two Midwestern Poets." *Milwaukee Journal*, April 22, 1962.

Huff, Robert. "The Lamb, the Clocks, the Blue Light." *Poetry* 109 (October 1966): 44–48.

Hughes, Elinor. "The Theater." *Boston Herald*, July 16, 1941.

Jacobsen, Josephine. "Two Poets." *Baltimore Sun*, May 5, 1955.

Janssen, Marian. *The Kenyon Review 1939–1970: A Critical History*. Baton Rouge: Louisiana State University Press, 1990.

——. "Postillion for Pegasus: Isabella Gardner and *Poetry*." In *Uneasy Alliance: Twentieth-Century American Literature, Culture and Biography*, edited by Hans Bak, 199–213. Amsterdam and New York: Rodopi, 2004.

Jarrell, Randall. "Recent Poetry." *Yale Review* 45, no. 1: 122–32.

Jesson, Henry. *And Beacons Burn Again: Letters from an English Soldier*. Edited by Leighton Rollins. New York and London: D. Appleton-Century Company, 1940.

Killorin, Joseph, ed. *Selected Letters of Conrad Aiken*. New Haven: Yale University Press, 1978.

Kinnell, Galway. "New Volumes from Two Poets." *Chicago Magazine* (June 1951): 61–62.

Kunitz, Stanley. "Five Points of the Compass." *Poetry* 88, no. 3 (June 1956): 183-91.

Logan, John. "The Celebration of Birthdays." *Sewanee Review* 64, no. 1 (Winter 1956): 161–63.

——. "Mother Cabrini's Bones." *Poetry* 81, no. 6 (March 1953): 350-51

——. "The Poetry of Isabella Gardner." *Sewanee Review* 70, no. 2 (Spring 1962): 250–53.

——. "Spring Chill." *Poetry* 81, no. 6 (1953): 350–51.

Logan, John, and A. Poulin Jr., eds. *A Ballet for the Ear: Interviews, Essays and Reviews*. Ann Arbor: University of Michigan Press, 1983.

Loring, Kathryn. "They Were There." *Chicago Daily Tribune,* September 30, 1953.

Lyndon, Marion. "Dinner before Large Dance: Affair for 50 Guests to Precede Ball in Honor of Isabella Stewart Gardner—Mrs. Theodore E. Brown also Entertaining." *Boston Globe,* December 19, 1933.

Lyon, Herb. "Tower Ticker." *Chicago Daily Tribune,* January 6, 1955.

McDermott, William V. *A Surgeon in Combat: European Theatre-World War II.* Dublin NH: William L. Bauhan, 1997.

Makowsky, Veronica A. *Caroline Gordon: A Biography.* New York: Oxford University Press, 1989.

Maritain, Jacques. *Creative Intuition in Art and Poetry.* New York: Pantheon Books, 1953.

Mazzaro, Jerome. "At the Start of the Eighties." *Hudson Review* 33, no. 3 (Autumn 1980): 455–68.

Michelson, Peter. "Sentiment and Artifice: Elizabeth Bishop and Isabella Gardner." *Chicago Review* 18, nos. 3 and 4 (1966): 188–96.

Millier, Brett. *Elizabeth Bishop: Life and the Memory of It.* Berkeley, Los Angeles, London: University of California Press, 1993.

Mills, Ralph J. Jr. "Three American Poets." *Modern Age* (Winter 1961–1962): 102–6.

Mitchell, Jack. "Capturing Emotion in Motion: Photographing Ballet Dance." *Dance Magazine,* December 1999, http://findarticles.com/p/articles/mi_m1083/is_12_73/ai_58050370/

Monks, John Peabody, *Roque Island, Maine: A History.* Edited by Diana Whitehill Laing. Boston: The Colonial Society of Massachusetts, 1964.

Morrow, Lance. *The Chief: A Memoir of Fathers and Sons.* New York: Random House, 1984.

Nims, John Frederick. "Poetry: Ironic to Romantic." *Chicago Sunday Tribune,* April 3, 1955.

Officer, Lawrence H., and Samuel H. Williamson. "Purchasing Power of Money in the United States from 1774 to 2008." MeasuringWorth, 2009. http://www.measuringworth.com/powerus/

Oostdijk, Diederik. "Karl Shapiro and *Poetry: A Magazine of Verse* (1950–1955)." PhD. diss., Radboud University, Nijmegen, 2000.

Ostriker, Alice. "American Poetry Now Shaped by Women." *New York Times Book Review,* March 9, 1986.

Page, Eleanor. "Junior League to Hear Tutor of Princess." *Chicago Daily Tribune,* March 21, 1951.

Palffy, Eleanor. *Largely Fiction.* Boston and Cambridge MA: Houghton Mifflin Company and The Riverside Press, 1948.

Parisi, Joseph, and Steven Young, comps. and eds. *Dear Editor: A History of Poetry in Letters. The First Fifty Years, 1912–1962.* Introduction by Billy Collins. New York and London: W. W. Norton and Company, 2002.

Phillips, Robert. "Queen Anne's Lace." In *Personal Accounts: New and Selected Poems, 1966–1986*, 54–56. Princeton NJ: Ontario Review Press, 1986.

Plath, Sylvia. *The Journals of Sylvia Plath.* Edited by Ted Hughes and Frances McCullough. New York: Ballantine Books, 1983.

Power, Fremont. "Voice from the Balcony." Clipping, IG Papers.

Quick, Dorothy. "Theater on Huntting Lane—The Leighton Rollins School of Acting." In *East Hampton Invents the Culture of Summer: The Legacy of the Woodhouse Family of Huntting Lane,* edited by Ellen R. Samuels, Robert A. M. Stern, Margaret Stocker, and Enez Whipple, 33–39. East Hampton NY: East Hampton Historical Society, 1994.

Rago, Henry. "A Statement by the New Editor." *Poetry* 87, no. 1 (1955): 39.

Ransom, John Crowe. "The Poet as Woman." Review of *Edna St. Vincent Millay and Her Times,* by Elizabeth Atkins. In *The World's Body,* 76–110. Baton Rouge: Louisiana State University Press, 1968. First published 1938 by Charles Scribner's Sons.

Rico, Diana. *Kovacsland: A Biography of Ernie Kovacs.* San Diego, New York, London: Harcourt Brace Jovanovich, 1990.

Robie, Burton A. Review of *My Sad Captains and Other Poems* by Thom Gunn and *The Looking Glass* by Isabella Gardner. *Library Journal* 86, no. 17 (October 1, 1961): 3286.

Rodman, Selden. "The Content and the Form." *New York Times,* May 22, 1955.

Rosenthal, M. L. "Comment." *Poetry* 151, nos. 1–2 (October-November 1987): 199-226.

Rubenstein, Bruce. "Danny's Boat." In *Greed, Rage, and Love Gone Wrong: Murder in Minnesota,* 109–30. Minneapolis: University of Minnesota Press, 2005.

Sarton, May. *A World of Light: Portraits and Celebrations.* New York: W. W. Norton and Company, 1988. First published 1976 by W. W. Norton and Company.

Selerie, Gavin, ed. "Gregory Corso." In *The Riverside Interviews: 3.* London: Binnacle Press, 1982.

Seymour, Daniel. *A Loud Song.* New York: Lustrum Press, 1971.

Seymour, Maurice. *Ballet Portraits.* New York: Pellegrini and Cudahy, 1952.

——. "Introduction." In *Seymour on Ballet: 101 Photographs,* unnumbered pages. Foreword by Leonide Massine. New York: Pellegrini and Cudahy, 1947.

Shapiro, Karl. "Dylan Thomas." *Poetry* 87 no. 2 (November 1955): 100-110.

——. *Edsel.* New York: Bernard Geiss Associates, 1971.

——. *In Defense of Ignorance.* New York: Random House, 1960.

——. *Reports of My Death.* Chapel Hill NC: Algonquin Books, 1990.

——. "Voices that Speak to the Critic in Very Different Rhythms." *New York*

Times Book Review, December 24, 1961.

Sitwell, Edith. "A Tidy, Natural Taste." *Saturday Review of Literature,* July 9, 1955, 14.

Smith, Hal. Review of *Best Poems of 1959: The Looking Glass* by Isabella Gardner and *My Sad Captains and Other Poems* by Thom Gunn. *Epoch* 11, no. 3 (Fall 1961): 187–90.

Stevens, Ashton. "Mr. Coward and Some High Spirits." Clipping, IG Papers.

Stitt, Peter. "In Praise of Isabella Gardner." *Minnesota Review* 6, no. 1 (1966): 93–96.

Stuart, Dabney. "Weights and Measures." *Shenandoah* 17, no. 2 (Winter 1966): 91–102.

Tharp, Louise Hall. *Mrs. Jack: A Biography of Isabella Stewart Gardner.* Boston MA: Little, Brown, 1965.

Thorndike, Joseph T. "Mrs. Jack and Her Back Bay Palazzo." *American Heritage Magazine* 29, no. 6 (October-November 1978). http://www.americanheritage.com/articles/magazine/ah/1978/6/1978_6_44.shtml

Turner, Florence. *At the Chelsea.* San Diego, New York, London: Harcourt Brace Jovanovich, 1987.

Underwood, Thomas. *Allen Tate: Orphan of the South.* Princeton NJ: Princeton University Press, 2000.

Waldron, Ann. *Close Connections: Caroline Gordon and the Southern Renaissance.* New York: Putnam, 1987.

Webster, Harvey Curtis. "Five Poets." *Poetry* 101, no. 3 (December 1962): 209–14.

Wecter, Dixon. *The Saga of American Society: A Record of Social Aspiration 1607–1937.* New York: Charles Scribner's Sons, 1937.

Whipple, Enez. *Guild Hall of East Hampton.* New York: Harry N. Abrams, Inc., 1993.

———. "Remembering Mary Woodhouse." In *East Hampton Invents the Culture of Summer: The Legacy of the Woodhouse Family of Huntting Lane,* edited by Ellen R. Samuels, Robert A.M. Stern, Margaret Stocker and Enez Whipple, 17–31. East Hampton NY: East Hampton Historical Society, 1994.

Wreszin, Michael. *A Rebel in Defense of Tradition: The Life and Politics of Dwight Macdonald.* New York: Basic Books, a Division of HarperCollins, 1994.

Wright, James. "Gravity and Incantation." *Minnesota Review* 2, no. 3 (Spring 1962): 424–27.

Young, John Nichols. *Erskine H. Childers, President of Ireland: A Biography.* Gerrards Cross: Colin Smythe, 1985.

Young, Vernon. "Hell and Death." *New York Times Book Review,* September 21, 1980.

Acknowledgments

Not at All What One Is Used To: The Life and Times of Isabella Gardner was long in the making. I started out in 1989 as a young Dutch scholar, just after I had finished my critical history of the *Kenyon Review*. I traveled all over the United States, doing archival research and talking to over a hundred people who had known Gardner. I had one of the best years of my life due principally to the munificent generosity of librarians and those I interviewed. On my return to the Netherlands, I was all set to start writing, but, instead, became the head of my university's international office. In between visits to all corners of the world, from Bolivia to Tanzania, from Djakarta to Tokyo, I managed to write some articles about Gardner and other American poets, but there was simply no time and rest for the concerted effort a biography requires. Thousands of copied letters became brittle, photographs faded, and the taped voices of my interviewees grew dim.

All that changed when, some fifteen years later, at the instigation of Gardner's Hotel Chelsea friend, the ever-kind Herbert Krohn, Richard Lingner of the Isabella Stewart Gardner Museum in Boston asked me if I would like to take part in an evening devoted to "The Other Isabella." I jumped at the chance and, together with Krohn and Gardner's brother Robert, told her dramatic life story. At dinner that night, Robert asked me if I ever was going to finish the biography, and I had to confess that Gardner would have to be my retirement project. The next day I received a letter in which I was offered a year's fellowship.

I immersed myself in my dusty research materials. Rereading Gardner's correspondence and listening to the interviews, I felt fortunate, grateful, and often sad, because many of those to whom I had talked have died since. Each interview was special, from the one at Gardner's palatial parental home with her beloved brother George, to the one at McDonald's with Gardner's protégé, ex-junkie poet Morty Sklar. Daniel Jones took me to St. Mark's and Gardner's grave and sent me many of the photographs in this book. Maurice Seymour spent almost two days with me and invited me to his granddaughter's wedding rehearsal dinner, where I first met Raoul Van Kirk, Gardner's grandson, then a teenager. Fifteen years later, Raoul flew from his home in California to Boston to attend the Isabella Gardner evening; and he, too, has been generous with information, photographs, and food. Seymour's daughter, Sydney Seymour Fingold, opened up her home and heart to me, as did his niece, Riva Blevitsky Berkovitz. Although Anabel Holland was troubled by a recent fire in her home and afflicted by health problems, she talked to me for hours and, later, sent the letter that starts this book. I spent a snowy New Year's weekend at Maurice Donohue's house in West Virginia; he became a friend. I never saw so many stars as the night I stayed at Butler's Point, Maine, with Robert Hall McCormick III and his wife, Mary, who served me a lobster dinner. Gardner's warm-hearted sister Rose and her husband, Philip, had me to lunch twice in their beautiful house in Marion, Massachusetts. Roland Flint, Gardner's literary executor before his early death, spent two days with me at Yaddo. In New York City, Michael Andre took me to the Metropolitan Opera, Robert Phillips to a Halloween Party with George Plimpton, and Ruth Herschberger to the White Horse Tavern. Thomas Underwood, Allen Tate's biographer, talked with me about the love of Gardner's life, shared his address book with me, and helped me buy my first car ever, which carried me across America. Tate's cousin, Lucas Myers, fed me a southern dinner, and Gardner's protégée, Shreela Ray, cooked an Indian one. Nina Kearns, Gardner's niece, though leaving the next day for a long stay in Japan, took time off to talk to me and show me her Billy Congdon paintings. When I met white-haired, piercingly blue-eyed Congdon himself in Italy it was as if his letters had come alive; in between religious exhortations and tales of sexual indiscretions he suggested that a little madness was an essential characteristic for Gardner's biographer. I saw many of Congdon's paintings in Italy and wish I owned one. Lorna Ritz, exceedingly thin, battling cancer, reminisced surrounded by her spacious, magnificent canvases. Her former lover, Jay Bolotin, entrusted me with Gardner's letters to him.

Here I list, in alphabetical order, all those others I interviewed—generally in person, sometimes on the telephone—who not only helped my understanding of Gardner and her times, but also often hosted me. I am very grateful to all of them. Daniel Aaron, Mary Baker, Mildred Baker, Rodolfo Balzarotti, Stanley Bard, Rosemarie Beck, Mr. and Mrs. Edmund Biddle, Ann Birstein, Tom and Martha Blagden, Philip Booth, Lucy Bowron, Constance Breuer, Elizabeth Brown, Myra Cholden Brown, Jean Burden, Pierce Butler, Larry Calcagno, Paul Carroll, John Clark, Marvin Cohen, William Cole, Allen Davis III, Fellowes Davis, Charles DeFanti, James Dickey, Kate Donahue, H. E. F. Donohue, Paul Earls, Richard Eberhart, Deirdre English, Fanita English, Helen Drutt English, Mary Ann Fick, Charles and Doris Foster, Joseph Frank, John L. Gardner Jr., Daniela Gioseffi, John Goetz, Vera Gold, Jean Gould, Hannah Green, Roy E. Grimm,

Marthe Hall, Nancy Hallinan, David Hallman, Pauline Hanson, Mrs. Sydney Harris, Patricia Haskell, Carol Hebald, Roger Hecht, Harry Holland, Barbara Howes, David Ignatow, Kim Young Ik, Josephine Jacobsen, Gerta Kennedy, Gyorgy Kepes, Milton Kessler, Galway Kinnell, Carolyn Kizer, Patricia Knowlton, Richard Kostelanetz, Paul Kresh, Janet Lees, Harry Levin, Mrs. John Luedtke-meyer, Gloria Macdonald, Alice McIntyre, Frank MacShane, Gerald Malanga, Paolo Mangini, Mary Manning, Martin Manulis, Jane Mayhall, Jerome Mazzaro, Gail Mazur, Maglet Myrhum, Howard Nemerov, Ned O'Gorman, William Packard, Molly Peacock, Robert Peters, Al Poulin Jr, John Prince, Eugene Pugatch, Gomer Rees, Harriet Rosenstein, Bruce Rubenstein, Frances Pole Sacco, Stephen Sandy, Gert Schiff, Evalyn Katz Shapiro, Harvey Shapiro, Karl and Sophie Shapiro, Alan Shields, Layle Silbert, Irving Silver, Peter Simpson, William Jay Smith, Barbara Van Rensselaer Spalding, Betty Farley Stockton, Eric Stange, Robert Stange, Helen Heinz Tate, Anita Thacher, Boyd and Maris Thomes, Phyllis Hoge Thompson, Leonard and Sherley Unger, Barbara Warren, Stella Waitzkin, Arnold Weinstein, Reed and Helen Whittemore, Mrs. Frank Wigglesworth, Galen Williams, Anne Runk Wright, and Harriet Zinnes.

I am grateful to the many people who answered my letters: Jonathan Aaron, Philip Appleman, Steven Gould Axelrod, Lady Ayer, Kent Bales, Rudolf Baranik, Julia Bartholomay, Carol Bergé, Harold Blumenfeld, Carol Bly, Mrs. George Brewster, Harry Brewster, Cleanth Brooks, David Brooks, Stanley Burnshaw, Alvaro Cardona-Hine, Constance Carrier, Anthony Chapin, Julia Child, Rlene Dahlberg, Pierre Delattre, Reuel Denney, Richard Elman, Constance Fearing, Wallace Fowlie, Paul Genega, Allen Ginsberg, Anthony Hecht, Verna Hobson, Margo Hoff, Edwin Honig, Michael James, Mary Brewster Kennedy, Frank Kermode, Jascha Kessler, Mrs. Arthur Kinsolving, William Knott, David Levine, Fred Licht, Lyn Lifshin, William McDermott, Leo Marx, James Merrill, William Merwin, Ralph Mills Jr., Peter E. Murphy, Arthur Naftalin, John Frederick Nims, Gordon O'Brien, Alicia Ostriker, David Ray, Rochelle Ratner, Piers Paul Read, David Riesman, Ned Rorem, Edward W. Rosenheim, M. L. Rosenthal, Norman Rosten, Alice Ryerson, Arthur Schlesinger Jr., Grace Schulman, Lee Seldes, Timothy Seldes, Patrick Shaw, Sayre Sheldon, Mr. and Mrs. Melvin Shestack, Brother Benedict Simmonds, Eileen Simpson, William Stafford, Richard Stern, May Stevens, Peter Stitt, Carolyn Stoloff, Mark Strand, Louise Talma, Martin Tucker, Mona Van Duyn, Julie Van Kirk, Ann Waldron, Warren Woesner, Nancy and Percy Wood, Mrs. Charles Woodard, Frances Wyatt.

This book is also based to a large extent on original manuscript materials, listed in works cited. The librarians at the depositories were unfailingly helpful and courteous. I would like to thank in particular Holly Hall, Anne Posega, and Kevin Ray at the Washington University Libraries, whose kindnesses were legion. I wish to single out the late Holly Hall: not only did she start it all, but she hosted me at her home several times and allowed me to join her family for a Fourth of July celebration.

A number of institutions helped fund my research: the American Council of Learned Societies, Documentary Educational Resources (DER), Foundation Doctor Catherine van Tussenbroek, The Netherlands Organization for Scientific Research, and Radboud University Nijmegen. Thank you. I was a very happy visiting scholar at Harvard University and the University of California at Berkeley. In California, my friend Inez Hollander Lake was most helpful in matters both mundane and academic. Sara Davis, my editor at the University of Missouri Press, assisted me spiritedly and accurately across the ocean; we never got to meet—I am sure we would have become fast friends.

Robert Gardner deserves special mention. From the first, he encouraged me to write about his sister's life. He shared his memories, allowed me to copy over a hundred letters from Gardner to him without checking them first, and showed me the old home movies their father had made, although they were almost too painful for him to watch. Talking to him, watching his extraordinary lyrical films, reading his poetic books, seeing his impulse to preserve, his need to communicate, his struggle with death in life, I came to know part of Gardner, their talents and insecurities being much the same. Instrumental in getting me the DER fellowship, which allowed me to finish the biography, he never in any way tried to influence my writing. I have great admiration and affection for him and hope this book does not disappoint him. I am glad, now, that it took me so long to write it, for had I finished it fifteen years ago, I would have—I tell myself—been more judgmental and have understood Gardner less.

This book is for Ger, who introduced me to American literature and has been a close reader of this text as it took shape. And, of course, it is for the love of our lives, our young son Alexander, red-haired like Isabella, who once wondered: "How can you stand it? You sit in front of a computer all day, typing, and the next day you delete almost everything you have written. Your life is utterly boring." Gardner's life was not.